SYSTEMATIC THEOLOGY

SYSTEMATIC
THEOLOGY

VOLUME III

Life and the Spirit
History and the Kingdom of God

PAUL TILLICH

THE UNIVERSITY OF CHICAGO PRESS

FOR HANNAH

THE COMPANION OF MY LIFE

The University of Chicago Press, Chicago 60637

© 1963 by The University of Chicago. All rights reserved
Published 1963. Paperback edition 1976
Printed in the United States of America

01 00 99 98 97 96 95 94 93 92   9 10 11 12 13 14

Library of Congress Catalog Card Number: 51-2235

ISBN: 3 vols. in 1, 0-226-80336-8 (cloth);
vol. 1, 0-226-80337-6 (paper); vol. 2, 0-226-80338-4 (paper);
vol. 3, 0-226-80339-2 (paper)

PREFACE

WITH THE third volume, my *Systematic Theology* is completed. The last volume appears six years after the second volume, which itself appeared six years after the first one. The long periods between the dates of publication were caused not only by the qualitative and quantitative immensity of the subject but also by demands on my time in connection with my work as a systematic theologian. These demands involved developing particular problems in smaller and less technical books and presenting my views in lectures and discussions at many places in this country and abroad. I considered these demands as justified and tried to fulfil them although this meant delays in the completion of my main work.

But finally, in view of my age, a further delay was not permissable, in spite of the fact that one never feels enough work has been done on a book that struggles with so many problematic subjects. However, at some time, the author must accept his finitude and with it the incompleteness of the completed. A strong motive to do so came from the doctoral students who over the years have asked that the still fragmentary manuscript of the third volume be opened to them because they had to write theses on my theology. This questionable procedure had to come to an end and, beyond this, a large number of requests for the third volume had finally to be satisfied. My friends and I sometimes feared that the system would remain a fragment. This has not happened, although even at its best this system is fragmentary and often inadequate and questionable. Nevertheless, it shows the stage at which my theological thought has arrived. Yet a system should be not only a point of arrival but a point of departure as well. It should be like a station at which preliminary truth is crystallized on the endless road toward truth.

I want to express my thanks to Mrs. Elizabeth Boone, who did the necessary "Englishing" of my style with its unavoidable Germanisms, to William Crout, who read the galley proof, and to Mrs. Elizabeth Stoner and Mrs. Maria Pelikan, who helped prepare the index. I also want

PREFACE

to thank my assistant, Clark Williamson, who was the special editor
for this volume, for the hard work he put into the difficult task and for
the fruitful discussions we had about particular problems. And I am
grateful to the publishers, who very graciously and patiently awaited
the slow growth of the three volumes.

East Hampton, Long Island

TABLE OF CONTENTS

INTRODUCTION

PART IV. LIFE AND THE SPIRIT

PART V. HISTORY AND THE KINGDOM OF GOD

TABLE OF CONTENTS

INDEX

INTRODUCTION

INTRODUCTION

THE QUESTION "Why a system?" has been asked ever since the first volume of my systematics appeared. In one of the books that deals critically with my theology, *The System and the Gospel*, by Kenneth Hamilton, the fact of the system itself, more than anything stated within the system, is characterized as the decisive error of my theology. Of course, such an argument could be used against all of the theological systems that have been created in the history of Christian thought, from Origen, Gregory, and John of Damascus, to Bonaventura, Thomas, and Ockham, and finally to Calvin, Johann Gerhard, and Schleiermacher, not to mention innumerable others. There are many reasons for aversion to the systematic-constructive form in theology; one is the result of confusion of a deductive, quasi-mathematical system, like those of Lullus in the Middle Ages and Spinoza in modern times, with the systematic form as such. But there are very few examples of deductive systems, and even in them the deductive form remains external to the experienced material. Spinoza's influence is prophetic and mystical as well as metaphysical. There are, however, other reasons for aversion to a system. In theology the systematic form is often considered an attempt to rationalize revelatory experiences. But this confuses the justifiable demand to be consistent in one's statements with the unjustifiable attempt to derive theological statements from sources that are strange to revelatory experiences.

For me, the systematic-constructive form has meant the following. First, it forced me to be consistent. Genuine consistency is one of the hardest tasks in theology (as it probably is in every cognitive approach to reality), and no one fully succeeds. But in making a new statement, the necessity of surveying previous statements in order to see whether or not they are mutually compatible drastically reduces inconsistencies. Second, and very surprisingly, the systematic form became an instrument by which relations between symbols and concepts were discovered that otherwise would not have been apparent. Finally, the systematic construction has led me to conceive the object of theology in its wholeness, as a *Gestalt* in which many parts and elements are united by determining principles and dynamic interrelations.

3

To emphasize the importance of the systematic form is not to deny that every concrete system is transitory and that none can be final. New organizing principles appear, neglected elements acquire central significance, the method may become more refined or completely different, with the result that a new conception of the structure of the whole emerges. This is the fate of every system. But this is also the rhythm in which the history of Christian thought has moved through the centuries. The systems were points of crystallization toward which the discussion of particular problems moved and from which new discussions and fresh problems arose. It is my hope that, in however limited a way, the present system may perform the same function.

A special characteristic of these three volumes, much noticed and often criticized, is the kind of language used in them and the way in which it is used. It deviates from the ordinary use of biblical language in systematic theology—that is, to support particular assertions with appropriate biblical quotations. Not even the more satisfactory method of building a theological system on the foundation of a historical-critical "biblical theology" is directly applied, although its influence is present in every part of the system. Instead, philosophical and psychological concepts are preferred, and references to sociological and scientific theories often appear. This procedure seems more suitable for a systematic theology which tries to speak understandably to the large group of educated people, including open-minded students of theology, for whom traditional language has become irrelevant. Of course, I am not unaware of the danger that in this way the substance of the Christian message may be lost. Nevertheless, this danger must be risked, and once one has realized this, one must proceed in this direction. Dangers are not a reason for avoiding a serious demand. It sometimes appears in these days that the Roman Catholic church is more open to the demand for reformation than are the churches of the Reformation. Certainly, these three books would not have been written if I had not been convinced that the event in which Christianity was born has central significance for all mankind, both before and after the event. But the way in which this event can be understood and received changes with changing conditions in all periods of history. On the other hand, this work would not have come into existence either, if I had not tried during the larger part of my life to penetrate the meaning of the Christian symbols, which have become increasingly problematic within the cultural context of our time. Since the split between a faith unacceptable to culture and a culture unacceptable to faith was not possible for me, the only alternative was to attempt to interpret the symbols of faith through expressions of our own culture. The result of this attempt is the three volumes of *Systematic Theology*.

Several critical books and many critical articles concerning my theology appeared before this final volume was finished. I did not feel that I should deal with them in terms of direct answers, since that would overload this volume with polemical material and I believed that the volume itself, especially the section on the doctrine of the Spirit, implicitly answers many of the criticisms. Others could not be answered except by repeating the arguments of the former volumes. And in some cases, as in those criticisms arising from traditional supranaturalism or exclusive Christocentrism, I could only answer, No!

Long after I had written the sections on life and its ambiguities, I happened to read Pierre Teilhard de Chardin's book *The Phenomenon of Man*. It encouraged me greatly to know that an acknowledged scientist had developed ideas about the dimensions and processes of life so similar to my own. Although I cannot share his rather optimistic vision of the future, I am convinced by his description of the evolutionary processes in nature. Of course, theology cannot rest on scientific theory. But it must relate its understanding of man to an understanding of universal nature, for man is a part of nature and statements about nature underlie every statement about him. The sections in this book on the dimensions and ambiguities of life attempt to make explicit what is implicit in even the most antiphilosophical theologies. Even if the questions about the relation of man to nature and to the universe could be avoided by theologians, they would still be asked by people of every place and time—often with existential urgency and out of cognitive honesty. And the lack of an answer can become a stumbling block for a man's whole religious life. These are the reasons why I ventured to enter, from the theological point of view, the field of a philosophy of life, fully aware of the cognitive risks involved.

A system is not a *summa*, and this system is not even complete. Some subjects are less fully treated than others: for example, atonement, trinity, and particular sacraments. But I hope that there are not too many problems that are totally neglected. My choice was mostly dependent on the urgency of the actual problem-situation, as reflected mainly in public discussions. This factor is also responsible for the presentation of some questions and answers in rather traditional terms, whereas for others, new roads of thought as well as of language were tried. The latter method was applied in some of the eschatological chapters which conclude this volume and which turn the whole system back to its beginning in the sense of Romans 11:36. "For *of* him, and *through* him, and *to* him, are all things." In these chapters the attempt has been made, not to solve the mystery of the "to him," but to interpret it in such a way as to provide a meaningful alternative to the primitive and often superstitious imaginings about the *eschaton*, whether the *eschaton* is conceived individually or universally.

The church-historical situation in which the system has been written is characterized by developments which surpass in religious significance everything solely theological. Most significant is the encounter of the historical religions with secularism and with the "quasi-religions" born out of it (for a treatment of this subject, see my recent book, *Christianity and the Encounter of the World Religions*). A theology which does not deal seriously with the criticism of religion by secular thought and some particular forms of secular faith, such as liberal humanism, nationalism, and socialism, would be "a-*kairos*"—missing the demand of the historical moment. Another important characteristic of the present situation is the less dramatic but increasingly significant exchange between the historical religions, dependent partly on the need for a common front against the invading secular forces and partly on the conquest of spatial distance between different religious centers. Again I must say that a Christian theology which is not able to enter into a creative dialogue with the theological thought of other religions misses a world-historical occasion and remains provincial. Finally, Protestant systematic theology must take into consideration the present, more affirmative relation between Catholicism and Protestantism. Contemporary theology must consider the fact that the Reformation was not only a religious gain but also a religious loss. Although my system is very outspoken in its emphasis on the "Protestant principle," it has not ignored the demand that the "Catholic substance" be united with it, as the section on the church, one of the longest in the whole system, shows .There is a *kairos*, a moment full of potentialities, in Protestant-Catholic relations; and Protestant theology must become and remain conscious of it.

Since the twenties of this century several systems of Protestant theology have been elaborated—some over a period of three decades and more. (I consider my lectures on "Systematic Theology" in Marburg, Germany, in 1924 as the beginning of my work on this system.) This approach was very different from that of the immediately preceding period, especially for American Protestantism, in which philosophical criticism, on the one hand, and denominational traditionalism, on the other hand, inhibited the rise of a constructive systematic theology. This situation has drastically changed. The impact of the world-historical events as well as the threat coming from the historical-critical method of biblical research have subjected Protestant theology to the necessity of a positive revision of its whole tradition. And this can be done only through systematic construction.

PART IV
LIFE AND THE SPIRIT

I

LIFE, ITS AMBIGUITIES, AND THE QUEST FOR UNAMBIGUOUS LIFE

A. THE MULTIDIMENSIONAL UNITY OF LIFE

1. Life: Essence and Existence

THE FACT that more than ten different meanings of the word "life" are given in an ordinary dictionary makes it understandable why many philosophers hesitate to use the word "life" altogether and why others restrict its use to the realm of living beings, thus implying the contrast of life with death. On the other hand, in Continental Europe, toward the turn of the century, a large philosophical school was concerned with "philosophy of life." It included such people as Nietzsche, Dilthey, Bergson, Simmel, and Scheler, and it influenced many others, notably the existentialists. At the same time in America the "philosophy of process" developed, foreshadowed by the pragmatism of James and Dewey and fully elaborated by Whitehead and his school. The term "process" is much less equivocal than the term "life" but also much less expressive. The living and the dead body are equally subject to "process," but in the fact of death, "life" includes its own negation. The emphatic use of the word "life" serves to indicate the conquest of this negation—as in "life reborn" or in "eternal life." Perhaps it is not too bold to assume that the words for life first arose through the experience of death. In any case, the polarity of life and death has always colored the word "life." This polar concept of life presupposes the use of the word for a special group of existing things, i.e., "living beings." "Living beings" are also "dying beings," and they exhibit special characteristics under the predominance of the organic dimension. This *generic* concept of life is the pattern after which the ontological concept of life has been formed. The observation of a particular potentiality of beings, whether it is that of a species or of individuals actualizing themselves in time and space, has led to the *ontological* concept of life—life as the "actuality of being." This concept of life unites the two main qualifications of being which underlie this whole system; these two main qualifications of being are the essential and the existential. Potentiality is that kind of being which has the power, the dynamic, to become actual (for example, the potentiality of every tree is treehood). There are other essences which do not have this power, such as geometrical forms (for example, the triangle). Those which become actual, however, subject themselves to the conditions of existence, such as finitude, estrangement, conflict, and so on. This does not mean that they lose their essential character (trees remain trees), but it does mean that they fall under the structures of existence and are open to growth, distortion, and death. We use the word "life" in this sense of a "mixture" of essential and existential elements. In terms of the history of philosophy we can say that we envisage the Aristotelian distinction between *dynamis* and *energeia*, between potentiality and actuality, from an existentialist viewpoint. Certainly this is not too different from Aristotle's own view, which emphasizes the lasting ontological tension between matter and form in all existence.

The ontological concept of life underlies the *universal* concept used by the "philosophers of life." If the actualization of the potential is a structural condition of all beings, and if this actualization is called "life," then the universal concept of life is unavoidable. Consequently, the genesis of stars and rocks, their growth as well as their decay, must be called a life process. The ontological concept of life liberates the word "life" from its bondage to the organic realm and elevates it to the level of a basic term that can be used within the theological system only if interpreted in existential terms. The term "process" is not open to such interpretation, although in many instances it is helpful to speak of life processes.

The ontological concept of life and its universal application require two kinds of consideration, one of which we should call "essentialist" and the other "existentialist." The first deals with the unity and diversity of life in its essential nature. It describes what I venture to call "*the multidimensional unity of life*." Only if this unity and the relation of the dimensions and realms of life are understood, can we analyze the existential ambiguities of all life processes correctly and express the quest for unambiguous or eternal life adequately.

2. The Case against "Levels"

The diversity of beings has led the human mind to seek for unity in diversity, because man can perceive the encountered manifoldness of things only with the help of uniting principles. One of the most universal principles used for this purpose is that of a hierarchical order in which every genus and species of things, and through them every individual thing, has its place. This way of discovering order in the seeming chaos of reality distinguishes grades and levels of being. Ontological qualities, such as a higher degree of universality or a richer development of potentiality, determine the place which is ascribed to a level of being. The old term "hierarchy" ("holy order of rulers, disposed in rank of sacramental power") is most expressive for this kind of thinking. It can be applied to earthly rulers as well as to genera and species of beings in nature, for example, the inorganic, the organic, the psychological. In this view reality is seen as a pyramid of levels following each other in vertical direction according to their power of being and their grade of value. This imagery of rulers (*archoi*) in the term "hierarchy" gives to the higher levels a higher quality but a smaller quantity of exemplars. The top is monarchic, whether the monarch is a priest, an emperor, a god, or the God of monotheism.

The term "level" is a metaphor which emphasizes the equality of all objects belonging to a particular level. They are "leveled," that is, brought to a common plane and kept on it. There is no organic movement from one to the other; the higher is not implicit in the lower, and the lower is not implicit in the higher. The relation of the levels is that of interference, either by control or by revolt. Certainly, in the history of thought (and social structures), the intrinsic independence of each level from the others has been modified, as, for instance, in Thomas Aquinas' definition of the relation of nature and grace ("grace fulfilling, not denying nature"). But the way in which he describes the grace which fulfils nature shows the continuing dominance of the hierarchical system. It was not until Nicolaus Cusanus formulated the principle of the "coincidence of opposites" (for example, of the infinite and the finite) and Luther formulated the principle of "justification of the sinner" (calling the saint a sinner and the sinner a saint if accepted by God) that the hierarchical principle lost its power and was replaced. Its place was taken in the religious realm by the doctrine of the priesthood of all believers and in the social-political realm by the democratic principle of equal human nature in every man. Both the Protestant and the democratic principles negate the mutually independent and hierarchically organized levels of the power of being.

The metaphor "level" betrays its inadequacy when the relation of different levels is under consideration. The choice of the metaphor had far-reaching consequences for the whole cultural situation. And, conversly, the choice itself expressed a cultural situation. The question of the relation of the organic to the inorganic "level" of nature leads to the recurrent problem of whether biological processes can be fully understood through the application of methods used in mathematical physics or whether a teleological principle must be used to explain the inner-directedness of organic growth. Under the dominance of the metaphor "level" the inorganic either swallows the organic (control) or the inorganic processes are interfered with by a strange "vitalist" force (revolt) —an idea which naturally produces passionate and justified reactions from the physicists and their biological followers.

Another consequence of the use of the metaphor "level" appears in considering the relation of the organic and the spiritual, usually discussed as the relation of body and mind. If body and mind are levels, the problem of their relation can be solved only by reducing the mental to the organic (biologism and psychologism) or by asserting the interference of mental activities in the biological and psychological processes; this latter assertion produces the passionate and justifiable reaction of biologists and psychologists against the establishment of a "soul" as a separate substance exercising a particular causality.

A third consequence of the use of the metaphor "level" is manifest in the interpretation of the relation between religion and culture. For instance, if one says that culture is the level on which man creates himself, whereas it is in religion that he receives the divine self-manifestation, which gives religion ultimate authority over culture, then destructive conflicts inevitably appear between religion and culture—as the pages of history indicate. Religion as the superior level tries to control culture or some cultural functions such as science, the arts, ethics, or politics. This suppression of the autonomous cultural functions has led to revolutionary reactions in which culture has tried to engulf religion and subject it to the norms of autonomous reason. Here again it is obvious that the use of the metaphor "level" is a matter not of inadequacy alone but of decision about the problems of human existence.

The preceding example can lead to the question of whether the relation of God and man (including his world) can be described, as in religious dualism and theological supranaturalism, in terms of two levels—the divine and the human. Arrival at the decisive answer to this question is simplified through the attempt to demythologize religious language. Demythologization is not directed against the use of genuine mythical images as such but against the supranaturalistic method which takes these images literally. The enormity of the superstitious consequences following from this kind of supranaturalism sufficiently demonstrates the danger which the metaphor "level" poses in theological thought.

3. DIMENSIONS, REALMS, DEGREES

The result of these considerations is that the metaphor "level" (and such similar metaphors as "stratum" or "layer") must be excluded from any description of life processes. It is my suggestion that it be replaced by the metaphor "dimension," together with correlative concepts such as "realm" and "grade." The significant thing, however, is not the replacement of one metaphor by another but the changed vision of reality which such replacement expresses.

The metaphor "dimension" is also taken from the spatial sphere, but it describes the difference of the realms of being in such a way that there cannot be mutual interference; depth does not interfere with breadth, since all dimensions meet in the same point. They cross without disturbing each other; there is no conflict between dimensions. Therefore, the replacement of the metaphor "level" by the metaphor "dimension" represents an encounter with reality in which the unity of life is seen above its conflicts. These conflicts are not denied, but they are not derived from the hierarchy of levels; they are consequences of the ambiguity of all life processes and are therefore conquerable without the destruction of one level by another. They do not refute the doctrine of the multidimensional unity of life.

One reason for using the metaphor "level" is the fact that there are wide areas of reality in which some characteristics of life are not manifest at all, for instance, the large amount of inorganic materials in which no trace of the organic dimension can be found and the many forms of organic life in which neither the psychological nor the spiritual dimension is visible. Can the metaphor "dimension" cover these conditions? I believe it can. It can point to the fact that, even if certain dimensions of life do not appear, nonetheless they are potentially real. The distinction of the potential from the actual implies that all dimensions are always real, if not actually, at least potentially. A dimension's actualization is dependent on conditions which are not always present.

The first condition for the actualization of some dimensions of life is that others must already have been actualized. No actualization of the organic dimension is possible without actualization of the inorganic, and the dimension of spirit would remain potential without the actualization of the organic. But this is only one condition. The other one is that in the realm which is characterized by the already actualized dimension particular constellations occur which make possible the actualization of a new dimension. Billions of years may have passed before the inorganic realm permitted the appearance of objects in the organic dimension, and millions of years before the organic realm permitted the appearance of a being with language. Again, it took tens of thousands of years before the being with the power of language became the historical man whom we know as ourselves. Potential dimensions of being became actual in all these cases because conditions were present for the actualization of that which had always been potentially real.

One can use the term "realm" to indicate a section of life in which a particular dimension is predominant. "Realm" is a metaphor like "level" and "dimension," but it is not basically spatial (although it is this, too); it is basically social. One speaks of the ruler of a realm, and just this connotation makes the metaphor adequate, because in the metaphorical sense a realm is a section of reality in which a special dimension determines the character of every individual belonging to it, whether it is an atom or a man. In this sense one speaks of the vegetable realm or the animal realm or the historical realm. In all of them, all dimensions are potentially present, and some of them are actualized. All of them are actual in man as we know him, but the special character of this realm is determined by the dimensions of the spiritual and historical. Only the inorganic dimension is actualized in the atom, but all the other dimensions are potentially present. Symbolically speaking, one could say that when God created the potentiality of the atom within himself he created the potentiality of man, and when he created the potentiality of man he created the potentiality of the atom—and all other dimensions between them. They are all present in every realm, in part potentially, in part (or in full) actually. Of the dimensions which are actual, one characterizes the realm, because the others which are also actual in it are there only as conditions for the actualization of the determining dimension (which itself is not a condition for the others). The inorganic can be actual without actuality of the organic but not vice versa.

This leads to the question of whether there is a gradation of value among the different dimensions. The answer is affirmative: That which presupposes something else and adds to it is by so much the richer. Historical man adds the historical dimension to all other dimensions which are presupposed and contained in his being. He is the highest grade from the point of view of valuation, presupposing that the criterion of such value judgment is the power of a being to include a maximum number of potentialities in one living actuality. This is an ontological criterion, according to the rule that value judgments must be rooted in qualities of the objects valued, and it is a criterion which should not be confused with that of perfection. Man is the highest being within the realm of our experience, but he is by no means the most perfect. These last considerations show that the rejection of the metaphor "level" does not entail the denial of value judgments based on degrees of power of being.

4. THE DIMENSIONS OF LIFE AND THEIR RELATIONS

a) The dimensions in the inorganic and organic realms.—We have mentioned different realms of the encountered reality as being determined by special dimensions, for example, the inorganic, the organic, the historical. We must now ask what the principle is for establishing a dimension of life as a dimension. First of all, there is no definite number of them, for dimensions of life are established under flexible criteria. One is justified in speaking of a particular dimension when the phenomenological description of a section of encountered reality shows unique categorical and other structures. A "phenomenological" description is one which points to a reality as it is given, before one goes to a theoretical explanation or derivation. In many cases that encounter of mind and reality which produces words has prepared the way for a precise phenomenological observation. In other cases such observation leads to the discovery of a new dimension of life or, conversely, to the reduction of two or more assumed dimensions to one. With these criteria in mind, and without any claim to finality, several obvious dimensions of life may be distinguished. The purpose of discussing them in the context of a theological system is to show the multidimensional unity of life and to determine concretely the source and the consequences of the ambiguities of all life processes.

The particular character of a dimension which justifies its establishment as a dimension can best be seen in the modification of time, space, causality, and substance under its predominance. These categories have universal validity for everything that exists. But this does not mean that there is only *one* time, space, and so on. For the categories change their character under the predominance of each dimension. Things are not *in* time and space; rather they *have* a definite time and space. Inorganic space and organic space are different spaces; psychological time and historical time are different times; and inorganic and spiritual causality are different causalities. However, this does not mean that the categories, for example, in their inorganic character disappear in the organic realm or that clock time is annihilated by historical time. The categorical form which belongs to a conditioning realm, such as the inorganic in relation to the organic, enters the new categorical form as an element within it. In historical time or causality, all preceding forms of time or causality are present, but they are not the same as they were before. Such considerations provide a solid basis for the rejection of all kinds of reductionist ontology, both naturalistic and idealistic.

If, in agreement with tradition, we start by calling the inorganic the first dimension, the very use of the negative term "inorganic" points to the indefiniteness of the field which this term covers. It might be possible and adequate to distinguish more than one dimension in it, as one formerly distinguished the physical and chemical realms and still does for special purposes in spite of their growing unity. There are indications that one could speak of special dimensions in the macrocosmic as well as the microcosmic realm. In any case, this whole field, which may or may not constitute *one* realm, is phenomenologically different from the realms which are determined by the other dimensions.

The religious significance of the inorganic is immense, but it is rarely considered by theology. In most theological discussions the general term "nature" covers all particular dimensions of the "natural." This is one of the reasons why the quantitatively overwhelming realm of the inorganic has had such a strong antireligious impact on many people in the ancient and the modern worlds. A "theology of the inorganic" is lacking. According to the principle of the multidimensional unity of life, it has to be included in the present discussion of life processes and their ambiguity. Traditionally, the problem of the inorganic has been discussed as the problem of matter. The term "matter" has an ontological and a scientific meaning. In the second sense, it is usually identified with that which underlies the inorganic processes. If the whole of reality is reduced to inorganic processes, the result is the non-scientific ontological theory which is called materialism or reductionist naturalism. Its peculiar contention is not that there is matter in everything that exists—every ontology must say this including all forms of positivism—but that the matter we encounter under the dimension of the inorganic is the only matter.

In the inorganic dimension, potentialities become actual in those things in time and space which are subject to physical analysis or which can be measured in spatial-temporal-causal relations. However, as indicated before, such measurements have their limitations in the realms of the very large and the very small, in the macrocosmic and microcosmic extensions. Here time, space, causality in the ordinary sense, and the logic based on them are not sufficient to describe the phenomena. If one followed the principle that, under certain conditions, quantity becomes quality (Hegel), one would be justified in distinguishing the dimensions of the subatomic, of the astronomical, and of that between them which appears in the ordinary human encounter with reality. If, however, one denies the transition of quantity into quality, one may speak of *one* dimension in the inorganic realm and consider the ordinary encounter as a particular case of the micro- or macrocosmic structures.

Special characteristics of the dimension of the inorganic will appear in its comparison with characteristics of the other dimensions and, above all, their relation to the categories, and through a discussion of the life processes in all dimensions. For the inorganic has a preferred position among the dimensions in so far as it is the first condition for the actualization of every dimension. This is why all realms of being would dissolve were the basic condition provided by the constellation of inorganic structures to disappear. Biblically speaking: "You return to the ground, for out of it you were taken" (Genesis 3:19 [R.S.V.]). This is also the reason for the above-mentioned "reductionist naturalism," or materialism, which identifies matter with inorganic matter. *Materialism*, in this definition, *is an ontology of death*.

The dimension of the organic is so central for every philosophy of life that linguistically the basic meaning of "life" is organic life. But in a way more obvious than in the inorganic realm, the term "organic life" actually embraces several dimensions. The structural difference between a typical representative of the vegetable realm and one of the animal realm makes the establishment of two dimensions advisable, despite the indefiniteness of the transition between them. This decision is supported by the fact that in the realm which is determined by the animal dimension, another dimension makes its appearance: the self-awareness of life—the psychic (if this word can be saved from its occultist connotations). The organic dimension is characterized by self-related, self-preserving, self-increasing, and self-continuing *Gestalten* ("living wholes").

The theological problem arising from the differences between the organic and the inorganic dimensions is connected with the theory of evolution and the misguided attacks on it on the part of traditional religion. The conflict arose not only over the significance of the evolutionary doctrine for the doctrine of man but also over the transition from the inorganic to the organic. Some theologians argued for the existence of God on the basis of our ignorance of the genesis of the organic out of the inorganic; they asserted that the "first cell" can be explained only in terms of a special divine interference. Obviously, biology had to reject the establishment of such a supranatural causality and to attempt to narrow our ignorance about the conditions for the appearance of organisms —an attempt which has been largely successful. The question of the source of the species of organic life is more serious. Here two points of view are in conflict, the Aristotelian and the evolutionary; the first emphasizes the eternity of the species in terms of their *dynamis*, their potentiality, and the second emphasizes the conditions of their appearance in *energeia*, actuality. Formulated in the following way, the difference obviously need not create a conflict: the dimension of the organic is essentially present in the inorganic; its actual appearance is dependent on conditions the description of which is the task of biology and biochemistry.

An analogous solution must be given for the problem of the transition from the dimension of the vegetative to that of the animal, especially to the phenomenon of an individual's "inner awareness" of himself. Here again, the distinction of the potential from the actual provides the solution: potentially, self-awareness is present in every dimension; actually, it can appear only under the dimension of animal being. The attempt to pursue self-awareness back into the vegetative dimension can be neither rejected nor accepted, since it can in no way be verified, whether by intuitive participation or by reflexive analogy to expressions similar to those man finds in himself. Under these circumstances, it seems wiser to restrict the assumption of inner awareness to those realms in which it can be made highly probable, at least in terms of analogy, and emotionally certain in terms of participation—most obviously in the higher animals.

Under special conditions the dimension of inner awareness, or the psychological realm, actualizes within itself another dimension, that of the personal-communal or the "spirit." Within reach of present human experience, this has happened only in man. The question of whether it has happened anywhere else in the universe cannot yet be answered positively or negatively. (For the theological significance of this problem, see *Systematic Theology*, II, 95, 96.)

b) The meaning of spirit as a dimension of life.—The word "spirit" in this title raises an important problem of terminology. The Stoic term for spirit is *pneuma*, and the Latin, *spiritus*, with its derivations in modern languages—in German it is *Geist*, in Hebrew *ru'ach*. There is no semantic problem in these languages, but there is one in English, because of misuse of the word "spirit" with a small "s." The words "Spirit" and "Spiritual" are used only for the divine Spirit and its effects in man, and are written with a capital "S." The question then is, Should and can the word "spirit," designating the particularly human dimension of life, be reinstated? There are strong arguments for trying to do so; and I shall attempt it throughout the discussions of the present part of the theological system.

In the Semitic as well as in the Indo-Germanic languages, the root of the words designating spirit means "breath." It was in the experience of breathing and above all in the cessation of breathing in the corpse that man's attention was drawn to the question, What keeps life alive? His answer was: breath. Where there is breath, there is the power of life; where it vanishes, the power of life vanishes. As the *power* of life, spirit is not identical with the inorganic substratum which is animated by it; rather, spirit is the power of animation itself and not a part added to the organic system. Yet some philosophical developments, allied with mystical and ascetic tendencies in the later ancient world, separated spirit and body. In modern times this trend came to its fulfilment in Descartes and

English empiricism. The word received the connotation of "mind," and "mind" itself received the connotation of "intellect." The element of power in the original meaning of spirit disappeared, and finally the word itself was discarded. In contemporary English it is largely replaced by "mind," and the question is whether the word "mind" can be de-intellectualized and fully replace the word "spirit."

According to some, it is possible, but the majority of those who answer this question take the opposite position. They see the necessity of restoring the term "spirit" to denote the unity of life-power and life in meanings, or in condensed form, the "unity of power and meaning." The fact that the term "Spirit" has been preserved in the religious sphere is due partly to the strength of tradition in the religious realm and partly to the impossibility of depriving the divine Spirit of the element of power (for example, the hymn "Veni, *Creator* Spiritus"). "God is Spirit" can never be translated as "God is Mind" or "God is Intellect." And even Hegel's *Phaenomenologie des Geistes* should never have been translated as *Phenomenology of the Mind*. Hegel's concept of spirit unites meaning with power.

A new understanding of the term "spirit" as a dimension of life is a theological necessity. For every religious term is a symbol using material from ordinary experience, and the symbol itself cannot be understood without an understanding of the symbolic material. (God as "Father" is meaningless for somebody who does not know what "father" means.) It is quite probable that the fading of the symbol "Holy Spirit" from the living consciousness of Christianity is at least partly caused by the disappearance of the word "spirit" from the doctrine of man. Without knowing what spirit is, one cannot know what Spirit is. This is the reason for the ghostly connotations of the words "divine Spirit" and for the absence of these words from ordinary talk, even within the church. It seems that, while it may be possible to rescue the term "spirit," the adjective "spiritual" is lost beyond hope. This book will not even attempt to re-establish it in its original meaning.

But there are other sources of the semantic confusion which darkens the meaning of the word "spirit." For instance, if one speaks of the spirit of a nation, of a law, or of an artistic style, one points to their essential character as expressed in their manifestations. The relation which this use of the word "spirit" has to its original meaning stems from the fact that the self-expressions of human groups are dependent on the dimension of spirit and its different functions. Another source of semantic confusion is the way in which one speaks of a "spiritual world," pointing to the realm of essences or ideas, in the Platonic sense. But the life "in" ideas, for which the word "spirit" is adequate, is different from the ideas themselves, which are potentialities of life but not life itself. Spirit is a dimension of life, but it is not the "universe of potentialities," which itself is not life. Mythically speaking, one could say that in the "paradise of dreaming innocence" there is potential but not actual spirit. "Adam before the fall" is also before the state of actualized spirit (and history).

A third source of semantic confusion is the concept of "spirits." If spirit is a dimension of life, one can certainly speak of living beings in which this dimension is actualized, and one can call them beings with spirit. But it is extremely misleading to call them "spirits," because this implies the existence of a "spirit" realm apart from life. Spirit becomes somewhat like inorganic matter and loses its character as a dimension of life which is potentially or actually present in all life. It assumes a "ghostly" character. This is confirmed by the so-called spiritualistic (in Continental languages, spiritistic) movements which try to make contact with the "spirits" or "ghosts" of the deceased and to provoke physical effects from them (noises, words, physical movements, visual appearances). Those who assert such experience are thus faced with the necessity of attributing physical causality to these "spirits." The way in which their manifestations are described points to a somehow transmuted psycho-physical existence of human beings after death. But such existence is neither Spiritual (determined by the divine Spirit) nor identical with what the Christian message calls "eternal life." Just like the question of extra-sensory perception, it is a matter of empirical investigations the results of which, whether positive or negative, have no direct bearing on the problem of man's spirit or of God as Spirit.

It is fortunate that in the word "spirited" the original element of power in the meaning of spirit is still preserved, although in a small corner of ordinary communication. The word is used as a translation of Plato's *thymoeides*, as describing that function of the soul which lies between rationality and sensuality and corresponds to the virtue of courage and to the social group of the aristocracy of the sword. This concept—which is often omitted from the picture of Plato's philosophy—is nearest to the genuine conception of spirit.

Since the dimension of spirit appears for us only in man, it is desirable to relate the term "spirit" to some other terms used in the doctrine of man, namely, "soul" (*psyche*), "mind" (*nous*), "reason" (*logos*). The word "soul" has suffered a fate similar to that of the term "spirit." It has been lost in that human endeavor which calls itself the "doctrine of the soul," namely, psychology. Modern psychology is psychology without *psyche*. The reason for this is the rejection of the soul as an immortal "substance" by modern epistemology since Hume and Kant. The word "soul" has been preserved mainly in poetry where it designates the seat of the passions and emotions. In the contemporary doctrine of man, the psychology of personality deals with phenomena attributed to the human soul. If spirit is defined as the unity of power and meaning, it can become a partial substitute for the lost concept of soul, although it transcends it in range, in structure, and especially, in dynamics. In any case, while the word "soul" is alive in biblical, liturgical, and poetic language, it has lost its usefulness for a strict theological understanding of man, his spirit, and its relation to the divine Spirit.

Although the word "mind" cannot become a substitute for "spirit," it has a basic function in the doctrine of life. It expresses the consciousness of a living being in relation to its surroundings and to itself. It includes awareness, perception, intention. It appears in the dimension of animality as soon as self-awareness appears; and in rudimentary or developed form, it includes intelligence, will, directed action. Under the predominance of the dimension of spirit, i.e., in man, it is related to the universals in perception and intention. It is structurally determined by reason (*logos*), the third of the terms to be considered.

The concept of reason has been fully discussed in the first part of the system, "Reason and Revelation." There, the difference between technical, or formal, and ontological reason was emphasized. Here, the question is that of the relation of both concepts to the dimension of spirit. Reason in the sense of *logos* is the principle of form by which reality in all its dimensions, and mind in all its directions, is structured. There is reason in the movement of an electron, and there is reason in the first words of a child—and in the structure of every expression of the spirit. Spirit as a dimension of life includes more than reason—it includes *eros*, passion, imagination—but without *logos*-structure, it could not express anything. Reason in the sense of technical reason or of reasoning is one of the potentialities of man's spirit in the cognitive sphere. It is the tool for the scientific analysis and technical control of reality.

Although these semantic considerations are far from complete, they may be sufficient to indicate the use of some key words in the following chapters and to provide, through agreement or disagreement, a stricter use of anthropological terms in theological statements.

c) The dimension of spirit in its relation to the preceding dimensions.—The semantic discussion in the last section interrupted the step-by-step consideration of distinguishable dimensions of life and their relations. There are two questions to be asked: the first concerns the relation of spirit to the psychological and biological dimensions, and the second concerns the question of the dimension which follows spirit in the order of conditioning, namely, the historical dimension. After a preliminary discussion, the second question will be fully considered in the last part of the system—"History and the Kingdom of God." At this point we must concentrate on the first, the relation of spirit to the psychological dimension—the dimension of inner awareness.

The appearance of a new dimension of life is dependent on a constellation of conditions in the conditioning dimension. Constellations of conditions make it possible for the organic to appear in the inorganic realm. Constellations in the inorganic realm make it possible for the dimension of self-awareness to become actual, and in the same way constellations under the predominance of the psychological dimension make it possible for the dimension of the spirit to become actual. The phrases "make it possible" and "provides for the conditions" for a dimension to become actual are crucial in these statements. The question is not how the conditions are provided; this is a matter of the interplay of freedom and destiny under the directing creativity of God, i.e., under the divine providence. The question is rather how the actualization of the potential follows from the constellation of conditions.

In order to answer this we must now consider the dynamics of life, or the historical dimension in an anticipatory way. This last and all-embracing dimension of life comes to its full actualization only in man, in whom as the bearer of the spirit the conditions for it are present. But the historical dimension is manifest—although under the predominance of other dimensions—in all realms of life. It is the universal character of actual being which, in the philosophies of life or process, has led to the elevation of the category of becoming to the highest ontological rank. But one cannot deny that the claim of the category of being to this rank is justified because, while becoming includes and overcomes relative non-being,

being itself is the negation of absolute non-being; it is the affirmation that there is anything at all. Indeed, it is under the protection of this affirmation that becoming and process are universal qualities of life. It is questionable, however, whether the words "becoming" and "process" are adequate for a view of the dynamics of life as a whole. They are lacking in a connotation which characterizes all life, and that is the creation of the new. This connotation is strongly present in references to the historical dimension, which is actual—even if subdued—in every realm of life, for history is the dimension under which the new is being created.

The actualization of a dimension is a historical event within the history of the universe, but it is an event which cannot be localized at a definite point of time and space. In long periods of transition the dimensions, metaphorically speaking, struggle with each other in the same realm. This is obvious concerning the transition of the inorganic to the organic, of the vegetative to the animal, of the biological to the psychological. This is also true of the transition from the psychological to the dimension of the spirit. If we define man as that organism in which the dimension of spirit is dominant, we cannot fix a definite point at which he appeared on earth. It is quite probable that for a long period the fight of the dimensions was going on in animal bodies which were anatomically and physiologically similar to those which are ours as historical man, until the conditions were given for that leap which brought about the dominance of the dimension of the spirit. But we must go one step farther. The same struggle of the dimensions which finally produced the sharp division between those beings who have language and those who have not now goes on within every human being as a lasting problem for the basis of the predominance of the spirit. Man cannot not be man, as animal cannot not be animal. But man can partly miss that creative act in which the dominance of the psychological is overcome by the dominance of the spirit. As we shall see, this is the essence of the moral problem.

These considerations reject implicitly the doctrine that at a precise moment of the evolutionary process God in a special act added an "immortal soul" to an otherwise complete human body, with this soul bearing the life of the spirit. This idea—in addition to being based on the metaphor "level" and a corresponding supranaturalistic doctrine of man—disrupts the multidimensional unity of life, especially the unity of the psychological and the spirit, thus making the dynamics of the human personality completely incomprehensible.

Instead of separating the spirit from the conditioning psychological realm, we shall try to describe the rise of an act of the spirit out of a constellation of psychological factors. Every act of the spirit presupposes given psychological material and, at the same time, constitutes a leap which is possible only for a totally centered self, that is to say, one that is free.

The relation of spirit to the psychological material can be observed in the cognitive as well as in the moral act. Every thought aiming at knowledge is based on sense impressions and conscious and unconscious scientific traditions and experiences, and conscious and unconscious authorities, besides volitional and emotional elements which are always present. Without this material, thinking would have no content. But in order to transform this material into knowledge, something must be done to it; it must be split, reduced, increased, and connected according to logical, and purged according to methodological, criteria. All this is done by the personal center which is not identical with any particular one of these elements. The transcendence of the center over the psychological material makes the cognitive act possible, and such an act is a manifestation of spirit. We said that the personal center is not identical with any one of the psychological contents, but neither is it another element added to them; if it were this, it would be psychological material itself and not the bearer of the spirit. Nor is the personal center strange to the psychological material. It is *their* psychological center, but transformed into the dimension of the spirit. The psychological center, the subject of self-awareness, moves in the realm of higher animal life as a balanced whole, organically or spontaneously (but not mechanically) dependent on the total situation. If the dimension of the spirit dominates a life process, the psychological center offers its own contents to the unity of the personal center. This happens through deliberation and decision. In doing so it actualizes its own potentialities, but in actualizing its own potentialities, it transcends itself. This phenomenon can be experienced in every cognitive act.

The same situation obtains in a moral act. Here, also, a large amount of material is present in the psychological center—drives, inclinations, desires, more or less compulsory trends, moral experiences, ethical traditions and authorities, relations to other persons, social conditions. But the moral act is not the diagonal in which all these vectors limit each other and converge; it is the centered self which actualizes itself as a personal self by distinguishing, separating, rejecting, preferring, connecting, and in doing so, transcending its elements. The act, or more exactly the whole complex of acts, in which this happens has the character of freedom, not freedom in the bad sense of the indeterminacy of an act of the will, but freedom in the sense of a total reaction of a centered self which deliberates and decides. Such freedom is united with destiny in such a way that the psychological material which enters into the moral act represents the pole of destiny, while the deliberating and deciding self represents the pole of freedom, according to the ontological polarity of freedom and destiny.

The preceding description of acts of the spirit implicitly refutes both a dualistic contrasting of the spirit with the psychological and a dissolution of the spirit into the psychological out of which it arises. The principle of multidimensional unity denies dualism as well as psychologistic (or biologistic) monism.

Friedrich Nietzsche expresses well the intricacies of the relation of the dimension of the spirit to the preceding dimensions of life, when he says of spirit that it is the life which cuts into life itself. Out of its pain it draws into fulfilment (*Thus Spake Zarathustra*).

d) Norms and values in the dimension of spirit.—In the description of the relation between spirit and its psychological presuppositions, the word "freedom" was used for the way in which the spirit acts upon the psychological material. Such freedom is possible only because there are norms to which the spirit subjects itself just in order to be free within the limits of its biological and psychological destiny. Freedom and subjection to valid norms are one and the same thing. Therefore the question arises: What is the source of these norms?

One can distinguish three main answers to this question, each of which has been represented in both past and present: the pragmatic, the value-theoretical, the ontological. They contradict each other in some respects, but they do not exclude each other. Each contributes an important element to the solution, although the ontological answer is decisive and implicit within the other two, whether or not this is realized by those who offer the answer.

According to the pragmatic derivation of norms, life is its own criterion. Pragmatism does not transcend life in order to judge life. The criteria of spirit are immanent in the life of the spirit. This is consistent with our doctrine of the multidimensional unity of life and our rejection of the metaphor "level": the norms of life do not originate outside of life. But pragmatism has no way of demonstrating how particular expressions of life can become norms for life as a whole. Whenever the pragmatic method is applied consistently to ethical, political, or aesthetic judgments, it selects criteria which themselves must be measured by higher, and finally highest, criteria, and when this point is reached, the pragmatic method is replaced, without explicit recognition, by an ontological principle which cannot be tested pragmatically because it is the criterion for all testing.

This situation is clearly recognized by the value theory of norms in the dimension of spirit. The value theory has a high standing in present philosophical thought and has largely influenced non-philosophical and even popular thought. Its great merit has been to establish the validity of norms without taking refuge in either heteronomous theology or that kind of metaphysics the breakdown of which has produced the value theory (in people like Lotze, Ritschl, the Neo-Kantians, and so on.) They wanted to save validity (*Geltung*) without pragmatic relativism or metaphysical absolutism. In their "hierarchies of values" they tried to establish norms for a society without *sacred* hierarchies. But they were and still are unable to answer the question: What is the basis for the claim of such values to control life? What is their relevance for the processes of life in the dimension of spirit for which they are supposed to be valid? Why should life, the bearer of spirit, care for them at all? What is the relation of obligation to being? This question has driven some philosophers of value back to the ontological problem.

The pragmatic solution must be restated and qualified: it is true that the criteria for life in the dimension of spirit are implicit in life itself—otherwise they would not be relevant for life; but life is ambiguous because it unites essential and existential elements. The essential or potential in man and his world is the source from which the norms for life in the dimension of spirit are derived. The essential nature of being, the *logos*-determined structure of reality, as Stoicism and Christianity would call it, is the "heaven of values" to which the value theory points.

But if this is accepted and the ontological answer thus restated, the question arises: How can we reach this "heaven"; how can we know about the *logos*-structure of being, about the essential nature of man and his world? We know about it only through its ambiguous manifestations in the mixture which is life. These manifestations are ambiguous in so far as they not only reveal but also conceal. There is no straight and certain way to the norms of action in the dimension of spirit. The sphere of the potential is partly visible, partly hidden. Therefore, the application of a norm to a concrete situation in the realm of the spirit is a venture and a risk. It requires courage and acceptance of the possibility of failure. The daring character of life in its creative functions holds true also in the dimension of the spirit, in morality, culture, and religion.

B. THE SELF-ACTUALIZATION OF LIFE AND ITS AMBIGUITIES

FUNDAMENTAL CONSIDERATION: THE BASIC FUNCTIONS OF LIFE AND THE NATURE OF THEIR AMBIGUITY

Life was defined as the actualization of potential being. In every life process such actualization takes place. The terms "act," "action," "actual," denote a centrally intended movement ahead, a going-out from a center of action. But this going-out takes place in such a way that the center is not lost in the outgoing movement. The self-identity remains in the self-alteration. The other (*alterum*) in the process of alteration is turned both away from the center and back toward it. So we can distinguish three elements in the process of life: self-identity, self-alteration, and return to one's self. Potentiality becomes actuality only through these three elements in the process which we call life.

This character of the structure of life processes leads to the recognition of the first function of life: self-integration. In it the center of self-identity is established, drawn into self-alteration and re-established with the contents of that into which it has been altered. There is centeredness in all life, both as reality and as task. The movement in which centeredness is actualized shall be called the self-integration of life. The syllable "self" indicates that it is life itself which drives toward centeredness in every process of self-integration. There is nothing outside life which could cause its movement from centeredness through alteration back to centeredness. The nature of life itself expresses itself in the function of self-integration in every particular life process.

But the process of actualization does not imply only the function of self-integration, the circular movement of life from a center and back to this center; it also implies the function of producing new centers, the function of self-creation. In it the movement of actualization of the potential, the movement of life, goes forward in the horizontal direction. In it also self-identity and self-alteration are effective, but under the predominance of self-alteration. Life drives toward the new. It cannot do this without centeredness, but it does it by transcending every individual center. It is the principle of growth which determines the function of self-creation, growth within the circular movement of a self-centered being and growth in the creation of new centers beyond this circle.

The word "creation" is one of the great symbol-words describing the relation of God to the universe. Contemporary language has applied the words "creative," "creativity," and even "creation" to human (and prehuman) beings, actions, and products. And it is consistent with this fashion to speak of the self-creative function of life. Of course, life is not self-creative in an absolute sense. It presupposes the creative ground out of which it comes. Nevertheless, as we can speak of Spirit only because we have spirit, so we can speak of Creation only because creative power is given to us.

The third direction in which the actualization of the potential goes is in contrast to the circular and the horizontal—the vertical direction. This metaphor stands for the function of life which we suggest calling the self-transcending function. In itself the term "self-transcendence" could also be used for the two other functions: self-integration, going from identity through alteration back to identity, is a kind of intrinsic self-transcendence within a centered being, and in every process of growth a later stage transcends a former one in the horizontal direction. But in both cases the self-transcendence remains within the limits of finite life. One finite situation is transcended by another; but finite life is not transcended. Therefore, it seems appropriate to reserve the term "self-transcendence" for that function of life in which this does occur—in which life drives beyond itself as finite life. It is *self*-transcendence because life is not transcended by something that is not life. Life, by its very nature as life, is both *in* itself and *above* itself, and this situation is manifest in the function of self-transcendence. For the way in which this elevation of life beyond itself becomes apparent, I suggest using the phrase "driving toward the sublime." The words "sublime," "sublimation," "sublimity" point to a "going beyond limits" toward the great, the solemn, the high.

Thus, within the process of actualization of the potential, which is called life, we distinguish the three functions of life: self-integration under the principle of centeredness, self-creation under the principle of growth, and self-transcendence under the principle of sublimity. The basic structure of self-identity and self-alteration is effective in each, and each is dependent on the basic polarities of being: self-integration on the polarity of individualization and participation, self-creation on the polarity of dynamics and form, self-transcendence on the polarity of freedom and destiny. And the structure of self-identity and self-alteration is rooted in the basic ontological self-world correlation. (The relation of the structure and the functions of life to the ontological polarities will receive a fuller treatment in the discussion of the particular functions.)

The three functions of life unite elements of self-identity with elements of self-alteration. But this unity is threatened by existential estrangement, which drives life in one or the other direction, thus disrupting the unity. To the degree in which this disruption is real, self-integration is countered by disintegration, self-creation is countered by destruction, self-transcendence is countered by profanization. Every life process has the ambiguity that the positive and negative elements are mixed in such a way that a definite separation of the negative from the positive is impossible: life at every moment is ambiguous. It is my intention to discuss the particular functions of life, not in their essential nature, separate from their existential distortion, but in the way they appear within the ambiguities of their actualization, for life is neither essential nor existential but ambiguous.

1. The Self-integration of Life and Its Ambiguities

a) *Individualization and centeredness.*—The first of the polarities in the structure of being is that of individualization and participation. It is expressed in the function of self-integration through the principle of centeredness. Centeredness is a quality of individualization, in so far as the indivisible thing is the centered thing. To continue the metaphor, the center is a point, and a point cannot be divided. A centered being can develop another being out of itself, or it can be deprived of some parts which belong to the whole; but the center as such cannot be divided—it can only be destroyed. A fully individualized being, therefore, is at the same time a fully centered being. Within the limits of human experience only man has these qualities fully; in all other beings, both centeredness and individualization are limited. But they are qualities of everything that is, whether limited or fully developed.

The term "centeredness" is derived from the geometrical circle and metaphorically applied to the structure of a being in which an effect exercised on one part has consequences for all other parts, directly or indirectly. The words "whole" or *Gestalt* have been used for things with such structure; and these terms have sometimes been applied to all dimensions except the inorganic ones. Occasionally, the inorganic dimensions have also been included. The line of thought we have followed leads to the more inclusive interpretation. Since individualization is an ontological pole, it has universal significance, and so has centeredness, which is the condition of the actualization of the individual in life. However, this makes the term "centeredness" preferable to wholeness or *Gestalt*. It does not imply an integrated *Gestalt*, or "whole," but only processes going out from and returning to a point which cannot be localized in a special place in the whole but which is the point of direction of the two basic movements of all life processes. In this sense, centeredness exists under the control of all dimensions of being, but as a process of outgoing and returning. For where there is a center, there is a periphery which includes an amount of space or, in non-metaphorical terms, which unites a manifoldness of elements. This corresponds to participation, with which individualization forms a polarity. Individualization separates. The most individualized being is the most unapproachable and the most lonely one. But, at the same time, he has the greatest potentiality of universal participation. He can have communion with his world and *eros* toward it. This *eros* can be theoretical as well as practical. He can participate in the universe in all its dimensions and draw elements of it into himself. Therefore the process of self-integration moves between the center and the manifoldness which is taken into the center.

This description of integration implies the possibility of disintegration. Disintegration means failure to reach or to preserve self-integration. This failure can occur in one of two directions. Either it is the inability to overcome a limited, stabilized, and immovable centeredness, in which case there is a center, but a center which does not have a life process whose content is changed and increased; thus it approaches the death of mere self-identity. Or it is the inability to return because of the dispersing power of the manifoldness, in which case there is life, but it is dispersed and weak in centeredness, and it faces the danger of losing its center altogether—the death of mere self-alteration. The function of self-integration ambiguously mixed with disintegration works between these two extremes in every life process.

b) *Self-integration and disintegration in general: health and disease.*— Centeredness is a universal phenomenon. It appears in the microcosmic as well as in the macrocosmic dimension of the inorganic realm, and it appears in the realm of our ordinary encounter with inorganic objects. It appears in atom and star, in molecule and crystal. It produces structures which inspire the enthusiasm of the artist and which confirm, poetically speaking, the Pythagorean symbol of the musical harmony of the astronomical spheres. This gives to every star as well as to every atom and crystal a kind of individuality. They cannot be divided; they can only be crushed—their centeredness disrupted and parts of their integrated unity lost and driven toward other centers. The full weight of these facts becomes manifest if one imagines a completely uncentered realm of inorganic being. It would be that chaos of which, in creation myths, water is the symbol. Individual centeredness in the microcosmic and macrocosmic spheres and in everything between them is the "beginning" of creation. But the process of self-integration is counteracted by the forces of disintegration: repulsion counteracts attraction (compare the centrifugal and centripetal forces); concentration—ideally in one point—is counteracted by expansion—ideally to an infinite periphery— and fusion is contrasted by splitting. The ambiguities of self-integration and disintegration are effective in these processes, and they are effective simultaneously in the same process. Integrating and disintegrating forces are struggling in every situation, and every situation is a compromise between these forces. This gives a dynamic character to the inorganic realm which cannot be described in exclusively quantitative terms. One could say: No-thing in nature is merely a thing—if "thing" here means that which is altogether conditioned, an object without any kind of "being in itself" or centeredness. Perhaps man alone is able to produce "things" by dissolving centered structures and reconnecting the pieces into technical objects. Yet, though the technical objects have no center in themselves, even they have a center which is imposed on them by man (for example, the computing machine). This view of the inorganic realm and its dimensions is a decisive step in overcoming the gap between the inorganic and the organic (and psychological). Just like every other dimension, the inorganic belongs to life, and it shows the integratedness and the possible disintegration of life in general.

Self-integration and disintegration are most manifest under the dimension of the organic. Every living being is sharply centered (at whatever point in the whole of natural processes one starts to speak of living beings); it reacts as a whole. Its life is a process of going out and returning to itself as long as it lives. It takes in elements of the encountered reality and assimilates them to its own centered whole, or it rejects them if assimilation is impossible. It pushes ahead into space as far as its individual structure permits, and it withdraws when it has overstepped this limit or when other living individuals force it to withdraw. It develops its parts in balance under the uniting center and is forced back into balance if one part tends to disrupt the unity.

The process of self-integration is constitutive for life, but it is so in a continuous struggle with disintegration, and integrating and disintegrating tendencies are ambiguously mixed in any given moment. The strange elements which must be assimilated have the tendency to become independent within the centered whole and to disrupt it. Many diseases, especially infectious ones, can be understood as an organism's inability to return to its self-identity. It cannot eject the strange elements which it has not assimilated. But disease can also be the consequence of a self-restriction of the centered whole, a tendency to maintain self-identity by avoiding the dangers of going out to self-alteration. The weakness of life expresses itself in the refusal of necessary movement, desirable food, participation in the environment, and so on. In order to be safe, the organism tries to rest in itself, but since this contradicts the life function of self-integration, it leads to disease and disintegration.

This view of disease compels us to reject biological theories which model their concepts of life after those phenomena in which life disintegrates, i.e., uncentered processes which are subject to quantitative-calculating methods of analysis. The stimulus-response theory has an important function in the science of life, but it becomes erroneous if raised to absolute validity. Whether the uncentered, calculable processes are produced by disease (for their production is the essence of disease) or whether they are artificially produced in the experimental situation, they are opposed to the normal processes of self-integration. They are not models of healthy life but of life in disintegration.

One distinguishes between lower and higher forms of life in the realm of the organic. Something must be said about this distinction from the theological point of view, because of the wide symbolic use to which all forms of organic life, especially the higher ones, are subject and because of the fact that man—against the protest of many naturalists—is often called the highest living being. First of all, one should not confuse the "highest" with the "most perfect." Perfection means actualization of one's potentialities; therefore, a lower being can be more perfect than a higher one if it is actually what it is potentially—at least in a high approximation. And the highest being—man—can become less perfect than any other, because he not only can fail to actualize his essential being but can deny and distort it.

So a higher living being is not in itself a more perfect one; rather, there are different degrees of lower and higher. The question then is: What are the criteria of high and low, and why is man the highest being in spite of his liability to the greatest imperfection? The criteria are the definiteness of the center, on the one hand, and the amount of content united by it, on the other. These are the criteria for the higher or lower rank of the dimensions of life. They decide the establishment of the animal dimension above the dimension of the vegetative. They decide that the dimension of inner awareness surpasses the biological and is surpassed by the dimension of the spirit. They decide that man is the highest being because his center is definite and the structure of its content is all-embracing. In contrast to all other beings, man does not have only environment; he has world, the structured unity of all possible content. This and its implications make him the highest being.

The decisive step in the self-integration of life—with respect to both the definite character of the center and the richness of the content—is the appearance of self-awareness somewhere in the animal realm. Self-awareness means that all encounters of a being with its environment are experienced as related to the individual being that is aware of them. Centered awareness implies a center which is definite, and at the same time, it implies a more embracing content than in even the most developed preconscious being. Without awareness there is only presence in encounter; with awareness a past and future are open in terms of remembrance and anticipation. The remoteness of the remembered or the anticipated may be very slight, but the fact that it appears irrefutably in animal life indicates the dominance of a new dimension, the psychological.

The self-integration of life in the psychological realm includes the basic movement of going out of and returning to itself in immediate experience. The center of a being under the dimension of self-awareness can be called the "psychological self." "Self," in this sense, must not be misunderstood as an object, the existence of which could be discussed, or as a part of a living being, but rather as the point to which all contents of awareness are related, in so far as "I" am aware of them. The acts which go out from this center are related to the environment as receiving it and reacting to it. This is an implication of the basic polar elements of individualization and participation in all reality, and it is a continuation of the same polar tension in the biological and inorganic realms. Under the dimension of self-awareness, it is effective as perceiving encountered reality and reacting upon it.

It is difficult to discuss the psychological realm and the functions of life within it because of the fact that man ordinarily experiences the dimension of self-awareness in unity with the dimension of the spirit. The psychological and the personal self are united in him. Only in such special situations as dream, intoxication, half-sleep, and so on, does a partial separation occur, and this separation is never so complete that a sharply distinct description of the psychological is possible. To avoid this difficulty, one approaches the process of self-integration under the dimension of self-awareness by way of animal psychology. The limits of this approach lie in man's ability to participate empathetically in the psychological self of even the highest animals in such a way that, for example, he can fully understand psychological health and disease. Artificially induced psychic disintegration in animals, such as exaggerated anxiety or exaggerated hostility, can be observed only indirectly in so far as they are expressed biologically. Self-awareness is, so to speak, submerged in both dimensions, the biological dimension on the one side and that of the spirit on the other side, and can be approached through analyses and conclusions only, not by direct observation.

Conscious of these limitations, one may say that the structure of health and disease, of successful or unsuccessful self-integration in the psychological sphere, is dependent on the working of the same factors which work in the preceding dimensions: the forces driving toward self-identity and those driving toward self-alteration. The psychological self can be disrupted by its inability to assimilate (i.e., to take into the centered unity an extensively or intensively overpowering number of impressions), or by its inability to resist the destructive impact of impressions drawing the self in too many or too contradictory directions, or by its inability under such impacts to keep particular psychological functions balanced by others. In these ways self-alteration may prevent or disrupt self-integration. The opposite derangement is caused by the psychological self's fear of losing itself, with the result that it becomes indifferent to stimuli and ends in a stupor which prevents any self-alteration and transforms self-identity into a dead form. The ambiguities of psychic self-integration and disintegration occur between these poles.

c) The self-integration of life in the dimension of spirit: morality, or the constitution of the personal self.—In man complete centeredness is essentially given, but it is not actually given until man actualizes it in freedom and through destiny. The act in which man actualizes his essential centeredness is the moral act. Morality is the function of life by which the realm of the spirit comes into being. Morality is the constitutive function of spirit. A moral act, therefore, is not an act in which some divine or human law is obeyed but an act in which life integrates itself in the dimension of spirit, and this means as personality within a community. Morality is the function of life in which the centered self constitutes itself as a person; it is the totality of those acts in which a potentially personal life process becomes an actual person. Such acts happen continuously in a personal life; the constitution of the person as a person never comes to an end during his whole life process.

Morality presupposes the potentially total centeredness of him in whom life is actualized under the dimension of spirit. "Total centeredness" is the situation of having, face to face with one's self, a world to which one, at the same time, belongs as a part. This situation liberates the self from the bondage to the environment on which every being in the preceding dimensions is dependent. Man lives in an environment, but he has a world. Theories which try to explain his behavior solely by reference to his environment reduce man to the dimension of the organic-psychological and deprive him of participation in the dimension of spirit, thus making it impossible to explain how he can have a theory which claims to be true—of which the environmental theory itself is an instance. But man has a world, *i.e.*, a structured whole of infinite potentialities and actualities. In his encounter with his environment (*this* home, *this* tree, *this* person), he experiences both environment and world, or more exactly, in and through his encounter with the things of his environment he encounters a world. He transcends their merely environmental quality. If this were not so, he could not be completely centered.

In some part of his being he would be a part of his environment, and this part would not be an element in his centered self. But man can oppose his self to every part of his world, including himself as a part of his world.

This is the first presupposition of morality and of the dimension of the spirit in general. The second follows from it. Because man has a world which he faces as a totally centered self, he can ask questions and receive answers and commands. This possibility, which characterizes the dimension of the spirit, is unique, because it implies both freedom from the merely given (environment) and norms which determine the moral act through freedom. As shown above, these norms express the essential structure of reality, of self and world, over against the existential conditions of mere environment. Again it becomes manifest that freedom is the openness for norms of unconditional, or essential, validity. They express the essence of being, and the moral side of the function of self-integration is the totality of acts in which the commands coming from the essence of the encountered world are obeyed or disobeyed. One can also say that man is able to respond to these commands and that this ability is what makes him responsible. Every moral act is a responsible act, a response to a valid command, but man can refuse to respond. If he refuses, he gives way to the forces of moral disintegration; he acts against the spirit in the power of the spirit. For he can never get rid of himself as spirit. He constitutes himself as a completely centered self even in his anti-essential, antimoral actions. These actions express moral centeredness even while they tend to dissolve the moral center.

Before continuing the discussion of the constitution of the personal self, it may be useful to discuss a semantic problem. "Moral" and its derivatives have accumulated so many bad connotations that it seems impossible to use them in any positive sense. Morality is reminiscent of moralism, of immorality with its sexual connotations, of conventional morals, and so on. For this reason, it has been suggested (especially in Continental theology) that the term "morals" be replaced by the term "ethics." But this offers no real solution because after a short time the negative connotations of "moral" would fall upon the new word. It is more useful to reserve the term "ethics" and its derivatives to designate the "science of morals," which deals theoretically with the moral function of the spirit. Of course, this presupposes that the term "moral" can be liberated from the negative connotations which have increasingly distorted its meaning since the eighteenth century. The preceding and following discussions are an attempt to work in this direction.

The moral act in which the realm of the spirit comes into being presupposes the freedom to receive commands, to obey and to disobey them. The source of these commands is the moral norms, that is, the essential structures of encountered reality, in man himself and in his world. The first question that arises at this point is: How does man become aware of the ought-to-be in his encounter with being? How does it happen that he experiences the moral commands as commands of unconditional validity? In contemporary ethical discussions the answer has been given with increasing unanimity on the basis of Protestant and Kantian insights: in the encounter of a person who is already and not yet a person with another in the same condition, both are constituted as real persons. "Oughtness" is basically experienced in the ego-thou relation. This situation can also be described in the following way: man, facing his world, has the whole universe as the potential content of his centered self. Certainly, there are actual limits because of the finitude of every being, but the world is indefinitely open to man; everything can become a content of the self. This is the structural basis for the endlessness of libido in the state of estrangement; it is the condition for man's desire to "win the whole world."

But there is one limit to man's attempt to draw all content into himself—the other self. One can subject and exploit another in his organic basis, including his psychological self, but not the other self in the dimension of the spirit. One can destroy it as a self, but one cannot assimilate it as a content of one's own centeredness. The attempt to do so by totalitarian rulers has never succeeded. Nobody can deprive a person of his claim to be a person and to be dealt with as a person. Therefore, the other self is the unconditional limit to the desire to assimilate one's whole world, and the experience of this limit is the experience of the ought-to-be, the moral imperative. The moral constitution of the self in the dimension of the spirit begins with this experience. Personal life emerges in the encounter of person with person and in no other way. If one can imagine a living being with the psychosomatic structure of man, completely outside any human community, such a being could not actualize its potential spirit. It would be driven in all directions, limited only by its finitude, but it would not experience the ought-to-be. Therefore, the self-integration of the person as a person occurs in a community, within which the continuous mutual encounter of centered self with centered self is possible and actual.

The community itself is a phenomenon of life which has analogies in all realms. It is implied by the polarity of individualization and participation. Neither pole is actual without the other. This is as true of the function of self-creation as it is of the function of self-integration, and there is no self-transcendence of life except through the polar interdependence of individualization and participation.

It would be possible to continue the discussion of centeredness and self-integration in relation to participation and community, but this would anticipate descriptions which belong to the dimension of the historical, and such anticipation would be dangerous for understanding the life processes. For example, it would support the false assumption that the moral principle refers to the community in the same way that it refers to the personality. But the structure of the community, including its structure of centeredness, is qualitatively different from that of the personality. The community is without complete centeredness and without the freedom which is identical with being completely centered. The confusing problem of social ethics is that the community consists of individuals who are bearers of the spirit, whereas the community itself, because of its lack of a centered self, is not. Where this situation is recognized, the notion of a personified community put under moral commands is impossible—as in some forms of pacifism. These considerations lead to the decision that the functions of life with respect to the community must be discussed in the context of the most embracing dimension, the historical. At this point the object of discussion is the question of the way in which the person becomes a person. Considering the communal quality of the person does not mean considering the community.

d) *The ambiguities of personal self-integration: the possible, the real, and the ambiguity of sacrifice.*—As does any other form of self-integration, the personal moves between the poles of self-identity and self-alteration. Integration is the state of balance between them, disintegration the disruption of this balance. Both trends are always effective in actual life processes under the conditions of existential estrangement. Personal life is ambiguously pulled between forces of essential centeredness and of existential disruption. There is no moment in a personal life process in which one or the other force is exclusively dominant.

As in the organic and the psychological realms, the ambiguity of life in the function of self-integration is rooted in the necessity for a being to take the encountered content of reality into its centered unity without being disrupted by its quantity or quality. Personal life is always the life of somebody—as in all dimensions, life is the life of some individual being, according to the principle of centeredness. I speak of my life, of your life, of our lives. Everything is included in my life which belongs to me: my body, my self-awareness, my memories and anticipations, my perceptions and thoughts, my will, and my emotions. All this belongs to the centered unity which I am. I try to increase this content by going out and try to preserve it by returning to the centered unity which I am. In this process I encounter innumerable possibilities, each of which, if accepted, means a self-alteration and consequently a danger of disruption. For the sake of my present reality, I must keep many possibilities outside of my centered self, or I must give up something of what I now am for the sake of something possible which may enlarge and strengthen my centered self. So my life process oscillates between the possible and the real and requires the surrender of the one for the other—the sacrificial character of all life.

Every individual has essential potentialities which he tends to actualize, according to the general movement of being from the potential to the actual. Some of these potentialities never reach the stage of concrete possibilities; historical, social, and individual conditions reduce the possibilities drastically. From the point of view of human potentialities, a Central American rural Indian may have the same human potentialities as a North American college student, but he does not have the same possibilities of actualizing them. His choices are much more limited, although he also has to sacrifice possibilities for realities and vice versa.

Examples illustrating this situation are abundant. We must sacrifice possible interests for those which are or could become real. We must surrender possible work and possible vocations for the one we have chosen. We must sacrifice possible human relations for the sake of real ones or real ones for the sake of possible ones. We must choose between a consistent but self-limiting building-up of our life and a breaking-through of as many limits as possible with a loss of consistency and direction. We must continuously decide between abundance and poverty and between special kinds of abundance and special kinds of poverty. There is the abundance of life into which one is driven by the anxiety of remaining poor in some respect, or in many respects; but this abundance may surpass our power of doing justice to it and to us, and then the abundance becomes an empty repetition. If thereupon the opposite anxiety, that of losing oneself in life, leads to a partial resignation or complete withdrawal from abundance, the poverty becomes empty self-relatedness— the centered unity of the personal self comprises many different trends, each of which tends to dominate the center. We have mentioned this already in connection with the psychological self and have pointed to the structure of compulsion; the same ambiguity of self-integration is present under the dimension of spirit. It is usually described as the struggle of values in a personal center; in ontological terms it can be called the conflict of essences within an existing self. One of the many ethical norms, strengthened by experiences with the encountered world, takes hold on the personal center and shakes the balance of essences within the centered unity. This can result in a failure of self-integration in personalities with a strong but narrow morality—just as it may lead to disrupting conflicts between the dominating and the suppressed ethical norms. The ambiguity of sacrifice is apparent even in the moral function of the spirit.

The self-integration of life includes the sacrifice of the possible for the real, or of the real for the possible, as an inescapable process in all dimensions other than that of the spirit and as an inescapable decision within the dimension of the spirit. In the common judgment, sacrifice is unambiguously good. In Christianity, in which God himself makes the sacrifice according to Christian symbolism, the act of sacrifice seems to transcend any ambiguity. But this is not true, as theological thoughts and penitential practice well know. They know that every sacrifice is a moral risk and that hidden motives may even make a seemingly heroic sacrifice questionable. This does not mean that there should not be sacrifice; the moral life demands it continuously. But the risk must be taken with awareness that it is a risk and not something unambiguously good on which an easy conscience can rely. One of the risks is the decision whether to sacrifice the real for the possible or the possible for the real. The "anxious conscience" tends to prefer the real to the possible, because the real is at least familiar, whereas the possible is unknown. But the moral risk in sacrificing an important possibility can be equally as great as the risk in sacrificing an important reality. The ambiguity of sacrifice also becomes visible when the question is asked, What is to be sacrificed? Self-sacrifice may be worthless if there is no self worthy of being sacrificed. The other one, or the cause, for which it is sacrificed may receive nothing from it, nor does he who makes the sacrifice achieve moral self-integration by it. He may merely gain the power which weakness gives over the strong one for whom the sacrifice is made. If, however, the self which is sacrificed is worthy, the question arises whether that for which it is sacrificed is worthy to receive it. The cause which receives it may be evil, or the person for whom it is offered may use it for selfish exploitation. Thus the ambiguity of sacrifice is a decisive and all-permeating expression of the ambiguity of life in the function of self-integration. It shows the human situation in the mixture of essential and existential elements and the impossibility of separating them as good and evil in an unambiguous way.

e) *The ambiguities of the moral law: the moral imperative, the moral norms, the moral motivation.*—The discussion of the conflict of norms and the necessity of risking the sacrifice of some of them for the sake of others has shown that the ambiguities of personal self-integration are ultimately rooted in the character of the moral law. Since morality is the constitutive function of the spirit, the analysis of its nature and the proof of its ambiguity are decisive for the understanding of the spirit and the predicament of man. Obviously, such inquiry relates the present discussion to the biblical and classical theological judgments about the law's meaning in the relation of God and man. The three functions of the spirit—morality, culture, and religion—will be treated separately in this and the following sections. Only after this has been done will their essential unity, their actual conflicts, and their possible reunion be considered. This sequence is called for by the fact that they can only be reunited by that which transcends each of them, i.e., the new reality or the divine Spirit. Under the dimension of spirit as it is actual in human life, no reunion is possible.

Three main problems of the moral law confront ethical inquiry: the unconditional character of the moral imperative, the norms of moral action, and moral motivation. The ambiguity of life in the dimension of the spirit is manifest in all three.

As we have seen, the moral imperative is valid because it represents our essential being over against our state of existential estrangement. For this reason the moral imperative is categorical, its validity not dependent on external or internal conditions; it is unambiguous. But this unam-

biguity does not refer to anything concrete. It only says that if there is
a moral imperative it is unconditional. The question then is whether
and where there is a moral imperative. Our first answer was: The encounter with another person implies the unconditional command to
acknowledge him as a person. The validity of the moral imperative is
basically experienced in such encounters. But this does not say what
kind of encounter provides for such an experience, and to answer this a
qualifying description is needed. There are innumerable non-personal
encounters in reality (walking together in a crowd, reading about people
in a newspaper) which are potentially personal encounters but which
never become actual. The transition from the potentially personal encounter to the actual one is a field with countless ambiguities, many of
which put before us painful decisions. The question—Who is my neighbor?—with all its problems, remains valid in spite—or more exactly
because—of the *one* answer given by Jesus in the story of the Good
Samaritan. This answer shows that the abstract notion of "acknowledging the other one as a person" becomes concrete only in the notion of
participating in the other one (which follows from the ontological
polarity of individualization and participation). Without participation
one would not know what "other self" means; no empathy discerning
the difference between a thing and a person would be possible. Even the
word "thou" in the description of the ego-thou encounter could not be
used, because it implies the participation that is present whenever one
addresses somebody as a person. So one must ask, What kind of participation is it in which the moral self is constituted and which has unconditional validity? It certainly cannot be a participation in the particular
characteristics of another self with one's own particular characteristics.
This would be the more or less successful convergence of two particularities which could lead to sympathy or antipathy, to friendship or
hostility; this is a matter of chance, which does not constitute a moral
imperative. The moral imperative demands that one self participate in
the center of the other self and consequently accept his particularities
even if there is no convergence between the two individuals as individuals. This acceptance of the other self by participating in his personal
center is the core of love in the sense of *agape*, the New Testament term.
The preliminary formal answer, that the unconditional character of the
moral imperative is experienced in the encounter of person with person,

has now become embodied in the material answer, that it is *agape* which gives concreteness to the categorical imperative, centeredness to the person and the foundation of the life of the spirit.

Agape, as the ultimate norm of the moral law, is beyond the distinction of formal and material. But, because of the material element in *agape*, this assertion reveals the ambiguity of the moral law—and it does so just in the term "law of love." The problem can be formulated in this manner: How is participation in the center of the other self related to participation in or rejection of his particular characteristics? Do they support, or exclude, or limit each other? For instance, what is the essential and what is the existential relation of *agape* and libido, and what does the mixture of both relations in a moral act mean for the validity of *agape* as ultimate norm? These questions are asked in order to show the ambiguity of the moral law from the point of view of its validity, and at the same time they lead to the question of the ambiguity of the moral law from the point of view of its content—the actual commandments.

The commandments of the moral law are valid because they express man's essential nature and put his essential being against him in his state of existential estrangement. This raises the question: How is moral self-integration possible within the ambiguous mixture of essential and existential elements which characterizes life? We answered: By love in the sense of *agape*! For love includes the ultimate, though formal, principle of justice, and love applies it in an ever changing way to the concrete situation.

This solution is decisive for the question of the content of the moral law. But it can be attacked from two sides. One can defend the pure formalism of ethics, as it appears, for example, in Kant and reject *agape* as ultimate principle just because it leads to ambiguous decisions which are lacking in unconditional validity. But actually, not even Kant was able to maintain the radical formalism he intended, and in his elaboration of the moral imperative he appears as a liberal heir of Christianity and Stoicism. It seems that radical ethical formalism is logically impossible because the form always keeps traits of that from which it has been abstracted. Under these circumstances, it is more realistic to name the content from which the form is abstracted but to formulate the principles in such a way that the radicalism of the pure form is united in them with the concrete content. And in spite of the ambiguities in its application, this is just what *agape* does.

The content of the moral law is historically conditioned. This fact is the reason why Kant attempted to liberate the ethical norm from all concrete contents, and—in contrast—it is also the reason why most kinds of naturalism reject absolute principles of moral action. According to them, the content of the moral imperative is determined by biological and psychological necessities or by sociological and cultural realities. This precludes absolute ethical norms and admits only a calculating ethical relativism.

The truth of ethical relativism lies in the moral law's inability to give commandments which are unambiguous, both in their general form and in their concrete application. Every moral law is abstract in relation to the unique and totally concrete situation. This is true of what has been called natural law and of what has been called revealed law. This distinction between natural and revealed law is ethically irrelevant, because according to classical Protestant theology, the Ten Commandments, as well as the commandments of the Sermon on the Mount, are restatements of the natural law, the "law of love," after periods in which it was partly forgotten, partly distorted. Their substance is the natural law, or in our terminology, man's essential nature standing against him in his existential estrangement. If formulated in commandments, this law never reaches the here and now of a particular decision. With respect to it, the commandment may be right in a special situation, mainly in its prohibitive form, but it may be wrong in another situation just because of its prohibitive form. Every moral decision demands a partial liberation from the stated moral law. Every moral decision is a risk because there is no guarantee that it fulfils the law of love, the unconditional demand coming from the encounter with the other one. This risk must be taken, but if it is taken the question arises, How is it possible to reach personal self-integration under these conditions? There is no answer to this question within the realm of man's moral life and its ambiguities.

The ambiguity of the moral law with respect to ethical content even appears in the abstract statements of the moral law and not only in their particular application. For instance, the ambiguity of the Ten Commandments is rooted in the fact that, in spite of their universalist form, they are historically conditioned by the Israelitic culture and its development out of the surrounding cultures. Even the ethical statements of the New Testament, including those of Jesus, reflect the condition of the Roman Empire and the radical withdrawal of the individual from the problems of social and political existence, and this situation was repeated in all periods of the history of the church. Ethical questions and answers changed, and every answer or statement of the moral law in each period of human history remained ambiguous. Man's essential nature and the ultimate norm of *agape* in which it is expressed are both hidden and manifest in the processes of life. We have no unambiguous approach to the created nature of man and its dynamic potentialities. We have only an indirect and ambiguous approach through the revelatory experiences which underlie the ethical wisdom of all nations, but which are not unambiguous even though they are revelatory. The human reception of every revelation makes the revelation itself ambiguous for man's action.

A practical consequence of these considerations is that the moral conscience is ambiguous in what it commands us to do or not to do. In view of innumerable historical and psychological cases, one cannot deny that there is an "erring conscience." The conflicts between tradition and revolution, between nomism and liberality, between authority and autonomy, make a simple reliance on the "voice of conscience" impossible. It is a risk to follow one's conscience; it is a greater risk to contradict it. But if it is uncertain, this greater risk is required. Therefore, although it is safer to follow one's conscience, the result may be disastrous, revealing the ambiguity of conscience and leading to the quest for a moral certainty which in temporal life is given only fragmentarily and through anticipation.

The principle of *agape* expresses the unconditional validity of the moral imperative, and it gives the ultimate norm for all ethical content. But it has still a third function: it is the source of moral motivation. It necessarily commands, threatens, and promises, because fulfilment of the law is reunion with one's essential being, or integration of the centered self. The law is "good," as Paul says. But just at this point its deepest and most dangerous ambiguity appears, that which drove Paul, Augustine, and Luther to their revolutionary experiences. The law as law expresses man's estrangement from himself. In the state of mere potentiality or created innocence (which is not a historical stage), there is no law, because man is essentially united with that to which he belongs: the divine ground of his world and of himself. What ought to be and what is are identical in the state of potentiality. In existence, this identity is broken, and in every life process the identity and non-identity of what is and what ought to be are mixed. Therefore, obedience and disobedience to the law are mixed; the law has the power to motivate partial fulfilment, but in so doing it also drives to resistance, because by its very character as law it confirms our separation from the state of fulfilment. It produces hostility against God, man, and one's self. This leads to different attitudes toward the law. The fact that it has some motivating power leads to the self-deception that it can produce reunion with our essential being, i.e., a complete self-integration of life in the realm of the spirit. This self-deception is conspicuously represented by those who are called variously the righteous ones, the pharisees, the puritans, the pietists, the moralists, the people of good will. They *are* righteous, and they deserve to be admired. On a limited basis they are well-centered, strong, self-certain, dominating. They are persons who radiate judgment even when they do not express it in words. Yet just by their righteousness they are often responsible for the distintegration of those whom they encounter and who feel their judgment.

The other attitude toward the law, probably that of the majority of people, is a resigned acceptance of the fact that its motivating power is limited and that it cannot bring about a full reunion with what we ought to be. They do not deny the validity of the law; they do not fall into anti-nomianism, and so they compromise with its commandments. This is the attitude of those who try to obey the law and oscillate between fulfilment and non-fulfilment, between a limited centeredness and a limited dispersion. They are good in the sense of conventional legality, and their fragmentary fulfilment of the law makes the life of society possible. But their goodness, like that of the righteous ones, is ambiguous—only with less self-deception and with less moral arrogance.

There is a third attitude toward the law, one which combines a radical acceptance of the validity of the law with a complete despair about its motivating power. This attitude is the result of passionate attempts to be a "righteous one" and to fulfil the law without compromise in its uncon-ditional seriousness. If these strivings are followed by the experience of failure, the centered self is disrupted in the conflict between willing and doing. One is aware of the fact (which has been rediscovered and methodologically described by present-day analytic psychology) that the unconscious motives of personal decisions are not transformed by com-mandments. The motivating power of the law is defied by them, some-times by direct resistance, sometimes by the process of rationalization and—in the social realm—by the production of ideologies. The motivating power of the divine law is wrecked by what Paul calls the op-posing "law in our members." And this is not changed by the reduction of the whole law to the law of *agape*, because if *agape* (toward God, man, and oneself) is imposed on us as law, the impossibility of fulfilling it becomes more obvious than in the case of any particular law. The ex-perience of this situation leads to the quest for a morality which fulfils the law by transcending it, that is, *agape* given to man as reuniting and integrating reality, as new being and not as law.

2. THE SELF-CREATIVITY OF LIFE AND ITS AMBIGUITIES

a) *Dynamics and growth.*—The second polarity in the structure of being is that of dynamics and form. It is effective in the function of life which we have called self-creativity, and it is effective in the principle of growth. Growth is dependent on the polar element of dynamics in so far as growth is the process by which a formed reality goes beyond itself to another form which both preserves and transforms the original reality. This process is the way in which life creates itself. It does not create itself in terms of original creation. It is given to itself by the divine creativity which transcends and underlies all processes of life. But on this basis, life creates itself through the dynamics of growth. The phenomenon of growth is fundamental under all dimensions of life. It is frequently used as the ultimate norm by philosophers who openly reject all ultimate norms (for example, pragmatists). It is used for processes under the dimension of the spirit and for the work of the divine Spirit. It is a main category in individual as well as social life, and in the "philosophies of process" it is the hidden reason for their preference of "becoming" to "being."

But dynamics is held in a polar interdependence with form. Self-creation of life is always creation of form. Nothing that grows is without form. The form makes a thing what it is, and the form makes a creation of man's culture into what it is: a poem or a building or a law, and so on. However, a continuous series of forms alone is not growth. Another element, coming from the pole of dynamics, makes itself felt. Every new form is made possible only by breaking through the limits of an old form. In other words, there is a moment of "chaos" between the old and the new form, a moment of no-longer-form and not-yet-form. This chaos is never absolute; it cannot be absolute because, according to the structure of the ontological polarities, being implies form. Even relative chaos has a relative form. But relative chaos with relative form is transitional, and as such it is a danger to the self-creative function of life. At this crisis life may fall back to its starting point and resist creation, or it may destroy itself in the attempt to reach a new form. Here one thinks of the destructive implications of every birth, whether of individuals or species, of the psychological phenomenon of repression, and of the creation of a new social entity or a new artistic style. The chaotic element which appears here is already manifest in the creation myths, even in the creation stories of the Old Testament. Creation and chaos belong to each other, and even the exclusive monotheism of biblical religion confirms this structure of life. It is echoed in the symbolic descriptions of the divine life, of its abysmal depth, of its character as burning fire, of its suffering over and with the creatures, of its destructive wrath. But in the divine life the element of chaos does not endanger its eternal fulfilment, whereas in the life of the creature, under the conditions of estrangement, it leads to the ambiguity of self-creativity and destructiveness. Destruction can then be described as the prevalence of the elements of chaos over against the pole of form in the dynamics of life.

But there is no pure destruction in any life process. The merely negative has no being. In every process of life structures of creation are mixed with powers of destruction in such a way that they cannot be unambiguously separated. And in the actual processes of life, one never can establish with certainty which process is dominated by one or the other of these forces.

One could consider integration as an element of creation and disintegration as a form of destruction. And one could ask why integration and disintegration should be understood as a special function of life. However, they must be distinguished—as must the two polarities on which they are dependent. Self-integration constitutes the individual being in its centeredness; self-creation gives the dynamic impulse which drives life from one centered state to another under the principle of growth. Centeredness does not imply growth, but growth does presuppose coming from and going to a state of centeredness. Likewise, disintegration is possibly, but not necessarily, destruction. Disintegration takes place within a centered unity; destruction can occur only in the encounter of centered unity with centered unity. Disintegration is represented by disease, destruction by death.

b) Self-creativity and destruction outside the dimension of spirit: life and death.—Like centeredness, growth is a universal function of life. But while the concept of centeredness is taken from the dimension of the inorganic and its geometrical measurement, the concept of growth is taken from the organic dimension and is one of its basic characteristics. In both cases, the concept is used metaphorically to indicate the universal principle under which one of the three basic functions of life works, but it is also used literally in the realm from which it is taken.

"Growth" is used metaphorically whenever it refers to the inorganic realms—the macrocosmic, the microcosmic, and that of ordinary experience. The problem of growth and decay in the macrocosmic sphere is as old as mythology and as new as recent astronomy. For instance, it was envisaged in the rhythmic process of the burning and renewal of a "cosmos," in the discussions about "entropy" and the threat of the "death" of the world by the loss of warmth, or in the indications given by contemporary astronomy that we live within an expanding world. Such ideas show that mankind has always been aware of the ambiguity of self-creativity and destruction in the processes of life in general, including the inorganic dimension. The religious significance of these ideas is obvious, but they should never be abused (as has the doctrine of entropy) by basing arguments for the existence of a highest being on them.

The ambiguity of creation and destruction is equally visible in the microcosmic, especially the subatomic, sphere. The continuous genesis and decay of the smallest particles of matter, mutual annihilation as expressed in the conception of "countermatter," the exhaustion of radiating materials—in all these hypothetical concepts, life is seen as creating itself and being destroyed under the predominance of the inorganic dimension. These microcosmic developments are the background for developments of growth and decay within the realm of the inorganic materials ordinarily encountered, even those which actually and symbolically give the impression of unchangeable duration (rocks, metals, and so on).

The concepts of self-creativity and destruction, growth and decay, come into their own in the realms which are dominated by the dimensions of the organic, for it is here that life and death are experienced. It is not necessary to confirm the fact as such, but it is important to point out the ambiguous interweaving of self-creation and destruction in all realms of the organic. In every process of growth, the conditions of life are also the conditions of death. Death is present in every life process from its beginning to its end, although the actual death of a living being does not depend only on the ambiguity of its own individual life process but also on its position within the totality of life. But death from outside could have no power over a being if death from inside were not continuously at work.

Therefore one must affirm that the moment of our conception is the moment in which we begin not only to live but also to die. The same cellular constitution which gives a being the power of life drives toward the extinction of this power. This ambiguity of self-creation and destruction in all life processes is a fundamental experience of all life. Living beings are consciously aware of it, and the face of every living being expresses the ambiguity of growth and decay in its life process.

The ambiguity of self-creation and destruction is not limited to the growth of the living being in itself but also to its growth in relation to other life. Individual life moves within the context of all life; in each moment of a life process, strange life is encountered, with both creative and destructive reactions on both sides. Life grows by suppressing or removing or consuming other life. Life lives on life.

This leads to the concept of struggle as a symptom of the ambiguity of life in all realms but most properly speaking in the organic realm and most significantly in its historical dimension (see Part V of the system). Every look at nature confirms the reality of struggle as an ambiguous means of the self-creation of life—a fact classically formulated by Heraclitus when he called "war" the father of all things. One could write a "phenomenology of encounters" showing how the growth of life at every step includes conflicts with other life. One could point to the necessity for the individual to push ahead in trial, defeat, and triumph in order to actualize himself, and to the inevitable clash with like attempts and experiences of other life. In push and counterpush, life effects a preliminary balance in all dimensions, but there is no a priori certainty about the outcome of these conflicts. The balance achieved in one moment is destroyed in the next.

This is the case in the relation between organic beings, even of the same species. Yet the struggle becomes even more conspicuously a tool of growth in the encounter of species where one feeds on the other. A life-and-death-struggle is going on in all of what we call "nature," and because of the multidimensional unity of life, it is going on also between

men, within man, and in the history of mankind. It is a universal structure of life, and disregard of this fact is the underlying reason for the
theoretical error and practical failure of legalistic pacifism, which tries
to abolish this characteristic of the self-creation of all life—at least in
historical mankind.

Life lives on life, but it also lives through life, being defended,
strengthened, and driven beyond itself by struggle. The survival of the
strongest is the means by which life in the process of self-creation
reaches its preliminary balance, a balance which is continuously threatened by the dynamics of being and the growth of life. It is only by the
waste of innumerable seeds of generative power and actual individuals
that a preliminary balance in nature is maintained. Without such waste
a whole complex of natural life would be destroyed, as happens when
climatic conditions or human activities interfere. The conditions of
death are also the conditions of life.

The individual life process transcends itself in two directions, by
labor and by propagation in the self-creation of life. The curse laid on
Adam and Eve in the story of the Fall powerfully expresses the ambiguity of labor as a form of the self-creation of life. In English the word
"labor" is used both for the pangs of childbirth and for the toil of
tilling the land. Labor as the result of being thrown out of paradise is
imposed on the woman and the man. There is little positive valuation
of labor in the Old Testament and not much in the New Testament or
in the medieval church (even for the monastic life); certainly, there is
no glorification of it as there is in Protestantism, industrial society, and
socialism. In the attiudes of these latter the burden of labor has often
been concealed, especially in educational contexts, and sometimes even
repressed, as by the contemporary activistic ideology and by people who
feel a vacuum the moment they stop working. These extremes in the
valuation of labor show its ambiguity, an ambiguity which appears in
every life process under the dimension of the organic.

Individualized and separated from the encountered reality, life goes
beyond itself to assimilate other life, whether it is under the inorganic or
under the organic dimension. But in order to go out, it must submit to
the surrender of a well-preserved self-identity. It must surrender the
blessedness of a fulfilled resting in itself; it must toil. Even if driven by
libido or *eros*, it cannot escape the labor of destroying a potential balance
for an actual creative imbalance. In the concrete-symbolic language of

the Old Testament, even God has been thrown out of his blessed balance and forced into labor by human sin. It is in this context that the romantic devaluation of technical progress must be rejected. In so far as it liberates innumerable human beings from a toil which ruins their bodies and prevents the actualization of the potentialities of their spirit, technical progress is a healing power in view of the wounds caused by the destructive implications of labor.

But there is another side to the ambiguity of labor. Labor prevents the self-identity of a living individual from losing its dynamics and becoming empty. This is the reason why the laborless blessedness of heaven, as it appears in mythological symbols, is abhorred by many people who identify it with the hell of eternal ennui and prefer to it the hell of eternal pain. This shows that for a being whose life is conditioned by time and space, the burden of labor is an expression of its real life and as such a blessing superior to the imaginary one of dreaming innocence or mere potentiality. Sighing under the burden of every labor is ambiguously mixed with anxiety about losing it, witnessing to the ambiguity of the self-creation of life.

The most conspicuous and mysterious ambiguity in the function of the self-creation of life is that of propagation, or concretely, that of sexual differentiation and reunion. The self-creative process of life under the dimension of the organic reaches its highest power and its deepest ambiguity in it. Individual organisms are driven toward each other to experience the highest ecstasy, but in this experience the individuals disappear as separate individuals and sometimes die or are killed by their mates. The sexual union of the separate is the most conspicuous form of the self-creation of life, and here the life of the species which is actual in individuals both fulfils and negates the individuals. This holds true not only of the individuals within a species but also of the species itself. In producing individuals it also produces from time to time those which represent the transition to a new species, anticipating the ambiguity of life in the historical dimension.

The discussion of the ambiguity of propagation, like that of the ambiguity of labor, has touched on the realm which represents the transition from the dimension of the organic to that of the spirit—the realm of self-awareness, the psychological. As shown above, it is difficult to separate it from the two between which it is a bridge; nevertheless, one can abstract some elements from them and discuss them independently.

The ambiguity of self-creation appears in terms of self-awareness in the ambiguities of pleasure and pain and in the ambiguities of "life instinct" and "death instinct." With respect to the first, it seems evident that every self-creative process of life is—if it reaches awareness—a source of pleasure, and every destructive process of life a source of pain. From this simple and seemingly unambiguous statement, the psychological law has been derived according to which every life process is a pursuit of pleasure and a flight from pain. The inference is thoroughly false. Healthy life follows the principle of self-creation, and in the moment of creativity the normal living being disregards both pain and pleasure. They may be present in or as consequences of the creative act, but they are not objects of pursuit or flight within the act itself. Therefore, it is totally misleading to ask: Does not the creative act itself provide a pleasure of a higher order, even if pain is connected with it, and does this not confirm the pleasure principle? It does not, because this principle asserts an intentional pursuit of happiness, and there is no such intention in the creative act itself. It certainly fulfils something toward which life is driven by its inner dynamics, the classical name of which is *eros*. This is the reason why successful production gives joy, but there would be no creative act and no joy of fulfilment if the act were intended as a means to bring about joy. Creative *eros* implies surrender to the object of *eros*, and it is destroyed by reflection upon its possible consequences in terms of joy or pain. The pain-pleasure principle is valid only in sick, uncentered, and therefore unfree and uncreative life.

The ambiguity of pain and pleasure is most conspicuous in a phenomenon which is often called morbid but which is universally present in healthy as well as sick life—the experience of pain in pleasure and of pleasure in pain. The psychological material substantiating this ambiguity in the self-creation of life is extensive but not fully understood. In itself it is not a matter of an unambiguous distortion of life—as the term morbid would indicate—but rather an ever present symptom of the ambiguity of life under the dimension of self-awareness. It appears most strikingly in two of the characteristics of the self-production of life—in struggle and in sex.

In the ambiguity of pain and pleasure, there is an anticipation of the ambiguity of life instinct and death instinct. The latter two phrases are questionable tools for grasping phenomena which are deeply rooted in the self-creative function of life. It is one of the contradictions of nature that a living being affirms its life and denies it. The self-affirmation of life is usually taken for granted, its negation rarely, and if the latter is taught, as in Freud's doctrine of *Todestrieb* (poorly translated by "death instinct"), even otherwise orthodox pupils rebel. But the facts, given in immediate self-awareness, prove the ambiguity of life as described by Freud (and seen by Paul when he speaks of the sadness of this world which leads to death). In every conscious being, life is aware of its exhaustibility; it dimly feels that it must come to an end, and the symptoms of its exhaustion not only make it conscious of this fact but also awaken a longing for it. It is not an acute state of pain which produces the desire to be rid of oneself in order to be rid of the pain (although this may also happen); it is the existential awareness of one's finitude which poses the question of whether the continuation of finite existence is worth the burden of it. But as long as there is life, this tendency is counterbalanced by the self-affirmation of life, the desire to maintain its identity even if it is the identity of the life of a finite, exhaustible individual. Thus suicide actualizes an impulse latent in all life. This is the reason for the presence of suicidal fantasies in most people but the comparative rarity of actual suicide. It makes unambiguous what, according to the nature of life, is valid only in its ambiguity.

All these factors have been considered without regard to the dimensions of spirit and of history, but they have laid the foundations for a description of the self-creation of life under these dimensions.

c) The self-creativity of life under the dimension of spirit: culture

(1) THE BASIC FUNCTIONS OF CULTURE: LANGUAGE AND THE TECHNICAL ACT.—Culture, *cultura*, is that which takes care of something, keeps it alive, and makes it grow. In this way, man can cultivate everything he encounters, but in doing so, he does not leave the cultivated object unchanged; he creates something new from it—materially, as in the technical function; receptively, as in the functions of *theoria*; or reactively, as in the functions of *praxis*. In each of these three cases, culture creates something new beyond the encountered reality.

The new in man's cultural activity is first of all the double creation of language and technology. They belong together. In the first book of the Bible, man in paradise is requested by God to give names to the animals (language) and to cultivate the garden (technology). Socrates discusses the meaning of words by referring to the technical problems of craftsmen and of military and political technicians. In pragmatism, the validity of concepts is measured by their technical applicability. Speaking and using tools belong together.

Language communicates and denotes. Its communicative power is dependent upon such non-denotative means of communication as sounds and gestures, but communication reaches its fulfilment only when there is denotation. In language, communication becomes mutual participation in a universe of meanings. Man has the power of such communication because he has a world in correlation to a completely developed self. This liberates him from bondage to the concrete situation, that is, to the particular here and now of his environment. He experiences world in everything concrete, something universal in everything particular. Man has language because he has a world, and he has a world because he has language. And he has both because in the encounter of self with self he experiences the limit which stops him in his unstructured running from one "here and now" to the next and throws him back on himself and enables him to look at the encountered reality as a world. Here lies the common root of morality and culture. A confirmation of this statement can be observed in the effects of some mental disturbances—when a person loses his capacity for encountering other persons as persons, he also loses the capacity for meaningful talk. A stream of words without denotative structure or communicative power pours out of him; he is never aware of the "wall" of the listening thou. To a lesser degree, this is a danger for everyone. The inability to listen is both a cultural distortion and a moral fault.

We have not placed language at the basis of our analysis of culture in order to present a philosophy of language. In view of the tremendous amount of work done in this field by earlier and contemporary philosophers, such an attempt would be preposterous and, furthermore, unnecessary for our purpose. But language has been put at the beginning of our discussion of the self-creation of life under the dimension of spirit because it is fundamental for all cultural functions. It is present in all of them, whether technical or political, cognitive or aesthetic, ethical or religious. In order to actualize this omnipresence, language is endlessly variable, both with respect to the particular cultural function in which it appears and with respect to the encounter with the reality which it expresses. In both respects language reveals the basic characteristics of man's cultural activities and affords a useful approach to their nature and their differences. If taken in this larger sense semantics could and should become a door to life in the dimension of the spirit. Some indications of its significance for systematic theology may be given here.

Language grasps the encountered reality in terms of "being at hand"—in the literal sense of being as an object for "handling" or managing in order to reach ends (which may become means for other ends). This is what Heidegger has called *Zuhandensein* (being at disposal) in contrast to *Vorhandensein* (being in existence); the first form denotes a technical, the second a cognitive, relationship to reality. Each has its particular language—not excluding the other but trespassing on it. The language of "being at hand" is the ordinary, often very primitive and limited language, and the others borrow from it.

But in a temporal sense, it is perhaps not the first language. Mythological language seems to be equally old, combining the technical grasp of objects with the religious experience of a quality of the encountered that has highest significance even for daily life but transcends it in such a way that it demands another language, that of the religious symbols and their combination, the myth. Religious language is symbolic-mythological, even when it interprets facts and events which belong to the realm of the ordinary technical encounter with reality. The contemporary confusion of these two kinds of language is the cause of one of the most serious inhibitions for the understanding of religion, as it was in the prescientific period for the understanding of the ordinarily encountered reality, the object of technical use.

The language of myth, as well as the language of the ordinary technical encounter with reality, can be translated into two other kinds of language, the poetic and the scientific. Like religious language, poetic language lives in symbols, but poetic symbols express another quality of man's encounter with reality than religious symbols. They show in sensory images a dimension of being which cannot be shown in any other way, although like religious language they use the objects of ordinary experience and its linguistic expression. Again, the confusion of these kinds of language (the poetic with the religious and the technical with the poetic) is prohibitive for understanding the functions of the spirit to which both belong.

This is especially true of the cognitive function and the language created by it. It has been confused with all the others, partly because it is present in them in a prescientific form, partly because it gives a direct answer to the question which is asked indirectly in all functions of man's cultural self-creativity—the question of truth. But the methodological search for empirical truth and the artificial language used for this purpose must be sharply distinguished from the truth implied in the technical, mythological, and poetic encounters with reality and their natural or symbolic kinds of language.

Another characteristic of culture which is universal and prefigured in language is the triad of elements in cultural creativity: subject matter, form, and substance. Out of the inexhaustible manifoldness of encountered objects, language chooses some which are of significance in the universe of means and ends or in the religious, poetic, and scientific universe of expression. They constitute the subject matter in cultural activities although differently in each.

The differences are caused by the form, the second and decisive element in a cultural creation. The form makes a cultural creation what it is—a philosophical essay, a painting, a law, a prayer. In this sense form is the essence of a cultural creation. Form is one of those concepts which cannot be defined, because every definition presupposes it. Such concepts as this can be explained only by being put into configuration with other concepts of the same character.

The third element can be called the substance of a cultural creation. Whereas its subject matter is chosen and its form is intended, its substance is, so to speak, the soil out of which it grows. Substance cannot be intended. It is unconsciously present in a culture, a group, an individual, giving the passion and driving power to him who creates and the significance and power of meaning to his creations. The substance of a language gives it its particularity and its expressive ability. This is the reason that translation from one language to another is fully possible only in those spheres in which form is predominant over substance (as in mathematics) and becomes difficult or impossible when substance is predominant. In poetry, for example, translation is essentially impossible because poetry is the most direct expression of the substance through an individual. The encounter with reality on which one language is based differs from the encounter with reality in any other language, and this encounter in its totality and its depth is the substance in the cultural self-creation of life.

The word "style" is ordinarily used in relation to works of art, but it is sometimes applied to a particular qualification of the form by the substance in all other functions of man's cultural life, so that one may speak of a style of thinking, of research, of ethics, of law, of politics. And if one applies the term in this way, one often finds that analogies with respect to style can be discovered in all the cultural functions of a particular period, group, or cultural orbit. This makes style a key to understanding the way in which a particular group or period encounters reality, although it is also a source of conflicts between the demands of form-creation and of the expression of the substance.

The interpretation of language anticipates structures and tensions of cultural creativity which will frequently recur in the following discussion. The fundamental importance of language for the self-creation of life under the dimension of spirit is mirrored in this way. In analyzing the different kinds of language, we started with language that expresses the ordinary technical encounter with reality, but, as indicated above, the technical function is itself one of the functions through which life creates itself under the dimension of spirit. As language liberates from bondage to the "here and now" through universals, so the technical handling of encountered reality liberates from bondage to the naturally given conditions of existence by the production of tools. Higher animals also use things at hand as tools under particular conditions, but they do not create tools as tools for unlimited use. In their production of nests, caves, hills, and so forth, they are bound to a definite plan, and they cannot use these tools beyond the scope of this plan. Man produces tools as tools, and for this the conception of universals is presupposed, i.e., the power of language. The power of tools is dependent on the power of language. Logos precedes everything. If man is called *homo faber*, he is implicitly called *anthropos logikos*, i.e., man who is determined by the logos and who is able to use the meaningful word.

The liberating power of the production of tools consists in the possibility of actualizing purposes which are not implied in the organic processes themselves. Preservation and growth in the organic dimension are surpassed wherever tools as tools appear. The decisive difference is that the inner aims (*tele*) of the organic process are determined by the process, whereas the external aims (purposes) of technical production are not determined but represent infinite possibilities. Space travel is a technical aim and somehow a technical possibility, but it is not determined by the organic needs of a living being. It is free, a matter of choice. However, this leads to a tension from which many conflicts of our contemporary culture arise: the perversion of the relation of means and ends by the unlimited character of the technical possibilities. Means become ends simply because they are possible. But if possibilities become purposes only because they are possibilities, the genuine meaning of purpose is lost. Every possibility may be actualized. No resistance is forthcoming in the name of an ultimate end. The production of means becomes an end in itself, as in the case of the compulsive talker talking becomes an end in itself. Such distortion may affect a whole culture in which the production of means becomes the end beyond which there is no end. This problem, intrinsic in technical culture, does not deny the significance of technology but shows its ambiguity.

(2) THE FUNCTIONS OF "THEORIA": THE COGNITIVE AND THE AESTHETIC ACTS.—By their duality, the two basic functions of culture, the word and the technical act, point to a general duality in the cultural self-creation of life. This duality is based on the ontological polarity of individualization and participation and is actual in the life processes under all dimensions. Every individual being has the quality of being open for other individual beings. Beings "receive each other" and, by doing so, change each other. They receive and react. In the realm of the organic, this is called stimulus and response; under the dimension of self-awareness, it is called perception and reaction; under the dimension of spirit, I suggest calling it *theoria* and *praxis*. The original Greek forms of the words "theory" and "practice" are used because the modern forms have lost the meaning and power of the ancient words. *Theoria* is the act of looking at the encountered world in order to take something of it into the centered self as a meaningful, structured whole. Every aesthetic image or cognitive concept is such a structured whole. Ideally, the mind drives toward an image which embraces all images and a concept which contains all concepts, but in reality the universe never appears in a direct vision—it only shines through particular images and concepts. Therefore every particular creation of *theoria* is a mirror of encountered reality, a fragment of a universe of meaning. This is implied in the fact that language moves in universals. World breaks through environment in every universal. He who says, "This is a tree," has grasped treehood in an individual tree and with it a fragment of the universe of meaning.

In this example, language is given as a cognitive expression of *theoria*, but the same example can also be used for the aesthetic sense of the term. If Van Gogh paints a tree, it becomes an image of his dynamic vision of the world. He contributes to the creation of the universe of meanings by creating an image both of treehood and of the universe as reflected in the particular mirror of a tree.

The terms "images" and "concepts" for the two ways in which *theoria* receives reality through the aesthetic and cognitive functions need some justification. Both words are used in a very wide sense: images for all aesthetic creations, concepts for all cognitive creations. Most would probably agree that the visual, as well as the literary, arts create images, sensory or imaginary, but the application of the term "image" to music might be questioned. A justification for this enlargement of the meaning of "image" is that one can speak of musical "figures," thus transferring a term that is visual by definition to the sphere of sounds. And the movement is not one-sided: one speaks of colors, ornaments, poems, and plays in musical terms. Therefore, in spite of its visual origin, we use the term "image" for the whole of aesthetic creativity (as Plato used the visual term *eidos*, or "idea," universally).

The question whether a concept or a proposition is the most important tool of knowledge seems to me empty, because in every defined concept numerous propositions are implicit and at the same time every structured proposition leads in the direction of new concepts which presuppose old ones.

The distinction between the aesthetic and the cognitive has been explained before in connection with the description of the structure of reason,[1] but the structure of reason is only one element in the dynamics of life and the functions of spirit. It is the static element in the self-creation of life under the dimension of spirit. When we spoke about the existential conflicts of reason in "Reason and Revelation" (Part I of the system), we might better have spoken, in a less condensed manner, of the existential conflicts produced by the ambiguous application of rational structures in the dynamics of the spirit. For reason is the structure of both mind and world, whereas spirit is their dynamic actualization in personality and community. Strictly speaking, ambiguities cannot occur in reason, which is structure, but only in spirit, which is life.

Most of the problems connected with the cognitive function of man's life have been discussed under "Reason and Revelation." Here we need only point to the basic tension in the nature of the cognitive processes which leads to their ambiguities. In the act of the cognitive creativity of life (as, analogously, in all functions of the self-creation of life under the

[1] *Systematic Theology*, I, 77–78.

dimension of spirit, including morality and religion), there is a fundamental conflict between that which is intended and the situation that
both causes the intention and at the same time prevents its fulfilment.
This conflict is based on the estrangement between subject and object,
an estrangement which is, at the same time, a condition for culture as the
whole of creative, receiving, or transforming acts.

Therefore, one can say that the cognitive act is born out of the desire
to bridge the gap between subject and object. The equivocal term for the
result of such reunion is "truth." The word is claimed by both science and
religion and sometimes even by the arts. If one of these claims is accepted
exclusively, new words for the other claims must be found—which, it
seems to me, is unnecessary because the basic phenomenon is the same in
all cases: the fragmentary reunion of the knowing subject with the
known object in the act of knowledge.

The intention of finding truth is only one element in the aesthetic
function. The main intention is to express qualities of being which can
be grasped only by artistic creativity. The result of such creativity has
been called the beautiful and has sometimes been combined with truth,
sometimes with the good, sometimes with both, in a triad of highest
values. As a term, "beauty" has lost the power it had in the Greek combination of the beautiful and the good (*kalon k'agathon*), and in recent
aesthetics it has been almost unanimously rejected because of its connections with the decadent phase of the classical style—beautifying
naturalism. Perhaps one could speak of expressive power or expressiveness. This would not exclude aesthetic idealism or naturalism but would
point to the aim of the aesthetic function, that is, to express. The tension
which arises in the aesthetic function is that beween expression and the
expressed. One could speak of expressive truth or untruth. But one
should instead speak of the authenticity of the expressive form or of its
unauthenticity. It can be unauthentic for two reasons: either because it
copies the surface instead of expressing the depth or because it expresses
the subjectivity of the creating artist instead of his artistic encounter with
reality. A work of art is authentic if it expresses the encounter of mind
and world in which an otherwise hidden quality of a piece of the
universe (and implicitly of the universe itself) is united with an otherwise hidden receptive power of the mind (and implicitly of the person
as a whole). Innumerable combinations, which determine the artistic
styles as well as the individual work, are possible betwen the two ele-

ments of the aesthetic encounter. The tension in the aesthetic function is different in character from that in the cognitive function. To be sure, it is also ultimately rooted in the existential estrangement of self and world which, in the cognitive function, is the separation of subject and object. But a real union of self and world is achieved in the aesthetic encounter. There are degrees of depth and authenticity in this union, depending on the creative powers of the artists, but there is always some kind of union. This is the reason that philosophers, for example, in the Kantian school (classical as well as Neo-Kantian), have seen in art the highest self-expression of life and the answer to the question implied in the limitations of all other functions. And this is the reason that sophisticated cultures tend to replace the religious by the aesthetic function. But this attempt is untrue to the human situation and to the nature of aesthetics. A work of art is a union of self and world within limitations both on the side of the self and on the side of the world. The limitation on the side of the world is that although in the aesthetic function as such *one*, otherwise hidden, quality of the universe is reached, ultimate reality, which transcends all qualities, is not reached; the limitation on the side of the self is that in the aesthetic function the self grasps reality in images and not with the totality of its being. The effect of this double limitation is to give union in the aesthetic function an element of unreality. It is "seeming"; it anticipates something that does not yet exist. The ambiguity of the aesthetic function is its oscillation between reality and unreality.

The aesthetic function is not restricted to artistic creativity, as the cognitive function is not restricted to scientific creativity. We have pre-scientific and pre-artistic functions of the spirit. They permeate the whole life of man, and it would be very wrong were the term "creative" to be applied only to vocational, scientific, and artistic creativity. For instance, the knowledge and expressive power embodied in myth—often experienced at a very early age—has become for most people the door into all aspects of culture. And ordinary observation of facts and events, as well as direct aesthetic experience with nature and man, are effective daily in the self-creation of life under the dimension of the spirit.

(3) THE FUNCTIONS OF "PRAXIS": THE PERSONAL AND THE COMMUNAL ACTS.—*Praxis* is the whole of cultural acts of centered personalities who as members of social groups act upon each other and themselves. *Praxis* in this sense is the self-creation of life in the personal-communal realm.

Therefore, it includes the acts of persons on themselves and on other persons, on the groups to which they belong and through them on other groups, and indirectly on mankind as a whole.

In the functions of *praxis*, life creates itself in a particular way under the dimension of spirit. There are tensions in all of the functions which lead to ambiguities and the quest for the unambiguous. It is difficult to find traditional names for them, for there is much overlapping and a frequent lack of differentiation between the activities themselves and their scholarly interpretations. One can speak of social relations, of law, of administration, of politics, and one can speak of personal relations and personal development. And in so far as there are norms directing the cultural acts in all these modes of transformation, one could subsume the whole realm under the term "ethics" and distinguish between individual and social ethics. But the term "ethics" designates primarily the principles, validity, and motivation of the moral act as described earlier, and it is probably more expedient for our understanding of the functions of the spirit to define ethics as the science of the moral act and to subsume the theory of the cultural functions of *praxis* under the whole of a "theory of culture." The decisive reason for such a semantic distinction is the fundamental position which the moral act assumes when understood as the self-constitution of spirit. At the same time this terminology makes it obvious that the special content of morality is a creation of the *cultural* self-creativity of life.

Praxis is action aiming at growth under the dimension of spirit; as such it uses means for ends and, in this respect, is a continuation of the technical act (as *theoria* is the continuation of the word which grasps encountered reality). In this connection, "continuation" means that the different functions of *praxis* employ tools adequate to their purposes and transcend the production of physical tools by which, in union with the word, man was first liberated from bondage to his environment. Some of the most important technical activities are economy, medicine, administration, and education. They are complex functions of the spirit, combining ultimate norms, scientific material, human relations, and a large accumulation of technical experience. Their high valuation in the Western world is caused partly by the Jewish-Christian symbol of the Kingdom of God's subjecting encountered reality to its purposes.

Under the heading of *theoria*, we found truth and authentic expressiveness as aims of cultural creativity. Now we would like to discover the corresponding terms under the heading of *praxis*. The first is "the good," the *agathon*, the *bonum*; and the good must be defined as the essential nature of a thing and the fulfilment of the potentialities implied in it. However, this applies to everything that is and describes the inner aim of creation itself. It does not provide a special answer to the question of the good toward which *praxis* aspires. To supply this we need other concepts which are subordinate to the good but which express a particular quality of it. One of these concepts is justice. It corresponds to truth in the sphere of *theoria*. Justice is the aim of all cultural actions which are directed toward the transformation of society. The word can also be applied to the individual, in so far as he behaves in a just way. But more frequently another term, namely, righteous, is used in this sense: he who is righteous exercises justice. But this does not end the search for a term which designates the personal good in the same way that justice covers the social good. One must regret that the Greek word *arete* (in Latin *virtus*, in English "virtue") has so completely lost its original power that today it has ridiculous connotations. It would be a confusing anticipation of later discussions were such religious terms as pious, justified, holy, spiritual, and so forth, to be used here, because they are dependent on the Christian answer to the questions implied in the ambiguities of *praxis*.

Such a term as *arete* (virtue) points to the actualization of essential human potentialities. In view of this, it might be possible to speak directly of the fulfilment of human potentialities and to call the inner aim of *praxis*, directed toward individuals as individuals, "humanity." Yet the use of "humanity" is also problematical because of the different meanings of "humanity" in ordinary language and because of the philosophical connotation of "humanism" as a special interpretation of the potentialities of man. In view of this connotation, humanity, as the aim of man's *praxis*, could be contrasted with divinity as the aim, in the sense of "becoming similar to God." In spite of these dangers, I suggest using the word "humanity" in the sense of the fulfilment of man's inner aim with respect to himself and his personal relations, in co-ordination with justice as the fulfilment of the inner aim of social groups and their mutual relations.

At this point the question arises as to what produces the tensions in the nature of humanity and justice, from which the ambiguities of their actualization result. The general answer is the same as that given in the description of the self-creation of life under the dimension of spirit: the infinite gap between subject and object under the conditions of existential estrangement. In the functions of *theoria* the gap lies between the knowing subject and the object to be known and between the expressing subject and the object to be expressed. In the functions of *praxis* the gap lies between the existing human subject and the object for which he strives—a state of essential humanity—and the gap between the existing social order and the object toward which it strives—a state of universal justice. This practical gap between subject and object has the same consequences as the theoretical gap; the subject-object scheme is not only the epistemological but also the ethical problem.

Every cultural act is the act of a centered self and is based on the moral self-integration of the person within the community. In so far as the person is the bearer of the cultural self-creation of life, he is subjected to all the tensions of culture we have discussed and all the ambiguities of culture we will discuss in the following sections. A person who participates in a culture's movement, growth, and possible destruction is culturally creative. In this sense, every human being is culturally creative, simply by virtue of speaking and using tools. This universal characteristic should be distinguished from original creativity, which in the full sense of the word "original" can be applied to only a few; but despite the necessity for this distinction, it should not be distorted into a mechanical division. There are unnoticeable transitions.

Therefore, everyone is subjected to the ambiguities of culture, both in the subjective and the objective senses. They are inseparable from historical destiny.

d) *The ambiguities of the cultural act: the creation and the destruction of meaning*

(1) THE AMBIGUITIES IN THE LINGUISTIC, COGNITIVE, AND AESTHETIC SELF-CREATION OF LIFE.—The word is the bearer of meaning; therefore, language is the first result of the self-creation of life under the dimension of spirit. It permeates every cultural act and, indirectly, all functions of the spirit. But it has a special relation to the functions of *theoria*—cognition and expression—as the technical act, though present in every function of cultural self-creation, has a special relation to the functions of *praxis*. For this reason I want to discuss the ambiguities of the word together with the ambiguities of truth and expressiveness and the ambiguities of the technical act together with the ambiguities of humanity and justice.

As the bearer of meaning, the word liberates from bondage to the environment, a bondage to which life in all previous dimensions is subjected. Meaning presupposes a self-awareness of life which has transpsychological validity. Something universally valid is intended in every meaningful sentence, even if the subject spoken about is particular and transitory. Cultures live in such meanings. The meanings are as like and as different as are the languages of particular social groups. The meaning-creating power of the word depends on the different ways in which the mind encounters reality, as expressed in language from the mythical to that of daily life and, between these, as expressed in the scientific and the artistic functions. All this is continuous activity of the self-creation of life in producing a universe of meaning. Logic and semantics deal scientifically with the structures and norms through which this universe is created.

The ambiguity that enters into this process results from the fact that the word, while creating a universe of meaning, also separates the meaning from the reality to which it refers. The act of grasping objects by the mind, on which language is based, opens up a gap between the object grasped and the meaning created by the word. The inherent ambiguity of language is that in transforming reality into meaning it separates mind and reality. Countless examples could be given, but one can distinguish the following main kinds of ambiguity of the word: the poverty in the midst of richness that falsifies that which is grasped through neglect of innumerable other possibilities; the limitation on universality imposed by expressing a definite encounter with reality in a particular structure that is strange to other linguistic structures, and the indefiniteness within definite meaning that leads to the betrayal of the mind by words, the ultimately uncommunicative character of this main tool of communication as a result of the unintended as well as intended connotations in the self of the centered person; the unlimited character of the freedom of language when limitations by persons or objects are rejected, the empty talk and the reaction against it, the flight into silence; the manipulation of language for the sake of purposes with no basis in reality, such as flattery, polemics, intoxication, or propaganda; and finally, the perversion of language to the exact opposite of the function intended by the self-creative power of life through hiding, distorting, and contradicting that which it is supposed to present.

These are examples of processes going on in all speech in one way or another, despite the continuous, but only fragmentarily successful, fights against avoidable ambiguities waged by semantic analysis. This makes it understandable that in biblical thought the word is united with power in the Creator, that it becomes a historical personality in the Christ, and that it is ecstatic self-manifestation in the Spirit. In these symbols the word not only grasps encountered reality; it is itself reality beyond the split between subject and object.

The ambiguities of the cognitive act of the self-creation of life are rooted in the split between subject and object. This split is the precondition of all knowledge and, at the same time, the negative power in all knowledge. The whole history of epistemology is a cognitive attempt to bridge this split by showing the ultimate unity of subject and object, either by annihilating one side of the gap for the sake of the other or by establishing a uniting principle which contains both of them. All this was and is being done in order to explain the possibility of knowledge. The reality of the split, of course, cannot be avoided; every act of cognitive existence is determined by it. And cognitive existence as an act of cultural self-creation is the subject matter of our inquiry.

Again, only a limited number of examples can be mentioned. We may start with the "ambiguity of observation," the observation which is usually understood as the solid basis of all knowledge, although its solidity does not prevent ambiguity. In history as well as in physics, in ethics as well as in medicine, the observer wants to regard the phenomenon as it "really" is. "Really" means independent of the observer. However, there is no such thing as independence from the observer. The observed changes in being observed. This has always been obvious in philosophy, the humanities, and history, but now it has also become so in biology, psychology, and physics. The result is not the "real" but encountered reality, and from the point of view of the meaning of absolute truth, encountered reality is distorted reality.

The next example of the ambiguity of the self-creation of life in the cognitive function of culture is the "ambiguity of abstraction." Cognition tries to reach the essence of an object or a process by abstraction from the many particulars in which this essence is present. This is so even in history where such all-embracing concepts as "Renaissance" or "Chinese art" include, interpret, and hide innumerable concrete facts. Every concept shows this ambiguity of abstraction, which has frequently resulted in a pejorative use of the word "abstract." But every concept is an abstraction—and according to the neurologist, Kurt Goldstein, it is the power of abstraction that makes man man.

Much discussion has resulted from the "ambiguity of truth as a whole." Obviously, every statement about an object uses concepts which themselves need definition, and the same is true of the concepts used in these definitions, and so on, ad infinitum. Every particular assertion is preliminary, because a finite being cannot comprehend the whole, and if he claims to, as some metaphysicians have, he deceives himself. Therefore, the only truth given to man in his finitude is fragmentary, broken, and untrue if measured by the truth embodied in the whole. But to apply this measure is itself untrue, for it would exclude man from any truth, even from the truth of this statement. The ambiguity of the conceptual pattern leads deep into a metaphysical discussion. Today it is predominantly a problem in physics, where some physicists interpret the determining physical patterns, such as atom, power field, and so on, as mere products of the human mind without any *fundamentum in re* (foundation in reality), whereas others attribute such a foundation to them. The same problem has arisen in sociology with the concept of social classes, in psychology with the concept of complexes, and in history with the names for historical periods. The ambiguity lies in the fact that in creating large conceptual patterns the cognitive act changes the encountered reality in such a way that it becomes unrecognizable.

Finally, one must point to the "ambiguity of argumentation," in which a chain of arguments is intended to conceptualize the structure of things but in which undiscussed assumptions that are unnoticed by the cognitive subject play a determining role. This is true of the historical context in which the argument takes place, of the unnoticed influence of the cognitive subject's sociological position on the argument—an influence called ideology—and finally, of the unconscious impact of the cognitive subject's psychological situation, which is called rationalization. Every argument depends on these forces, even if a strong scientific discipline is practiced. The basic gap between subject and object cannot be bridged by method.

These examples explain why those who are aware of the ambiguities of the cognitive act often try to escape them by transcending the gap in the direction of a mystical unity; truth for them is the mystical conquest of the subject-object scheme.

Another attempt to find the unambiguous is made in images created by the arts. In artistic intuition and its images, a reunion of *theoria* and reality, which otherwise could not be reached, is believed possible. But the aesthetic image is no less ambiguous than the cognitive concept and the grasping word. In the aesthetic function the gap between expression and that which is expressed represents the split between the acts of *theoria* and encountered reality. The ambiguities resulting from this split can be shown in the conflicts of stylistic elements which characterize every work of art—and indirectly, every aesthetic encounter with reality. These elements are the naturalistic, the idealistic, and the expressionistic. Each of these terms suffers under several of the ambiguities of language mentioned before, but we cannot dispense with them. Naturalism in this context refers to the artistic impulse to present the object as ordinarily known or scientifically sharpened or drastically exaggerated. If this impulse is radically followed through, subject matter overpowers expression and results in a questionable imitation of nature—the "ambiguity of stylistic naturalism." Idealism in this context refers to the contrary artistic impulse, that of going beyond ordinarily encountered reality in the direction of what things essentially are and therefore ought to be. It is the anticipation of a fulfilment that cannot be found in an actual encounter and that is, theologically speaking, eschatological. Most of what we call classical art is strongly determined by this impulse, although not exclusively, for no style is completely ruled by any one of the three stylistic elements. But here also the ambiguities are manifest; the natural object, the expression of which is the aim of the aesthetic self-creation of life, is lost in the anticipated idea of it, and this is the "ambiguity of stylistic idealism." An ideal without realistic foundation is set up against the encountered reality, which is beautified and corrected to conform with the ideal in a manner which combines sentimentality and dishonesty. This is what has marred the religious art of the last hundred years. Such art still expresses something, although not encountered reality—the low taste of a culturally empty period.

(2) THE AMBIGUITIES OF TECHNICAL AND PERSONAL TRANSFORMATION. —All ambiguities of the self-creation of life in the functions of *theoria* are ultimately dependent on the cleavage between subject and object under the conditions of existence: the subject tries to bridge the gap by receiving the object in words, concepts, and images, but never achieves this aim. There is reception, grasp, and expression, but the gap remains and the subject remains within itself. The opposite happens in the self-

creation of life by the functions of *praxis*, including their technical element. In them it is the object that is to be transformed according to concepts and images, and it is the object which causes the ambiguous character of cultural self-creation.

We have linked together the liberating power of the word and of the technical act, i.e., in the production of tools as tools. Language and techniques enable the mind to set and pursue purposes which transcend the environmental situation. But in order to produce tools, one must know and comply with the inner structure of the materials used and their behavior under anticipated conditions. The tool which liberates man also subjects him to the rules of its making.

This consideration leads to three ambiguities of all technical production, whether it involves the hammer which helps to produce a hut or the set of machines which help to produce a man-made satellite. The first is the "ambiguity of freedom and limitation" in technical production; the second is the "ambiguity of means and ends"; and the third is the "ambiguity of self and thing." From mythical times to our own period, these ambiguities have largely determined the destiny of mankind, but perhaps no period has been as aware of this as ours.

The ambiguity of freedom and limitation in technical production is powerfully expressed in myths and legends. It underlies the biblical story of the tree of knowledge from which Adam eats against the will of the gods and in the Greek myth of Prometheus, who brings fire to men, also against their will. Perhaps the story of the Tower of Babel, telling of man's desire to be united under a symbol in which his finitude is overcome and the divine sphere reached, is nearest to our own situation. In all these cases, the result is both creative and destructive; and this remains the destiny of technical production in all periods. It opens up a road along which no limit can be seen, but it does so through a limited, finite being. Awareness of this conflict is clearly expressed in the myths referred to, and it is also voiced today by our scientists, who are aware of the destructive possibilities into which their creation of scientific knowledge and technical tools has thrown all mankind.

The second ambiguity, that of "means and ends," is related to this basic ambiguity of technical production. It renders concrete the limitlessness of technical freedom by asking: For what? So long as this question is answered by the basic needs of man's physical existence, the problem is hidden, though not absent, since the question of what a basic need is cannot be answered with assurance. But the problem comes into the open if, after the satisfaction of basic needs, new needs are endlessly engendered and satisfied and—in a dynamic economy—engendered in order to be satisfied. Technical possibility becomes social and individual temptation in this situation. The production of means—of gadgets—becomes an end in itself, since no superior end is visible. This ambiguity is largely responsible for the emptiness of contemporary life. But it is not possible to change this by simply saying: Do not continue production! This is as impossible as saying to the scientist, with respect to the ambiguity of freedom and limitation: Do not continue research! Ambiguities cannot be overcome by cutting off an element which essentially belongs to the process of the self-creation of life.

This is also true of the "ambiguity of self and thing." A technical product, in contrast to a natural object, is a "thing." There are no "things" in nature, that is, no objects which are nothing but objects, which have no element of subjectivity. But objects that are produced by the technical act *are* things. It belongs to man's freedom in the technical act that he can transform natural objects into things: trees into wood, horses into horsepower, men into quantities of workpower. In transforming objects into things, he destroys their natural structures and relations. But something also happens to man when he does this, as it happens to the objects which he transforms. He himself becomes a thing among things. His own self loses itself in objects with which he cannot communicate. His self becomes a thing by virtue of producing and directing mere things, and the more reality is transformed in the technical act into a bundle of things, the more the transforming subject himself is transformed, He becomes a part of the technical product and loses his character as an independent self. The liberation given to man by technical possibilities turns into enslavement to technical actuality. This is a genuine ambiguity in the self-creation of life, and it cannot be overcome by a romantic, that is, pre-technical, return to the so-called natural. For man, the technical is something natural, and enslavement to natural primitivism would be unnatural. The third ambiguity of technical production cannot be overcome by annihilating technical production. With the other ambiguities, it leads to the quest for unambiguous relations of means and ends, that is, for the Kingdom of God.

The technical act permeates all functions of *praxis* and contributes in part to their ambiguities. But they have their own sources of creation and destruction, the discussion of which will deal first with the personal and then with the communal ambiguities of *praxis*.

In the realm of the personal self-creation of life, we must distinguish between the personal in itself and the personal in relation, although in reality they are inseparable. In both respects the aim of the cultural act is the actualization of the potentialities of man as man. It is "humanity" in the sense of this definition. Humanity is attained by self-determination and other-determination in mutual dependence. Man strives for his own humanity and tries to help others reach humanity, an attempt which expresses his own humanity. But both sides—determining one's self by one's self and being determined by others—manifest the general ambiguity of the personal self-creation of life. It is the relation of the one who determines and the one who is determined. Semantically speaking, even the term "self-determination" points to the ambiguity of *identity* and *non-identity*. The determining subject can determine only in the power of what it essentially is. But under the conditions of existential estrangement, it is separated from what it essentially is. Therefore, self-determination into fulfilled humanity is impossible; nevertheless, it is necessary, because a self determined completely from outside would cease to be a self—it would become a thing. This is the "ambiguity of self-determination," the dignity and the despair of every responsible personality ("responsible" in the sense of responding to the "silent voice" of one's essential being). One could also speak of the "ambiguity of the good will." In order to will the good, the will itself must be good. Self-determination must make it good, which is to say that the good will must create the good will, and so on ad infinitum in an endless regression. In light of these considerations, such terms as "self-education," "self-discipline," "self-healing," show their profound ambiguity. They imply either that their objects have already been reached or that they must be rejected altogether, and the absurd concept of self-salvation is completely ruled out.

In contrast to self-determination, one can speak of "other-determination," meaning personal self-creation in so far as it depends on actions of one person upon another. This happens unintentionally in every act of personal participation and intentionally wherever unorganized or organized education, or a guiding impulse, is at work. An ambiguity appears in these relations which can be formulated in the following way: working toward the growth of a person is at the same time working toward his depersonalization. Trying to enhance a subject as subject makes it into an object. First of all, one can observe the practical problems implied in this ambiguity in educational activity, whether it is unintentional or intentional. In communicating cultural contents by education, the extremes of totalitarian indoctrination and liberal unconcern are rarely reached, but they are always present as elements and cause the attempt to educate the person as a person to be one of a culture's most ambiguous tasks. The same is true of the attempt to educate the person by inducting him into the actual life of the educational group. Here the extremes of authoritarian discipline and liberal permissiveness, although rarely practiced to the full, appear as elements in the educational process and tend either to break the person as person or to prevent him from reaching any definite form. In this respect the main problem of education is that every method, however refined, increases the "objectifying" tendency which it tries to avoid.

Another example of the "ambiguity of personal growth" is the guiding activity. The term "guiding" is used here in the sense of "helper" in the growth of a person. This help can be psychotherapy or counseling; it can be the aid which is a basic part of family relationships; it can be that which is unintentionally present in friendship and in all educational activities (to the extent that the latter are a consequence of the helping activity). The most conspicuous example today is psychoanalytic practice and its ambiguities. One of the great achievements of psychoanalytic theory is its insight into the depersonalizing consequences of the phenomenon of transference, not only on the patient, but also on the analyst, and into the attempts to overcome this situation by methods finally removing the transference in the healing process. However, this can be successful only if the ambiguity of working for personal growth is overcome. And this is possible only if the subject-object scheme is conquered. Unambiguous life is impossible wherever the subject-object scheme is unbroken.

If we now turn to the realm of human relations, we find the ambiguities of the self-creation of life in the "ambiguity of personal participation." This refers above all to the relationship of person to person, but it also includes the relation of the person to the non-personal. The ambiguity of participation is present in innumerable forms between the extremes of self-seclusion and self-surrender. In every act of participation there is an element of holding one's self back and an element of giving one's self. In the attempts to know the other one, self-seclusion expresses itself in the projection of images of the other's being which disguise his real being and are only projections of the one who attempts to know. The screen of images between person and person makes every knowing participation between persons profoundly ambiguous (as, for instance, the analysis of childrens' images of parents has abundantly shown). And there is the other possibility of relinquishing one's images of the other one and receiving the images he either actually has of himself or wants to impose on those who try to participate cognitively in him.

Emotional participation is also subject to the ambiguities of self-seclusion and self-surrender. In reality, emotional participation in the other one is emotional oscillation within one's self, created by an assumed participation in the other one. Much so-called romantic love is of this character. It manifests the ambiguity of missing the other person just by the attempt to enter emotionally into his secret being. And there is also the opposite movement, the chaotic self-surrender which, in an act of throwing one's self away shamelessly, brings everything to the other one; but he who receives it cannot use it, because it has lost its secrecy and uniqueness. Again we must say that profound ambiguities are effective in every act of emotional participation which, together with the cognitive ambiguities, are responsible for the inexhaustible creative-destructive situations in the relation of person to person.

It is inevitable that active participation shows analogous structures. The self-produced images of the other one and the emotional self-seclusion in the gown of participation bring about manifold patterns of mutual destruction in the encounter of person with person. If the other one is attacked, it is his image and not his self that is attacked. It is one's own desire for self-surrender that is more often satisfied in surrender to the other one and not his. Participation, sought for, turns into self-seclusion after the experience of rejection, real or imagined. The innumerable mixtures of hostility and surrender are some of the most conspicuous examples of the ambiguity of life.

(3) THE AMBIGUITIES OF COMMUNAL TRANSFORMATION.—The frame in which cultural self-creation occurs is the life and growth of the social group under the dimension of spirit. Discussion of this framework has been deferred to this point because of the difference in structure between the personal self and the community.

Whereas the centered self is the knowing, deliberating, deciding, and acting subject in every personal act, a social group has no such center. One can only call the seat of authority and power the "center" of a group by analogy, for in many cases authority and power are split, although the cohesion of the group persists, being rooted in life processes that may reach back into the past or that may be determined by unconscious forces which are stronger than any political or social authority. A person's free act makes him responsible for the consequences of the act. An act of the representative of authority in a group may be highly responsible, or completely irresponsible, with the whole group's having to bear the consequences. But the group is not a personal unity which becomes responsible for acts which, for example, are forced upon it against the will of the majority or through the preliminary superiority of one part in a situation where power is split. The life of a social group belongs under the historical dimension, which unites the other dimensions, adding to them the direction toward the future. Although we intend to deal with the historical dimension in Part V of the present system, at this point we must deal with the ambiguities which follow from the principle of justice as such, without entering upon a discussion of justice in the historical dimension.

Under the dimension of spirit and in the function of culture, life creates itself in human groups whose nature and development is the subject matter of sociology and historiography. Here we ask the normative question: What are social groups intended to be by their essential nature, and what ambiguities appear in the actual processes of their self-creation? Whereas in the previous descriptions we have shown the ambiguities of the growth of the person toward humanity, we must now discuss the ambiguities of the growth of the social group toward justice.

One may distinguish between social organisms and the organizational forms which special human activities take to enable them to grow toward justice. Families, friendship groups, local and vocational communities, tribal and national groups, have grown naturally within the cultural self-creation of life. But as parts of cultural creativity they are, at the same time, objects of organizing activity; in fact, they are never the one without the other. This distinguishes them from flocks in the organic-psychological dimension. The justice of a flock or a grove of trees is the natural power of the more powerful ones to force their potentialities into actualization against the natural resistance of the others. In a human group the relation of the members is ordered under traditional rules, conventionally or legally fixed. The natural differences in the power of being are not excluded in the organizational structure, but they are ordered according to the principles implied in the idea of justice. The interpretation of these principles is endlessly varied, but justice itself is the point of identity in all interpretations. The relations of man and wife, parents and children, relatives and strangers, members of the same local group, citizens of the same nation, and so on, are ordered by rules which, consciously or unconsciously, seek to express some form of justice. This is true even in the relation of the conquering group to the conquered within the same social context. The justice given to the slave is still justice, however unjust slavery may be from a higher point of view. According to the polarity of dynamics and form, a social group could not have being without form. And the social group's form is determined by the understanding of justice effective in the group.

The ambiguities of justice appear wherever justice is demanded and actualized. The growth of life in social groups is full of ambiguities which—if not understood—lead either to an attitude of despairing resignation of all belief in the possibility of justice or to an attitude of utopian expectation of a complete justice, which is later frustrated.

The first ambiguity in the actualization of justice is that of "inclusiveness and exclusion." A social group is a group because it includes a particular kind of people and excludes all others. Social cohesion is impossible without such exclusion. At this point the ambiguities of self-integration and self-creation must be discussed together, prior to an introduction of the historical dimension of life processes. The special character of social groups, as described before, makes it impossible to subsume them totally under the dimension of spirit. Their life does not possess the moral centeredness of the personal self, and for this reason, one often separates the social-political from the cultural self-creation of life. But this is also impossible, since, on the one hand, the element of justice present in all groups is created by acts of the spirit and, on the other hand, all realms dominated by the dimension of the spirit are, in their cultural forms, partly dependent on the social-political forces. It is inherent in the essential justice of a group to preserve its centeredness, and the group tries to establish a center in all acts in which it actualizes itself. A center does not precede growth in the life of social groups, but self-integration and self-creation are identical at every moment. The difference in this respect is obvious, both from the dimensions preceding that of the spirit and from the dimension of the spirit itself. In the historical dimension, self-integration and self-creation are one and the same act of life. The processes of life coincide under the all-embracing dimension of the historical.

A consequence of the convergence of the life processes under the historical dimension is the application of the "ambiguity of social cohesion and social exclusion" both to the process of self-integration and to the process of self-creation. This is the subject of countless sociological inquiries, and the practical consequences of every suggested solution are very great. The ambiguity of cohesion implies that in every act by which social cohesion is strengthened individuals or groups on the boundary line are expelled or rejected and, conversely, that every act in which such individuals or groups are retained or accepted weakens the cohesion of the group. Those on the boundary line include individuals from a different social class, individuals who enter closed family and friendship groups, national or racial strangers, minority groups, dissenters, or newcomers simply because they are newcomers. In all these cases, justice does not demand unambiguous acceptance of those who would possibly disturb or destroy group cohesion, but it certainly does not permit their unambiguous rejection.

The second ambiguity of justice is that of "competition and equality." Inequality in the power of being between individuals and groups is not a matter of static differences but of continuous dynamic decisions. This happens in every encounter of being with being, in every glimpse of each other, in every conversation, in every demand, question, or appeal. It happens in the competitive life in family, school, work, business, intellectual creation, social relations, and the struggle for political power. There is a pushing ahead in all these encounters, a trying, a withdrawing into an existing unity, a pushing out of it, a coalescing, a splitting, a continuous alteration between victory and defeat. These dynamic inequalities are actual under all dimensions from the beginning of each life process to its end. Under the dimension of the spirit, they are judged by the principle of justice and the element of equality in it. The question is, In what respect does justice include equality?

There is *one* unambiguous answer: every person is equal to every other, in so far as he is a person. In this respect there is no difference between an actually developed personality and a mentally diseased one who is merely a potential personality. By the principle of justice incarnate in them, they both demand to be acknowledged as persons. The equality is unambiguous up to this point, and the implications are also logically unambiguous: equality before the law in all those respects in which the law determines the distribution of rights and duties, chances and limitations, goods and burdens, and in just returns for obedience to or defiance of the law, for merit and demerit, for competence and incompetence.

However, although the logical implications of the principle of equality are unambiguous, every concrete application is ambiguous. Past and present history incontestably documents this fact. In the past not even the recognition of a mentally diseased individual of the human genus as a potential person has been acknowledged, and there are still limits to this recognition in the present. In addition, there are the terrifying relapses which have occurred in the demonic destruction of justice in our century. However, even if this situation should change in the future, it could not change the ambiguities of competition, which work continuously for inequality in the encounters of people in daily life, in the stratification of society, and in the political self-creation of life. The very attempt to apply the principle of equality, as contained unambiguously in the acknowledgment of the person as person, can have destructive consequences for the realization of justice. It may deny the right embodied in a particular power of being and give it to individuals or groups whose power of being does not warrant it. Or it may keep individuals or groups under conditions which make growth of their potentialities technically impossible. Or it may prevent one kind of competition and foster another kind, thus removing one source of unjust inequality only to produce another. Or it may apply unjust power in order to crush unjust power. These examples make it clear that a state of unambiguous justice is a figment of the utopian imagination.

The third ambiguity in the self-actualization of a social group is "the ambiguity of leadership." It runs through all human relations from the parent-child to the ruler-subject relationship. And in its many forms it shows the ambiguity of creativity and destruction which characterizes all life processes. "Leadership" is a structure which starts rather early in the organic realm and which is effective under the dimensions of inner awareness, of the spirit, and of history. It is very poorly interpreted if it is derived from the existence of different degrees of strength and the drive of the stronger to enslave the weaker. This is a permanent abuse of the principle of leadership and not its essence. Leadership is the social analogy to centeredness. As we have seen, it is only an analogy, but it is a valid one. For without the centeredness given by leadership, no self-integration and self-creation of a group would be possible. This function of leadership can be derived from the very fact that would seem to be its refutation—the personal centeredness of the individual member of the group. Without a leader or leading group, a group could be united only through a psychological power, directing all individuals in a way similar to mass shock reactions, by which spontaneity and freedom would be lost in the movement of a mass in which the particles had no independent decision. Propagandists of all kinds try to produce such behavior. They do not want to be leaders but managers of a causally-determined mass movement. But just this possibility of using the power of leadership for transforming leadership into mass-management shows that this is not the intrinsic nature of leadership, which presupposes and preserves the centered person whom it leads. The possibility just mentioned shows the ambiguity of leadership. The leader represents not only the power and justice of the group but also himself, his power of being, and the justice implied in it. This applies not only to him as an individual but to the particular social stratum in which he stands and which, willingly or unwillingly, he also represents. This situation is the permanent source of the ambiguity of every ruling power, whether it is a dictator, an aristocracy, or a parliament. And this is true also of voluntary groups whose chosen leaders manifest the same ambiguous motives as do political rulers. The ambiguity of rationalization or ideology production is present in every leadership structure. But the attempt to remove such a structure, for example, in a state of anarchy, is self-defeating because chaos breeds dictatorship and the ambiguities of life cannot be conquered by producing a vacuum.

Leaders in special functions have been called "authorities," but this is a misleading application of a term which has a more fundamental meaning than leadership and, consequently, more conspicuous ambiguities. "Authority," first of all, denotes the ability to start and to augment (*augere, auctor*) something. In this sense, there are authorities in all realms of cultural life. They result from the "division of experience" and are necessary because of every individual's finite range of knowledge and ability. There is nothing ambiguous in this situation, but the ambiguity of leadership in the sense of authority starts the moment that actual authority, which is based on the division of experience, is frozen into an authority bound to a particular social position, for example, to scholars as scholars, kings as kings, priests as priests, or parents as parents. In these cases, persons with less knowledge and ability come to exert authority over some who have more, and thus the genuine meaning of authority is distorted. This, however, is not only a regrettable fact which could and should be prevented but also an inevitable ambiguity, because of the unavoidable transformation of actual into established authority. This is most obvious in the case of parental authority but is also true of the relations of age-classes in general, of the professions to those whom they serve, and of representatives of power to those whom they direct or rule. All institutional hierarchy is based on this transformation of actual into established authority. But authority is authority over persons and therefore open to rejection in the name of justice. Established authority tries to prevent such rejection, and here an ambiguity appears: a successful rejection of authority would undercut the social structure of life, whereas a surrender to authority would destroy the basis of authority—the personal self and its claim for justice.

The fourth ambiguity of justice is the "ambiguity of legal form." We have discussed the ambiguity of the moral law, its right and its inability to create what it is supposed to create—the reunion of man's essential being with his existential being. The ambiguities of the legal form as expressed in the laws of states, for example, in civil and criminal law, are similar. They are supposed to establish justice but instead give rise to both justice and injustice. The ambiguity of the legal form has two causes, one external, the other internal. The external cause is the relation between the legal form and the legalizing, interpreting, and executing powers. There the ambiguities of leadership exert their influence on the character of the legal form. It claims to be the form of justice, but it is the legal expression of a particular—individual or social—power of being. This in itself is not only unavoidable; it is also true to the essential nature of being, that is, the multidimensional unity of life.

Every creation under the dimension of spirit unites expression with validity. It expresses an individual or social situaion, which is indicated by the particular style. The legal style of a law-establishing group in a special period tells us not only about logical solutions of legal problems but also about the nature of the economic and social stratification existing at the time and about the character of the ruling classes or groups. Nevertheless, the logic of the law is not replaced by the will to power and the pressure of ideologies which serve the preservation of or the attack on the existing power structure. The legal form is not used simply for other purposes; it retains its own structural necessities and can serve those other purposes only because it retains its own structure, for power without valid legal form destroys itself.

The internal ambiguity of the legal form is independent of the lawgiving, interpreting, and executing authorities. Like the moral law, it is abstract and, consequently, inadequate to any unique situation, for according to the principle of individualization every situation is unique—even if very similar to others in some respects. Many legal systems are aware of this fact and have built-in safety measures against the abstract equality of everyone before the law, but they can only partly remedy the injustice which is based on the abstract character of the law and the uniqueness of every concrete situation.

e) *The ambiguity of humanism.*—Culture, creating a universe of meaning, does not create this universe in the empty space of mere validity. It creates meaning as the actualization of what is potential in the bearer of the spirit—in man. This statement has already been defended against the anti-ontological philosophers of value. It must now be discussed in one of its decisive consequences, that is, the answer it implies to the question of the ultimate aim of the cultural self-creation of life: What is the meaning of the creation of a universe of meaning?

Following from the ontological derivation of values, the answer has two sides, the one macrocosmic, the other microcosmic. The macrocosmic can be expressed in the following way: the universe of meaning is the fulfilment of the potentialities of the universe of being. Thus, in the human world, the unfulfilled potentialities of matter, as they appear, for example, in the atom, are actualized. However, they are not actualized in the atoms, or molecules, or crystals, or plants, or animals themselves, but only in so far as parts and forces that are actualized under these dimensions are present in man. This leaves the question of the fulfilment of the universe as a whole open for the consideration of the self-transcendence of life, its ambiguities, and the symbol of unambiguous or eternal life.

In the microcosmic answer, man is seen as the point at which and the instrument through which a universe of meaning is actualized. Spirit and man are bound to each other, and only in man does the universe reach up to an anticipatory and fragmentary fulfilment. This is the root of the humanistic idea as the microcosmic answer to the question of the aim of culture, and this is the justification of humanism, which is not the principle of a particular philosophical school, but is common to all of them. However, we must make the limiting statement that the humanistic idea can be maintained only if its ambiguities, together with the ambiguities of all cultural self-creation, are emphasized and if humanism is followed up to the point at which it asks the question of unambiguous life.

Humanism is a more embracing concept than humanity. We have defined humanity as the fulfilment of the personal life as personal and have co-ordinated it with justice and, in the larger view which includes all functions of the spirit, with truth and expressiveness. Humanism embraces these principles and relates them to the actualization of man's cultural potentialities. Humanity, like justice, is a concept, subordinated to humanism, which designates the intrinsic aim of all cultural activity.

Humanism cannot be criticized as rationalism. It cannot be criticized at all in so far as it asserts that the aim of culture is the actualization of the potentialities of man as the bearer of spirit. But a humanistic philosophy which tries to hide the ambiguities in the idea of humanism must be rejected. The ambiguities of humanism are based on the fact that, as humanism, it disregards the self-transcending function of life and absolutizes the self-creative function. This does not mean that humanism ignores "religion." Ordinarily, though not always, it subsumes religion under the human potentialities and considers it accordingly as a cultural creation. But in doing so humanism actually denies the self-transcendence of life and with it the innermost character of religion.

Since humanism as a term and as an attitude is intimately connected with education, it is most illuminating to demonstrate its ambiguities by considering an ambiguity of education which applies to both the personal and the communal realms. "Educating" means leading out from something—that is, from the state of "rudeness," as the word "e-rudition" indicates. But neither these words nor present educational practice answer the question: Leading into what? Unqualified humanism would reply: Into the actualization of all human potentialities.

However, since the infinite distance between the individual and the species makes this impossible, the answer, in the humanistic view, would have to be: the actualization of those human potentialities which are possible in terms of the historical destiny of this particular individual. This qualification, however, is fatal for the humanist ideal in so far as it claims to give the final answer to the educational and general cultural question. Because of human finitude, no one can fulfil the humanist ideal, since decisive human potentialities will always remain unrealized. But even worse, the human condition always excludes—whether under aristocratic or democratic systems—the vast majority of human beings from the higher grades of cultural form and educational depth. The intrinsic exclusiveness of the humanist ideal prevents it from being the final aim of human culture. It is the ambiguity of humanistic education that it isolates individuals and groups from the masses, and the more it isolates them, the more successful it is. But in doing so, it diminishes its own success, for the community of man to man, as an ever open possibility, belongs to the humanist ideal itself. If such openness is reduced by humanist education, such education defeats itself. Therefore the question "Educating into what?" must be answered in a way which includes everyone who is a person. But culture cannot do that by itself—just because of the ambiguities of humanism. Only a self-transcending humanism can answer the question of the meaning of culture and the aim of education.

In addition, we must remember (Part III, Sec. I E, 2) the failure of the humanist ideal to consider the human predicament and its existential estrangement. Without self-transcendence the demand of humanist fulfilment becomes a law and falls under the ambiguities of the law. Humanism itself leads to the question of culture transcending itself.

3. The Self-transcendence of Life and Its Ambiguities

a) *Freedom and finitude.*—The polarity of freedom and destiny (and its analogies in the realms of being which precede the dimension of the spirit) creates the possibility and reality of life's transcending itself. Life, in degrees, is free from itself, from a total bondage to its own finitude. It is striving in the vertical direction toward ultimate and infinite being. The vertical transcends both the circular line of centeredness and the horizontal line of growth. In the words of Paul (Romans 8:19–22), the longing of all creation for the liberation from the "subjection to futility" (R.S.V.) and "the shackles of mortality" (N.E.B.) is described with a profound poetic empathy. These words are a classical expression of the self-transcendence of life under all dimensions. One can also think of Aristotle's doctrine that the movements of all things are caused by their *eros* toward the "unmoved mover."

The question as to how the self-transcendence of life manifests itself cannot be answered in empirical terms, as is possible in the case of self-integration and self-creativity. One can speak about it only in terms which describe the reflection of the inner self-transcendence of things in man's consciousness. Man is the mirror in which the relation of everything finite to the infinite becomes conscious. No empirical observation of this relation is possible, because all empirical knowledge refers to finite interdependences, not to the relation of the finite to the infinite.

The self-transcendence of life is contradicted by the profanization of life, a tendency which, like self-transcendence, cannot be described empirically but only through the mirror of man's consciousness. But profanization appears in man's consciousness, like self-transcendence, as an experience which has been expressed and was extremely effective in all epochs of man's history. Man has witnessed to the conflict between the affirmation and the denial of the holiness of life wherever he has reached full humanity. And even in such ideologies as communism, the attempt toward a total profanization of life has resulted in the unexpected consequence that the profane itself received the glory of holiness. The term "profane" in its genuine meaning expresses exactly what we call "resisting self-transcendence," that is, remaining before the door of the temple, standing outside the holy, although in English "profane" has received the connotation of attacking the holy in vulgar or blasphemous terms and consequently has come to mean vulgar language in general. In religious terminology (though not in German and the Romance languages), "profane" has been replaced by "secular," derived from *saeculum* in the sense of "world." But this does not express the contrast to the holy as graphically as "profane" does, and therefore I wish to keep the word for the important function of expressing the resistance against self-transcendence under all dimensions of life.

The general assertion may be made that in every act of the self-transcendence of life profanization is present or, in other words, that life transcends itself ambiguously. Although this ambiguity is most conspicuous in the religious realm, it is manifest under all dimensions.

b) Self-transcendence and profanization in general: the greatness of life and its ambiguities.—Life, transcending itself, appears in the mirror of man's consciousness as having greatness and dignity. Greatness can be used as a quantitative term and in this sense can be measured; however, the greatness of life in the sense of self-transcendence is qualitative. The great in the qualitative sense shows a power of being and meaning that makes it a representative of ultimate being and meaning and gives it the dignity of such representation. The classical example is the Greek hero, who represents the highest power and value within the group to which he belongs. Through his greatness he comes near to the divine sphere in which the fulfilment of being and meaning is seen in divine figures. But if he trespasses the limits of his finitude, he is thrown back upon it by the "anger of the gods." Greatness implies risk and the willingness of the great to take tragedy upon themselves. If they perish in these tragic consequences, this does not diminish their greatness and their dignity. Only smallness, the fear of reaching beyond one's finitude, the readiness to accept the finite because it is given, the tendency to keep one's self within the limits of the ordinary, the average existence and its security—only smallness radically conflicts with the greatness and dignity of life.

Human literature abounds in praise of the greatness of the physical universe, but "greatness" in this respect is not usually defined. In this case the word obviously includes the quantitative vastness of the universe in time and space. But it points more emphatically to the qualitative mystery of the structures of every particle of the physical universe as well as to the structure of the whole. "Mystery" here means the infinity of questions with which every answer confronts the human mind. Reality, every bit of reality, is inexhaustible and points to the ultimate mystery of being itself which transcends the endless series of scientific questions and answers. The greatness of the universe lies in its power of resisting ever threatening chaos, of which the myths, including the biblical stories, manifest a keen awareness. The same awareness is expressed in ontology and the cosmological interpretations of history in a rationalized form. It underlies the feeling for reality in all sensitive forms of poetry and the visual arts.

But where the holy is, there is also the profane. Life in the inorganic realm is not only great; it is also small in its greatness, hiding its potential holiness and manifesting only its finitude. It is, in religious language, "dust and ashes"; it is, as the cyclical interpretation of history asserts, fuel for the final burning of the cosmos; and it is, as technical use of it implies, material for analysis and calculation, for the production of tools. Far from being great, life under the dimension of the inorganic is nothing but the material out of which things are being made. And some philosophers see the whole physical universe as a large thing—a divinely created (or eternally given) cosmic machine. The universe is completely profanized, first in the inorganic realm and, then, by reduction of everything else to the latter, in its entirety. It belongs to life's ambiguity that both qualities, the holy and the profane, are always present in its structures.

To find a conspicuous example of this ambiguity in the inorganic sphere, we may look at the technical structures which as mere things are open to distortion, dismemberment, and the ugliness of dirt and waste. But technical things can also manifest a sublime adequacy to their purpose, an aesthetic expressiveness not due to external ornamentation but intrinsic to their form. In this way things which are mere things can transcend themselves toward greatness.

Self-transcendence in the sense of greatness implies self-transcendence in the sense of dignity. It might seem that this term belongs exclusively to the personal-communal realm because it presupposes complete centeredness and freedom. But one element of dignity is inviolability, which is a valid element of all reality, giving dignity to the inorganic as well as to the personal. The sense in which life in the personal realm is inviolable lies in the unconditional demand of a person to be acknowledged as a person. Although it is technically possible to violate anybody, morally it is impossible because it violates the violator and destroys him morally. But the question is whether dignity in the sense of inviolability can be ascribed to all life, including the inorganic realm. Myth and poetry express such a valuation of the whole of encountered reality, including the inorganic, especially the four elements and their manifestation in nature. A derivation of polytheism from the overwhelming greatness of natural powers has been attempted. But the gods never represent greatness alone; they also represent dignity. They not only act; they also command, and a basic commandment in all religions is to acknowledge the superior dignity of the god. If a god represents one of the basic elements of being, this element is honored and its violation is revenged by the wrath of the god. This is the way in which the dignity of reality under the predominance of its inorganic elements was recognized by mankind. The elements were represented by gods, and they could be so represented only because they participate in the self-transcending function of all life. The self-transcendence of life in all dimensions makes polytheism possible. The hypothesis that man first encountered reality as the totality of things and then elevated these things to divine dignity is more absurd than the absurdities it attributes to primitive man. Actually, mankind encountered the sublimity of life, its greatness and dignity, but he encountered it in ambiguous unity with profanization, smallness, and desecration. The ambiguities of the polytheistic gods represent the ambiguities of the self-transcendence of life. This is the lasting and irrepressible validity of polytheistic symbolism. It expresses the self-transcendence of life under all dimensions against an abstract monotheism which, in order to give all power and honor to one god, transforms everything into mere objects, thus depriving reality of its power and its dignity.

The foregoing discussion anticipates the analysis of religion and its ambiguities, and is justified by the multidimensional unity of life and the necessity of going back from analogous concepts to that to which they are analogous. Only in this way can anything at all be said about such terms as "greatness" and "dignity" in their application to the inorganic realm. But a question remains from the discussion of the greatness of life—that of how the technical use of the inorganic (and organic) undermines its greatness and its dignity. The problem of the technical use of organic or inorganic material has usually been discussed from the point of view of its effect on man, but some romantic philosophers have discussed it from the point of view of the material itself. It is easy to dismiss these philosophers as romanticists, but it is not so easy to dismiss the question in light of the symbol of creation. If a created section of reality is pressed into a tool, is it dishonored? Perhaps the answer to this uninvestigated question could be that the total movement of the inorganic universe contains innumerable encounters of particles and masses in which some of them undergo the loss of their identity. They are burned or frozen or taken into another entity. The technical act of man is a continuation of these processes. But beyond this, man introduces another conflict, that between the intensification of potentialities (as in electrical light, airplanes, chemical components) and the unbalancing of the structure of smaller or larger parts of the universe (as when wastelands are produced or the atmosphere is poisoned). Here technical sublimation of matter includes its profanization. Such ambiguities lie behind the anxiety of myth-creating mankind about man's overstepping his limits and the anxiety of recent scientists about the same problem: a taboo is broken.

Much of what has been said about greatness and dignity in the inorganic universe is immediately valid in the organic realm and its several dimensions. The greatness of a living being and the infinite sublimity of its structure have been expressed by poets, painters, and philosophers in all ages. The inviolability of living beings is expressed in the protection given to them in many religions, in their importance for polytheistic mythology, and in the actual participation of man in the life of plants and animals, practically and poetically. All this is so much a part of universal human experience that it does not require expanded comment, but the ambiguities implied in it call for a full discussion, because of their own significance and because they anticipate ambiguities in the dimensions of spirit and history.

The holiness of a living being, its greatness and dignity, is ambiguously united with its profanization, its smallness, and its violability. The general rule that all organisms live through the assimilation of other organisms implies that they become "things" for each other, "food-things," so to speak, to be digested, absorbed as nourishment, and thrown out as debris. This is radical profanization in terms of their independent life. This law of life-living-from-life has even been practiced by men against men in anthropophagy. But here the reaction started on the basis of the person-to-person encounter. Man ceased to be transformed into a food-thing, although he still remained a "labor-thing." But in the relation of man to all other living beings a change took place only where the relation of man to some animals (or, as in India to animals in general) became analogous to the relation of man to man. This shows most clearly the ambiguity between the dignity or inviolability of life and the actual violation of life by life. The biblical vision of peace in nature envisages an unambiguous self-transcendence in the realm of the organic which would change the actual conditions of organic life (Isaiah 11:6–9).

Under the dimension of self-awareness, self-transcendence has the character of intentionality; to be aware of one's self is a way of being beyond one's self. The subject-element in all life becomes a subject, and the object-element in all life becomes an object—something that is thrown opposite the subject (*ob-jectum*). The greatness of this event in the history of nature is tremendous, and so is the new dignity following from it. The state of being beyond one's self in terms of self-awareness, even the most rudimentary, is a mark of greatness surpassing that in all preceding dimensions. The expression of this situation is the polarity of pleasure and pain, which now receives a new valuation. Pleasure can be considered as the awareness of one's self as a subject in the sense in which it was discussed earlier as the bearer of creative *eros*. Pain must then be considered as the awareness of one's self made into an object deprived of self-determination; the animal which is being made into a food-thing suffers and tries to escape it. Some higher animals and all men experience pain if their dignity as subject is violated. They suffer feelings of shame if they are made into things to be looked at, bodily or psychologically, or if they are treated as objects of valuating judgments, even if the judgment is favorable, or if they are punished in consequence of condemning judgments, the shame in this case being more painful than the physical suffering. In all these cases the sublime center of self-awareness is deprived of its greatness and its dignity. It is not the dimension of the spirit which is here referred to but that of self-awareness, which, however, reaches into the dimensions both of the organic and of the spirit.

This valuation of the subject-object scheme as a decisive moment in the self-transcendence of life seems to contradict the mystical tendency of identifying self-transcendence with the transcendence of the subject-object split. But there is no contradiction in this, for even in the most outspoken form of mysticism the mystical self-transcendence has nothing in common with the vegetative state under the dimension of the organic. Its very nature is to overcome the subject-object split after it has fully developed in the personal realm—not to annihilate it, but to find something above the split in which it is conquered and preserved.

c) The great and the tragic.—The self-transcendence of life, which reveals itself to man as the greatness of life, leads under the conditions of existence to the tragic character of life, to the ambiguity of the great and the tragic. Only the great is able to have tragedy. In Greece the heroes, the bearers of highest value and power, and the great families are the subjects of tragedy in myths as well as in plays. The small ones, or those who are ugly or evil, are below the level at which tragedy starts. But there is a limit to this aristocratic feeling: every Athenian citizen was asked by the government to participate in the performance of the tragedies, thus implying that no human being is without some greatness, that is, the greatness of being of divine nature. The performance of the tragedy, appealing to every citizen, is an act of democratic valuation of man as man, as a potential subject of tragedy, and therefore as a bearer of greatness.

We may ask whether something analogous can be said of greatness under all dimensions of life, and the question may be answered affirmatively. All beings affirm themselves in their finite power of being; they affirm their greatness (and dignity) without being aware of it. They do it in their relation to other beings and, in doing so, bring upon themselves the reaction of the logos-determined laws, which push back anything that trespasses the limits given to it. This is the tragic explanation of suffering in nature, an explanation which is neither mechanistic nor romantic but realistic in terms of the spontaneous character of life processes.

But in spite of these natural analogies to the human situation, consciousness of the tragic, and therefore pure tragedy, is possible only under the dimension of the spirit. The tragic, though first formulated in the context of the Dionysian religion, is, like the Apollonian logos, a universally valid concept. It describes the universality of man's estrangement and its inescapable character, which nevertheless is a matter of responsibility. We have used the term *hubris* to describe one element in man's estrangement; the other element is "concupiscence." In the description of existence (in Part III of *Systematic Theology*), *hubris* and concupiscence appear merely as negative elements. In the present part, dealing with life processes, they appear in their ambiguity—*hubris* ambiguously united with greatness and concupiscence with *eros*. *Hubris* in this sense is not pride—the compulsive overcompensation of actual smallness—but the self-elevation of the great beyond the limits of its finitude. The result is both the destruction of others and self-destruction.

If greatness is inescapably connected with tragedy, it is natural that people should try to avoid tragedy by avoiding greatness. This, of course, is an unconscious process, but it is the most widespread of all life processes under the dimension of the spirit. In many respects it is possible to avoid tragedy by avoiding greatness, although not ultimately, for every man has the greatness of being partially responsible for his destiny. And if he avoids the amount of greatness that is possible for him he becomes a tragic figure. This anxiety of avoiding tragedy throws him into the tragic loss of himself and of the greatness to be a self.

It belongs to the ambiguity of greatness and tragedy that the subjects of tragedy are not aware of their situation. Several great tragedies are tragedies of the revelation of the human predicament (as in the case of Oedipus, who blinds himself after his eyes have seen himself in the mirror held before him by the messengers); and there have been entire civilizations, such as the later ancient and the modern Western, whose tragic *hubris* has been revealed by prophetic messengers at the moment that its catastrophe was approaching (for example, the pagan and Christian seers of the end of the empire in late ancient Rome and the existentialist prophets of the arrival of Western nihilism in the nineteenth and early twentieth centuries). If one asks what the guilt of the tragic hero is, the answer must be that he perverts the function of self-transcendence by identifying himself with that to which self-transcendence is directed— the great itself. He does not resist self-transcendence, but he resists the demand to transcend his own greatness. He is caught by his own power of representing the self-transcendence of life.

It is impossible to speak meaningfully of tragedy without understanding the ambiguity of greatness. Sad events are not tragic events. The tragic can be understood only on the basis of the understanding of greatness. It expresses the ambiguity of life in the function of self-transcendence, including all dimensions of life but becoming conscious only under the dominance of the dimension of spirit.

But under the dimension of the spirit something else happens. The great reveals its dependence on its relation to the ultimate, and with this awareness the great becomes the holy. The holy is beyond tragedy, although those who represent the holy stand with all other beings under the law of greatness and its consequence, tragedy (compare the section on the tragic involvement of the Christ, Vol. II, pp. 132–34).

d) Religion in relation to morality and culture.—Since the concept of the holy has been discussed in the second part of the theological system, and since implicit definitions of religion are present in every part of it, we can restrict ourselves at this point to a discussion of religion in its basic relation to morality and culture. In this way the highly dialectical structure of man's spirit and its functions will appear. Logically, this could be the place for a fully developed philosophy of religion (including an interpretation of the history of religion). But practically this is impossible in the limits of this system, which is not a *summa*.

In accordance with their essential nature, morality, culture, and religion interpenetrate one another. They constitute the unity of the spirit, wherein the elements are distinguishable but not separable. Morality, or the constitution of the person as person in the encounter with other persons, is essentially related to culture and religion. Culture provides the contents of morality—the concrete ideals of personality and community and the changing laws of ethical wisdom. Religion gives to morality the unconditional character of the moral imperative, the ultimate moral aim, the reunion of the separated in *agape*, and the motivating power of grace. Culture, or the creation of a universe of meaning in *theoria* and *praxis*, is essentially related to morality and religion. The validity of cultural creativity in all its functions is based on the person-to-person encounter in which the limits to arbitrariness are established. Without the force of the moral imperative, no demand coming from the logical, aesthetic, personal, and communal forms could be felt. The religious element in culture is the inexhaustible depth of a genuine creation. One may call it substance or the ground from which culture lives. It is the element of ultimacy which culture lacks in itself but to which it points. Religion, or the self-transcendence of life under the dimension of spirit, is essentially related to morality and culture. There is no self-transcendence under the dimension of the spirit without the constitution of the moral self by the unconditional imperative, and this self-transcendence cannot take form except within the universe of meaning created in the cultural act.

This picture of the essential relation of the three functions of the spirit is both "transhistorical remembrance" and "utopian anticipation." As such, it judges their actual relations under the conditions of existence. But it is more than an external judge. It is actual in so far as essential and existential elements are mixed in life and since the unity of the three functions is as effective as their separation. It is just this that is the root of all ambiguities under the dimension of the spirit. And only because the essential element is effective in life—though ambiguously—can its image be drawn as the criterion of life.

The three functions of life under the dimension of spirit separate in order to become actual. In their essential unity there is no moral act which is not at the same time an act both of cultural self-creation and of religious self-transcendence. There is no independent morality in "dreaming innocence." And in the essential unity of the three functions, there is no cultural act which is not at the same time an act of moral self-integration and religious self-transcendence. There is no independent culture in dreaming innocence. And in the essential unity of the three functions, there is no religious act which is not at the same time an act of moral self-integration and cultural self-creation. There is no independent religion in dreaming innocence.

But life is based on the loss of dreaming innocence, on the self-estrangement of essential being and the ambiguous mixture of essential and existential elements. In the actuality of life, there is separated morality with the ambiguities it implies; there is separated culture with its ambiguities; and there is separated religion with its most profound ambiguities. We must now turn to these.

Religion was defined as the self-transcendence of life under the dimension of spirit. This definition makes the image of the essential unity of religion with morality and culture possible, and it also explains the ambiguities of the three functions in their separation. The self-transcendence of life is effective in the unconditional character of the moral act and in the inexhaustible depth of meaning in all meanings created by culture. Life is sublime in every realm dominated by the dimension of the spirit. The self-integration of life in the moral act and the self-creativity of life in the cultural act are sublime. Within them, life transcends itself in the vertical direction, the direction of the ultimate. But because of the ambiguity of life, they are also profane; they resist self-transcendence. And this is inevitable because they are separated from their essential unity with religion and are actualized independently.

The definition of religion as self-transcendence of life in the dimension of the spirit has the decisive implication that religion must first of all be considered as a quality of the two other functions of the spirit and not as an independent function. Such a consideration is logically necessary, for self-transcendence of life cannot become a function of life beside others, because if it did it would have to be itself transcended, and so on in endless repetition. Life cannot genuinely transcend itself in one of its own functions. This is the argument against religion as a function of the spirit, and one cannot deny that theologians who advance this argument have a strong point. Therefore, if religion is defined as a function of the human mind, they are consistent in rejecting the concept of religion altogether in a theology which is supposed to be based on revelation.

But these assertions make incomprehensible the fact that there is religion in life under the dimension of the spirit, not only as a quality in morality and culture, but also as an independent reality beside them. This fact of the existence of religion in the ordinary sense of the word is one of the great stumbling blocks in life under the dimension of the spirit. According to the definition of religion as the self-transcendence of life, there should be no religion, individual or organized, as a particular function of the spirit. Every act of life should in itself point beyond itself, and no realm of particular acts should be necessary. But, as in all realms of life, self-transcendence is resisted by profanization in the realm of the spirit. Morality and culture in existential separation from religion become what is usually called "secular." Their greatness is contradicted by their profanity. Under the pressure of profanization the moral imperative becomes conditional, dependent on fears and hopes, a result of psychological and sociological compulsion; an ultimate moral aim is replaced by utilitarian calculations, and the fulfilment of the law is a matter of futile attempts at self-determination. The self-transcendence of the moral act is denied; morality is activity between finite possibilities. In the sense of our basic definition it is profanized—even if, in conflict with the meaning of grace, it is as restrictive as some forms of religious morality. It is unavoidable that such morality should fall under the ambiguities of the law. Under the analogous pressure of profanization, the cultural creation of a universe of meanings loses the substance which is received in self-transcendence—an ultimate and inexhaustible meaning. This phenomenon is well known and has been widely discussed by the analysts of our present civilization, usually under the heading of the secularization of culture. They have often rightly referred to the analogous phenomenon in ancient civilization and derived a general rule about the relation of religion and culture from these two examples of Western intellectual history. With the loss of its religious substance, culture is left with an increasingly empty form. Meaning cannot live without the inexhaustible source of meaning to which religion points.

Out of this situation religion arises as a special function of the spirit. The self-transcendence of life under the dimension of spirit cannot become alive without finite realities which are transcended. Thus there is a dialectical problem in self-transcendence in that something is transcended and at the same time not transcended. It must have concrete existence, otherwise nothing would be there to be transcended; yet it should not "be there" anymore but should be negated in the act of being transcended. This is exactly the situation of all religions in history. Religion as the self-transcendence of life needs the religions and needs to deny them.

e) *The ambiguities of religion*

(1) THE HOLY AND THE SECULAR (PROFANE).—In contrast to all other realms in which the ambiguities of life appear, the self-transcendence of life in religion shows a double ambiguity. The first has already been mentioned as one which is a universal characteristic of life, the ambiguity of the great and the profane. We have seen how in the process of profanization life, in all cultural acts of self-creativity and in the moral act of self-integration, loses its greatness and dignity. And we have seen why, in order to maintain itself as self-transcendent, life under the dimension of spirit expresses itself in a function which is defined by self-transcendence, that is, religion.

But this character of religion leads to a reduplication of ambiguities. Religion, as the self-transcending function of life, claims to be the answer to the ambiguities of life in all other dimensions; it transcends their finite tensions and conflicts. But in doing so, it falls into even profounder tensions, conflicts, and ambiguities. Religion is the highest expression of the greatness and dignity of life; in it the greatness of life becomes holiness. Yet religion is also the most radical refutation of the greatness and dignity of life; in it the great becomes most profanized, the holy most desecrated. These ambiguities are the central subject of any honest understanding of religion, and they are the background with which church and theology must work. They are the decisive motive for the expectation of a reality which transcends the religious function.

The first ambiguity of religion is that of self-transcendence and profanization in the religious function itself. The second ambiguity of religion is the demonic elevation of something conditional to unconditional validity. One can say that religion always moves between the danger points of profanization and demonization, and that in every genuine act of the religious life both are present, openly or covertly.

The profanization of religion has the character of transforming it into a finite object among finite objects. In religion as a particular function of the spirit, it is the process of the profanization of the holy to which we refer. If in religion the great is called the holy, this indicates that religion is based on the manifestation of the holy itself, the divine ground of being. Every religion is the receptive answer to revelatory experiences. This is its greatness and its dignity; this makes religion and its expressions holy in *theoria* as well as in *praxis*. In this sense one can speak of Holy Scriptures, holy communities, holy acts, holy offices, holy persons. These predicates mean that all these realities are more than they are in their immediate finite appearance. They are self-transcendent, or, seen from the side of that to which they transcend—the holy—they are translucent toward it. This holiness is not their moral or cognitive or even religious quality but their power of pointing beyond themselves. If the predicate "holiness" refers to persons, the actual participation of the person in it is possible in many degrees, from the lowest to the highest. It is not the personal quality that decides the degree of participation but the power of self-transcendence. Augustine's great insight in the Donatist struggle was that it is not the quality of the priest that makes a sacrament effective but the transparency of his office and the function he performs. Otherwise the religious function would be impossible, and the predicate of the holy could not be applied at all.

From this it follows that the ambiguity of religion is not identical with the "paradox of holiness" to which we have referred and shall refer more fully in connection with the image of the Christian and the church. The first ambiguity of religion is the presence of profanized elements in every religious act. There are two opposite ways in which this is true, the one institutional, the other reductive. The institutional way is not restricted to so-called institutionalized religion, for, as psychology has shown, there are institutions in the inner life of the individual, "ritual activities" as Freud has called them, which produce and preserve methods of action and reaction. The relentless attacks on "organized religion" are mostly based on a deeply rooted confusion, for life is organized in all its self-actualizations; without form it could not even have dynamics, and this is true of the personal as well as the communal life. But the real object of honest attacks on organized religion is the ambiguity of religion in the context of its institutional form. Instead of transcending the finite in the direction of the infinite, institutionalized religion actually becomes a finite reality itself—a set of prescribed activities to be performed, a set of stated doctrines to be accepted, a social pressure group along with others, a political power with all the implications of power politics. The critics cannot see the self-transcendent, great, and holy character of religion in this structure, which is subject to the sociological laws which govern all secular groups. But even if all this is internalized and performed by individuals in their personal religious life, the institutional character is not removed. The content of the personal religious life is always taken from the religious life of a social group. Even the silent language of prayer is formed by tradition. The critics of such profanized religion are justified in their criticism and often serve religion better than those whom they attack. It would, however, be a utopian fallacy to attempt to use these criticisms to remove the profanizing tendencies in the religious life and to retain pure self-transcendence of holiness. Insight into the inescapable ambiguity of life prevents such a fallacy. In all forms of communal and personal religion, profanizing elements are effective; and conversely, the most profanized forms of religion draw their power to continue from the elements of greatness and holiness within them. The pettiness of average daily-life religion is no argument against its greatness, and the way in which it is drawn down to the level of undignified mechanization is no argument against its dignity. Life, transcending itself, at the same time remains within itself, and the first ambiguity of religion follows from this tension.

The preceding description deals with only one way in which religion shows its ambiguity, the "institutional" way. There is another, the "reductive" way, based on the fact that culture is the form of religion and that morality is the expression of its seriousness. This fact can lead to the reduction of religion to culture and morality, whereby its symbols are interpreted as results merely of cultural creativity, whether as veiled concepts or as images. If one takes away the veil of self-transcendence, one finds cognitive insight and aesthetic expression. In this view the myths are a combination of primitive science and primitive poetry; they are creations of *theoria* and as such have lasting significance, but their claim to express transcendence must be discarded. The same kind of interpretation is given of the manifestations of religion in *praxis*: the holy personality and the holy community are developments of personality and community which must be judged by the principles of humanity and justice, but their claim to transcend these principles must be rejected.

As it appears in such ideas, the reduction of religion is not radical. Religion is given a place in the whole of man's cultural creativity, and its usefulness for moral self-actualization is not denied. But this is a preliminary state in the process of a reductionist profanization of religion. It soon becomes clear either that the claim of religion must be accepted or that it has no claim to a place among the functions of cultural creativity and morality has no need of it. Religion, which in principle has a home in every function of the spirit, has become homeless in all of them. The benevolent treatment it has received from those who reject its claim to self-transcendence does not help it, and its benevolent critics soon become much more radical. Religion is explained away in the cognitive realm as being derived from psychological or sociological sources and is considered as illusion or ideology, while in the aesthetic realm, religious symbols are replaced by finite objects in the different naturalistic styles, especially in critical naturalism and some types of non-objective art. Education does not initiate into the mystery of being to which religion points, but introduces people only into the needs of a society whose needs and ends remain finite in spite of their endlessness. All communities become agents for the actualization of such a society, rejecting any kind of self-transcending symbols and trying to dissolve the churches into the organizations of secular life. Within large sections of contemporary mankind, this reductive way of profanizing religion, reduction by annihilation, is tremendously successful—not only in the communist East, but also in the democratic West. In the world-historical view, one must say that in our period this way is much more successful than the institutional way of profanizing religion.

Nevertheless, here also the ambiguity of life resists an unambiguous solution. First of all, we must remind ourselves of the fact that the profanizing forces are not simply the negation of religion as a function of the spirit but that they are present in its very nature: actual religion lives in the cognitive forms, from language to ontology, which are the results of cultural creativity. In using language, historical research, psychological descriptions of human nature, existentialist analyses of man's predicament, prephilosophical and philosophical concepts, it uses the secular material which becomes independent in the processes of reductive profanization. Religion can be secularized and finally dissolved into secular forms only because it has the ambiguity of self-transcendence.

But when this is attempted, the ambiguity of religion shows its effect on these processes of reductive profanation, just as it shows its effect in the center of religious self-transcendence. The way in which this happens suggests the larger concept of religion as experience of the unconditional, both in the moral imperative and in the depth of culture. The ambiguity of radical secularism is that it cannot escape the element of self-transcendence which appears in these two experiences. Often these experiences are rather hidden and any expression of them is carefully avoided; but if the radically secular philosopher is asked by a tryrannical power—dictatorial or conformist—to give up his secularism, he resists such a demand, experiencing the unconditional imperative of honesty up to total self-sacrifice. In the same way, if the radically secular writer whose novel has been written with the totality of his being sees that it is being used as a mere piece of entertainment, he feels this as an abuse and as profanization. Reductive profanization may succeed in abolishing religion as a special function, but it is not able to remove religion as a quality that is found in all functions of the spirit—the quality of ultimate concern.

(2) THE DIVINE AND THE DEMONIC.—In religion the ambiguity of self-transcendence appears as the ambiguity of the divine and the demonic. The symbol of the demonic does not need justification as it did thirty years ago, when it was reintroduced into theological language. It has become a much-used and much-abused term to designate antidivine forces in individual and social life. In this way it has frequently lost the ambiguous character implied in the word itself. Demons in mythological vision are divine-antidivine beings. They are not simply negations of the divine but participate in a distorted way in the power and holiness of the divine. The term must be understood against this mythological background. The demonic does not resist self-transcendence as does the profane, but it distorts self-transcendence by identifying a particular bearer of holiness with the holy itself. In this sense all polytheistic gods are demonic, because the basis of being and meaning on which they stand is finite, no matter how sublime, great, or dignified it may be. And the claim of something finite to infinity or to divine greatness is the characteristic of the demonic. Demonization of the holy occurs in all religions day by day, even in the religion which is based on the self-negation of the finite in the Cross of the Christ. The quest for unambiguous life is, therefore, most radically directed against the ambiguity of the holy and the demonic in the religious realm.

The tragic is the inner ambiguity of human greatness. But the subject of tragedy does not *aspire* to divine greatness. He does not intend "to be like God." He touches, so to speak, the divine sphere, and he is rejected by it into self-destruction, but he does not claim divinity for himself.

Wherever *this* is done, the demonic appears. A main characteristic of the tragic is the state of being blind; a main characteristic of the demonic is the state of being split.

This is easily understandable on the basis of the demonic's claim to divinity on a finite basis: the elevation of one element of finitude to infinite power and meaning necessarily produces the reaction from other elements of finitude, which deny such a claim or make it for themselves. The demonic self-elevation of one nation over against all the others in the name of her God or system of values produces the reaction from other nations in the name of *their* God. The demonic self-elevation of particular forces in the centered personality and the claim of their absolute superiority leads to the reaction of other forces and to a split consciousness. The claim of *one* value, represented by *one* God, to be the criterion of all others leads to the splits in polytheistic religion.

A consequence of these splits, connected with the nature of the demonic, is the state of being "possessed" by the power which produces the split. The demoniacs are the possessed ones. The freedom of centeredness is removed by the demonic split. Demonic structures in the personal and communal life cannot be broken by acts of freedom and good will. They are strengthened by such acts—except when the changing power is a divine structure, that is, a structure of grace.

Wherever the demonic appears, it shows religious traits, even if the appearance is moral or cultural. This is a logical consequence of the mutual immanence of the three functions of life in the dimension of spirit and of the dual concept of religion as unconditional concern and as a realm of concrete symbols that express concrete concerns. Here also examples are abundant: the unconditional demands of commitment by states which vest themselves with religious dignity, by cultural functions which control all others (as in scientific absolutism), by individuals who seek idolization of themselves, by particular drives in the person which take over the personal center—in all these cases, distorted self-transcendence takes place.

A revealing example of the ambiguity of the demonic in the cultural realm is the Roman empire, whose greatness, dignity, and sublime character was universally acknowledged, but which became demonically possessed when it vested itself with divine holiness and produced the split which led to the antidemonic struggle of Christianity and the demonic persecution of the Christians.

This historical reminder furnishes a transition to the discussion of religion in the narrower sense of the word and its demonization. The basic ambiguity of religion has a deeper root than any of the other ambiguities of life, for religion is the point at which the answer to the quest for the unambiguous is received. Religion in this respect (that is, in the respect of man's possibility of receiving this answer) is unambiguous; the actual reception, however, is profoundly ambiguous, for it occurs in the changing forms of man's moral and cultural existence. These forms participate in the holy to which they point, but they are not the holy itself. The claim to be the holy itself makes them demonic.

This is the reason why theologians have protested against applying the term "religion" to Christianity. They have contrasted religion with revelation and have described religion as man's attempt to glorify himself. This is, indeed, a correct description of demonized religion, but it ignores the fact that every religion is based on revelation and that every revelation expresses itself in a religion. In so far as religion is based on revelation it is unambiguous; in so far as it receives revelation it is ambiguous. This is true of all religions, even those which their followers call revealed religion. But no religion is revealed; religion is the creation and the distortion of revelation.

The concept of religion cannot be avoided in any theology, although the criticism of religion is an element in the history of all religions. The revelatory impact behind the religions awakens people everywhere to an awareness of the contrast between the unambiguous life toward which the self-transcendence of life is directed and the often terrifying ambiguities of actual religions. One can read the history of religion, especially of the great religions, as a continuous inner religious struggle against religion for the sake of the holy itself. Christianity claims that in the Cross of the Christ the final victory in this struggle has been reached, but even in claiming this, the form of the claim itself shows demonic traits; that which is rightly said about the Cross of the Christ is wrongly transferred to the life of the church, whose ambiguities are denied, although they have become increasingly powerful throughout its history.

But at this point it is the demonization of religion in general of which we want to give some examples. Religion as a historical reality uses cultural creations both in *theoria* and *praxis*. It uses some and rejects others, and in doing so it establishes a realm of religious culture which lies

alongside the other cultural creations. But religion as the self-transcendence of life in all realms claims a superiority over them which is justified
in so far as religion points to that which transcends all of them, but the
claim to superiority becomes demonic when religion as a social and personal reality makes this claim for itself and the finite forms by which
it points to the infinite.

We can show this in the four functions of man's cultural creativity
discussed before (but in reverse order): the communal, the personal,
the aesthetic, the cognitive. Religion is actual in social groups which are
united with or separated from political groups. In both cases they constitute a social, legal, and political reality which is consecrated by the
holy embodied in them. In the power of this consecration they consecrate
the other communal structures and in this way try to control them. In
case of their resistance, they try to destroy them. The power of the bearers
of the holy is the unconditional character of the holy, in whose name they
break the resistance of all those who do not accept the symbols of self-
transcendence under which the religious community lives. This is the
source of the power of those who represent a religious community, as it is
the source of the solidity of the holy institutions, sacred customs, divinely
ordered systems of law, hierarchical orders, myths and symbols, and so
on. But this very solidity betrays its divine-demonic ambiguity; it is able
to reject all criticisms which are raised in the name of justice. It overrules
them in the name of the holy, which has the principle of justice within
itself, breaking the minds and bodies of those who try to resist. No
examples need be given for this ambiguity of religion, for they fill the
pages of world history. It is enough to show why the quest for unambiguous life must transcend religion, even though the answer is given
in religion.

In the realm of the personal life, the divine-demonic ambiguity of
religion appears in the idea of the saint. Here is reflected the conflict
between humanity and holiness and the divine support and demonic suppression of personal development toward humanity. These conflicts
with their integrating, disintegrating, creative, and destructive consequences go on first of all within the individual person. One of the ways
religion uses its own consecrated idea of personality to suppress the idea
of humanity within the individual is by engendering an uneasy conscience in him who does not accept the absolute claim of religion. The

psychologist knows the devastation in personal development which is caused by this conflict. Very often in the history of religion it is the negative, ascetic principle which receives religious consecration and which stands as a condemning judge against the positive implications of the idea of humanity. But the power contained in the religious image of personal holiness would not exist if there were not the other side—the impact on the development of the person coming from the divine, anti-demonic (and antiprofane) character of the holy to which religion points. But again one must say that the answer to the quest for unambiguous life is not in the idea of the saint, although the answer can be received only in the depth of the self-transcending personality—religiously speaking, in the act of faith.

The discussion about the divine-demonic ambiguity in the relation of religion to *theoria* naturally focuses on the problem of religious doctrine, particularly when it appears in the form of an established dogma. The conflict arising here is one between the consecrated truth of the dogma and the truth which unites dynamic change and creative form. But it is not the theoretical conflict as such in which the divine-demonic ambiguity appears but in its significance for the holy community and holy personality. The demonic suppression of honest obedience to the structures of truth is at stake here. What is happening in this respect to the cognitive function happens equally to the aesthetic function; the suppression of authentic expressiveness in art and literature is equal to the suppression of honest cognition. It is done in the name of a religiously consecrated truth and a religiously consecrated style. There is no doubt that self-transcendence opens the eyes to cognitive truth and aesthetic authenticity. Divine power lies behind religious doctrines and religious art. But the demonic distortion begins when new insight presses toward the surface and is trodden down in the name of the dogma, the consecrated truth, or when new styles seek to express the drives of a period and are prevented from doing so in the name of religiously approved forms of expression. In all these cases the resisting community and the resisting personalities are victims of the demonic destruction of truth and expressiveness in the name of the holy. As in relation to justice and to humanity directly, so in relation to truth and to expressiveness indirectly —religion is *not* the answer to the quest for unambiguous life, although the answer can only be received through religion.

C. THE QUEST FOR UNAMBIGUOUS LIFE AND THE SYMBOLS OF ITS ANTICIPATION

In all life processes an essential and an existential element, created goodness and estrangement, are merged in such a way that neither one nor the other is exclusively effective. Life always includes essential and existential elements; this is the root of its ambiguity.

The ambiguities of life are manifest under all dimensions, in all processes and all realms of life. The question of unambiguous life is latent everywhere. All creatures long for an unambiguous fulfilment of their essential possibilities; but only in man as the bearer of the spirit do the ambiguities of life and the quest for unambiguous life become conscious. He experiences the ambiguity of life under all dimensions since he participates in all of them, and he experiences them immediately within himself as the ambiguity of the functions of the spirit: of morality, culture, and religion. The quest for unambiguous life arises out of these experiences; this quest is for a life which has reached that toward which it transcends itself.

Since religion is the self-transcendence of life in the realm of the spirit, it is in religion that man starts the quest for unambiguous life and it is in religion that he receives the answer. But the answer is not identical with religion, since religion itself is ambiguous. The fulfilment of the quest for unambiguous life transcends any religious form or symbol in which it is expressed. The self-transcendence of life never unambiguously reaches that toward which it transcends, although life can receive its self-manifestation in the ambiguous form of religion.

Religious symbolism has produced three main symbols for unambiguous life: Spirit of God, Kingdom of God, and Eternal Life. Each of them and their relation to each other require a short preliminary consideration. The Spirit of God is the presence of the Divine Life within creaturely life. The Divine Spirit is "God present." The Spirit of God is not a separated being. Therefore one can speak of "Spiritual Presence" in order to give the symbol its full meaning.

The word "presence" has an archaic connotation, pointing to the place where a sovereign or a group of high dignitaries is. In capitalizing it, we indicate that it is supposed to express the divine presence in creaturely life. "Spiritual Presence," then, is the first symbol expressing unambiguous life. It is directly correlated to the ambiguities of life under the dimension of spirit although, because of the multidimensional unity of life, it refers indirectly to all realms. In it both "Spiritual" and "Presence" are capitalized, and the word "Spiritual" is used for the first time in this part of *Systematic Theology*. It has *not* been used as an adjective from spirit with a small "s," designating a dimension of life. This symbol will guide our discussion in the fourth part of the system.

The second symbol of unambiguous life is the "Kingdom of God." Its symbolic material is taken from the historical dimension of life and the dynamics of historical self-transcendence. Kingdom of God is the answer to the ambiguities of man's historical existence but, because of the multidimensional unity of life, the symbol includes the answer to the ambiguity under the historical dimension in all realms of life. The dimension of history is actualized, on the one hand, in historical events which reach out of the past and determine the present, and on the other hand, in the historical tension which is experienced in the present, but runs irreversibly into the future. Therefore, the symbol of the Kingdom of God covers both the struggle of unambiguous life with the forces which make for ambiguity, and the ultimate fulfilment toward which history runs.

This leads to the third symbol: unambiguous life is Eternal Life. Here the symbolic material is taken from the temporal and spatial finitude of all life. Unambiguous life conquers the servitude to the categorical limits of existence. It does not mean an endless continuation of categorical existence but the conquest of its ambiguities. This symbol, together with that of the Kingdom of God, will be the leading notions in the fifth part of the theological system: "History and the Kingdom of God."

The relation of the three symbols, "Spiritual Presence," "Kingdom of God," and "Eternal Life" can be described in the following way: all three are symbolic expressions of the answer revelation gives to the quest for unambiguous life. Unambiguous life can be described as life under the Spiritual Presence, or as life in the Kingdom of God, or as Eternal Life. But as shown before, the three symbols use different symbolic material and in doing so express different directions of meaning within the same idea of unambiguous life. The symbol "Spiritual Presence" uses the dimension of spirit, the bearer of which is man, but in order to be present in the human spirit, the Divine Spirit must be present in all the dimensions which are actual in man, and this means, in the universe.

The symbol Kingdom of God is a social symbol, taken from the historical dimension in so far as it is actualized in man's historical life. But the historical dimension is present in all life. Therefore, the symbol "Kingdom of God" embraces the destiny of the life of the universe, just as does the symbol "Spiritual Presence." But history's quality of running irreversibly toward a goal introduces another element into its symbolic meaning, and that is the "eschatological" expectation, the expectation of the fulfilment toward which self-transcendence strives and toward which history runs. Like Spiritual Presence, the Kingdom of God is working and struggling in history; but as eternal fulfilment of life, the Kingdom of God is above history.

The symbolic material of the third symbol of unambiguous life, Eternal Life, is taken from the categorical structure of finitude. Unambiguous life is Eternal Life. As with Spiritual Presence and Kingdom of God, Eternal Life is also a universal symbol, referring to all dimensions of life and including the two other symbols. Spiritual Presence creates Eternal Life in those who are grasped by it. And the Kingdom of God is the fulfilment of temporal life in Eternal Life.

The three symbols for unambiguous life mutually include each other, but because of the different symbolic material they use, it is preferable to apply them in different directions of meaning: Spiritual Presence for the conquest of the ambiguities of life under the dimension of the spirit, Kingdom of God for the conquest of the ambiguities of life under the dimension of history, and Eternal Life for the conquest of the ambiguities of life beyond history. Yet in all three of them we find a mutual immanence of all. Where there is Spiritual Presence, there is Kingdom of God and Eternal Life, and where there is Kingdom of God there is Eternal Life and Spiritual Presence, and where there is Eternal Life there is Spiritual Presence and Kingdom of God. The emphasis is different, the substance is the same—life unambiguous.

The quest for such unambiguous life is possible because life has the character of self-transcendence. Under all dimensions life moves beyond itself in the vertical direction. But under no dimension does it reach that toward which it moves, the unconditional. It does not reach it, but the quest remains. Under the dimension of the spirit it is the quest for an unambiguous morality and an unambiguous culture reunited with an unambiguous religion. The answer to this quest is the experience of revelation and salvation; they constitute religion above religion, although they become religion when they are received. In religious symbolism they are the work of the Spiritual Presence or of the Kingdom of God or of Eternal Life. This quest is effective in all religions and the answer received underlies all religions, giving them their greatness and dignity. But both quest and answer become matters of ambiguity if expressed in the terms of a concrete religion. It is an age-old experience of all religions that the quest for something transcending them is answered in the shaking and transforming experiences of revelation and salvation; but that under the conditions of existence even the absolutely great—the divine self-manifestation—becomes not only great but also small, not only divine but also demonic.

II

THE SPIRITUAL PRESENCE

A. THE MANIFESTATION OF THE SPIRITUAL PRESENCE IN THE SPIRIT OF MAN

1. The Character of the Manifestation of the Divine Spirit in the Human Spirit

a) Human spirit and divine Spirit in principle.—We have dared to use the almost forbidden word "spirit" (with a small "s") for two purposes: first, in order to give an adequate name to that function of life which characterizes man as man and which is actualized in morality, culture, and religion; second, in order to provide the symbolic material which is used in the symbols "divine Spirit" or "Spiritual Presence." The dimension of spirit provides this material. As we have seen, spirit as a dimension of life unites the power of being with the meaning of being. Spirit can be defined as the actualization of power and meaning in unity. Within the limits of our experience this happens only in man—in man as a whole and in all the dimensions of life which are present in him. Man, in experiencing himself as man, is conscious of being determined in his nature by spirit as a dimension of his life. This immediate experience makes it possible to speak symbolically of God as Spirit and of the divine Spirit. These terms, like all other statements about God, are symbols. In them, empirical material is appropriated and transcended. Without this experience of spirit as the unity of power and meaning in himself, man would not have been able to express the revelatory experience of "God present" in the term "Spirit" or "Spiritual Presence." This shows again that no doctrine of the divine Spirit is possible without an understanding of spirit as a dimension of life.

The question of the relation between Spirit and spirit is usually answered by the metaphorical statement that the divine Spirit dwells and works in the human spirit. In this context, the word "in" implies all the problems of the relation of the divine to the human, of the unconditional to the conditioned, and of the creative ground to creaturely existence. If the divine Spirit breaks into the human spirit, this does not mean that it rests there, but that it drives the human spirit out of iself. The "in" of the divine Spirit is an "out" for the human spirit. The spirit, a dimension of finite life, is driven into a successful self-transcendence; it is grasped by something ultimate and unconditional. It is still the human spirit; it remains what it is, but at the same time, it goes out of itself under the impact of the divine Spirit. "Ecstasy" is the classical term for this state of being grasped by the Spiritual Presence. It describes the human situation under the Spiritual Presence exactly.

We described the nature of the revelatory experience, its ecstatic character, and its relation to the cognitive side of the human spirit, in the section on "Reason and Revelation" (Part I of the system). In that section, we also gave a similar description of the nature of the saving experience, which is an element in the revelatory experience precisely as the latter is an element in the saving experience. The Spiritual Presence creates an ecstasy in both of them which drives the spirit of man beyond itself without destroying its essential, i.e., rational, structure. Ecstasy does not destroy the centeredness of the integrated self. Should it do so, demonic possession would replace the creative presence of the Spirit.

Although the ecstatic character of the experience of Spiritual Presence does not destroy the rational structure of the human spirit it does something the human spirit could not do by itself. When it grasps man, it creates unambiguous life. Man in his self-transcendence can reach for it, but man cannot grasp it, unless he is first grasped by it. Man remains in himself. By the very nature of his self-transcendence, man is driven to ask the question of unambiguous life, but the answer must come to him through the creative power of the Spiritual Presence. "Natural theology" describes man's self-transcendence and the questions implied in his consciousness of its ambiguity. But "natural theology" does not answer the question.

This illustrates the truth that the human spirit is unable to compel the divine Spirit to enter the human spirit. The attempt to do so belongs directly to the ambiguities of religion and indirectly to the ambiguities of culture and morality. If religious devotion, moral obedience, or scientific honesty could compel the divine Spirit to "descend" to us, the Spirit which "descended" would be the human spirit in a religious disguise. It would be, and often is, simply man's spirit ascending, the natural form of man's self-transcendence. The finite cannot force the infinite; man cannot compel God. The human spirit as a dimension of life is ambiguous, as all life is, whereas the divine Spirit creates unambiguous life.

This drives us to the question as to how the thesis of the multidimensional unity of life is related to the Spiritual Presence. The multidimensional unity of life has functioned to preclude dualistic and supranaturalistic doctrines of man in himself and in his relation to God. Now it is unavoidable that the question should arise as to whether the contrast between human spirit and divine Spirit reintroduces a dualistic-supranatural element. The basic answer to this question is that the relation of the finite to that which is infinite—and which is therefore above all comparison to the finite—is incommensurable and cannot adequately be expressed by the same metaphor which expresses the relations between finite realms. On the other hand, there is no way to express any relation to the divine ground of being other than by using finite material and the language of symbols. This difficulty cannot be completely overcome, for it reflects the human situation itself. But it is possible in theological language to indicate an awareness of the human situation, including the inevitable limitations on all attempts to express the relation to the ultimate. One way to do this is to use the metaphor "dimension," but to use it with the radical qualification implied in speaking of the "dimension of depth" or of the "dimension of the ultimate" or of "the eternal" (as I myself have done on several occasions). It is obvious that the metaphor "dimension" as it is used in these phrases means something other than what it means in the series of the dimensions of life we have described. It is not one dimension in this series, dependent for its actualization upon that of the preceding one, but it is the ground of being of them all and the aim toward which they are self-transcendent. Therefore, if the term "dimension" is used in such combinations as "dimension of depth" (which has become quite popular), it means the dimension in which all dimensions are rooted and negated and affirmed. However, this transfo.ms the metaphor into a symbol, and it is doubtful whether this double use of the same word is to be recommended.

Another way to deal with the difficulty of expressing the relation of the human spirit to the divine Spirit is by replacing the metaphor "dimension" with the statement that, since the finite is potentially or essentially an element in the divine life, everything finite is qualified by this essential relation. And since the existential situation in which the finite is actual implies both separation from and resistance to the essential unity of the finite and the infinite, the finite is no longer actually qualified by its essential unity with the infinite. It is only in the self-transcendence of life that the "memory" of the essential unity with the infinite is preserved. The dualistic element implied in such a terminology is, so to speak, preliminary and transitory; it simply serves to distinguish the actual from the potential and the existential from the essential. Thus it is neither a dualism of levels nor supranaturalistic.

It has been asked if the substitution of the metaphor "dimension" for the metaphor "level" does not contradict the method of correlation of existential questions with theological answers. This would indeed be the case were the divine Spirit to represent a new dimension within the series of life's dimensions. But this is not intended and should rather be precluded by the preceding consideration. "Dimension," like the categories and polarities, is used symbolically when it is applied to God. Therefore, in the phrase "the dimension of the ultimate," it is used symbolically, whereas in reference to the different dimensions of life, it is used metaphorically. Man's existential situation requires the method of correlation and prohibits the dualism of levels. In the human spirit's essential relation to the divine Spirit, there is no correlation, but rather, mutual immanence.

b) Structure and ecstasy.—The Spiritual Presence does not destroy the structure of the centered self which bears the dimension of spirit. Ecstasy does not negate structure. This is one of the consequences of the doctrine of "transitory dualism," discussed in the last few paragraphs. A dualism of levels logically leads to the destruction of the finite, for example, the human spirit for the sake of the divine Spirit. But, religiously speaking, God does not need to destroy his created world, which is good in its essential nature, in order to manifest himself in it. We discussed this in connection with the meaning of "miracle." We rejected miracles in the supranaturalistic sense of the word, and we also rejected the miracle of ecstasy created by the Spiritual Presence when this is understood as inviting the destruction of the structure of the spirit in man (*Systematic Theology*, I, 111-14).

However, should we give a "phenomenology" of the Spiritual Presence, we should find in the history of religion a large number of reports and descriptions which indicate that ecstasy as the work of the Spirit disrupts created structure. The Spiritual Presence's manifestations since the earliest times, as well as in biblical literature, have a miraculous character.

The Spirit has bodily effects: the transference of a person from one place to another, changes within the body, such as generation of new life in it, penetration of rigid bodies, and so on. The Spirit also has psychological effects of an extraordinary character which endow the intellect or will with powers not within the scope of a person's natural capacity, such as knowledge of strange tongues, penetration into the innermost thoughts of another person, and healing influences even at a distance. However questionable their historical reliability may be, these reports point to two important qualities of Spiritual Presence: its universal and extraordinary character. The universal impact of the Spiritual Presence on all realms of life is expressed in these reports of miracles in all dimensions; in supranaturalistic language they point to the truth of the unity of life. Spiritual presence answers questions implied in the ambiguities of all life's dimensions: spatial and temporal separation and bodily and psychological disorders and limitations are overcome. We shall develop this more fully later in "demythologized" terms.

The two terms "inspiration" and "infusion" express the way in which man's spirit receives the impact of Spiritual Presence. Both terms are spatial metaphors and involve, respectively, "breathing" and "pouring" into the human spirit. In the discussion of revelation, we sharply rejected the distortion which occurs when the experience of inspiration is turned into an informative lesson about God and divine matters. The Spiritual Presence is not that of a teacher but of a meaning-bearing power which grasps the human spirit in an ecstatic experience. After the experience, the teacher can analyse and formulate the element of meaning in the ecstasy of inspiration (as the systematic theologian does), but when the analysis of the teacher begins, the inspirational experience has already passed.

The other term which describes the impact of the Spiritual Presence in a spatial metaphor is "infusion." This concept is central in the early church and later in the Catholic church, where it describes the relation of the divine Spirit to the human spirit. Such terms as *infusio fidei* or *infusio amoris* derive faith and love from *infusio Spiritus Sancti* ("the infusion of the Holy Spirit"). Protestantism was and remains suspicious of this terminology because of the magic-materialistic perversion to which the idea was subjected in the later Roman church. The Spirit became a substance the reality of which was not necessarily noticed by the centered self-awareness of the person. It became a kind of "matter"

which was transmitted by the priest in the performance of the sacraments, provided that the receiving subject did not resist. This a-personal-
istic understanding of the Spiritual Presence resulted in an objectivation
of the religious life which culminated in the business practice of selling
indulgence. For Protestant thinking, the Spirit is always personal. Faith
and love are impacts of the Spiritual Presence on the centered self, and
the vehicle of this impact is the "word," even within the administration
of the sacraments. This is why Protestantism is reluctant to use the term
"infusion" for the impact of the Spiritual Presence.

But this reluctance is not wholly justified, and Protestantism is not
wholly consistent about it. When reading and interpreting the story of
Pentecost and similar stories in the New Testament, especially in the
book of Acts and in passages of the Epistles (particularly Paul's), the
Protestant also uses the metaphor of the "outpouring" of the Holy Spirit.
And he does so rightly, because even if we prefer "in-spiration," we do
not escape a substantial metaphor, for "breath" is also a substance entering him who receives the Spirit. But there is another reason for using the
term "infusion" as well as "inspiration," and that is contemporary psychology's rediscovery of the significance of the unconscious and the
consequent re-evaluation of symbols and sacraments that has taken place
in contrast to the traditional Protestant emphasis on the doctrinal and
moral word as the medium of the Spirit.

But if the ecstatic reception of the Spiritual Presence is described as
"inspiration" or "infusion" or as both, we must observe the basic rule
that the Spiritual Presence's reception can only be described in such a
way that ecstasy does not disrupt structure. The unity of ecstasy and
structure is classically expressed in Paul's doctrine of the Spirit. Paul is
primarily the theologian of the Spirit. His Christology and his eschatology are both dependent on this central point in this thinking. His doctrine of justification through faith by grace is a matter of support and
defense of his main assertion that with the appearance of the Christ a
new state of things came into being, created by the Spirit. Paul strongly
emphasizes the ecstatic element in the experience of the Spiritual Presence, and he does so in accordance with all the New Testament stories
in which it is described. These experiences, which he acknowledges in
others, he claims also for himself. He knows that every successful prayer,
i.e., every prayer which reunites with God, has ecstatic character. Such a
prayer is impossible for the human spirit, because man does not know

how to pray; but it is possible for the divine Spirit to pray through man, even should man not use words ("unspeakable sighs"—Paul). The formula—being in Christ—which Paul often uses, does not suggest a psychological empathy with Jesus Christ; rather it involves an ecstatic participation in the Christ who "is the Spirit," whereby one lives in the sphere of this Spiritual power.

At the same time, Paul resists any tendency that would permit ecstasy to disrupt structure. The classical expression of this is given in the first letter to the Corinthians where Paul speaks of the gifts of the Spirit and rejects ecstatic speaking in tongues if it produces chaos and disrupts the community, the emphasis on personal ecstatic experiences if they produce *hubris*, and the other charismata (gifts of the Spirit) if they are not subjected to *agape*. He then discusses the greatest creation of the Spiritual Presence, *agape* itself. In the hymn to *agape* in I Corinthians, chapter 13, the structure of the moral imperative and the ecstasy of the Spiritual Presence are completely united. Similarly, the first three chapters of the same letter indicate a way to unite the structure of cognition with the ecstasy of the Spiritual Presence. The relation to the divine ground of being through the divine Spirit is not agnostic (as it is not amoral); rather it includes the knowledge of the "depth" of the divine. However, as Paul shows in these chapters, this knowledge is not the fruit of *theoria*, the receiving function of the human spirit, but has an ecstatic character, as indicated by the language Paul uses in these chapters as well as in the chapter on *agape*. In ecstatic language Paul points to *agape* and *gnosis*— forms of morality and knowledge in which ecstasy and structure are united.

The church had and continues to have a problem in actualizing Paul's ideas, because of concrete ecstatic movements. The church must prevent the confusion of ecstasy with chaos, and it must fight for structure. On the other hand, it must avoid the institutional profanization of the Spirit which took place in the early Catholic church as a result of its replacement of *charisma* with office. Above all. it must avoid the secular profanization of contemporary Protestantism which occurs when it replaces ecstasy with doctrinal or moral structure. The Pauline criterion of the unity of structure and ecstasy stands against both kinds of profanization. The use of this criterion is an ever present duty and an ever present risk for the churches. It is a duty, because a church which lives in its institutional forms and disregards the Spiritual Presence's ecstatic side opens the door to the chaotic or disrupting forms of ecstasy and is even responsible for the growth of secularized reactions against the Spiritual Presence. On the other hand, a church which takes ecstatic movements seriously risks confusing the Spiritual Presence's impact with that of a psychologically determined overexcitement.

This danger can be reduced by investigating ecstasy's relation to the different dimensions of life. The ecstasy which is created by the divine Spirit occurs under the dimension of spirit, as discussed in the preceding chapter on the relations of the human spirit and the divine Spirit. However, because of the multidimensional unity of life, all dimensions, as they are effective in man, participate in the Spirit-created ecstasy. This refers directly to the dimension of self-awareness and indirectly to the organic and inorganic dimensions. It is a reductionist profanization of self-transcendence to attempt to derive religion, especially in its ecstatic side, from psychological dynamics. This takes place predominantly with regard to those aspects which are evaluated negatively and are assumed to be susceptible to removal through psychotherapy. Religious movements of emotional character in our society, as well as in former societies, give much weight to such reductionist attempts, and ecclesiastical authoritarianism is always ready to co-operate with these attacks from the opposite side. Spirit-movements find it difficult to defend themselves against this alliance of ecclesiastical and psychological critics. This whole part of the present system is a defense of the ecstatic manifestations of the Spiritual Presence against its ecclesiastical critics; in this defense, the whole New Testament is the most powerful weapon. Yet, this weapon can be used legitimately only if the other partner in the alliance—the psychological critics—is also rejected or at least put into proper perspective.

The doctrine of the multidimensional unity of life provides the basis for this defense. The psychological (and biological) basis of all ecstasy is accepted as a matter of course in the context of this doctrine. But because the dimension of the spirit is potentially present in the dimension of self-awareness, the dynamics of the psychological self can be the bearer of meaning in the personal self. This happens whenever a mathematical problem is solved, a poem is written, or a legal decision is rendered. It occurs in every prophetic pronouncement, every mystical contemplation, and every successful prayer: the dimension of the spirit actualizes itself within the dynamics of self-awareness and under its biological conditions.

In the last examples, we have pointed to experiences of Spirit-created ecstasy. At this point, however, a special phenomenon must be considered. Ecstasy, in its transcendence of the subject-object structure, is the great liberating power under the dimension of self-awareness. But this liberating power creates the possibility of confusing that which is "less" than the subject-object structure of the mind with that which is "more" than this structure. Whether it takes biological or emotional form, intoxication does not reach the actuality of self-awareness. It is always less than the structure of objectivation. Intoxication is an attempt to escape from the dimension of spirit with its burden of personal centeredness and responsibility and cultural rationality. Although ultimately it can never succeed, for the reason that man bears the dimension of spirit, it does give temporary release from the burden of personal and communal existence. In the long run, however, it is destructive, heightening the tensions it wants to avoid. Its main distinguishing feature is that it lacks both spiritual productivity and Spiritual creativity. It returns to an empty subjectivity which extinguishes these contents coming from the objective world. It makes the self a vacuum.

Ecstasy, similarly to the productive enthusiasm of cultural dynamics in *theoria* as well as in *praxis*, has in itself the manifold richness of the objective world, transcended by the Spiritual Presence's inner infinity. He who pronounces the divine Word is, as is the keenest analyst of society, aware of the social situation of his time, but he sees it ecstatically under the impact of the Spiritual Presence in the light of eternity. He who contemplates is aware of the ontological structure of the universe, but he sees it ecstatically under the impact of the Spiritual Presence in light of the ground and aim of all being. He who prays earnestly is aware of his own situation and his "neighbor's," but he sees it under the Spiritual Presence's influence and in the light of the divine direction of life's processes. In these experiences, nothing of the objective world is dissolved into mere subjectivity. Rather, it is all preserved and even increased. But it is not preserved under the dimension of self-awareness and in the subject-object scheme. A union of subject and object has taken place in which the independent existence of each is overcome; new unity is created. The best and most universal example of an ecstatic experience is the pattern of prayer. Every serious and successful prayer—which does not talk to God as a familiar partner, as many prayers do—is a speaking to God, which means that God is made into an object for him who prays. However, God can never be an object, unless he is a subject at the same time. We can only pray to the God who prays to himself through us. Prayer is a possibility only in so far as the subject-object structure is overcome; hence, it is an ecstatic possibility. Herein lies both the greatness of prayer and the danger of its continuous profanization. The term "ecstatic," the use of which ordinarily carries many negative connotations, can perhaps be saved for a positive meaning if it is understood as the essential character of prayer.

The criterion which must be used to decide whether an extraordinary state of the mind is ecstasy, created by the Spiritual Presence, or subjective intoxication is the manifestation of creativity in the former and the lack of it in the latter. The use of this criterion is not without risk, but it is the only valid criterion the church can employ in "judging the Spirit."

c) The media of the Spiritual Presence

(1) SACRAMENTAL ENCOUNTERS AND THE SACRAMENTS.—According to theological tradition the Spiritual Presence is effective through the Word and the sacraments. Upon these, the church is founded and their administration makes the church the church. It is our twofold task to interpret this tradition in terms of our understanding of the relation of Spirit to spirit and to enlarge the question of the media of the divine Spirit so that it will include all personal and historical events in which the Spiritual Presence is effective. The duality of Word and sacrament would not be as significant as it is if it did not represent the primordial phenomenon that reality is communicated either by the silent presence of the object as object or by the vocal self-expression of a subject to a subject. In both ways, communication can be received by beings under the dimensions of self-awareness and spirit. An encountered reality can impress itself upon a subject through the indirect means of giving signs of itself as a centered subjectivity. This occurs through sounds which become words under the dimension of the spirit. Because of the sequence of the dimensions, the objective sign precedes the subjective, which in this context means that the sacrament is "older" than the Word.

The terms "word" and "sacrament" designate the two modes of communication in relation to the Spiritual Presence. Words which communicate the Spiritual Presence become the Word (with a capital "W"), or in traditional terms, the Word of God. Objects which are vehicles of the divine Spirit become sacramental materials and elements in a sacramental act.

As indicated, the sacrament is older than the word, although the word is implicit in the completely silent sacramental material. This is so because the experience of sacramental reality belongs to the dimension of the spirit and concretely to its religious function. Therefore, it cannot be without the word even if it remains voiceless. The term "sacramental," in this larger sense, needs to be freed from its narrower connotations. The Christian churches, in their controversies over the meaning and number of the particular sacraments, have disregarded the fact that the concept "sacramental" embraces more than the seven, five, or two sacraments that may be accepted as such by a Christian church. The largest sense of the term denotes everything in which the Spiritual Presence has been experienced; in a narrower sense, it denotes particular objects and acts in which a Spiritual community experiences the Spiritual Presence; and in the narrowest sense, it merely refers to some "great" sacraments in the performance of which the Spiritual Community actualizes itself. If the meaning of "sacramental" in the largest sense is disregarded, sacramental activities in the narrower sense (sacramentalia) lose their religious significance—as happened in the Reformation—and the great sacraments become insignificant—as happened in several Protestant denominations. This development is rooted in a doctrine of man which has dualistic tendencies, and can only be overcome by an understanding of man's multidimensional unity. If the nature of man is conceived simply in terms of conscious self-awareness, of intellect and will, then only words, doctrinal and moral words, can bear the Spiritual Presence. No Spirit-bearing objects or acts, nothing sensuous which affects the unconscious, can be accepted. Sacraments, if retained, become obsolete rudiments of the past. But it is not only the emphasis on the conscious side of the psychological self that is responsible for the disappearance of sacramental thinking; magical distortion of the sacramental experience, even in Christianity is also responsible. The Reformation was a concentrated attack on Roman Catholic sacramentalism. The argument was that the doctrine of *"opus operatum"* in the Roman church distorted the sacraments into non-personal acts of magical technique. If the sacrament has effects by virtue of its mere performance, the centered act of faith is not essential to its saving power. (Only conscious resistance to the meaning of the sacrament would annihilate its effect.) According to the judgment of the Reformation, this perverts religion into magic in order to gain objective grace from the divine power.

Therefore, it is important to draw the boundary line between the impact of a sacrament on the conscious through the unconscious self and magical techniques which influence the unconscious without the consent of the will. The difference is that in the first case the centered self consciously participates in the experience of the sacramental act, whereas in the second case the unconscious is influenced directly without participation of the centered self. Although magic as a technical method has been replaced since the late Renaissance by technical sciences, the magical element in the relation between human beings is still a reality—however scientifically it might be explained. It is an element in most human encounters, including such encounters as those of the listeners to a sermon or a political speech with the speaker, of the counseled with the counselor, of the spectator with the actor, of the friend with the friend, of the beloved with the lover. As an element in a larger whole which is determined by the centered self, it expresses the multidimensional unity of life. But if it is exercised as a particular, intentional act—by-passing the personal center—it is a demonic distortion. And every sacrament is in danger of becoming demonic.

The fear of such demonization has induced reformed Protestantism and many of the so-called sectarian groups, in contrast to Lutheranism, to reduce the sacramental mediation of the Spirit drastically or even totally. The result is either an intellectualization and moralization of the Spiritual Presence or, as in Quakerism, a mystical inwardness. In light of the twentieth-century rediscovery of the unconscious, it is now possible for Christian theology to re-evaluate positively the sacramental mediation of the Spirit. One could even say that a Spiritual Presence apprehended through the consciousness alone is intellectual and not truly Spiritual. This means that the Spiritual Presence cannot be received without a sacramental element, however hidden the latter may be. In religious terminology, one could say that God grasps every side of the human being through every medium. The formula "Protestant principle and Catholic substance" refers definitively to the sacrament as the medium of the Spiritual Presence. The concept of the multidimensional unity of life provides for this formula. Catholicism has always tried to include all dimensions of life in its system of life and thought; but it has sacrificed the unity, that is, the dependence of life in all dimensions, including the religious, on the divine judgment. The sacramental material is not a sign pointing to something foreign to itself. To put it in terms of the theory of symbolism, the sacramental material is not a sign but a symbol. As symbols the sacramental materials are intrinsically related to what they express; they have inherent qualities (water, fire, oil, bread, wine) which make them adequate to their symbolic function and irreplaceable. The Spirit "uses" the powers of being in nature in order to "enter" man's spirit. Again, it is not the quality of the materials as such which makes them media of the Spiritual Presence; rather, it is their quality as brought into sacramental union. This consideration excludes both the Catholic doctrine of transubstantiation which transforms a symbol into a thing to be handled, and the reformed doctrine of the sign character of the sacramental symbol. A sacramental symbol is neither a thing nor a sign. It participates in the power of what it symbolizes, and therefore, it can be a medium of the Spirit.

Concrete sacraments develop over long periods of time. No part of encountered reality is excluded beforehand from the possibility that it might become sacramental material; anything may prove adequate for it in certain constellations. Often a magic tradition is transformed into a religious one (the sacramental "food"), and sometimes a historical moment is remembered and transformed into a sacred legend (the Last Supper). Ordinarily, sacramental symbolism is connected with great moments in the individual's life, birth, maturity, marriage, and imminent death, or with special religious events, such as entering a religious group and being assigned special tasks within it. Above all, sacramental symbolism is associated with the ritual activities of the group itself. Events in both series often become identical.

In view of this situation one must ask whether the Spiritual Community is bound to definite media of the Spiritual Presence. The answer must unite an affirmative and a negative element: In so far as the Spiritual Community actualizes the New Being in Jesus as the Christ no sacramental act can take place in it which is not subject to the criterion of that reality on which the community is based. This excludes all demonized sacramental acts, such as bloody sacrifices. A second limitation must be added to this. The sacramental acts through which the Spirit of the New Being in Christ is mediated must refer to the historical and doctrinal symbols in which revelatory experiences leading to the central revelation have been expressed, for example, the crucifixion of the Christ or eternal life. But within these limits the Spiritual Community is free to appropriate all symbols which are adequate and which possess symbolic power. The debate over the number of sacraments is justified only if it is the form in which genuine theological problems are discussed, for example, the Spiritual problems of marriage and divorce or of priesthood and laity. Otherwise, the Protestant reduction of the number of the sacraments from seven to two is not theologically justifiable. And the biblicistic argument that they are prescribed by Jesus will not stand. The Christ has not come to give new ritual laws. He is the end of the law. The definitive selection of great sacraments from the large number of sacramental possibilities depends on tradition, evaluation of importance, and criticism of abuses. However, the decisive question is whether they possess and are able to preserve their power of mediating the Spiritual Presence. For example, if a large number of the Spiritual Community's serious members are no longer grasped by certain sacramental acts, however old they are and however solemn their performance, it must be asked whether a sacrament has lost its sacramental power.

(2) WORD AND SACRAMENT.—In our analysis of the sacramental character of objects or acts, we found that they are not without words even if voiceless, because language is the fundamental expression of man's spirit. Therefore the word is the Spirit's other and ultimately more important medium. If human words become vehicles of the Spiritual Presence they are called the "Word of God." We discussed this term and its many meanings in the first part of the system (Part I, Sec. II D, 13). In connection with the doctrine of the Spirit the following points must be repeated: first, one should emphasize that the "Word of God" is a term which qualifies human words as media of the Spiritual Presence. God does not use a particular language, and special documents written in Hebrew, Aramaic, Greek, or any other language are not as such words of God. They can become the Word of God if they become mediators of the Spirit and have the power to grasp the human spirit. This applies both positively and negatively to biblical as well as to all other literature. The Bible does not contain words of God (or as Calvin has said divine "oracles"), but it can and in a unique way has become the "Word of God." Its uniqueness resides in the fact that it is the document of the central revelation, with respect to both its giving and its receiving sides. Every day, by its impact on people inside and outside the church, the Bible proves that it is the Spirit's most important medium in the Western tradition. But it is not the only medium, nor is everything in it always such a medium. In many of its parts it is always

a potential medium, but it only becomes an actual medium to the degree that it grasps the spirit of men. No word is the Word of God unless it is the Word of God for someone; nor is it, in our present terminology, unless it is a medium whereby the Spirit enters the spirit of someone.

This enlarges indefinitely the number of words which can become the Word of God. It includes all religious and cultural documents, that is, the whole of human literature—not only that which is sublime, great, and dignified, but also that which is average, small, and profane—if it hits the human mind in such a way that an ultimate concern is created. Even the spoken word of an ordinary conversation can become a medium of the Spirit—as an ordinary object can acquire sacramental qualities—in a special configuration of physical and psychological circumstances.

Again, however, we must establish a criterion to use against the false elevation of human words to the dignity of the Word of God. The biblical words are this criterion. They constitute the ultimate touchstone for what can and cannot become the Word of God for someone. Nothing is the Word of God if it contradicts the faith and love which are the work of the Spirit and which constitute the New Being as it is manifest in Jesus as the Christ.

(3) THE PROBLEM OF THE "INNER WORD."—The preceding discussion has related the working of the Spiritual Presence to media which, however internal their impact on the human spirit may be, also have an external objective side: objects, acts, sounds, letters. The question now arises as to whether or not such media are necessary at all or whether it is not possible to have an internal working of the Spirit without external vehicles. This question has been raised with great power by Spirit-movements in all periods of Christianity, most conspicuously in the Reformation period. The liberation of the Christian conscience from the church's authority by the reformers also produced the desire for liberation from the new authorities, i.e., from the letter of the Bible and the creedal statements of its theological interpreters. It was an attack, in the name of the Spirit, both on the pope of Rome and on the new pope—the Bible and its scholarly guardians. Since the Spirit means "God present," no human form of life and thought can be shut off from the Spirit. God is not bound to any of his manifestations. The Spiritual Presence breaks through the established Word and the established sacrament. The conclusion drawn by the Spirit-movement is that the Spirit

does not need such mediations. He dwells in the depth of the person, and when he speaks he speaks through the "inner word." He who listens to it receives new and personal revelations, independent of the churches' revelatory traditions. When regarded in light of the doctrine of the Spirit, as we have developed it, the truth in these ideas is their emphasis on the Spirit's freedom from any of the ambiguous forms in which it is received in religion. At this point, I must confess that the present system is essentially, but indirectly, influenced by the Spirit-movements, both through their impact on Western culture in general (including such theologians as Schleiermacher) and through their criticism of the established forms of religious life and thought. But some critical remarks are in order precisely because of this influence.

First, the term "inner word" is unfortunate. When the Franciscan theologians of the thirteenth century insisted on the divine character of the principles of truth in the human mind or when German mystics of the fourteenth century insisted on the Logos' presence in the soul, they expressed motifs of the Spirit-movements of past and future. In spite of this, however, they did not cut off the Spirit's working in the individual from the revelatory tradition. Yet the term "inner word" can have the connotation of this "cutting-off" of the Spirit's work from the revelatory tradition, and this leads us to the question: Is not "word" by its very definition a means of communication between two beings with centered self-awareness? If there are not two centers, what does the "inner word" mean? Is the implication that God or the Logos or the Spirit is this other self? This certainly can be said symbolically, as in the claims of the prophets to have heard the "voice of Jahweh" in an ecstatic experience and in the claims of many people at all times to similar experiences. Even the "voice of conscience" (which is voiceless) has been interpreted as the divine Spirit's speaking to the human spirit. However, if "inner word" has this meaning, it is not completely inner, because what has happened in that other finite self, which is a necessary condition of all human language, is replaced by the divine "self." However, even in symbolic language, this is a questionable way of talking. Certainly, if we ascribe omniscience, love, wrath, and mercy to God, we speak in symbols, applying material to God which is taken from a centered self as we experience it. But "self" is a structural concept and not adequate symbolic material. When the New Testament says that God is Spirit or when Paul speaks of the witness of the divine Spirit to our spirit, the self-structure we need for religious symbolism is implicit. But it is misleading if made explicit. (Of the basic polarity of self and world, neither pole can be applied symbolically to God.) If God speaks to us, this is not the "inner word"; rather, it is the Spiritual Presence grasping us from "outside." But this "outside" is above outside and inside; it transcends them. If God were not also in man so that man could ask for God, God's speaking to man could not be perceived by man. The categories "inner" and "outer" lose their meaning in the relation of God and man.

We must give a negative answer to the question: Does God speak to man without a medium? The medium of the word is always present, because man's life under the dimension of spirit is determined by the word, whether or not this word has a voice. The thinking mind thinks in words. It speaks in the mode of silence, but it does not speak to itself in order to communicate something to itself. Man remembers what has been spoken to him since his life's beginning and organizes it into a meaningful whole. Therefore the speeches and writings of all prophets and mystics and of all those who claim to have had a divine inspiration are couched in the language of the tradition from which they come but are driven in the direction of the ultimate. When God spoke to the prophets, he did not give them new words or new facts, but he put the facts known to them in the light of ultimate meaning and instructed them to speak out of this situation in the language they knew. When the enthusiasts of the Reformation period expressed the "inner word" they had received in their language, it was the word of the Bible, of the tradition, and of the reformers, but illuminated by their own experience of the Spiritual Presence. By this light they gained insight into the social situation of the lowest classes in their society and further insights into the Spirit's freedom to work in the personal life over against ecclesiastical and biblicistic heteronomy, just as it had worked in the reformers themselves. The first-mentioned insight's prophetic character foreshadowed many Christian social movements in the last centuries up to the social gospel and the religious socialist movements of our own time. The other insights were the source of mystical tendencies such as those of the Quakers and the philosophies of religion in which religious "experience" is the decisive principle.

This analysis shows that the concept of the "inner word" is misleading.

The inner word is the refocusing into contemporary relevance of the words from traditions and former experiences. This refocusing occurs under the impact of the Spiritual Presence. The medium of the word is not excluded.

But the reformers' opposition to the Spirit-movements of their time had still another motive. The reformers (in agreement with the whole tradition of the church) were afraid that the ultimate criterion of all revelatory experiences—the New Being in Jesus as the Christ—would be lost in the name of the immediacy of the Spirit. Therefore they bound the Spirit to the Word, to the biblical message of the Christ. Certainly, this is theologically sound, for theology is based on the revelation in Jesus Christ as the central revelation. But it became unsound the moment revelation in the Christ was identified with a forensic doctrine of justification "by" faith, in which the Spiritual Presence's impact was replaced by an intellectual acknowledgment of the doctrine of forgiveness by grace alone. This certainly was not the intention, but it was the effect of the principle of "the Word alone." The Spirit's function was described ambiguously as the Spirit's testimony to the truth of the biblical message or to the truth of the biblical words. The former understanding of the doctrine is adequate to its genuine meaning, for the Spiritual Presence elevates the human spirit into the transcendent union of unambiguous life and gives the immediate certainty of reunion with God. The latter understanding of the doctrine reduces the Spirit's work to the one act of establishing a conviction of the literal truth of the biblical words, a function which contradicts the nature of the Spirit and therefore amounts to a security-seeking surrender to authority. This disregards the continuity of the Spiritual Presence and its impact on personality and community in conquering the ambiguities of life. Here again, the Spirit-movements pointed to a biblical characteristic which was present in the early Luther and which has been lost in the latter's victory over the Spirit in the orthodox development of the Reformation. In the ensuing struggles, the Spirit-movements lost something which justified orthodoxy's resistance. They concentrated on the inner movements of their souls under the impact of the Spirit instead of looking outside themselves, in Luther's manner, at the divine acceptance in spite of their actual unacceptability. They misinterpreted the Word spoken to them as the words of piety which they spoke to themselves. But this consideration transcends the problem of the media of the Spiritual Presence.

2. The Content of the Manifestation of the Divine Spirit in the Human Spirit: Faith and Love

a) The transcendent union and the participation in it.—All ambiguities of life are rooted in the separation and interplay of essential and existential elements of being. Therefore, the creation of unambiguous life brings about the reunion of these elements in life processes in which actual being is the true expression of potential being, an expression, however, which is not immediate, as in "dreaming innocence," but which is realized only after estrangement, contest, and decision. In the reunion of essential and existential being, ambiguous life is raised above itself to a transcendence that it could not achieve by its own power. This union answers the question implied in the processes of life and the function of the spirit. It is the direct answer to the process of self-transcendence—which in itself remains a question.

The "transcendent union" answers the general question implied in all ambiguities of life. It appears within the human spirit as the ecstatic movement which from one point of view is called "faith," from another, "love." These two states manifest the transcendent union which is created by the Spiritual Presence in the human spirit. The transcendent union is a quality of unambiguous life, a quality which we shall meet again in our discussion of the Kingdom of God and eternal life.

The two points of view determining the two terms can be distinguished in the following way: faith is the state of being *grasped* by the transcendent unity of unambiguous life—it embodies love as the state of being *taken into* that transcendent unity. From this analysis, it is obvious that faith logically precedes love, although in actuality neither can be present without the other. Faith without love is a continuation of estrangement and an ambiguous act of religious self-transcendence. Love without faith is an ambiguous reunion of the separated without the criterion and the power of the transcendent union. Neither of them is a creation of the Spiritual Presence, but both result from religious distortions of an original Spiritual creation.

These statements presuppose a full discussion of faith and love in order to be understandable. Such discussion could fill a large volume. [I myself have dealt with faith and love, each in a small book.[1]] However, this is not the present task, which is to determine the place of the two

[1] Faith: *Dynamics of Faith* (New York: Harper & Bros., 1957); love: *Love, Power, and Justice* (New York: Oxford University Press, 1954).

concepts within the theological system and to show in this way their relation to other theological concepts and religious symbols. Their central position in Christian life and theological thought has always been acknowledged since the time of the New Testament but, as is evident from the state of the contemporary discussion, they have not always been equally or adequately interpreted.

b) The Spiritual Presence manifest as faith.—There are few words in the language of religion which cry for as much semantic purging as the word "faith." It is continually being confused with belief in something for which there is no evidence, or in something intrinsically unbelievable, or in absurdities and nonsense. It is extremely difficult to remove these distorting connotations from the genuine meaning of faith. One of the reasons is that the Christian churches have often preached the message of the New Being in Christ as an "absurdity" which must be accepted on biblical or ecclesiastical authority whether the statements of the message are comprehensible or not. Another reason is the readiness of religion's many critics to concentrate their forces upon such a distorted image of faith as an easy object of attack.

Faith must be defined both formally and materially. The formal definition is valid for every kind of faith in all religions and cultures. Faith, formally or generally defined, is the state of being grasped by that toward which self-transcendence aspires, the ultimate in being and meaning. In a short formula, one can say that faith is the state of being grasped by an ultimate concern. The term "ultimate concern" unites a subjective and an objective meaning: somebody is concerned about something he considers of concern. In this formal sense of faith as ultimate concern, every human being has faith. Nobody can escape the essential relation of the conditional spirit to something unconditional in the direction of which it is self-transcendent in unity with all life. However unworthy the ultimate concern's concrete content may be, no one can stifle such concern completely. This formal concept of faith is basic and universal. It refutes the idea that world history is the battlefield between faith and un-faith (if it is permissible to coin this word in order to avoid the misleading term "unbelief"). There is no un-faith in the sense of something antithetical to faith, but throughout all history and, above all, in the history of religion, there have been faiths with unworthy contents. They invest something preliminary, finite, and conditioned with the dignity of the ultimate, infinite, and unconditional.

The continuing struggle through all history is waged between a faith directed to ultimate reality and a faith directed toward preliminary realities claiming ultimacy.

This leads us to the material concept of faith as formulated before. Faith is the state of being grasped by the Spiritual Presence and opened to the transcendent unity of unambiguous life. In relation to the christological assertion, one could say that faith is the state of being grasped by the New Being as it is manifest in Jesus as the Christ. In this definition of faith, the formal and universal concept of faith has become material and particular; it is Christian. However, Christianity claims that this particular definition of faith expresses the fulfilment toward which all forms of faith are driven. Faith as the state of being opened by the Spiritual Presence to the transcendent unity of unambiguous life is a description which is universally valid despite its particular, Christian background.

Such a description, however, bears little resemblance to the traditional definitions in which the intellect, will, or feeling is identified with the act of faith. In spite of the psychological crudeness of these distinctions, they remained decisive in both scholarly and popular conceptions of faith. It is therefore necessary to make some statements about faith's relation to the mental functions.

Faith, as the Spiritual Presence's invasion of the conflicts and ambiguities of man's life under the dimension of the spirit, is not an act of cognitive affirmation within the subject-object structure of reality. Therefore it is not subject to verification by experiment or trained experience. Nor is faith the acceptance of factual statements or valuations taken on authority, even if the authority is divine, for then the question arises, On the basis on what authority do I call an authority divine? Such a statement as "a being, called God, does exist" is not an assertion of faith but a cognitive proposition without sufficient evidence. The affirmation and the negation of such statements are equally absurd. This judgment refers to all attempts that would give divine authority to statements of fact in history, mind, and nature. No such assertions have the character of faith, nor can they be made in the name of faith. Nothing is more undignified than to make faith do duty for evidence which is lacking.

An awareness of this situation has led to the establishment of a more intimate relationship between faith and moral decision. An endeavor is made to overcome the shortcomings of the cognitive-intellectual understanding of faith by a moral-voluntaristic understanding. In such an endeavor, "faith" is defined as the result of a "will to believe" or as the fruit of an act of obedience. But one asks: The will to believe what? Or, obedience to whom? If these questions are taken seriously, the cognitive interpretation of faith is re-established. Faith cannot be defined as "will to believe at large," and it cannot be defined as "obedience to order at large." But in the moment in which the contents of the will to believe or of the obedience to order are sought, the shortcomings of the cognitive interpretation of faith reappear. For instance, if one is asked to accept the Word of God in obedience—and if this acceptance is called "obedience of faith"—one is asked to do something which can be done only by one already in the state of faith who acknowledges the word heard to be the Word of God. The "obedience of faith" presupposes faith but does not create it.

The most popular identification is that of faith with feeling. Moreover, it is not only popular but also readily accepted by scientists and philosophers who reject the religious claim to truth but who cannot deny its tremendous psychological and sociological power. This they ascribe to the indefinite yet indisputable realm of "oceanic" or other feeling and oppose it only when it tries to surpass its limits and trespass upon the solid land of knowledge and action. Certainly, faith as an expression of the whole person includes emotional elements, but it does not consist solely of them. It draws every element of *theoria* and *praxis* into itself and its ecstatic openness toward the Spiritual Presence; beyond these, it also includes elements of the life processes under all dimensions. As classical theology has rightly taught, there is "assent" in faith—there is cognitive acceptance of truth, not of true statements about objects in time and space but of the truth about our relation to that which concerns us ultimately and the symbols expressing it. (The full development of this assertion has been given in the first part of the system, "Reason and Revelation.")

There is also obedience in faith, a point in which Paul and Augustine, Thomas and Calvin, agree. But "obedience of faith" is not the heteronomous subjection to a divine-human authority. It is the act of keeping ourselves open to the Spiritual Presence which has grasped us and opened us. It is obedience by participation and not by submission (as in love relations).

Finally, there is an emotional element in the state of being grasped by the Spiritual Presence. This is not the feeling of a completely indefinite character referred to above. It is the oscillation between the anxiety of one's finitude and estrangement and the ecstatic courage which overcomes the anxiety by taking it into itself in the power of the transcendent unity of unambiguous life.

The preceding discussion of faith and the mental function has shown two things: first, that faith can neither be identified with nor derived from any of the mental functions. Faith cannot be created by the procedures of the intellect, or by endeavors of the will, or by emotional movements. But, second, faith comprehends all this within itself, uniting and subjecting it to the Spiritual Presence's transforming power. This implies and confirms the basic theological truth that in relation to God everything is by God. Man's spirit cannot reach the ultimate, that toward which it transcends itself, through any of its functions. But the ultimate can grasp all of these functions and raise them beyond themselves by the creation of faith.

Although created by the Spiritual Presence, faith occurs within the structure, functions, and dynamics of man's spirit. Certainly, it is not *from* man, but it is *in* man. Therefore, in the interest of a radical transcendence of the divine activity, it is wrong to deny that man is aware of his being grasped by the divine Spirit, or as it has been said, "I only believe that I believe." Man is conscious of the Spiritual Presence's work in him. But that phrase does serve to provide us with a warning against self-assurance about the state of being in faith.

Considered as material concept, faith has three elements: first, the element of being opened up by the Spiritual Presence; second, the element of accepting it in spite of the infinite gap between the divine Spirit and the human spirit; and third, the element of expecting final participation in the transcendent unity of unambiguous life. These elements are within one another; they do not follow one after the other, but they are present wherever faith occurs. The first element is faith in its receptive character, its mere passivity in relation to the divine Spirit. The second element is faith in its paradoxical character, its courageous standing in the Spiritual Presence. The third element characterizes faith as anticipatory, its quality as hope for the fulfilling creativity of the divine Spirit. These three elements express the human situation and the situation of life in general in relation to the ultimate in being and meaning. They reflect the characterization of the New Being (as it is given in the christological section of Part III [Sec. II]) as "regeneration," "justification," and "sanctification." These three elements will reappear in subsequent descriptions of the Spiritual Presence's conquest of life's ambiguities.

Faith is actual in all life processes—in religion, in the other functions of the spirit, and in the preceding realms of life—in so far as they condition the actualization of the spirit. At this point, however, it is relevant to elaborate only the essential nature and basic structure of faith. Faith's actual function of conquering the ambiguities of life in the power of its Spiritual origin is a subject of the last section of this part of the system (Part IV). It is to be noted that this dealing with faith as a kind of independent reality has biblical support, just as the vision of sin as a kind of mythological power ruling the world is also in the line of biblical, especially Pauline, thought. The subjective actualization of sin and faith and the problems arising therein are secondary to the objectivity of the two powers although the objective and subjective sides cannot be separated in reality.

c) *The Spiritual Presence manifest as love.*—Whereas faith is the state of being grasped by the Spiritual Presence, love is the state of being taken by the Spiritual Presence into the transcendent unity of unambiguous life. Such a definition requires a semantic as well as an ontological explanation. Semantically speaking, love, as faith, must be purged from many distorting connotations. The first is the description of love as emotion. Later, we shall speak about the genuine emotional element in love. Here we need state only that love is actual in all functions of the mind and that it has roots in the innermost core of life itself. Love is the drive toward the reunion of the separated; this is ontologically and therefore universally true. It is effective in all three life processes; it unites in a center, it creates the new, and it drives beyond everything given to its ground and aim. It is the "blood" of life and therefore has many forms in which dispersed elements of life are reunited. We have pointed to the ambiguities in some of these forms and to the disintegrating forces in the processes of integration. But in discussing the person-to-person encounter and the moral imperative intrinsic to it, we also asked the question of an unambiguous reunion, the question of love as participation in the other one through participation in the transcendent unity of unambiguous life. The answer to this question is given in the Spiritual Presence's creation of *agape*. *Agape* is unambiguous love and therefore impossible for the human spirit by itself. As faith, it is an ecstatic participation of the finite spirit in the transcendent unity of unambiguous life. He who is in the state of *agape* is drawn into this unity.

This description makes it possible to resolve the Catholic-Protestant controversy about the relation of faith and love. We have already indicated that faith logically precedes love, because faith is, so to speak, the human reaction to the Spiritual Presence's breaking into the human spirit; it is the ecstatic acceptance of the divine Spirit's breaking-up of the finite mind's tendency to rest in its own self-sufficiency. This view affirms Luther's statement that faith is receiving and nothing but receiving. At the same time, the Catholic-Augustinian emphasis on love is asserted with equal strength, by virtue of the insight into the essential inseparability of love and faith in the participation in the transcendent unity of unambiguous life. In this view, love is more than a consequence of faith, albeit a necessary one; it is one side of the ecstatic state of being of which faith is the other. A distortion of this relation occurs only if the acts of love are understood as conditioning the act by which the Spiritual Presence takes hold of man. The Protestant principle—that in relation to God everything is done by God—remains the weapon against such a distortion.

At this point an answer may be given to another question: Why does this presentation of the fundamental creation of the divine Spirit not add hope to faith and love rather than consider it as the third element of faith, that is, as the anticipatory direction of faith? The answer is that if hope were considered systematically (and not only homiletically, as in Paul's formula) as a third creation of the Spirit, its standing in man would be on a par with faith. It would be an independent act of anticipatory expectation whose relation to faith would be ambiguous. It would fall under the attitude of "believing that," an attitude which is in sharp contrast with the meaning of "faith." Hope is either an element of faith or a pre-Spiritual "work" of the human mind. Of course, this discussion strengthens the insight into the essential unity of faith and love. Love also becomes a pre-Spiritual "work" of the human spirit if we deny the essential inseparability of faith and love.

Love is not an emotion, but strong emotional elements are implied in it, as are the other functions of the human mind. For this reason it is justifiable to open the discussion of love and the mental functions with the question of the relation of love to emotion (as we started the discussion of faith and the mental functions with the question of the relation of faith and intellect). The emotional element in love is, as emotion always is, the participation of the centered whole of a being in the process of reunion, whether it is in anticipation or in fulfilment. It would be incorrect to say that the anticipated fulfilment is the driving power in love. Driving power toward reunion also exists in dimensions where awareness, and therefore anticipation, is lacking. And even where there is full consciousness, the drive toward reunion is not caused by the anticipation of an expected pleasure (as it would be on the basis of the pain-pleasure principle which we have rejected), but the drive for reunion belongs to the essential structure of life and, consequently, is experienced as pleasure, joy, or blessedness, according to the different dimensions of life. As the ecstatic participation in the transcendent unity of unambiguous life, *agape* is experienced as blessedness (*makaria* or *beatitudo* in the sense of the beatitudes). Therefore *agape* can be applied symbolically to the divine life and its trinitarian movement, making the symbol of the divine blessedness concrete. The emotional element cannot be separated from love; love without its emotional quality is "good will" toward somebody or something, but it is not love. This is also true of man's love of God, which cannot be equated with obedience, as some antimystical theologians teach.

But love is not only related to emotion; it is the whole being's movement toward another being to overcome existential separation. As such it includes a volitional element under the dimension of self-awareness, i.e., the will to unite. Such a will is essential in every love relation, because the wall of separation could not be pierced without it. The emotional element alone is not strong enough if desire and fulfilment do not coincide. As this is always the case under the conditions of existence, there is resistance on both sides of a love relationship. It is this volitional element in love to which the great commandment primarily refers. Love without the will to love, relying solely on the force of emotion, can never penetrate to the other person.

The relation between love and the intellectual function of the mind is most fully developed in Greek and Hellenistic-Christian thought against a mystical background. Plato's *eros*-doctrine points to love's function in creating the knower's awareness of his own emptiness as against the abundance of the known. In Aristotle the *eros* of everything moves the universe toward the pure form. In Hellenistic-Christian language, the word *gnosis* means knowledge, sexual intercourse, and mystical union. And the German word *erkennen*, which means to know, is also used for sexual union. Love includes the knowledge of the beloved, but it is not the knowledge of analysis and calculating manipulation; it is rather the participating knowledge which changes both the knower and the known in the very act of loving knowledge. Love, as faith, is a state of the whole person; all functions of the human mind are alive in every act of love.

While the word "faith" has a predominantly religious meaning, the word "love" is so equivocal that in many cases it is necessary to substitute the New Testament word *agape* for love as a creation of the Spiritual Presence. This is not always feasible, however, especially in homiletic and liturgical contexts, and beyond this limitation, there is a systematic problem in the equivocal use of the word "love" in English and other modern languages. In spite of the many kinds of love, which in Greek are designated as *philia* (friendship), *eros* (aspiration toward value), and *epithymia* (desire), in addition to *agape*, which is the creation of the Spirit, there is one point of identity in all these qualities of love which justifies the translation of them all by "love"; and that identity is the "urge toward the reunion of the separated," which is the inner dynamics of life. Love in this sense is one and indivisible. The attempt has been made to establish an absolute contrast between *agape* and *eros* (comprising the three other kinds of love); but as a result *agape* was reduced to a moral concept, not only in relation to God, but also in relation to man, and *eros* (which includes, in this terminology, *philia* and *epithymia* or *libido*) became profanized in a merely sexual direction and deprived of possible participation in unambiguous life. Nevertheless, one important truth stands out in the contrast of *agape* with the other kinds of love: *agape* is an ecstatic manifestation of the Spiritual Presence. It is possible only in unity with faith and is the state of being drawn into the transcendent unity of unambiguous life. For this reason, it is independent of the other qualities of love and is able to unite with them, to judge them, and to transform them. Love as *agape* is a creation of the Spiritual Presence which conquers the ambiguities of all other kinds of love.

Agape has this power because, similarly to faith, it has the basic structure of the New Being: the receptive, paradoxical, and anticipatory character. In the case of *agape*, the first quality is evident in its acceptance of the object of love without restrictions; the second quality is disclosed in *agape*'s holding fast to this acceptance in spite of the estranged, profanized, and demonized state of its objects, and the third quality is seen in *agape*'s expectation of the re-establishment of the holiness, greatness, and dignity of the object of love through its accepting him. *Agape* takes its object into the transcendent unity of unambiguous life.

All this is said of *agape* as Spiritual power, prior to any personal or social actualization. In this, it is the equal of sin and faith as powers controlling life. But there is a difference between *agape* and the two others (which makes *agape* greater than faith, in the words of Paul). *Agape* characterizes the divine life itself, symbolically and essentially. Faith characterizes the New Being in time and space but it does not characterize the divine life, and sin characterizes only estranged being. *Agape* is first of all the love God has toward the creature and through the creature toward himself. The three characteristics of *agape* must first be ascribed to God's *agape* toward his creatures and then to the *agape* of creature toward creature.

However, this leaves one relation still to be understood, and this is the love of the creature toward God. The New Testament uses the word *agape* for this relation also, disregarding the three elements in the *agape* of God toward the creatures and of the creatures toward each other. None of these elements is present in the love of man for God. Nevertheless, love as the drive toward the reunion of the separated can be used most emphatically of man's love for God. It unites all kinds of love and yet is something else beyond them all. The best way of characterizing it is to say that in relation to God the distinction between faith and love disappears. Being grasped by God in faith and adhering to him in love is one and the same state of creaturely life. It is participation in the transcendent unity of unambiguous life.

B. THE MANIFESTATION OF THE SPIRITUAL PRESENCE IN HISTORICAL MANKIND

1. Spirit and New Being: Ambiguity and Fragment

The Spiritual Presence, elevating man through faith and love to the transcendent unity of unambiguous life, creates the New Being above the gap between essence and existence and consequently above the ambiguities of life. In the preceding chapter we have described the manifestation of the divine Spirit in the human spirit. We must now determine the place in historical mankind in which the New Being as the creation of the Spiritual Presence is manifest. Of course this cannot be done without reference to the historical dimension of life which has been reserved as the subject of the last part of the system, "History and the Kingdom of God." But references to history are frequent in all parts of the theological system. Such concepts as revelation, providence, and the New Being in Jesus as the Christ, are possible only in the historical context. Yet it is one thing to see theological problems in their historical implications and another thing to make a theological problem of history as such. While the latter is reserved for the last part of this system, the former approach must be made here as it has been at many previous points of the discussion.

The divine Spirit's invasion of the human spirit does not occur in isolated individuals but in social groups, since all the functions of the human spirit—moral self-integration, cultural self-creation, and religious self-transcendence—are conditioned by the social context of the ego-thou encounter. It is therefore necessary to show the working of the divine Spirit at those points in history which are decisive for its self-manifestation within mankind.

The Spiritual Presence is manifest in all history; but history as such is not the manifestation of the Spiritual Presence. As in the spirit of the individual, there are particular marks which indicate the Spiritual Presence in a historical group. First, there is the effective presence of symbols in *theoria* and *praxis* through which a social group expresses its openness to the impact of the Spirit, and second, there is the rise of personalities and movements which fight against the tragically unavoidable profanization and demonization of these symbols. These two marks of the Spiritual Presence are found in religious as well as in quasi-religious groups, and in a sense they are a single phenomenon. This is so because a successful struggle for the purification of the symbols transforms them and creates a changed social group.

The most familiar example of these dynamics is the fight of the prophets in Israel and Judah against the profanization and demonization of the desert religion of Jahweh, and the radical transformation of the social group under the impact of the Spiritual Presence communicated by the prophets. Similar developments, especially radical movements

of purification with their impact on the social group, are found everywhere in historical mankind. The mark of the Spiritual Presence is not
lacking at any place or time. The divine Spirit or God, present to man's
spirit, breaks into all history in revelatory experiences which have both
a saving and transforming character. We have already pointed to this
fact in the discussion of universal revelation and the idea of the holy.
Now we relate it to the doctrine of the divine Spirit and its manifestations, and we can assert: Mankind is never left alone. The Spiritual
Presence acts upon it in every moment and breaks into it in some great
moments, which are the historical *kairoi*.

Since mankind is never left alone by God, since it is continuously under the impact of the Spiritual Presence, there is always New Being in
history. There is always participation in the transcendent union of
unambiguous life. But this participation is fragmentary. We must give
some attention to this concept; it is quite a different thing from ambiguity. When we say "Spiritual Presence" or "New Being" or *agape*, we
point to something unambiguous. It may be drawn into the ambiguous
actualizations of life, especially of life under the dimension of the spirit.
But in itself it is unambiguous. However, it is fragmentary in its manifestation in time and space. The fulfilled transcendent union is an
eschatological concept. The fragment is an anticipation (as Paul speaks
of the fragmentary and anticipatory possession of the divine Spirit, of
the truth, of the vision of God, and so on). The New Being is fragmentarily and anticipatorily present, but in so far as it is present it
is so unambiguously. The fragment of a broken statue of a god points
unambiguously to the divine power which it represents. The fragment
of a successful prayer elevates to the transcendent union of unambiguous life. The fragmentary character of a group's acceptance of the
Spirit makes this group, in the moment of acceptance, a holy community.
The fragmentary experience of faith and the fragmentary actualization
of love create the individual's participation in the transcendent union of
unambiguous life. This distinction between the ambiguous and the
fragmentary makes it possible for us to give full affirmation and full
commitment to the manifestations of the Spiritual Presence while remaining aware of the fact that in the very acts of affirmation and commitment the ambiguity of life reappears. Awareness of this situation is
the decisive criterion for religious maturity. It belongs to the quality of
the New Being that it puts its own actualization in time and space

under the criteria by which it judges the ambiguities of life in general. Yet in doing so, the New Being does conquer (though fragmentarily) the ambiguities of life in time and space.

2. THE SPIRITUAL PRESENCE AND THE ANTICIPATION OF THE NEW BEING IN THE RELIGIONS

One could give a whole history of religion under this heading, because it provides a key with which one can discover meaning in the seemingly chaotic religious life of mankind. And one could also find many quasi-religious phenomena in which it is possible to see manifestations of the Spiritual Presence. But such a program oversteps the limits of a theological system. Only a few typical manifestations of the Spirit can be discussed, and even they are subject to the serious limitation that existential knowledge presupposes participation. One can learn many things about strange religions and cultures by means of detached observation and even more through empathetic understanding. But neither way leads to the central experience of an Asian religion for one who has grown within the Christian-humanist civilization of the West. Serious encounters between representatives of the two worlds prove this. In view of the popular superficial reception of, for example, Buddhist attitudes, one should be warned by the statement of a great interpreter of Chinese ideas that after thirty years of living among the Chinese he has just begun to understand a little of their Spiritual life. The only authentic way to it is through actual participation. Typological considerations such as the following are justified only by the identity of the dimension of spirit in every articulate being with whom, therefore, communication is possible and the person-to-person encounter is demanded. From this common source spring similarities under the dimension of the spirit, which make possible a certain amount of existential participation. Every great religion has elements in its total structure which are subordinate in one religion and dominant in another. The Christian theologian can understand Eastern mysticism only to the degree in which he has experienced the mystical element in Christianity. But since the dominance or subordination of one of the elements changes the whole structure, even this limited way of understanding by participation can be deceptive. The following statements must be read with this in mind.

It seems that the original *mana* religion places a strong emphasis on the Spiritual Presence in the "depth" of everything that is. This divine power in all things is invisible, mysterious, approachable only through definite rituals, and known to a particular group of men, the priests. This early substantial vision of the Spiritual Presence survives with many variations in almost all the so-called high religions, even in some forms of Christian sacramentalism, and is secularized in the romantic philosophy of nature (in which ecstasy becomes aesthetic enthusiasm).

Another example is the religion of the great mythologies, such as those of India and Greece. The divine powers are separated from the world of existence although they rule it, either in part or as a whole. Their manifestations have an extraordinary character, physical as well as psychological. Nature and mind become ecstatic when the Spiritual Presence manifests itself. The influence of this mythological stage of Spiritual experience on all later stages, including Christianity, is obvious and is justified by the fact that the experience of the Spiritual Presence is ecstatic. For this reason, all radical attempts to demythologize religion are in vain. What one can and should do is to "deliteralize" them for those who are able and willing to apply rational criteria to the meaning of religious symbols.

At the mythological stage of religion (which itself is the result of a purifying impulse arising in the premythological stage, as discussed before), forces that fight its profanized and demonized forms appear and transform the reception of the Spiritual Presence in several directions. The Greek and Hellenistic mystery cults provide an example. The divine is embodied in them in the concrete figure of a mystery-god. The mystery element is emphasized more than it is in ordinary polytheism, which is very much open to profanization, and ecstatic participation in the god's destiny provides a pattern which is used by monotheistic Christianity to express its experience of the Spiritual Presence in the Christ.

The fight against the demonization of the Spirit appears conspicuously in the dualistic purifications of the mythological stage. The great attempt of religious dualism, which was made first in Persia, then in Manichaeism (the Mithraist cult, the Cathari, and similar groups), to concentrate demonic potentiality in one figure was supposed to liberate the opposite divine figure from any demonic contamination. Although it was not ultimately successful in this respect (because it assumed a split in the creative ground of being), its influence on such monotheistic religions as late Judaism and Christianity was and still is very great. Anxiety over the demonization of the Spiritual Presence is expressed in the fear of Satan "and all his works" (the baptism and confirmation vow) and in the fact that the classical Christian language still abounds in dualistic symbolism.

The two most important examples of the experience of Spiritual Presence are mysticism, Asian as well as European, and the exclusive monotheism of Judaism and the religions based upon it.

Mysticism experiences the Spiritual Presence as above its concrete vehicles, which characterize the mythological stage, and its various transformations. Both the divine figures and the concrete realities—personal, communal, and apersonal—in which the divine figures enter temporal and spatial reality lose their ultimate significance, in spite of the fact that they often retain a preliminary importance as grades on a Spiritual stairway to the ultimate. But the Spiritual Presence is fully experienced only when the grades are left behind and the mind is grasped in ecstasy. In this radical sense, mysticism transcends every concrete embodiment of the divine by transcending the subject-object scheme of man's finite structure, but for this very reason, it is in danger of annihilating the centered self, the subject of the ecstatic experience of the Spirit. Communication between East and West is most difficult at this point, with the East affirming a "formless self" as the aim of all religious life, and the West (even in Christian mysticism) trying to preserve in the ecstatic experience the subjects of faith and love: personality and community.

This attitude is rooted in the prophets' way of fighting against the Spiritual Presence's profanization and demonization in the priestly religion of their time. In the religion of the Old Testament the divine Spirit does not eliminate centered selves and their encounters, but it does sublimate them into states of mind which transcend their ordinary possibilities and which are not produced by their toil or good will. The Spirit grasps them and drives them to the heights of prophetic power.

This attitude toward personality and community (and consequently, in contrast to the mystical religions, to sin and forgiveness) is rooted in the fact that for the prophetic religion the Spiritual Presence is the presence of the God of humanity and justice. The story of the conflict between the prophet Elijah and the priests of Baal is significant, for it shows different kinds of ecstasy. The ecstasy produced by the presence of the Baal Spirit in the minds and bodies of his priests is connected with self-intoxication and self-mutilation, whereas the ecstasy of Elijah is that of a person-to-person encounter in prayer which certainly transcends ordinary experiences in intensity and effect but which neither extinguishes nor disintegrates the personal center of the prophet and does not produce physical intoxication. In all its parts the Old Testament follows this line. There is no pure Spiritual Presence where there is no humanity and justice. Without them—and this is the judgment of the prophets against their own religion—there is demonized or profanized Spiritual Presence. This judgment is taken up in the New Testament and reappears in church history in all purification movements, of which the Protestant Reformation was one.

3. The Spiritual Presence in Jesus as the Christ: Spirit Christology

The divine Spirit was present in Jesus as the Christ without distortion. In him the New Being appeared as the criterion of all Spiritual experiences in past and future. Though subject to individual and social conditions his human spirit was entirely grasped by the Spiritual Presence; his spirit was "possessed" by the divine Spirit or, to use another figure, "God was in him." This makes him the Christ, the decisive embodiment of the New Being for historical mankind. Although the christological problem was the central subject of the third part of this theological system, the problem appears in all parts, and in connection with the doctrine of the divine Spirit, several additions to the earlier christological statements are necessary.

The Synoptic stories show that the earliest Christian tradition was determined by a Spirit-Christology. According to this tradition, Jesus was grasped by the Spirit at the moment of his baptism. This event confirmed him as the elected "Son of God." Ecstatic experiences appear again and again in the Gospel stories. They show the Spiritual Presence driving Jesus into the desert, leading him through the visionary experiences of temptation, giving him the power of divination with respect to people and events, and making him the conqueror of demonic powers and the Spiritual healer of mind and body. The Spirit is the force behind the ecstatic experience on the mount of transfiguration. And the Spirit gives him the certainty about the right hour, the *kairos*, for acting and suffering. As a consequence of this understanding, the question arose as to how the divine Spirit could find a vessel in which to pour itself so fully, and the answer came in the form of the story of Jesus' procreation by the divine Spirit. This story was justified by the insight into the psychosomatic level at which the Spiritual Presence works and the legitimate conclusion that there must have been a teleological predisposition in Jesus to become the bearer of the Spirit without limit. However, this conclusion does not necessarily require an acceptance of this half-Docetic legend, which deprives Jesus of his full humanity by excluding a human father from his conception. The doctrine of the multidimensional unity of life answers the question of the psychosomatic basis of the bearer of the Spirit without such ambiguity.

We can now consider faith and love—the two manifestations of the Spiritual Presence—and their unity in the transcendent union of unambiguous life in relation to the appearance of Jesus as the Christ. Christ's self-sacrificial love is the center of the Gospels as well as of their apostolic interpretations. This center is the principle of *agape* embodied in his being and radiating from him into a world in which *agape* was and is known only in ambiguous expressions. The New Testament witness and the assertion of the greatest theologians in the history of the church are unanimous in this respect, in spite of many varieties of interpretations.

References to the faith of Jesus are rare in biblical literature as well as in later theology, although they are not altogether lacking. The reason for this seems to be that the term "faith" includes an element of "in spite of" which could not be applied to the one who as the Son is in continuous communication with the Father. Of course, this trend was strengthened by the Logos-Christology and its presuppositions in Paul's Christology. Such words as "I believe, help my unbelief" could not be put into the mouth of the Logos-Incarnate. Nor can more recent descriptions of faith—as a leap, as an act of courage, as a risk, as embracing itself and the doubt about itself—be applied to him who says that he and the Father are one. But we must ask whether this does not imply a tendency in church history which could be called "crypto-Monophysitic" and which runs the risk of depriving Jesus of his real humanity. This problem exists even in Protestantism, where the Monophysitic danger is substantially reduced by the reformers' emphasis on the "humble Christ" and the image of the "suffering servant." But the meaning of faith in Protestantism is determined by the doctrine of "justification through faith by grace," and it includes the paradox of the acceptance as just of him who is unjust—the forgiveness of sins. Faith, in this sense, can certainly not be applied to the Christ. One cannot attribute to the Christ the paradox of faith, because the Christ himself is the paradox.

The problem can be resolved in terms of the basic definition of faith as the state of being grasped by the Spiritual Presence and through it by the transcendent union of unambiguous life. We also have seen that faith in this sense is a Spiritual reality above its actualization in those who possess it. The faith of the Christ is the state of being grasped unambiguously by the Spiritual Presence.

At this point the most important implication of our distinction between ambiguous and fragmentary becomes obvious. It makes the faith of the Christ understandable. The dynamic picture of this faith which we receive in the Gospel stories expresses the fragmentary character of his faith, wherein the elements of struggle, exhaustion—even despair—often appear. Yet this never leads to a profanization or demonization of his faith. The Spirit never leaves him; the power of the transcendent union of unambiguous life always bears him up. If we call this "the faith of the Christ," the word "faith" may be used, though essentially qualified by its unambiguous character. The word "faith" cannot be applied to the Christ unless it is taken in its biblical meaning of a Spiritual reality in itself. Only if this meaning is preserved can one speak properly of "the faith of the Christ," just as one speaks of "the love of the Christ,"—thus qualifying both faith and love by the words "of the Christ."

The Spirit-Christology of the Synoptic Gospels has two further theological implications. One is the assertion that it is not the spirit of the man Jesus of Nazareth that makes him the Christ, but that it is the Spiritual Presence, God in him, that possesses and drives his individual spirit. This insight stands guard against a Jesus-theology which makes the man Jesus the object of Christian faith. This can be done in seemingly orthodox terms, as in Pietism, or in humanist terms, as in theological liberalism. Both distort or disregard the Christian message that it is Jesus *as* the Christ in whom the New Being has appeared. And they contradict Paul's Spirit-Christology, which emphasizes that "the Lord is the Spirit" and that we do not "know" him according to his historical existence (flesh) but only as the Spirit who is alive and present. This saves Christianity from the danger of a heteronomous subjection to an individual as an individual. The Christ is Spirit and not law.

The other implication of the Spirit-Christology is that Jesus, the Christ, is the keystone in the arch of Spiritual manifestations in history. He is not an isolated event—something which, so to speak, fell from heaven. Again, it is pietistic and liberal thought that denies an organic relation between the appearance of Jesus and the past and future. Spirit-Christology acknowledges that the divine Spirit which made Jesus into the Christ is creatively present in the whole history of revelation and salvation before and after his appearance. The event "Jesus as the Christ" is unique but not isolated; it is dependent on past and future, as they are dependent on it. It is the qualitative center in a process which proceeds from an indefinite past into an indefinite future which we call, symbolically, the beginning and the end of history.

The Spiritual Presence in the Christ as the center of history makes possible a fuller understanding of the manifestation of the Spirit in history. The New Testament writers and the church were aware of this problem and gave significant answers to it. The general assertion was that the Spiritual Presence in history is essentially the same as the Spiritual Presence in Jesus as the Christ. God in his self-manifestation, wherever this occurs, is the same God who is decisively and ultimately manifest in the Christ. Therefore, his manifestations anywhere before or after Christ must be consonant with the encounter with the center of history.

In this context, "before" does not mean before the year A.D. 30 but before an existential encounter with Jesus as the Christ—which probably will never happen universally at any one time in history. For even were all pagans and Jews to accept Jesus as the answer to their ultimate question, movements away from him would arise in the midst of Christianity as they always have arisen. "Before" Christ means "before an existential encounter with the New Being in him." The assertion that Jesus is the Christ implies that the Spirit, which made him the Christ and which became his Spirit (with a capital "S"), was and is working in all those who have been grasped by the Spiritual Presence before he could be encountered as a historical event. This has been expressed in the Bible and the churches by the scheme of "prophecy and fulfilment." The often absurd distortion of this idea in primitive as well as theological literalism should not prevent us from perceiving its truth, which is the assertion that the Spirit who created the Christ within Jesus is the same Spirit who prepared and continues to prepare mankind for the encounter with the New Being in him. The way in which this happens has been described positively and critically in the preceding chapter. That description is also valid for those who are directly or indirectly under the influence of an existential encounter with the New Being in Jesus as the Christ. There is always the state of being grasped by the Spiritual Presence, followed by the profanization and demonization in the process of reception and actualization and by the prophetic protest and renewal.

Nevertheless, since biblical times, serious theological discussions have arisen concerning the exact relation of the Spirit of Jesus as the Christ and the Spirit working in those who are grasped by the Spiritual Presence after his manifestation to them. The question is discussed in the Fourth Gospel in the form of Jesus' announcement concerning the coming of the Holy Spirit as the "Comforter." The question was bound to arise after the Spirit-Christology had been replaced by the Logos-Christology in the Fourth Gospel. The answer is two-sided and has determined the church's attitude ever since: After the return of the Logos-Incarnate to the Father, the Spirit will take his place and reveal the implication of his appearance. In the divine economy, the Spirit follows the Son, but in essence, the Son *is* the Spirit. The Spirit does not himself originate what he reveals. Every new manifestation of the Spiritual Presence stands under the criterion of his manifestation in Jesus as the Christ. This is a criticism of the claim of old and new Spirit-theologies which teach that the revelatory work of the Spirit qualitatively transcends that of the Christ. The Montanists, the radical Franciscans, and the Anabaptists are examples of this attitude. The "theologies of experience" in our time belong to the same line of thought. To them progressive religious experience, perhaps in terms of an amalgamation of the world religions, will go qualitatively beyond Jesus as the Christ—and not only quantitatively, as the Fourth Gospel acknowledges. Obviously, such an expectation's realization would destroy the Christ-character of Jesus. More than one manifestation of the Spiritual Presence claiming ultimacy would deny the very concept of ultimacy; they would, instead, perpetuate the demonic split of consciousness.

Another facet of the same problem appears in the argument between the Eastern and Western churches about the so-called *processio* of the Spirit from God the Father and God the Son. The Eastern church asserted that the Spirit proceeds from the Father alone, whereas the Western church insisted on the procession of the Spirit from the Father *and* the Son (*filioque*). In its scholastic form this discussion seems completely empty and absurd to us, and we can hardly understand how it could have been taken seriously enough to contribute to the final schism between Rome and the Eastern churches. But stripped of its scholastic form, the discussion has a profound meaning. The Eastern church, when it asserted that the Spirit proceeds from the Father alone, left open the possibility of a direct theocentric mysticism (of course, a "baptized mysticism"). The Western church, in contrast, insisted upon applying the Christocentric criterion to all Christian piety; and since the application of this criterion is the prerogative of the pope as the "vicar of Christ," the Roman church became less flexible and more legalistic than the Eastern churches. In Rome the freedom of the Spirit is limited by canon law. The Spiritual Presence is legally circumscribed. Certainly, this was not the intention of the writer of the Fourth Gospel when he had Jesus announce the coming of the Spirit who will lead into all truth.

4. THE SPIRITUAL PRESENCE AND THE NEW BEING
   IN THE SPIRITUAL COMMUNITY

a) The New Being in Jesus as the Christ and in the Spiritual Community.—As we have emphasized in the christological part of the system, the Christ would not be the Christ without those who receive him as the Christ. He could not have brought the new reality without those who have accepted the new reality in him and from him. Therefore, the creativity of the Spiritual Presence in mankind must be seen as a threefold one: in mankind as a whole in preparation for the central manifestation of the divine Spirit, in the divine Spirit's central manifestation itself, and in the manifestation of the Spiritual Community under the creative impact of the central event. We do not use the word "church" for the Spiritual Community, because this word has been used, of necessity, in the frame of the ambiguities of religion. At this point we speak instead of that which is able to conquer the ambiguities of religion—the New Being—in anticipation, in central appearance, and in reception. Such words as "body of Christ," "assembly (*ecclesia*) of God" or "of Christ," express the unambiguous life created by the divine Presence, in a sense similar to that of the term "Spiritual Community." Its relation to what is called "Church" or "church" in a rather equivocal terminology will be discussed later.

The Spiritual Community is unambiguous; it is New Being, created by the Spiritual Presence. But, although it is a manifestation of unambiguous life, it is nonetheless fragmentary, as was the manifestation of unambiguous life in the Christ and in those who expected the Christ. The Spiritual Community is an unambiguous, though fragmentary, creation of the divine Spirit. In this context, "fragmentary" means appearing under the conditions of finitude but conquering both estrangement and ambiguity.

The Spiritual Community is also Spiritual in the sense in which Luther often uses the word, that is, "invisible," "hidden," "open to faith alone," but nevertheless real, unconquerably real. This is analogous to the New Being's hidden presence in Jesus and in those who were vehicles of preparation for him. From the Spiritual Community's hiddenness, its "dialectical" relation (of identity and nonidentity) to the churches follows, just as the dialectical relation of Jesus and the Christ and, to take a similar case, of the history of religion and revelation also follows from the same hiddenness. In all three cases only the "eyes of faith" see what is hidden or Spiritual, and the "eyes of faith" are the Spirit's creation: only Spirit can discern Spirit.

The relation of the New Being in Christ to the New Being in the Spiritual Community is symbolized in several central stories of the New Testament. The first one, which is most significant for the meaning of "Christ," is also most significant for the relation of Christ to the Spiritual Community. It is the story of Peter's confession to Jesus that he is the Christ at Caesarea Philippi and Jesus' answer that the recognition of him as the Christ is a work of God; this recognition is the result not of an ordinary experience but of the impact of the Spiritual Presence. It is the Spirit grasping Peter that enables his spirit to recognize the Spirit in Jesus which makes him the Christ. This recognition is the basis of the Spiritual Community against which the demonic powers are powerless and which Peter and the other disciples represent. Therefore we can say: As the Christ is not the Christ without those who receive him as the Christ, so the Spiritual Community is not Spiritual unless it is founded on the New Being as it has appeared in the Christ.

The story of Pentecost powerfully emphasizes the Spiritual Community's character. The story, of course, combines historical, legendary, and mythological elements, the distinction between which, in the light of probability, is a task for historical research. But the symbolic meaning of the story in all its elements is of first importance for our purposes. We may distinguish five such elements. The first is the ecstatic character of the creation of Spiritual Community. It confirms what has been said about the Spiritual Presence's character, that is, the unity of ecstasy and structure. The story of Pentecost is an example of this unity. It is ecstasy, with all the characteristics of ecstasy; but it is an ecstasy united with faith, love, unity, and universality, as the story's other elements show. In light of the element of ecstasy in the Pentecost story, we must say that without ecstasy there is no Spiritual Community.

The second element in the story of Pentecost is the creation of a faith which was threatened and almost destroyed by the crucifixion of him who was supposed to be the bearer of the New Being. If we compare the Pentecost story with the Pauline report of the appearances of the resurrected Christ, we find that in both cases an ecstatic experience reassured the disciples and released them from a state of total incertitude. The fugitives who had dispersed in Galilee were not a manifestation of the Spiritual Community. They became its manifestation only after the Spiritual Presence grasped them and re-established their faith. In light of the certainty which overcomes doubt in the story of Pentecost, we must say that without the certainty of faith there is no Spiritual Community.

The third element in the story of Pentecost is the creation of a love which expresses itself immediately in mutual service, especially toward those who are in need, including strangers who have joined the original group. In the light of the service created by love in the story of Pentecost, we must say that there is no Spiritual Community without self-surrendering love.

The fourth element in the story of Pentecost is the creation of unity. The Spiritual Presence had the effect of uniting different individuals, nationalities, and traditions and gathering them together for the sacramental meal. The disciples' ecstatic speaking with tongues was interpreted as the conquest of the disruption of mankind as symbolized in the story of the Tower of Babel. In light of the unity apparent in the story of Pentecost, we must say that there is no Spiritual Community without the ultimate reunion of all the estranged members of mankind.

The fifth element in the story of Pentecost is the creation of universality, expressed in the missionary drive of those who were grasped by the Spiritual Presence. It was impossible that they should not give the message of what had happened to them to everybody, because the New Being would not be the New Being were not mankind as a whole and even the universe itself included in it. In light of the element of universality in the story of Pentecost we must say that there is no Spiritual Community without openness to all individuals, groups, and things and the drive to take them into itself.

All these elements which will reappear in our discussion as the marks of the Spiritual Community are derived from the image of Jesus as the Christ and the New Being manifest in him. This is expressed symbolically in the image of him as the head and the Spiritual Community as his body. In a more psychological symbolism, it is expressed in the image of him as the bridegroom and the Spiritual Community as the bride. In a more ethical symbolism, it is expressed in the image of him as the Lord of the Spiritual Community. This imagery points to the fact, to which we have already referred, that the divine Spirit is the Spirit of Jesus as the Christ and that the Christ is the criterion to which every Spiritual claim must submit.

b) *The Spiritual Community in its latent and in its manifest stages.*— The Spiritual Community is determined by the appearance of Jesus as the Christ, but it is not identical with the Christian churches. The question then arises: What is the Spiritual Community's relation to the manifold religious communities in the history of religion? This question reformulates our discussion of the problem of universal and final revelation and of the Spiritual Presence in the period antecedent to the central manifestation of the New Being. In the present context, however, we are seeking the appearance of the Spiritual Community in the preparatory period and are thereby implying that where there is the impact of the Spiritual Presence and therefore revelation (and salvation) there must also be the Spiritual Community. If, on the other hand, the appearance of the Christ is the central manifestation of the divine Spirit, the Spiritual Community's appearance in the period of preparation must differ from its appearance in the period of reception. I propose to describe this difference as that between the Spiritual Community in its latency and in its manifestation.

The terms "latent" and "manifest" church have been used by me for many years, and they have been both accepted and rejected quite frequently. Sometimes they were confused with the classical distinction between the invisible and the visible church. But the two distinctions overlap. The qualities invisible and visible must be applied to the church both in its latency and in its manifestation. The distinction between the Spiritual Community and the churches suggested here may be helpful in avoiding possible confusions between latency and invisibility. It is the Spiritual Community that is latent before an encounter with the central revelation and manifest after such an encounter. This "before" and "after" has a double meaning. It points to the world-historical event, the "basic *kairos*," which has established the center of history once for all, and it refers to the continually recurring and derivative *kairoi* in which a religious cultural group has an existential encounter with the central event. "Before" and "after" in connection with the Spiritual Community's latency and manifestation refer directly to the second sense of the words and only indirectly to the first.

The concrete occasion for the distinction between the latent and the manifest church comes with the encounter of groups outside the organized churches who show the power of the New Being in an impressive way. There are youth alliances, friendship groups, educational, artistic, and political movements, and, even more obviously, individuals without any visible relation to each other in whom the Spiritual Presence's impact is felt, although they are indifferent or hostile to all overt expressions of religion. They do not belong to a church, but they are not excluded from the Spiritual Community. It is impossible to deny this if one looks at the manifold instances of profanization and demonization of the Spiritual Presence in those groups—the churches—which claim to be the Spiritual Community. Certainly the churches are not excluded from the Spiritual Community, but neither are their secular opponents. The churches represent the Spiritual Community in a manifest religious self-expression, whereas the others represent the Spiritual Community in secular latency. The term "latent" comprises a negative and a positive element. Latency is the state of being partly actual, partly potential; one cannot attribute latency to that which is merely potential, for example, the reception of Jesus as the Christ by those who have not yet encountered him. In the state of latency, there must be actualized elements and elements not actualized. And this is just what characterizes the latent Spiritual Community. There is the Spiritual Presence's impact in faith and love; but the ultimate criterion of both faith and love, the transcendent union of unambiguous life as it is manifest in the faith and the love of the Christ, is lacking. Therefore the Spiritual Community in its latency is open to profanization and demonization without an ultimate principle of resistance, whereas the Spiritual Community organized as a church has the principle of resistance in itself and is able to apply it self-critically, as in the movements of prophetism and Reformation.

It was the latency of the Spiritual Community under the veil of Christian humanism which led to the concept of latency, but the concept proved to possess a wider relevance. It could be applied to the whole history of religion (which is in most cases identical with the history of culture).

There is a latent Spiritual Community in the assembly of the people of Israel, in the schools of the prophets, in the community of the temple, in the synagogues in Palestine and the Diaspora, and in the medieval and modern synagogues. There is a latent Spiritual Community in the Islamic devotional communities, in the mosques and theological schools, and in the mystical movements of Islam. There is a latent Spiritual Community in the communities worshiping the great mythological gods, in esoteric priestly groups, in the mystery cults of the later ancient world, and in the half-scientific, half-ritual communities of the Greek philosophical schools. There is a latent Spiritual Community in classical mysticism in Asia and Europe and in the monastic and half-monastic groups to which the mystical religions gave rise. The impact of the Spiritual Presence, and therefore of the Spiritual Community, is in all of these and many others. There are elements of faith in the sense of being grasped by an ultimate concern, and there are elements of love in the sense of a transcendent reunion of the separated. The Spiritual Community, however, is still latent. The ultimate criterion, the faith and love of the Christ, has not yet appeared to these groups—whether they existed before or after the years 1 to 30. As a consequence of their lack of this criterion, such groups are unable to actualize a radical self-negation and self-transformation as it is present as reality and symbol in the Cross of Christ. This means that they are teleologically related to the Spiritual Community in its manifestation; they are unconsciously driven toward the Christ, even though they reject him when he is brought to them through the preaching and actions of the Christian churches. In their opposition to this form of his appearance, they may represent the Spiritual Community better than the churches, at least in some respects. They may become critics of the churches in the name of the Spiritual Community, and this is true even of such anti-religious and anti-Christian movements as world communism. Not even communism could live if it were devoid of all elements of the Spiritual Community. Even world communism is teleologically related to the Spiritual Community.

It is most important for the practice of the Christian ministry, especially in its missionary activities toward those both within and without the Christian culture, to consider pagans, humanists, and Jews as members of the latent Spiritual Community and not as complete strangers who are invited into the Spiritual Community from outside. This insight serves as a powerful weapon against ecclesiastical and hierarchical arrogance.

c) *The marks of the Spiritual Community.*—Latent or manifest, the Spiritual Community is the community of the New Being. It is created by the divine Spirit as manifest in the New Being in Jesus as the Christ. This origin determines its character: it is the community of faith and love. The several qualities inherent in its character demand special consideration for their own sake and because they furnish the criteria for describing and judging the churches, for the churches are both the actualization and the distortion of the Spiritual Community.

As the community of the New Being the Spiritual Community is a community of faith. The term "community of faith" indicates the tension between the faith of the individual member and the faith of the community as a whole. It is of the nature of the Spiritual Community that this tension does not lead to a break (as it does in the churches). The Spiritual Presence by which the individual is grasped in the act of faith transcends individual conditions, beliefs, and expressions of faith. It unites him with the God who can grasp men through all these conditions but who does not restrict himself to any one of them. The Spiritual Community contains an indefinite variety of expressions of faith and does not exclude any of them. It is open in all directions because it is based on the central manifestation of the Spiritual Presence. It is faith, nevertheless, overcoming the infinite gap between the infinite and the finite; it is in every moment fragmentary, a partial anticipation of the transcendent union of unambiguous life. Unambiguous itself, it is the criterion for the faith of the churches, conquering their ambiguities. The Spiritual Community is holy, participating through faith in the holiness of the Divine Life; and it gives holiness to the religious communities, i.e., the churches, of which it is the invisible Spiritual essence.

As the community of the New Being, the Spiritual Community is a community of love. As the Spiritual Community contains the tension between the faith of the individual members, with their indefinite variety of experiences, and that of the community, so it contains the tension between the indefinite variety of love relations and the *agape* which unites being with being in the transcendent union of unambiguous life. And as the variety of conditions of faith does not lead to a break with the faith of the community, so the variety of love relations does not prevent *agape* from uniting the separated centers in the transcendent union of unambiguous life. Nevertheless, it is multidimensional love, fragmentary in view of the separation of everything from everything else in time and space, but an anticipation of the perfect union in Eternal Life. As such it is the criterion of the love within the churches, unambiguous in its essence, conquering their ambiguities. The Spiritual Community is holy, participating through love in the holiness of the divine life, and it gives holiness to the religious communities—the churches—of which it is the invisible Spiritual essence.

The unity and universality of the Spiritual Community follow from its character as a community of faith and love. Its unity expresses the fact that the tension between the indefinite variety of the conditions of faith does not lead to a break with the faith of the community. The Spiritual Community can stand the diversities of psychological and sociological structures, of historical development, and of preferences as to symbols and devotional and doctrinal forms. This unity is not without tensions, but it is without break. It is fragmentary and anticipatory because of the limits of time and space, but it is unambiguous and, as such, the criterion for the unity of the religious groups, the churches of which the Spiritual Community is the invisible Spiritual essence. This unity is another expression of the Spiritual Community's holiness, which participates in the holiness of the Divine Life.

The universality of the Spiritual Community expresses the fact that the tension between the indefinite variety of love relations and the *agape* which unites being with being in the transcendent union of unambiguous life does not lead to a break between them. The Spiritual Community can stand the diversity of the qualities of love. There is no conflict in it between *agape* and *eros*, between *agape* and *philia*, between *agape* and *libido*. There are tensions, as there are implicitly in every dynamic process. The dynamics of all life, even the unambiguous life of the transcendent union, implies tensions. But only in the estrangement of ambiguous life do the tensions become conflicts. *Agape*, in the Spiritual Community, is not only itself united with the other qualities of love; it also creates unity among them. As a consequence, the immense diversity of beings with regard to sex, age, race, nation, tradition, and character—typological as well as individual—does not prevent their participation in the Spiritual Community. The figurative statement that all men are children of the same father is not incorrect, but it has a hollow sound, because it suggests mere potentiality. The real question is whether, in spite of the existential estrangement of the children of God from God and from each other, participation in a transcendent union is possible. This question is answered in the Spiritual Community and by the working of *agape* as a manifestation of the Spirit in it.

As is the case with faith, love, and unity in the Spiritual Community, its quality of universality is also unambiguous, albeit fragmentary and anticipatory. The limits of finitude restrict the actual universality in every moment of time and at every point of space. The Spiritual Community is not the Kingdom of God in ultimate fulfilment. It is actual in the religious communities as their invisible Spiritual essence and the criterion of their ambiguous life. Nevertheless, the Spiritual Community is holy, because it participates through its universality in the holiness of the Divine Life.

d) The Spiritual Community and the unity of religion, culture, and morality.—The transcendent union of unambiguous life in which the Spiritual Community participates includes the unity of the three functions of life under the dimensions of the spirit—religion, culture, and morality. This unity is pre-formed in man's essential nature, disrupted under the conditions of existence, and recreated by the Spiritual Presence in the Spiritual Community as it struggles with the ambiguities of life in religious and secular groups.

There is no religion as a special function in the Spiritual Community. Of the two concepts of religion, the narrower and the broader, the narrower does not apply to the Spiritual Community, for all acts of man's spiritual life are grasped by the Spiritual Presence. In biblical terms: There is no temple in the fulfilled Kingdom of God, for "now at last God has his dwelling among men! He will dwell among them and they shall be his people, and God himself will be with them." The Spiritual Presence which creates the Spiritual Community does not create a separate entity in terms of which it must be received and expressed; rather, it grasps all reality, every function, every situation. It is the "depth" of all cultural creations and places them in a vertical relation to their ultimate ground and aim. There are no religious symbols in the Spiritual Community because the encountered reality is in its totality symbolic of the Spiritual Presence, and there are no religious acts because every act is an act of self-transcendence. Thus, the essential relation between religion and culture—that "culture is the form of religion and religion the substance of culture"—is realized in the Spiritual Community. Although unambiguous, however, it is not without its dynamics and tensions; therefore, similarly to the other characteristics of the Spiritual Community, it is fragmentary and anticipatory. The biblical vision of the holy city without a temple is the vision of ultimate fulfilment; but as such it is also a description of the holy community in anticipation and fragmentary realization. The temporal process and the limited field of consciousness prevent the universal mutual inherence of cultural creation and religious self-transcendence. The alternating prevalence of one or the other cannot be avoided, but this spatial and temporal disparity does not necessitate mutual exclusion of a qualitative character. Such exclusion occurs in the separation of religion from culture and in the consequent ambiguities of the religious and cultural life. The unambiguous, though fragmentary, union of religion and culture in the Spiritual Community is the criterion of the religious and cultural communities and the hidden power within them which struggles against separation and ambiguity.

Although religion in the narrower sense is lacking in the Spiritual Community, religion in the broader sense is united with morality in an unambiguous way. We have defined morality as the constitution of the person as person in the encounter with the other person. If religion in the narrower sense is separated from morality, both are forced to defend their mutual independence: morality must defend its autonomous character against religious commandments imposed on it from outside, as, for example, Kant did in a monumental way, and religion must defend itself against attempts to explain it as an illusionary support of or a destructive interference with autonomous morals, as Schleiermacher did most impressively. There is no such conflict in the Spiritual Community. Religion, in the sense of being grasped by the Spiritual Presence, presupposes self-establishment of the person in the moral act—the condition of everything spiritual and Spiritual in man. The term "Spiritual Community" itself points to the personal-communal character in which the New Being appears. It could not appear in any other character, and it would destroy itself if it imposed religious commands that were external to the act of moral self-constitution. This possibility is excluded from the Spiritual Community because religion in the narrower sense is excluded from it. On the other hand, the unity of religion and morals expresses itself in the character of morals in the Spiritual Community. Morals in the Spiritual Community are "theonomous" in a twofold sense. If we ask for the source of the unconditional character of the moral imperative, we must give the following answer: that the moral imperative is unconditional because it expresses man's essential being. Affirming what we essentially are and being obedient to the moral imperative are one and the same act. But one could ask: Why should one affirm one's essential being rather than destroy one's self? The answer to this must be that the person becomes aware of his infinite value or, ontologically expressed, of his belonging to the transcendent union of unambiguous life which is the Divine Life; this awareness occurs under the impact of the Spiritual Presence. The act of faith and the act of accepting the moral imperative's unconditional character are one and the same act.

If we ask the question of the moral imperative's motivating power, the answer in light of the Spiritual Community is not the law but the Spiritual Presence, which, in relation to the moral imperative, is grace. The moral act, the act of personal self-constitution in the encounter with other persons, is based on participation in the transcendent union. This participation makes the moral act possible. By its Spiritual impact, the preceding transcendent union creates the actual union of the centered person with itself, the encountered world, and the ground of self and world. It is the quality of "preceding" that characterizes the Spiritual impact as grace: and nothing establishes the moral personality and community but the transcendent union which manifests itself in the Spiritual Community as grace. The self-establishment of a person as person without grace leaves the person to the ambiguities of the law. Morality in the Spiritual Community is determined by grace.

Nevertheless, the unity of religion and morality remains fragmentary, for it has temporal and spatial limits; and it remains anticipatory because it does not embrace the whole field of person-to-person relations.

Even the personality and community under grace, subject to the impact of the Spiritual Presence, is not the fulfilled personality and community. Yet these are the criteria of moral self-establishment in religious and secular persons and groups. The "ethics of the Kingdom of God" is the measure of the ethics in the churches and in society.

The unity of religion with culture and morality implies the unity of culture with morality. This applies first to the content which morality receives from culture. The unconditional character of the moral imperative does not yield the content of the imperative. The ethical content is a product of culture and shares all the relativities of cultural creativity. Its relativity has but one limit, and that is the act of the constitution of the personal self in the person-to-person encounter; and this has already led us to more than a merely abstract acknowledgment—to the multidimensional love which affirms the other one in an act of reunion. In it the moral imperative and the ethical content come together and constitute the theonomous morals of the Spiritual Community. Love is continually subject to change while remaining identical with itself as love. In the Spiritual Community there are no tables of commandments besides the Spiritual Presence, which creates love and which may also create documents of the wisdom of love (as the Decalogue). But these documents are not ethical law books. Love decides at every moment as to their validity and their application to the particular case. In this way morality is both dependent on the dynamics of cultural creativity and independent of it through the love which is created by the Spiritual Presence. The New Being unites morality and culture by participation in the transcendent union of unambiguous life.

Yet this unity, though unambiguous, is fragmentary and anticipatory, owing to the finitude of the individuals and groups who are its moral agents. Every moral decision imposed by the Spirit excludes other possible decisions. This does not mean that love's action is ambiguous but that every act of love is fragmentary, able merely to anticipate an ultimate—that is, an all-embracing-fulfilment. Nevertheless, this unity of morality and culture is the criterion of the moral-cultural situation in all religious and secular communities. It is, at the same time, the hidden Spiritual power within them which seeks to resolve the ambiguities which follow from the existential separation of morality and culture.

As culture gives content to morality, so morality gives seriousness to culture. The lack of seriousness toward cultural creativity was first called "aestheticism" by Kierkegaard. It is the detached attitude toward cultural creations that are valued merely for an enjoyment untouched by *eros* toward the creation itself. This attitude should not be confused with the element of play in cultural creation and reception. Play is one of the most characteristic expressions of the freedom of the spirit, and there is a seriousness in free playing not to be surpassed by the seriousness of necessary work. Where there is seriousness, there is the unconscious or conscious force of the unconditional character of the moral imperative. A culture which loses this orientation in its creative work becomes shallow and self-destructive, and a morality which establishes itself in opposition as "withdrawal to seriousness" negates its own seriousness by an empty personal and communal self-constitution, as in the case of a culture-defying moralism. In both cases it is lack of a uniting love which produces the conflict. In the Spiritual Community there is no aestheticist detachment; there is the seriousness of those who seek to experience the ultimate in being and meaning through every cultural form and task. The seriousness of moral self-integration and the richness of cultural self-creation are united in the Spiritual Presence, which answers the self-transcending drive in culture and morality. The conflict between the irresponsible enjoyment of cultural forms and activities and the attitude of moral superiority over culture assumed in the name of seriousness has no place in the Spiritual Community. But the tension out of which such a conflict arises does have its place, for although there is genuine unity of culture and morality in the theonomy of the Spiritual Community, it exists fragmentarily and by anticipation. The limits of human finitude prevent an all-embracing seriousness and an all-embracing cultural *eros*. Yet even within these limits the unity of moral seriousness and cultural openness is the criterion for the relation of morality to culture in all religious and secular groups. It is the Spiritual power that struggles against the ambiguities which follow the separation of morality and culture.

This description of the Spiritual Community shows it to be both as manifest and hidden as the New Being in all its expressions. It is as manifest and as hidden as the central manifestation of the New Being in Jesus as the Christ; it is as manifest and as hidden as the Spiritual Presence which creates New Being in the history of mankind and, indirectly, in the universe as a whole. This is the reason for the use of the term "Spiritual Community," for every thing Spiritual is manifest in hiddenness. It is open only to faith as the state of being grasped by the Spiritual Presence. As we have said before: Only Spirit discerns Spirit.

III

THE DIVINE SPIRIT AND THE
AMBIGUITIES OF LIFE

A. THE SPIRITUAL PRESENCE AND THE AMBIGUITIES
OF RELIGION

1. The Spiritual Community, the Church, and the Churches

a) *The ontological character of the Spiritual Community.*—The term "Spiritual Community" has been used to characterize sharply that element in the concept of the church which is called the "body of Christ" by the New Testament and the "church invisible or Spiritual" by the Reformation. In the previous discussion this element has sometimes been called the "invisible essence of the religious communities." Such a statement implies that the Spiritual Community is not a group existing beside other groups but rather a power and a structure inherent and effective in such groups, that is, in religious communities. If they are consciously based on the appearance of the New Being in Jesus as the Christ, these groups are called churches. If they have other foundations, they are called synagogues, temple congregations, mystery groups, monastic groups, cult groups, movements. In so far as they are determined by an ultimate concern, the Spiritual Community is effective in its hidden power and structure in all such groups. In the language of the New Testament, the manifestation of the Spiritual Community in the Christian church is described in the following way: The church in New Testament Greek is *ecclesia*, the assembly of those who are called out of all nations by the *apostoloi*, the messengers of the Christ, to the congregation of the *eleutheroi*, those who have become free citizens of the "Kingdom of the Heavens." There is a "church," an "assembly of God" (or the Christ), in every town in which the message has been successful and a Christian *koinonia*, or communion, has come into being. But there is also the over-all unity of these local assemblies in the Church universal, by virtue of which the particular groups become churches (local, provincial, national, or after the split of the Church universal, denominational). The Church universal, as well as the particular churches included in it, is seen in a double aspect as the "body of Christ," on the one hand—a Spiritual reality—and as a social group of individual Christians on the other. In the first sense, they show all the characteristics which we have attributed to the Spiritual Community in the preceding chapters: in the second sense, all the ambiguities of religion, culture, and morality that were already discussed in connection with the ambiguities of life in general are present.

For the sake of semantic clarification, we have used the term "Spiritual Community" as an equivalent of "the church" (as the body of Christ), avoiding the term "the Church" (with a capital "C") completely. Of course, this term cannot be removed from liturgical language; but systematic theology has the right to use non-biblical and non-ecclesiastical terms, if such use serves to free the genuine meanings of the traditional terms from confusing connotations which obscure their meaning. When the reformers distinguished sharply between the invisible and the visible church they did the same thing. They also had to resist dangerous and even demonic distortions of the true meaning of "church" and "churches."

It cannot be denied, however, that a new terminology, though helpful in one respect, may produce new confusions in another. This has certainly been the case in the distinction between the church visible and invisible, and it might happen to the distinction between the Spiritual Community and the churches. In the first case, the confusion is that the "church invisible" is understood as a reality beside the Church visible or, more precisely, beside the visible churches. But in the thought of the reformers, there was no invisible church alongside the historical churches. The invisible church is the Spiritual essence of the visible church; like everything Spiritual, it is hidden, but it determines the nature of the visible church. In the same way the Spiritual Community does not exist as an entity beside the churches, but it is their Spiritual essence, effective in them through its power, its structure, and its fight against their ambiguities.

To the question of the logical-ontological character of the Spiritual Community, one can answer that it is essentiality determining existence and being resisted by existence. Two mistakes must be avoided here. One is the interpretation of the Spiritual Community as an ideal—as against the reality of the churches—that is, as constructed from the positive elements in the ambiguities of religion and projected onto the screen of transcendence. This image creates the expectation that the actual churches will progress toward an approximation of this ideal picture of the Spiritual Community. But this raises the question: What justifies such an expectation? Or more concretely, Where do the churches get the power of establishing and actualizing such an ideal? The familiar answer is that they get it from the divine Spirit, working in the church. But this answer leads to the further question as to the way in which the divine Spirit is present. How does the Spirit use the word and the sacrament as media of his creative work? How can faith be created, except by the power of faith; and love, except by the power of love? Essential power must precede actualization. In biblical terms one would say that the church as the Body of Christ, or as the Spiritual Temple, is the New Creation into which the individual Christian and the particular church is taken. This kind of thinking is more strange to our time than it was to most periods in the history of the church, including the Reformation. But it is certainly biblical thinking, and as long as the churches affirm that Jesus is the Christ, the mediator of the New Being, it is theologically necessary.

However, there is another danger to be avoided, and that is a kind of Platonism or mythological literalism which interprets the Spiritual Community as an assembly of so-called Spiritual beings, angelic hierarchies, saints and the saved from all periods and countries, represented on earth by ecclesiastical hierarchies and sacraments. This idea is in the line of Greek Orthodox thinking. Whatever its symbolic truth may be, it is not what we have called the Spiritual Community. The "heavenly assembly of God" is a supranaturalistic counterpart to the earthly assembly of God, the church, but it is not this quality in the churches which makes them churches—it is their invisible, essential Spirituality.

This calls for a category to be used in interpreting reality which is neither realistic nor idealistic nor supranaturalistic but essentialistic—a category pointing to the power of the essential behind and within the existential. This analysis holds true of every life process: everywhere, the essential is one of the determining powers. Its power is not causal but directive. One could call it teleological, but this word has been misused in the sense of a further causality, which certainly must be rejected by both science and philosophy. And yet, it would be possible to say that the Spiritual Community is the inner *telos* of the churches and that as such it is the source of everything which makes them churches.

This essentialistic interpretation of the Spiritual Community can give to theology a category which is most adequate to interpret the unambiguous life as Eternal Life, for Spiritual life is Eternal Life in anticipation.

b) The paradox of the churches.—The paradox of the churches is the fact that they participate, on the one hand, in the ambiguities of life in general and of the religious life in particular and, on the other hand, in the unambiguous life of the Spiritual Community. The first consequence of this is that whenever they are interpreted and judged the churches must be seen under two aspects. The awareness of this necessity has been expressed in the distinction between the church invisible and visible, to which we have already referred. As long as one who uses these terms is aware that he does not speak of two churches but of two aspects of one church in time and space, this terminology is possible and even unavoidable, for it is necessary to emphasize the invisible character of the Spiritual Community, which is the essential power in every actual church. If, however, these terms are so abused as to suggest two distinct churches, the result is either a devaluation of the empirical church here and now or an ignoring of the invisible church as an irrelevant ideal. Both consequences have characterized many phases of Protestantism's history. The first consequence has appeared in certain types of Spirit-movements, the second in liberal Protestantism.

Therefore, it might be useful to speak in an epistemological language of the sociological and the theological aspects of the church (meaning every particular church in time and space). Every church is a sociological reality. As such it is subject to the laws which determine the life of social groups with all their ambiguities. The sociologists of religion are justified in conducting these inquiries in the same way as the sociologists of law, of the arts, and of the sciences. They rightly point to the social stratification within the churches, to the rise and fall of elites, to power struggles and the destructive weapons used in them, to the conflict between freedom and organization, to aristocratic esotericism in contrast to democratic exotericism, and so forth. Seen in this light, the history of the churches is a secular history with all the disintegrating, destructive, and tragic-demonic elements which make historical life as ambiguous as all other life processes. If this aspect is looked at to the exclusion of the other, one can deal with the churches polemically or apologetically. If the intention is polemical (often born of undiscerning expectations and the disappointments which inevitably ensue), the rather miserable reality of concrete churches is emphasized and this reality is compared with their claim to embody the Spiritual Community. The church at the street corner hides the church Spiritual from view.

If, conversely, the churches as sociological realities are cited for apologetic purposes, they are valued because of their social significance. They are praised as the largest and most effective social agencies dedicated to the enhancement of the good life. People are asked to join the churches, at least for a try, for the sake of psychological security, for example, and to participate in the work of helping others toward the same goal. In light of this view, the history of the churches is told as the history of humanity's progress. Of course, on this basis the churches' critics can point to the reactionary, superstitious, and inhuman impact of the churches on Western civilization, and this they have done with tremendous success. This contrast shows that judging the churches from the point of view of their sociological functions and their social influence, past or present, is utterly inadequate. A church which is nothing more than a benevolent, socially useful group can be replaced by other groups not claiming to be churches; such a church has no justification for its existence.

The other view of the churches is the theological. It does not refuse to recognize the sociological aspect, but it does deny its exclusive validity. The theological view points, within the ambiguities of the social reality of the churches, to the presence of the unambiguous Spiritual Community.

However, a danger, similar to that found with respect to the sociological view, threatens and distorts the theological: exclusiveness. Of course, the theological view cannot be exclusive in the sense that it simply denies the existence of the sociological characteristics of the churches and their ambiguities. But it can deny their significance for the Spiritual nature of the church. This is the official Roman Catholic doctrine, according to which the Roman church is a sacred reality above the sociological ambiguities of past and present. Church history, from this point of view, becomes sacred history, elevated above all other history in spite of the fact that the disintegrating, destructive, and demonic features of life are shown in it as strongly, and often even more strongly, than in secular history. This makes it impossible to criticize the Roman church in essentials—in doctrine, ethics, hierarchical organization, and so forth. Since the Roman church identifies its historical existence with the Spiritual Community, every attack on it (often even on non-essentials) is felt as an attack on the Spiritual Community and consequently on the Spirit itself. This is one of the main roots both of hierarchical arrogance and, in opposition to it, of anti-ecclesiastical and antihierarchical movements. The Roman church tries to ignore the ambiguities of its life and to submerge the church's sociological character in its theological character, but the relation of the two is paradoxical and cannot be understood either by eliminating the one or by subjecting the one to the other.

The churches' paradoxical character is evident in the way in which the marks of the Spiritual Community are taken as marks of the churches. Each of them can be ascribed to the churches only with the addition of "in spite of." We refer to the predicates of holiness, unity, and universality. (Faith and love will be discussed in connection with the life of the churches and the fight against its ambiguities.)

The churches are holy because of the holiness of their foundation, the New Being, which is present in them. Their holiness cannot be derived from the holiness of their institutions, doctrines, ritual and devotional activities, or ethical principles; all these are among the ambiguities of religion. Nor can the churches' holiness be derived from the holiness of their members; the churches' members are holy in spite of their actual unholiness, in so far as they want to belong to the church and have received what the church has received, i.e., the ground on which they are accepted in spite of their unholiness. The holiness of the churches and of Christians is not a matter of empirical judgment but rather of faith in the working of the New Being within them. One could say that a church is holy because it is a community of those who are justified through faith by grace—and the churches do indeed pronounce this message as "good news" to their members. However, this message is also valid for the churches themselves. The churches living in the ambiguities of religion are, at the same time, holy. They are holy because they stand under the negative and the positive judgments of the Cross.

This is just the point at which the gap between Protestantism and Roman Catholicism seems unbridgeable. The Roman church accepts (at least in principle) critical judgment of each of its members, including the "vicar of Christ," the pope himself, but it does not accept critical judgment of itself as an institution, of its doctrinal decisions, ritual traditions, moral principles, and hierarchical structure. It judges on the basis of its institutional perfection, but this basis itself is not judged. Protestantism cannot accept the predicate of holiness for its churches, if it is based on any kind of institutional perfection. The holy church is the distorted church, and this means every church in time and space.

If, as under Pope John XXIII through the Second Vatican Council, the Roman Catholic church revives the principle of reformation within itself, the question remains as to how far such a reformation can go. Pope John gave the first answer unmistakably: the doctrinal decisions of councils and popes are the unchangeable basis of the Catholic church. And the doctrinal decisions include statements concerning the hierarchical structure and the ethical system of the church. But there is a second answer, such as that given by Cardinal Bea, to the effect that, although the doctrines themselves are unchangeable, their interpretation must change. Only the future can show to what degree the principle of reformation will become effective within the Roman church through an interpretation under the guidance of the prophetic Spirit.

Nevertheless, the churches are embodiments of the New Being and creations of the Spiritual Presence, and their essential power is the Spiritual Community, which works toward unambiguous life through their ambiguities. Nor is this work without effect. There is regenerative power in the churches, even in their most miserable state. As long as they are churches and related in reception and reaction to the New Being in Jesus as the Christ, the Spiritual Presence works in them, and symptoms of this work can always be seen. This is the case most conspicuously in the movements of prophetic criticism and reformation to which we have already referred. It is generic to the churches' holiness that they have the principle of reformation within themselves: the churches are holy, but they are so in terms of an "in spite of" or as a paradox.

Unity is the second predicate of the churches which expresses the paradox of their nature. The churches are united because of the unity of their foundation, the New Being which is effective in them. But the churches' unity cannot be derived from their actual unity, nor can the predicate of unity be denied because of their present disunity. The predicate is independent of these empirical realities and possibilities. It is identical with the dependence of any actual church on the Spiritual

Community as its essence in power and structure. This is true of every particular local denominational and confessional church which is related to the event of the Christ as its foundation. The unity of the church is real in each of them in spite of the fact that all of them are separated from each other.

This contradicts the Roman Catholic church's claim to represent in its particularity the unity of the church and its rejection of any other group which claims to be a church. A consequence of this absolutism was that Rome prohibited co-operation of a purely religious kind with other Christian churches. In spite of some relaxation in this attitude, it expresses the Roman understanding of the church's unity, which could only be changed if the Roman church gave up its absolute claim and with it its own peculiar character.

Protestantism is aware of the paradoxical character of the predicate of unity. It considers the division of the churches as unavoidable in light of the ambiguities of religion but not as something which contradicts their unity with respect to the churches' foundation—their essential unity, which is paradoxically present in their ambiguous mixture of unity and disunity.

The fight against this ambiguity is waged in the power of the Spiritual Community, to which unambiguous unity belongs. It is manifest in all attempts to reunite the manifest churches and to draw what we have called the "latent churches" into this union. The most conspicuous of these attempts in our period is the work of the World Council of Churches. The ecumenical movement of which it is the organized representative powerfully expresses the awareness of the predicate of unity in many contemporary churches. In practical terms it is able to heal divisions which have become historically obsolete, to replace confessional fanaticism by interconfessional co-operation, to conquer denominational provincialism, and to produce a new vision of the unity of all churches in their foundation. But neither the ecumenical nor any other future movement can conquer the ambiguity of unity and division in the churches' historical existence. Even if it were able to produce the United Churches of the World, and even if all latent churches were converted to this unity, new divisions would appear. The dynamics of life, the tendency to preserve the holy even when it has become obsolete, the ambiguities implied in the sociological existence of the churches, and above all, the prophetic criticism and demand for reformation would bring about new and, in many cases, Spiritually justified divisions. The unity of the churches, similar to their holiness, has a paradoxical character. It is the divided church which is the united church.

Universality is the third predicate of the churches which expresses the paradox of their nature. The churches are universal because of the universality of their foundation—the New Being which is effective in them. The word "universal" replaces the classic word "catholic" (that which concerns all men), because since the split produced by the Reformation the latter word has generally been reserved for the Roman church or for such strongly sacramental churches as the Greek Orthodox and the Anglican. Although the word must be replaced, the fact yet remains that a church which does not claim catholicity has ceased to be a church.

Every church is universal—both intensively and extensively—because of its nature of actualizing the Spiritual Community. The intensive universality of the church is its power and desire to participate as church in everything created under all dimensions of life. Of course, such participation implies judgment of and fight against the ambiguities of life in the encountered realms of being. The predicate of intensive universality keeps the churches wide open—as wide as life universal. Nothing that is created and, therefore, essentially good is excluded from the life of the churches and their members. This is the meaning of the principle of the *complexio oppositorum*, of which the Roman church is rightly proud. There is nothing in nature, nothing in man, and nothing in history which does not have a place in the Spiritual Community and, therefore, in the churches of which the Spiritual Community is the dynamic essence. This is classically expressed in both the medieval cathedrals and the scholastic systems, in which all dimensions of being found their place, and even the demonic, the ugly, and the destructive appeared in a subdued role. The danger of this universality, of course, was that elements of ambiguity entered the life of the church, or, symbolically speaking, that the demonic revolted against its role of subjection to the divine. This danger induced Protestantism to replace the abundance of the *complexio oppositorum* by the poverty of sacred emptiness (in this point following Judaism and Islam). In doing so, Protestantism did not reject the principle of universality, because there can be a universality of emptiness as well as a universality of abundance. The predicate of universality is violated only if one of many possibilities is elevated to an absolute position and the other elements are excluded. When this happens the principle of universality disappears from the churches and is realized in the secular world. The fact that during the Reformation and Counter Reformation the churches largely cut themselves off from the universality of abundance and even of emptiness is partly responsible for the rise of a wide-open secularism in the modern world. The churches had become but segments of life and had lost their participation in life universal. Yet, however positive or negative the churches' attitude toward the predicate of universality, they are essentially universal in spite of their actual poverty in relation to the abundance of the encountered world. They may include music but exclude the visual arts; they may include work but exclude natural vitality; they may include philosophical analysis but exclude metaphysics; they may include particular styles of all cultural creations and exclude other styles. However universal they try to be, the universality of the churches is paradoxically present in their particularity.

All this is said about the intensive universality of the churches; but it is also valid of their extensive universality—that is, the validity of the church's foundation for all nations, social groups, races, tribes, and cultures. As the New Testament shows, this extensive universality is an immediate implication of the acceptance of Jesus as the bringer of the New Being. The tremendous emphasis which Paul places on this point is caused by his own experience as a Diaspora Jew who unites in himself Jewish, Greek, and Roman elements, as well as the syncretism of the Hellenistic period, and who brings all this into the church in himself and his congregation. The analogous situation in our time, stemming from national, racial, and cultural problems, forces contemporary theology to emphasize the universality of the churches as strongly as did Paul.

But there never is actual universality in the churches. The predicate of universality cannot be derived from the actual situation. In light of the historically conditioned particularity—even of the world churches and their councils—universality is paradoxical. Greek Orthodoxy identifies the universal Spiritual Community with the reception of the Christian message by Byzantine culture. Rome identifies the universal Spiritual Community with the church, ruled by the canonic law and its guardian, the pope. Protestantism shows its particularity by trying to subject foreign religions and cultures to contemporary Western civilization in the name of the universal Spiritual Community. And in many cases racial, social, and national particularities prevent the churches from actualizing the predicate of universality. Quantitative or extensive universality, like qualitative or intensive, is a paradoxical predicate of the churches. As was the case with respect to holiness and unity, we must also say of the churches' universality that it is present in their particularity. And it is certainly not without effect: since the earliest period, all churches have tried to overcome the ambiguity of universality, both intensively and extensively (often the two are identical).

It is one of the most regrettable traits of Protestant theology in the last hundred years that it has been conquered by a positivistic trend, of which Schleiermacher and Ritschl are examples. Positivism in theology is the resignation of the predicate of universality. That which is merely "positive," for example, a particular Christian church, cannot be considered universal. This is only possible if universality is conceived of as paradoxically present in the particular.

The ordinary layman who hears or confesses the words of the Apostles' Creed about the holiness, unity, and universality of the church often understands the paradox of the churches without the concept of the Spiritual Community. He is aware of the paradoxical meaning of those words as applied to the churches from his knowledge of his own. Usually he is even realistic enough to reject the idea that one day in the future these predicates will lose their paradoxical character and become empirically true. He knows the churches and their members (including himself) sufficiently to dismiss such utopian expectations. Nevertheless he is grasped by the power of the words in which the unambiguous side of the Church, the Spiritual Community, is expressed.

2. The Life of the Churches and the Struggle against the Ambiguities of Religion

a) Faith and love in the life of the churches

(1) THE SPIRITUAL COMMUNITY AND THE CHURCHES AS COMMUNITIES OF FAITH.—The Spiritual Community is the community of faith and love, participating in the transcendent unity of unambiguous life. The participation is fragmentary because of the finitude of life, and it is not without tensions because of the polarity of individualization and participation, which is never absent from any finite being. The Spiritual Community as the dynamic essence of the churches makes them existing communities of faith and love in which the ambiguities of religion are not eliminated but are conquered in principle. The phrase "in principle"

does not mean *in abstracto* but means (as do the Latin and Greek words *principium* and *arche*) the power of beginning, which remains the controlling power in a whole process. In this sense the Spiritual Presence, the New Being, and the Spiritual Community are principles (*archai*). The ambiguities of the religious life are conquered in principle in the churches' life; their self-destructive force is broken. They are not completely eliminated—they may even be present in demonic strength—but as Paul says in Romans, chapter 8, and other places: The appearance of the New Being overcomes the ultimate power of the demonic "structures of destruction." The ambiguities of religion in the churches are conquered by unambiguous life in so far as they embody the New Being. But this "in so far" warns us against identifying the churches with the unambiguous life of the transcendent union. Where the church is, there is a point at which the ambiguities of religion are recognized and rejected but not removed.

This is first of all true of the act in which the Spiritual Presence is received and the New Being actualized, the act of faith. Faith becomes religion in the churches—ambiguous, disintegrating, destructive, tragic, and demonic. But at the same time, there is a power of resistance against the manifold distortions of faith—the divine Spirit and its embodiment, the Spiritual Community. If we call the churches or any particular church a community of faith, we say that, according to its intention, it is founded on the New Being in Jesus as the Christ or that its dynamic essence is the Spiritual Community.

In discussing the Spiritual Community we indicated that there is a tension between the faith of those who are grasped by the Spiritual Presence and the faith of the community which consists of such individuals but is more than each of them and more than their totality. In the Spiritual Community this tension does not result in a break. In the churches a break is presupposed and leads to the ambiguities of religion, but it does so in such a way that these ambiguities are resisted and in principle overcome by the participation of the community of the church in the Spiritual Community. When we speak of the faith of the churches or of a particular church, what do we mean? Three aspects of the question must be considered. First, when in the early church individuals decided to enter the church and in doing so risked everything, including their lives, it was not too difficult to speak of the church as a community of faith. But as soon as many entered the church more as a matter of a religious shelter than as an existential decision, and later, when within a whole civilization everyone, including infants, belonged to the church, its characterization as a community of faith became questionable. The active faith, the *fides qua creditur*, could not be presupposed in most members. What was left was the creedal foundation of the church, the *fides quae creditur*. How are these two related? Whatever the answer, numerous ambiguities of the religious life reappeared, and the concept of faith itself became so ambiguous that there are good (though not sufficient) reasons for not using it at all.

The second difficulty in the concept of the community of faith is rooted in the history of the *fides quae creditur*, the creeds. This history is a typically ambiguous mixture between Spiritual creativity and the social forces which determine history. The social forces here under consideration are ignorance, fanaticism, hierarchical arrogance, and political intrigue. If the churches require that all their faithful members accept the formulas which came into existence in this way, they impose on them a burden which no one who is aware of the situation can honestly carry. It is a demonic and therefore destructive act for the community of faith to be interpreted as unconditional subjection to the doctrinal statements of faith as they have developed in the rather ambiguous history of the churches.

The third difficulty in the concept is the fact that a secular world has established itself which fosters a critical or sceptical or indifferent attitude toward the creedal statements—even among serious members of the churches. What does "community of faith" mean if the community, as well as the personalities of the individual members, is disrupted by criticism and doubt?

These questions show how powerful the ambiguities of religion are in the churches and how difficult the resistance of faith is.

There is one answer which underlies all parts of the present system and which is the basic content of the Christian faith, and that is that Jesus is the Christ, the bringer of the New Being. There are many possible ways of expressing this assertion, but in a church there is no way of avoiding it. Every church is based upon it. In this sense one can say that a church is a community of those who affirm that Jesus is the Christ. The very name "Christian" implies this. For the individual, this means a decision—*not* as to whether he, personally, can accept the assertion that Jesus is the Christ, *but* the decision as to whether he wishes to belong or not to belong to a community which asserts that Jesus is the Christ. If he decides against this, he has left the church, even if, for social or political reasons, he does not formalize his denial. Many formal members in all the churches more or less consciously do not want to belong to the church. The church can tolerate them, because it is not based on individual decisions but on the Spiritual Presence and its media.

In the opposite situation, there are some who unconsciously or consciously want to belong to the church, to such an extent that they cannot imagine not belonging to it, and who are in a state of such doubt about the basic assertion that Jesus is the Christ and its implications that they are on the verge of separating themselves from the church, at least inwardly. In our time, this is the predicament of many people, perhaps even the majority, though in various degrees. They belong to the church, but they doubt whether they belong. For them it must be said that the criterion of one's belonging to a church and through it to the Spiritual Community is the serious desire, conscious or unconscious, to participate in the life of a group which is based on the New Being as it has appeared in Jesus as the Christ. Such an interpretation can help people whose consciences are troubled by misgivings about the whole set of symbols to which they subject themselves in thought, devotion, and action. They can be assured that they fully belong to the church, and through it to the Spiritual Community, and can confidently live in it and work for it.

This solution is valid for all members of the church, including ministers and other representatives, but in the latter case problems of wisdom and tact arise, as in every organized group. It is obvious that one who denies, even tacitly, the basis and the aim of a function he is supposed to exercise must either separate himself from it or be forced out.

The above questions about the community of faith lead to another more difficult problem, especially difficult in light of the Protestant principle. The question is how the community of faith—which a church is supposed to be—is related to its creedal and doctrinal expressions in preaching and teaching and other utterances, especially those made by representatives of the church. This question must be answered in concrete decisions of the concrete church—ideally by the church universal, actually by the manifold centers between it and the local church. The creedal statements result from these decisions. Because it identifies itself with the Spiritual Community, the Roman church considers its creedal decisions unconditionally valid and regards every deviation from them as an heretical separation from the Spiritual Church. This produces a legally circumscribed reaction of the church against those considered to be heretics—formerly against all such members, today only against representatives of the church. The Protestant doctrine of the ambiguity of religion even in the churches makes such a reaction impossible; nevertheless, even Protestant churches must formulate their own creedal foundation and defend it against attacks from the side of its own representatives. However, a church which is conscious of its own ambiguities must acknowledge that its judgment, whether in pronouncing a creedal statement or in applying it to concrete cases, is itself ambiguous. The church cannot avoid fighting for the community of faith (as in the cases of the Nazi apostasy, the Communist heresy, relapses into Roman Catholic heteronomy, or rejection of the church's foundation in the New Being in the Christ), but in doing so the church may fall into disintegrating, destructive, or even demonic errors. This risk is inherent in the life of any church which puts itself not above but beneath the Cross of the Christ, i.e., in every church in which the prophetic-protestant principle has not been engulfed in hierarchical or doctrinal absolutism.

The question as to whether the affirmation of the church as the community of faith entails the affirmation of the concept of heresy remains. This question is burdened with connotations which the concept of heresy has acquired in the church's development. Originally used for deviations from officially accepted doctrine, the word came to signify, with the establishment of the canonic law, a breach of doctrinal law of the church, and with the acceptance of the canonic law as a part of the state law, it became the most serious criminal offense. The persecution of heretics has obliterated the original justified meaning of the word "heresy" for our conscious, and even more for our unconscious, reactions. It cannot be used in a serious discussion, and I am now convinced that we should not try to save the word, although we cannot avoid the problem to which it points.

The following may be said about the problem itself. The rejection of the foundation of a church, that is, of the Spiritual Community and its manifestation in the Christ, is not a heresy but a separation from the community in which the problem of heresy exists. The problem of heresy arises when the unavoidable attempt is made to formulate the implications of the basic Christian assertion conceptually. From the point of

view of the Protestant principle and the acknowledgment of the ambiguities of religion and in light of the always present latency of the
Spiritual Community, one can solve the problem in the following way:
the Protestant principle of the infinite distance between the divine
and the human undercuts the absolute claim of any doctrinal expression of the New Being. Certainly, a church's decision to base its
preaching and teaching on a particular doctrinal tradition or formulation is necessary; but if the decision is accompanied by the claim that it
is the only possible one, the Protestant principle is violated. It belongs
to the essence of the community of faith in Protestantism that a Protestant church can receive into its thinking and acting every expression
of thought and life created by the Spiritual Presence anywhere in the
history of mankind. The Roman church was more aware of this situation in its earlier than in its later development, but only since the Counter Reformation has it closed its doors against any doctrinal reappraisal
of the past. The prophetic freedom for essential self-criticism was lost.
Protestantism, born of the struggle for such freedom, lost it in the period
of theological orthodoxy and has recovered it again and again. Yet, with
this freedom and in spite of its endless denominational cleavages, Protestantism has remained a community of faith. It is aware, and should
always remain aware, of the two realities in which it participates—the
Spiritual Community, which is its dynamic essence, and its existence
within the ambiguities of religion. Awareness of these two poles of
Protestantism underlies the present attempt to develop a theological
system.

(2) THE SPIRITUAL COMMUNITY AND THE CHURCHES AS COMMUNITIES
OF LOVE.—At the same time that they are a community of faith the
churches are also a community of love, but this must be understood
within the ambiguities of religion and the Spirit's struggle with these
ambiguities. In his anti-Donatist writings Augustine decides that faith
is possible outside the church, for example, in schismatic groups, but that
love as *agape* is restricted to the community of the church. In saying
this he presupposes an intellectualistic concept of faith (for example,
acceptance of the formula of baptism) which separates faith from love.
But if faith is the state of being grasped by the Spiritual Presence, the
two cannot be separated. Yet Augustine is right in considering the
church as a community of love. We have discussed the nature of love
fully, especially in its quality as *agape*, in connection with the Spiritual

Community's character. Now we must describe its workings within and against the ambiguities of religion.

As the community of love, the church actualizes the Spiritual Community, which is its dynamic essence. In analyzing the act of the person's moral constitution as person, we found that this can happen only in the ego-thou encounter with the other person and that this encounter can become concrete only in terms of *agape*, the reuniting affirmation of the other one in terms of the eternal meaning of his being. The presupposition in the church is that every member has such a relation to every other member and that this relation becomes actual in spatial and temporal nearness (the "neighbor" of the New Testament). It expresses itself in mutual acceptance in spite of the separations which take place because the church is a sociologically determined group. This refers to political, social, economic, educational, national, racial, and above all, personal differences, preferences, sympathies, and antipathies. In some churches, such as the first church in Jerusalem and many sectarian groups, the concept "community of love" has led to an "ecstatic communism," a resignation of all differences, especially economic ones. But such an attitude fails to note the distinction between the theological and the sociological character of the church and fails to understand the nature of the latter and therefore of the ambiguities of every community of love. Often it is the ideological imposition of love which produces the most intensive forms of hostility. Like everything else in the nature of the churches, the community of love has the character of "in spite of"; love in the churches manifests the love of the Spiritual Community, but it does so under the condition of the ambiguities of life. A claim for political, social, and economic equality cannot be derived directly from the character of a church as a community. But it *does* follow from the church's character as a community of love that those forms of inequality which make an actual community of love and even of faith impossible—except for special heroic cases—must be attacked and transformed. This refers to political, social, and economic inequalities and forms of suppression and exploitation which destroy the potentialities for humanity in the individual and for justice in the group. The church's prophetic word must be heard against such forms of inhumanity and injustice, but first of all the church must transform the given social structure within itself. (See "The relating functions of the churches," pp. 212–16.) At the same time it must help the victims of a distorted social structure and of such forces as sickness and natural catastrophe both to experience the community of love and to attain the material goods which sustain their potentialities as men. This is that part of *agape* which is called charity and which is as necessary as it is ambiguous. It is ambiguous because it may substitute merely material contributions for the obligation toward human beings as human beings and because it can be used as a means for maintaining the social conditions which make charity necessary, even a thoroughly unjust social order. In contrast, true *agape* tries to create the conditions which make love possible in the other one. (It is not by chance that this has been declared the principle of psychotherapeutic healing, for example, by Erich Fromm.)

Every act of love implies judgment against that which negates love. The church as the community of love continuously exercises this judgment by its very existence. It exercises it against those outside as well as inside its community, and it *must* exercise it consciously and actively in both directions, although in doing so it becomes involved in the ambiguities of judging—authority and power. Since the church, in contrast to other groups in society, judges in the name of the Spiritual Community, its judging is in danger of becoming more radical, more fanatical, more destructive and demonic. On the other hand, and for this reason, there is present in the church the Spirit, which judges the church's judging and struggles against its distortions.

In relation to its own members, the church's judging occurs through the media of the Spiritual Presence, through the functions of the church, and finally through the discipline which in some churches, notably the Calvinistic ones, is considered as a medium of the Spiritual Presence, similar to the Word and the sacrament. Protestantism in general was hesitant about discipline because of its hierarchical and monastic abuses. Protestantism's main objection was to the practice and theory of excommunication. Under the Protestant principle, excommunication is impossible because no religious group has the right to put itself between God and man, either to unite man with God or to cut him off from God. The simple prayer of the excommunicated one may have more Spiritual power and more healing effect than any of the ecclesiastically approved sacraments from which he is excluded. Protestant discipline can consist only of counseling and, in the case of representatives of the church, exclusion from office. The decisive feature of the judging of love is that it has the one purpose of re-establishing the communion of love—not a cutting off, but a reuniting. Even a temporary cutting off makes a wound which can probably never be healed. Such removal may also take the form of social ostracism by the church community. This happens in Protestant churches and can be worse than excommunication in its destructive consequences, for it is an offense against the Spiritual Community and the church. An accommodation of the representatives of a church to social groups which exercise a predominant influence in it is equally, and in the long run more, dangerous. This is especially a problem of the minister, more so in the Protestant churches than in the Catholic church. The Protestant doctrine of the general priesthood of all believers deprives the minister of the taboo which protects the priest in the Roman church, and the significance of the laymen is correspondingly increased. This makes a prophetic judgment of the congregations, including their most powerful sociological groups, so difficult as to be almost impossible. The result is often the sociologically determined, class church so conspicuous in American Protestantism. In the name of a tactful and cautious approach (which in itself is desirable), the judging function of the community of love is suppressed. This situation probably hurts the church more than an open attack on its principles launched by deviating and erring members.

All this refers to the judging function of the community of love toward its members. The same criteria, of course, are valid, not only for the church's official representatives but also for members who have a priestly function in limited groups in the name of the community of love, for example, parents toward children and one parent to the other as parent, friends toward friends, leaders of voluntary groups to the members of their groups, teachers to their classes, and so on. The community of love must be actualized in affirmation, judgment, and reunion in all these cases, thus expressing the Spiritual Community. And in the power of the Spiritual Presence the church must fight against the ambiguities of the threefold manifestation of love through Spirit-determined individuals and movements. Each of the three manifestations is a creation of the Spiritual Presence, and in each of them the great "in spite of" of the New Being is effective; but it is most manifest in the third—the "reunion in spite of," the message and act of forgiveness. Like the judging element of love, the forgiving element is present in all the church's functions, in so far as they are dependent on the Spiritual Community. But the ambiguities of religion resist the dynamics of the Spirit in the act of forgiveness, too. Forgiveness can be a mechanical act, or mere permissiveness or the humilitation of him who is forgiven. Reunion in love is possible in none of these cases, because the paradox in forgiveness is disregarded.

The question of the relation of the particular church as a community of love to other communites outside of it is full of problems. Perhaps at no point are the ambiguities of religion more difficult to conquer than here. The first problem concerns individual members of all groups outside a church. The general answer to the question—What does love demand if they appear in the realm of the church?— is that they must be accepted as participants in the Spiritual Community in its latency and therefore as possible members of the particular church. But then the elements of love which we have called "judgment" and "reunion" pose the question: Under what conditions is their complete or partial acceptance as members possible? This is a profoundly problematic question. Does it mean conversion and, if so, to what? To Christianity, to one of its confessions or denominations, to the faith of the particular church? Our doctrine of the Spiritual Community in its latency suggests an answer: If someone desires to participate in the community of love in a particular church, then he may become a full member by accepting the creed and the order of that church; or he may remain in a particular church and become a fully accepted guest in another church; or he may remain in the latency of the Spiritual Community as a Jew, Mohammedan, humanist, mystic, and so on, who wants to be received into the community of love because he is aware of his own essential belonging to the Spiritual Community. In the last case, he would also be a guest or, more precisely, a visitor and friend. Such situations are frequent today. What is decisive, at least in the Protestant sphere, is the desire to participate in a group whose foundation is the acceptance of Jesus as the Christ; this desire takes the place of creedal statement and, in spite of the absence of conversion, opens the door into the community of love without reservation on the side of the church.

Another problem concerning the relation of the community of love to those outside is that of the relation of one particular church to another—local, national, denominational. Antagonism among churches, even to the extreme of fanatical persecution of one church by another, has social and political causes which are among the ambiguities of the churches in their sociological aspect. But there are other reasons derived from the Spiritual Presence's fight against profanization and demonization of the New Being. There is a profound anxiety in every church with a definite creed and order of life that the other one who asks to be taken into the community of love may distort this community by elements of profanization and demonization. In this situation fanaticism, as always, is a result of inner insecurity, and persecution, as always, is produced by anxiety. The suspicion and hate which appear in the relations between the communities of love are a consequence of the same fear which produced the witch and heresy trials. It is a genuine fear of the demonic and therefore cannot be overcome by an ideal of tolerance which is based on indifference or on an abstract minimization of differences. It is vulnerable only to the Spiritual Presence, which affirms and judges every expression of the New Being in the one community of love as well as in the others. In all of them, whether springing from latency or the manifest appearance of the Spiritual Community, there is creative Spiritual Presence, and in all of them profane and demonic possibilities are reality. Therefore, one church can recognize the community of love with another in the Spiritual Community as the dynamic essence of both by which the particularities of each are affirmed and judged. These considerations substantiate what was said earlier about the paradoxical character of the unity of the church.

b) The functions of the churches, their ambiguities, and the Spiritual Community

(1) THE GENERAL CHARACTER OF THE FUNCTIONS OF THE CHURCHES AND THE SPIRITUAL PRESENCE.—Having discussed in the previous sections the essential character of the churches in their relation to the Spiritual Community, we must now turn to their expression as living entities in a number of functions. Each of these functions is an immediate and necessary consequence of the nature of a church. They must be at work where there is a living church, even if periodically they are more hidden than manifest. They are never lacking, although the forms they take differ greatly from each other. One can distinguish the following three groups of church functions: the functions of constitution, related to the foundation of the churches in the Spiritual Community; the functions of expansion, related to the universal claim of the Spiritual Community; the functions of construction, related to the actualization of the Spiritual potentialities of the churches.

At this point a more general question arises—the question of the sense in which a doctrine of the churches and their functions is a subject matter of systematic theology and the sense in which it is a subject matter of practical theology. Of course, the first answer is that the boundary is not sharp. Nevertheless, one can distinguish between the theological principles governing the functions of the churches as churches and the practical tools and methods most adequate for their exercise. The task of systematic theology is to analyze the first; the task of practical theology is to suggest the second. (Of course, this distinction does not imply a division in the thinking of the systematic and the practical theologian; both think about both sets of problems, but each is committed to one of them in his work.) The following analyses of a systematic character will often overlap with descriptions of a practical character, as has already happened in the previous chapters.

The first statement to be made about the logical principles governing the churches' functions as churches is that they all participate in the paradox of the churches. They are all performed in the name of the Spiritual Community; yet they are also performed by sociological groups and their representatives. They are involved in the ambiguities of life—above all, of religious life—and their aim is to conquer these ambiguities through the power of the Spiritual Presence.

One can distinguish three polarities of principles which correspond to the three groups of functions. The functions of constitution stand under the polarity of tradition and reformation, the functions of expansion under the polarity of verity and adaptation, the functions of construction under the polarity of form-transcendence and form-affirmation. The ambiguities fought by the Spiritual Presence are also indicated in these polarities. The danger of tradition is demonic *hubris*; the danger of reformation is emptying criticism. The danger of verity is demonic absolutism; the danger of adaptation is emptying relativization. The danger of form-transcendence is demonic repression; the danger of form-affirmation is formalistic emptiness. In connection with a description of the respective functions, concrete examples of these polarities and of the dangers implied in them will be discussed; at this point only a few general remarks about each are necessary.

The principle of tradition in the churches is not a mere recognition of the sociological fact that the cultural forms of every new generation grow out of those produced by the preceding generations. This, of course, is also valid for the churches. But beyond this the principle of tradition in the church stems from the fact that the nature of the churches and the character of their life are determined by their function in the New Being as it has appeared in Jesus as the Christ and that the tradition is the link between this foundation and every new generation. This is not necessarily the case with national groups or cultural movements, whose beginnings may be rather irrelevant for their development. But the Spiritual Community is effective through every function of the church, and, therefore, all generations are ideally present—not only the generations who experienced the central manifestation, but also those who expected it. In this sense tradition is not particular, although it includes all particular traditions; it expresses the unity of historical mankind, of which the appearance of the Christ is the center.

The Greek Orthodox church considers itself as the church of the living tradition in contrast to the legally defined and papally determined tradition of the Roman church. The criticism which the Reformation leveled against many elements of both traditions, but especially the Roman, has made the concept itself suspect for Protestant feeling. Yet tradition is an element in the life of all churches. Even the Protestant criticism was possible only with the help of particular elements in the Roman Catholic tradition; the Bible, Augustine, the German mystics, the humanistic underground, and so on. It is a general characteristic of prophetic criticism of a religious tradition that it does not come from outside but from the center of the tradition itself, fighting its distortions in the name of its true meaning. There is no reformation without tradition.

The word "reformation" has two connotations: it points to a unique event in church history, the Protestant Reformation of the sixteenth century; and it points to a permanent principle, active in all periods, which is implied in the Spirit's fight against the ambiguities of religion. The historical Reformation occurred because the Roman church had successfully suppressed this principle at a moment when the prophetic Spirit called for a reformation of the church in "head and members." Obviously, there is no objective criterion for a movement of reformation; not even the Bible is such a criterion, since the Bible must be interpreted. There is, instead, the risk which is rooted in the awareness of the Spiritual freedom, and it is the prophetic Spirit which creates the courage for such a risk. Prostentantism takes this risk—even if it may mean the disintegration of particular churches. It takes the risk in the certainty that the Spiritual Community, the dynamic essence of a church, cannot be destroyed.

The polarity of tradition and reformation leads to a struggle of the Spiritual Presence with the ambiguities of religion. The principle of reformation is the corrective against the demonic suppression of the freedom of the Spirit by a tradition which is vested with absolute validity, in practice or by law; and since all churches have a tradition, this demonic temptation is actual and successful in all of them. Its success is caused by the taboo-producing anxiety about any deviation from that which is holy and has been proven to have saving power. The anticipation that, under the principle of reformation, the churches will fall into a profanizing criticism is implied in this anxiety. Schleiermacher's often quoted words, "The reformation goes on," are certainly true; but they raise the anxious question: What is the limit beyond which critical disintegration begins? This question gives the guardians of an absolutized tradition their power to suppress the desire for reform and to coerce the consciences of those who know better but do not have the courage to risk a new road. The two principles are united in the Spiritual Community. They are in tension but not in conflict. To the degree in which the dynamics of the Spiritual Community is effective in a church, the conflict is transformed into a living tension.

The second polarity of principles is essentially related to the functions of expansion in the life of the churches. It is the polarity of verity and adaptation. The problem is as old as the words of Paul in which he refers to his being a Jew to the Jews and a Greek to the Greeks while rejecting everyone who, against the truth of his message, tries to retransform the New Being (the "New Creation," as he calls it) into the old being of the Jewish law or of Greek wisdom. The existential conflict between verity and adaptation, as well as the fight of the Spiritual Presence to overcome it, is classically expressed in his sentences.

In the early church small groups demanded the subjection of the churches to the Jewish law, and the large majority, including most of the great theologians, demanded adaptation to the forms of thought which had been developed by classical Greek and Hellenistic philosophy. At the same time the masses accommodated themselves, under the permissive supervision of the church authorities, to the polytheistic trends in religion, whether in the veneration of images (icons) or in the invasion of the devotional life by a host of saints, especially the Holy Virgin. Without these adaptations the missionary work of the early church would have been impossible; but in the process of adaptation the content of the Christian message was in continual danger of being surrendered for the sake of accommodation. This danger of forsaking the pole of verity for the pole of adaptation was so real that most of the great struggles in the first millennium of the Christian churches can be seen in light of this conflict.

In the Middle Ages the adaptation of the Germanic-Romanic tribes to the feudal order was both a missionary and an educational necessity and was accompanied by a continual surrender of verity to accommodation. The struggle between emperor and pope must be understood partly as the reaction of the church against the feudal identification of the social with religious hierarchies; and the reaction of the personal piety of the late Middle Ages, including the Reformation, can be understood as resistance against the transformation of the church into the all-embracing feudal authority itself. Of course, none of these movements for verity as against accommodation escaped the necessity of adaptation themselves. In spite of the break between Luther and Erasmus, the humanist spirit entered Protestantism through Melanchthon, Zwingli, and in part, Calvin. In the following centuries the struggle between verity and adaptation continued with undiminished force and it is one of the most actual problems even today. These struggles, of course, are not restricted to missionary expansion toward foreign religions and cultures but refer even more immediately to expansion in the civilizations shaped by the Christian tradition. Both the change in the general cultural climate since the sixteenth century and the necessity of inducting new generations into the churches raise the inescapable problem that is involved in the polarity of verity and adaptation.

The danger of the pronouncement of verity without adaptation, as indicated above, is a demonic absolutism which throws the truth like stones at the heads of people, not caring whether they can accept it or not. It is what may be called the demonic offense the churches often give while claiming that they give the necessary divine offense. Without adaptation to the categories of understanding in those toward whom the expanding functions of the church are directed, the church not only does not expand but even loses what it has, because its members also live within the given civilization and can receive the verity of the message of the New Being only within the categories of that civilization.

If, on the other hand, the adaptation becomes an unlimited accommodation as in many periods of the history of the churches, the message's verity is lost, and a relativism takes hold of the church which leads to secularism, first merely empty and without ecstasy, but later open to a demonically distorted ecstasy. Missionary accommodation which surrenders the principle of verity does not conquer the demonic powers, whether they are religious or profane.

The third polarity of principles, related to the functions of construction, is that of form-transcendence and form-affirmation. The functions of construction use the different spheres of cultural creation in order to express the Spiritual Community in the life of the churches. This refers to *theoria* and *praxis* and, within them, to the aesthetic and the cognitive, the personal and the communal, spheres of life under the dimension of spirit. From all of them the churches take material, i.e., styles, methods, norms, and relations, but in a way which both affirms and transcends the cultural forms. If the churches engage in aesthetic or cognitive, personal or communal, construction, they do it as churches only if the relation of the Spiritual Presence is manifest in their works, and this means if there is an ecstatic, form-transcending quality in them. The churches do not act as churches when they act as a political party or a law court, as a school or a philosophical movement, as patrons of artistic production or of psychotherapeutic healing. The church shows its presence as church only if the Spirit breaks into the finite forms and drives them beyond themselves. It is this form-transcending, Spiritual quality that characterizes the functions of construction in the church: the functions of aesthetic self-expression, of cognitive self-interpretation, of personal self-realization, of social and political self-organization. It is not the subject matter as such which makes them functions of the church but their form-transcending, ecstatic character.

At the same time, the principle of form-affirmation must be observed. In every function of the church the essential form of the cultural realm must be used without a violation of its structural demands. This is implied in the earlier discussion of structure and ecstasy. In spite of the form-transcending character of religious art aesthetic rules must be obeyed; in spite of the form-transcending character of religious knowledge the cognitive rules must not be broken. The same is valid with respect to personal and social ethics, politics, and education. Some important problems arising out of this situation will be discussed later; at this point we must again refer to the two dangers between which the functions of construction in the life of the churches move. If the principle of form-transcendence is effective in separation from the principle of form-affirmation, the churches become demonic-repressive. They are driven to repress in everyone and every group that conscience of form which demands honest submission to the structural necessities of cultural creation. For example, they violate artistic integrity in the name of a sacred (or politically expedient) style; or they undercut the scientific honesty which leads to radical questions about nature, man, and history; or they destroy personal humanity in the name of a demonically distorted fanatical faith, and so forth.

At the other pole, there is the danger of profanization of the Spiritual creations and the emptiness which invites demonic invasions. A form which is too rigid to be transcended becomes by degrees more and more meaningless—though not wrong. It is first felt as a protection from transcendent interference, then as autonomous creativity, then as the embodiment of formal correctness, and last as empty formalism.

Where the Spiritual Presence is powerful in the churches the two principles, form-transcendence and form-affirmation, are united.

(2) THE CONSTITUTIVE FUNCTIONS OF THE CHURCHES.—Systematic theology has to deal with the functions of the church because they are part of its nature and add special elements to its characterization. If the functions of the church are of its very nature, they must always be present where there is a church; however, they can appear in different degrees of conscious care, intensity, and adequacy. Their exercise may be suppressed from outside, or they may coalesce with other functions, but they are always present as an element in the church's nature, pushing toward actualization.

However, they are not always organizationally present; functions and institutions are not necessarily interdependent. The institutions are dependent on the functions they serve, but the functions may exist even where no institutions serve them, and this is often the case. Most institutional developments have a spontaneous beginning. The nature of the church requires that a particular function make itself felt in Spiritual experiences and consequent actions, which finally lead to an institutional form. If an institution becomes obsolete, other ways of exercising the same function may grow up spontaneously and take shape in a new institutional form. This agrees with what we have said before about the freedom of the Spirit; it liberates the church from any kind of ritual legalism, in the power of the Spiritual Community. No institution, not even a priesthood or ministry, special sacraments or devotional services, follow necessarily from the nature of the church, but the functions for the sake of which these institutions have come into being do follow from it. They never are completely missing.

The first group of functions has been called the function of constitution. Since every church is dependent on the New Being as it is manifest in the Christ and real in the Spiritual Community, the constitutive function of a church is that of *receiving*. This applies to a church as a whole as well as to every individual member. If a church demands receptiveness of its members but itself as church refuses to receive, it becomes either a static hierarchical system, which claims to have received once and for all with no need ever to receive again, or it becomes a religious group with private experiences which make the transition into secularism. The function of reception includes the simultaneous function of mediation through the media of the Spiritual Presence, Word, and sacrament. He who receives mediates, and, on the other hand, he has received only because the process of mediation is going on continuously. In practice mediation and reception are the same: the church is priest and prophet to itself. He who preaches preaches to himself as listener, and he who listens is a potential preacher. The identity of reception and mediation excludes the possibility of the establishment of a hierarchical group which mediates while all the others merely receive.

The act of mediation occurs partly in communal services, partly in encounters between the priest who mediates and the laity who respond. But this division is never complete; whoever mediates must himself respond, and whoever responds mediates to his mediator. The "counselor," as the agent of the function of "taking care of souls" (*Seelsorge*) is in present terminology called, should never be subject only; he should never make of his counselee an object to be handled correctly and perhaps helped by an adequate treatment. If this happens, as it very often does in pastoral as well as in medical counseling, an ambiguity of religion has invaded the Spiritual function of mediation. But if the mediation is determined by the Spiritual Presence, the counselor subjects himself to the judgments and demands that he tries to communicate. He recognizes the truth that he is basically in the same predicament as the counselee.

And this may give him the possibility of finding the word of healing for him. He who is grasped by the Spirit can speak to one who needs his help in such a way that the Spirit can get hold of the other one through him, and thus help becomes possible. For Spirit can heal only what is open to Spirit.

The relation of pastoral counseling to psychotherapeutic help will be discussed later. Where there is reception and mediation, there is also response. The response is the affirmation of that which is received—the confession of faith—and the turning to the source from which it is received, i.e., worship. The term "confession of faith" has been misinterpreted by being identified with the acceptance of creedal statements and their repetition in ritual acts, but the function of responding and accepting accompanies all other functions of the church. It can be expressed in prose and in poetry, in symbols and in hymns. It can also be concentrated in creedal formulations and then elaborated by theological conceptualization. A church is not quite consistent when it avoids a statement of faith in terms of a creed and at the same time is unable to avoid expressing the content of its creed in every one of its liturgical and practical acts.

The other side of the function of response is worship; in it the church turns to the ultimate ground of its being, the source of the Spiritual Presence and the creator of the Spiritual Community, to God who is Spirit. Whenever He is reached in communal or personal experiences, Spiritual Presence has grasped those who experience Him. For only Spirit can experience Spirit, as only Spirit can discern Spirit.

Worship as the responding elevation of the church to the ultimate ground of its being includes adoration, prayer, and contemplation.

The adoration of a church, vocal in praise and thanksgiving, is the ecstatic acknowledgment of the divine holiness and the infinite distance of Him who at the same time is present in the Spiritual Presence. This acknowledgment is not a theoretical assertion but rather a paradoxical participation of the finite and estranged in the infinite to which it belongs. When a church praises the majesty of God for the sake of his glory, two elements are united: the complete contrast between the creaturely smallness of man and the infinite greatness of the creator, and the elevation into the sphere of the divine glory, so that the praise of His glory is at the same time a fragmentary participation in it. The unity of these elements is paradoxical and cannot be disrupted without producing a demonic image of God, on the one hand, and of miserable man, without genuine dignity, on the other. Such distortion of the meaning of adoration leads to the ambiguities of religion and is resisted by the Spiritual Presence, which, as Presence, includes the participation of him who adores in Him who is adored. Adoration in this sense is not the humiliation of man, but it would lose its meaning if it intended anything but the praise of God. Adoration performed for the sake of man's self-glorification is self-defeating. It never reaches God.

The second element in worship is prayer. The basic interpretation of prayer has been given in the section on God's directing creativity.[1] The central idea there was that every serious prayer produces something new in terms of creaturely freedom which is taken into consideration in the whole of God's directing creativity, as is every act of man's centered self. This newness, created by the prayer of supplication, is the Spiritual act of elevating the content of one's wishes and hopes into the Spiritual Presence. A prayer in which this happens is "heard," even if subsequent events contradict the manifest content of the prayer. The same is true of prayers of intercession which not only produce a new relation to those for whom the prayer is made but also introduce a change in the relation to the ultimate of the subjects and objects of intercession. It is therefore false to limit prayer to the prayer of thanks. This suggestion of the Ritschlian school is rooted in a profound anxiety about the magic distortion of prayer and its superstitious consequences for popular piety, but this anxiety is, systematically speaking, unfounded, although highly justified in practice. Thanksgiving to God is an expression of adoration and praise but not a formal acknowledgment which prejudices God to bestow further benefits upon those who are grateful. However, it would create a completely unrealistic relation to God if prayers of supplication were prohibited. In that case the expression of man's needs to God and the accusation of God by man for not answering (as in the Book of Job) and all the wrestling of the human spirit with the divine Spirit would be excluded from prayer. Certainly these comments are not the last word in the life of prayer, but the "last word" would be shallow and profanized, as innumerable prayers are, were the paradox of prayer to be forgotten by the churches and their members. Paul expresses the paradox of prayer classically when he speaks about the impossibility of the right prayer and about the divine

[1] *Systematic Theology*, I, 267.

Spirit's representing those who pray before God without an "objectifying" language (Romans 8:26). It is the Spirit which speaks to the Spirit, as it is the Spirit which discerns and experiences the Spirit. In all these cases the subject-object scheme of "talking to somebody" is transcended: He who speaks through us is he who is spoken to.

Spiritual prayer in this sense (and not a profanized conversation with another being called God) leads to the third element in the function of response—contemplation. Contemplation is the stepchild in Protestant worship. Only lately has the liturgical silence been introduced into some Protestant churches, and of course, there is no contemplation without silence. Contemplation means participation in that which transcends the subject-object scheme, with its objectifying (and subjectifying) words, and therefore the ambiguity of language as well (including the voiceless language of speaking to oneself). The Protestant churches' neglect of contemplation is rooted in their personal-centered interpretation of the Spiritual Presence. But Spirit transcends personality, if personality is identified with consciousness and moral self-integration. Spirit is ecstatic, and so are contemplation, prayer, and worship in general. The response to the impact of the Spirit must itself be Spiritual, and that means transcending in ecstasy the subject-object scheme of ordinary experience. This is most obvious in the act of contemplation, and one may demand that every serious prayer lead into an element of contemplation, because in contemplation the paradox of prayer is manifest, the identity and non-identity of him who prays and Him who is prayed to: God as Spirit.

The divine Spirit's presence in the experience of contemplation contradicts the idea we often find in medieval mysticism that contemplation must be reached by degrees, as in the movement from meditation to contemplation, and that it itself may be a bridge to mystical union. This gradualistic thinking belongs to the ambiguities of religion because it faces God as a besieged fortress to be surrendered to those who climb its walls. According the Protestant principle, God's surrender is the beginning; it is an act of his freedom by which he overcomes the estrangement between Himself and man in the one, unconditional, and complete act of forgiving grace. All the degrees of appropriation of grace are secondary, as growth is secondary to birth. Contemplation in the Protestant realm is not a degree but a quality, that is, a quality of a prayer which is aware that the prayer is directed to Him who creates the right prayer in us.

(3) THE EXPANDING FUNCTIONS OF THE CHURCHES.—The universality of the Spiritual Community demands the function of expansion of the churches. Since the universality of the Spiritual Community is implied in the confession of Jesus as the Christ, every church must participate in functions of expansion. The first function of expansion, historically and systematically, is missions. It is as old as the story of Jesus' sending the disciples to the towns of Israel, and it is as successful and unsuccessful as this first mission was. The majority of human beings is still—after two thousand years of missionary activity—non-Christian. Yet, there is no place on earth which is not somehow touched by Christian culture.

In spite of the fragmentary (and often ambiguous) character of the effects of missions, the function of expansion goes on during every moment in the church's existence. Whenever active members of the church encounter those outside the church, they are missionaries of the church, voluntarily or involuntarily. Their very being is missionary. The purpose of missions as an institutionalized function of the church is not to save individuals from eternal condemnation—as it was in some pietistic missions; nor is the purpose cross-fertilization of religions and cultures. The purpose of missions is rather the actualization of the Spiritual Community within concrete churches all over the world. One of the ambiguities of religion which endangers missions is the attempt of a religion to impose its own cultural forms upon another culture in the name of the New Being in the Christ. This necessarily leads to reactions which can destroy the whole effect of the expanding functions of the Christian churches. But it is hard for any church to separate the Christian message from the particular culture within which it is pronounced. In a sense it is impossible, because there is no abstract Christian message. It is always embodied in a particular culture. Even the most self-critical attempt of, for example, the Swiss or American missions to strip themselves of their cultural traditions would be a failure. Yet, if the Spiritual power is present in them, they would speak of that which concerns us ultimately through the traditional cultural categories. It is not a matter of formal analysis but of paradoxical transparence. Where there is Spiritual Presence, a missionary from any background can communicate the Spiritual Presence. (The world-historical meaning of missions will be discussed in the fifth part of the system, "History and the Kingdom of God.")

The second function of expansion is based on the desire of the churches to continue their life from generation to generation—the function of education. The problem of religious education has become one of the major issues in the contemporary churches. The many problems of the techniques of religious education do not concern us here, but the question of the meaning of the religious function of education has great importance for systematic theology. First of all, it must be emphasized that the educational function of the Christian church started the moment the first family was received in it, for this event put before the church the task of receiving the new generation into its communion. This task is a consequence of the self-interpretation of a church as the community of the New Being or the actualization of the Spiritual Community. The doubts of parents about the Christian education of their children reflect in part the difficulties of the educational process, in part the doubts of the parents themselves about the assertion that Jesus is the Christ. With respect to the first problem, educational theory can overcome psychological errors and lack of judgment. With respect to the second problem, only the Spiritual Presence can give the courage to affirm the Christian assertion and to communicate it to the new generation.

The educational function of the church does not consist in information about the history and the doctrinal self-expressions of the church. A confirmation-instruction which does merely that misses its purposes, although it may communicate useful knowledge. Neither does the educational function of the church consist in the awakening of a subjective piety, which may be called conversion but which usually disappears with its emotional causation. A religious education which tries to do this is not in line with the educational function of the church. The church's task is to introduce each new generation into the reality of the Spiritual Community, into its faith and into its love. This happens through participation in degrees of maturity, and it happens through interpretation in degrees of understanding. There is no understanding of a church's life without participation; but without understanding the participation becomes mechanical and compulsory.

The last of the functions of expansion is the evangelistic. It is directed toward the churches' estranged or indifferent members. It is missions toward the non-Christians within a Christian culture. Its two activities, which overlap but are distinguishable, are practical apologetics and evangelistic preaching. If the result of either is the desire for personal counseling, the function of mediation replaces that of expansion.

Practical apologetics is the practical application of the apologetic element in every theology. In the introductory part of the whole system we indicated that the type of theological thinking presented in this system is more apologetic than kerygmatic. As such it intends to give the theoretical foundation of practical apologetics. First of all, one must emphasize that practical apologetics is a continuous element in all expressions of the life of the church. The church, by reason of its paradoxical nature, is continually being asked questions about its nature which it must answer, and that is what apologetics means: the art of answering. Certainly, the most effective answer is the reality of the New Being in the Spiritual Community and in the life of the churches as far as they are determined by it. It is the silent witness of the community of faith and love which convinces the questioner who may be silenced but not convinced by even the most incontrovertible arguments. Nethertheless, arguments are needed, because they may serve to break through the intellectual walls of skepticism as well as of dogmatism with which the churches' critics protect themselves against the attacks of the Spiritual Presence. And since these walls are constantly being built in all of us and since they have separated masses of people on all levels of education from the churches, apologetics must be cultivated by the churches; otherwise they will not grow but will diminish in extension and increasingly become a small, ineffective section within a dynamic civilization. The psychological and sociological conditions of successful practical apologetics are dependent on many factors, to be valuated by practical theology, but the laying of the conceptual foundations on which practical apologetics is built is the task of systematic theology. Systematic theology must also stress its own limits as theoretical apologetics as well as the limits of even the most skillful apologetic practice. The acknowledgment of its own limits is itself an element in the apologetic function.

Evangelism by preaching, like apologetics, is directed toward people who have belonged or still belong to the realm of Christian civilization but who have ceased to be active members of the church or who have become indifferent or hostile toward it. Evangelism by preaching is more of a charismatic function than is apologetics; it is dependent on the emergence of people in the churches who are able to speak to the groups just characterized, in the name and power of the Spiritual Community but not in the way the churches do it, and who for this very reason have an impact on the listeners which ordinary preaching lacks. It would be unfair to say that this impact is "merely" psychological and predominantly emotional. The Spiritual Presence can use any psychological condition and every combination of factors to grasp the personal self, and it is an advantage of the metaphor "dimension" that it bridges the gap between the psychological and Spiritual (as well as the spiritual). However, it is not unfair, but true to the facts, to point out the dangers of evangelism as a religious phenomenon with the ambiguities of religion. The danger of evangelism against which the Spirit fights is the confusion of the subjective impact of evangelistic preaching with the Spiritual impact which transcends the contrast of subjectivity and objectivity. The criterion here is the creative character of the Spiritual Presence, that is, the creation of the New Being, which does not excite the subjectivity of the listener but transforms it. Mere excitement cannot create participation in the Spiritual Community even if it produces the different elements of conversion according to the traditional pattern. Repentance, faith, sanctity, and so on, are not what these words are taken to mean, and therefore their effect is only momentary and transitory. However, it would be wrong to reject evangelism, or even an individual evangelist, *in toto* because of these ambiguities. There must be evangelism, but it should not confuse excitement with ecstasy.

(4) THE CONSTRUCTING FUNCTIONS OF THE CHURCHES

(a) *The aesthetic function in the church.*—Those functions of the church are constructing functions in which it builds its life by using and transcending the functions of man's life under the dimension of the spirit. The church can never be without the functions of construction and, therefore, cannot forego the use of cultural creations in all basic directions. Those who indulge in contrasts of the divine Spirit with the human spirit in terms of exclusiveness cannot avoid contradicting themselves: in the very act of expressing this rejection of any contact between cultural creativity and Spiritual creativity, they use the whole apparatus of man's cognitive mind, even if they do it by quoting biblical passages, for the words used in the Bible are creations of man's cultural development. One can reject culture only by using it as the tool of such rejection. This is the inconsistency of what in recent discussions has been called "diastasis," i.e., the radical separation of the religious from the cultural sphere.

The churches are constructive in all those directions of man's cultural life which we have distinguished in the sections on the cultural self-creation of life. They are constructive in the realm of *theoria*, the aesthetic and the cognitive functions, and they are constructive in the realm of *praxis*, the personal and the communal functions. Later we shall discuss these functions in their immediate relation to the Spiritual Community; but at this point we must consider the problem of their part in the constructing functions of the churches. One question is central in all of them: How is the autonomous cultural form which makes them what they are related to their function as material for the self-construction of the churches? Does their functioning in the service of the ecclesiastical edifice distort the purity of their autonomous form? Must expressiveness, truth, humanity, and justice be bent in order to be built into the life of the churches? And if this demonic element in the ambiguities of religion is rejected, how can the human spirit be prevented from replacing the impact of the Spiritual Presence by self-creative acts of its own? How can the life of the churches be prevented from falling under the sway of the profane element in the ambiguities of religion? Instead of a general answer, we shall try to answer by dealing directly with each of the functions of construction and their particular problems.

The aesthetic realm is used by the church for the sake of the religious arts. In them the church expresses the meaning of its life in artistic symbols. The content of the artistic symbols (poetic, musical, visual) is the religious symbols given by the original revelatory experiences and by the traditions based on them. The fact that artistic symbols try to express in ever changing styles the given religious symbols produces the phenomenon of "double symbolization," an example of which is the symbol of "the Christ crucified" expressed in the artistic symbols of the Nordic Renaissance painter Matthias Grünewald—one of the rare pictures which is both Protestant in spirit *and* at the same time great art. We point to it as an example of double symbolization, but it is also an example of something else, i.e., the power of artistic expression to help transform what it expresses. The "Crucifixion" by Grünewald not only expresses the experience of the pre-Reformation groups to which he belonged, but has helped to spread the spirit of the Reformation and to create an image of the Christ radically opposite to that of Eastern mosaics, in which as an infant in Mary's lap he is already the ruler of the universe. It is understandable that such a picture as that of Grüne-wald would be censured by the authorities of the Eastern church, the church of the resurrection and not of the crucifixion. The churches knew that aesthetic expressiveness is more than a beautifying addition to devotional life. They knew that expression gives life to what is expressed—it gives power to stabilize and power to transform—and therefore they tried to influence and control those who produced religious art. This was carried through most strictly by the Eastern churches, but it is also practiced in the Roman church, especially in music, and even in the Protestant churches, particularly in hymnic poetry. Expression *does* something to what it expresses: this is the significance of religious art as a constructing function of the churches.

The problem implied in this situation is the possible conflict between the justified request of the churches that the religious art they accept express what they confess and the justified demands of the artists that they be permitted to use the styles to which their artistic conscience drives them. These two demands can be understood as two principles which control religious art, the principle of consecration and the principle of honesty. The first one is the power of expressing the holy in the concreteness of a special religous tradition (including its possibilities of reformation). The principle of consecration in this sense is an application of the larger principle of form-transcendence (as discussed before) to the sphere of religious art. It includes the use of religious symbols which characterize the particular religious tradition (for example, the Christ picture or the passion story) and stylistic qualities which distinguish the works of religious art from the artistic expression of the non-religious encounters with reality. The Spiritual Presence makes itself felt in the architectural space, the liturgical music and language, the pictorial and sculptural representations, the solemn character of the gestures of all participants, and so on. It is the task of aesthetic theory in co-operation with psychology to analyze the stylistic character of consecration. Whatever the general artistic style of a period may be, there are always some qualities which distinguish the sacred from the secular use of the style.

There is, however, a limit to the demands made on the artists in the name of the principle of consecration, and that limit is the demands of the principle of honesty. This principle is the application of the general principle of form-affirmation, as discussed before, to religious art. It is especially important in a period in which new artistic styles appear and the cultural consciousness is split in the fight between contradictory self-expressions. The principle of honesty is severely endangered in such situations, which have occurred frequently in the history of Western civilization. Consecrated forms of artistic expression claim absolute validity because they have impregnated the memory of ecstatic-devotional experiences, and they are defended against new stylistic developments in the name of the Spiritual Presence. Such claims drive artists into a deep moral conflict and church members into decisions which are religiously painful. Both feel, at least in some unconscious deeps, that the old stylistic forms, however consecrated they may be, no longer fulfil the function of expressiveness. They cease to express what happens in the religious encounter of those who are grasped by the Spiritual Presence in their concrete situation. But the new stylistic forms have not yet found qualities of consecration. In such a situation the demand of honesty on the artists may force them to refrain from trying to express the traditional symbols at all or, if they do try it, to acknowledge failure. On the other hand, the demand of honesty on those who receive the works of art is that they confess their uneasiness with the older stylistic forms, even if they are not yet able to estimate the new ones—perhaps just because there are not yet convincing forms with the quality of consecration. But both artists and non-artists are under the strict demand implied in the principle of honesty—not to admit imitations of styles which once had great consecrative possibilities but which have lost their religious expressiveness for an actual situation. The most famous—or infamous—example is the pseudo-Gothic imitation in church architecture.

Still another problem besetting the relation of the two principles of religious art must be mentioned: artistic styles may appear which by their very nature exclude consecrated forms and therefore have to be excluded from the sphere of religious art. One thinks of some types of naturalism or of the contemporary non-objective style. By their very nature both are excluded from the use of many traditional religious symbols: the non-objective style, because it excludes the organic figure and the human face; and naturalism, because in describing its objects it tries to exclude the self-transcendence of life. One could say that only styles which can express the ecstatic character of the Spiritual Presence lend themselves to religious art, and this would mean that some expressionistic element has to be present in a style in order to make it a tool for religious art. This is certainly correct, but it does not exclude any particular style, because in each of them elements are present which are expressionistic, pointing to the self-transcendence of life. The idealistic styles can become vehicles of religious ecstasy because none of them completely excludes the expressionistic element. But history shows that those styles in which the expressionistic quality is predominant lend themselves most readily to an artistic expression of the Spiritual Presence. They are best able to express the ecstatic quality of the Spirit. This is the reason why, in periods in which these styles were lost, great religious art did not appear. Most of the last considerations are derived from an interpretation of the visual arts, but with certain qualifications, they are valid also for the other arts.

If we look at the history of Protestantism, we find that it has continued and often surpassed the achievement of the early and medieval churches with respect to religious music and hymnical poetry but that it has fallen very short of their creative power in all the visual arts, including those in which hearing and seeing are equally important, as in religious dance and in religious play. This is related to the turn in the later Middle Ages from the emphasis on the eye to the emphasis on the ear. With the reduction of the sacraments in number and importance and the strengthening of the active participation of the congregation in the church services, music and poetry gained in importance, and the iconoclastic movements in early Protestantism and evangelical radicalism went so far as to condemn the use of the visual arts in the churches altogether. The background of this rejection of the arts of the eye is the fear—and even horror—of a relapse into idolatry. From early biblical times up to the present day, a stream of iconoclastic fear and passion runs through the Western and Islamic world, and there can be no doubt that the arts of the eye are more open to idolatrous demonization than the arts of the ear. But the difference is relative, and the very nature of the Spirit stands against the exclusion of the eye from the experience of its presence. According to the multidimensional unity of life, the dimension of spirit includes all other dimensions—everything visible in the whole of the universe. The spirit reaches into the physical and biological realm by the very fact that its basis is the dimension of self-awareness. Therefore, it cannot be expressed in spoken words only. It has a visible side, as is manifest in the face of man, which expresses bodily structure and personal spirit. This experience of our daily life is the premonition of the sacramental unity of matter and Spirit. One should remember that it was a mystic (Ötinger) who formulated all this when he said that "corporality (becoming body) is the end of the ways of God." The lack of the arts of the eye in the context of Protestant life is, though historically understandable, systematically untenable and practically regrettable.

When we pointed to the historical fact that the styles with a predominantly expressionistic element lend themselves best to religious art, we raised the question of the circumstances under which such a style can appear. The negative answer was completely clear: Religion cannot force any style upon the autonomous development of the arts. This would contradict the principle of artistic honesty. A new style appears in the course of the self-creation of life under the dimension of spirit. A style is created by the autonomous act of the individual artist and, at the same time, by historical destiny. But religion can influence historical destiny and autonomous creativity indirectly, and it does so whenever the impact of the Spiritual Presence on a culture creates cultural theonomy.

(*b*) *The cognitive function in the church.*—The cognitive realm appears in the churches as theology. In it the churches interpret their symbols and relate them to the general categories of knowledge. The subject matter of theology, like that of the religious arts, is the symbols given by the original revelatory experiences and by the traditions based on them. Yet, whereas the arts express the religious symbols in artistic symbols, theology expresses them in concepts which are determined by the criteria of rationality. In this way the doctrine and legally established dogmas of the churches arise and give impulse to further theological conceptualization.

The first thing to be said about the theological function of the churches is that, like the aesthetic function, it is never lacking. The statement that Jesus is the Christ contains in some way the whole theological system, as the telling of a parable of Jesus contains all artistic potentialities of Christianity.

It is not necessary at this point to deal with theology as such. That has been done in the introductory part of the system. But in light of the previous sections of this part of the system, a few remarks may be desirable: like all functions of the church, theology stands under the principles of form-transcendence and form-affirmation. In the aesthetic realm these principles appear as consecration and honesty. In an analogous way, one can speak, concerning the cognitive function, of the meditative and the discursive elements in theology. The meditative act penetrates the substance of the religious symbols; the discursive act analyzes and describes the form in which the substance can be grasped. In the meditative act (which can, in some moments, become contemplation) the cognitive subject and its object, the mystery of the holy, are united. Without such union the theological endeavor remains an analysis of structures without substance; on the other hand, meditation (including contemplative moments) without analysis of its contents and without their constructive synthesis cannot produce a theology. This is the limitation of "mystical theology." It can become theology only to the degree that it exercises the discursive function of cognition.

The meditative element in theological work is directed toward the concrete symbols originating in the revelatory experience from which they have arisen. Since theology is a function of the church, the church is justified in presenting to the theologian the concrete objects of its meditation and contemplation and in rejecting a theology in which these symbols are rejected or have lost their meaning. On the other hand, the discursive element of cognition is infinitely open in all directions and cannot be bound to a particular set of symbols. This situation seems to exclude theology altogether, and the history of the church shows a continuous series of antitheological movements, supported from both sides—by those who reject theology because its discursive element seems to destroy the concrete substance of the church embodied in its symbols, and by those who reject it because the meditative element seems to restrict the discourse to preconceived objects and solutions. If these assumptions were justified, no theology would be possible. But, certainly, theology is real and must have ways of overcoming the alternative of meditation and discourse.

The question is whether there are forms of the conceptual encounter with reality in which the meditative element is predominant and effective without suppressing the discursive strictness of thought. Is there an analogy to the relation of consecration and honesty in the relation of meditation and discourse? The answer is affirmative, because discursive thought does not exclude a theological sector within itself if the theological sector does not claim control over the other sectors. But one could ask whether there are not forms of discursive thinking which would make the theological sector not only relatively but absolutely impossible. Materialism, for example, has been called such a form of discursive thought. It has been asserted that a materialist cannot be a theologian. But such a view is rather superficial: first of all, materialism is not a position which is dependent merely on discourse; it is also dependent on meditation and has a theological element within itself. This is true of all philosophical positions; they are not only scientific hypotheses but also have a meditative element hidden under their philosophical arguments. This means that theology is always possible on the basis of any philosophical tradition. Nevertheless, there are differences in the conceptual material it uses. If the meditative element is strong in a philosophy, it can be compared with the artistic styles in which the expressionistic element is strong. Of such philosophies, we say today that they are existentialist or have important existentialist elements within their structures. The term "existentialist" in this connection designates philosophies in which the question of human existence in time and space and of man's predicament in unity with the predicament of everything existing is asked and answered in symbols or their conceptual transformation. In this sense, strong existentialist elements are present in Heraclitus, Socrates, Plato, the Stoics, and Neoplatonists. Such philosophers as Anaxagoras, Democritus, Aristotle, and the Epicureans are predominantly essentialist, dealing more with the structure of reality than with the predicament of existing. In the same way one can distinguish in modern times such men as Cusanus, Pico, Bruno, Boehme, Pascal, Schelling, Schopenhauer, Nietzsche, and Heidegger as predominantly existentialist and Galileo, Bacon, Descartes, Leibnitz, Locke, Hume, Kant, and Hegel as predominantly essentialist. These enumerations show that it is always a matter of emphasis and not of exclusiveness.

The division of "styles" of thought is analogous to the division of artistic styles. In both cases we have on one side the idealistic-naturalistic polarity, on the other side the expressionistic or existentialistic emphasis. In view of the ecstatic character of the Spiritual Presence, the churches can use for their own cognitive self-expression the systems of thought in which the existentialist emphasis is strong (note, for example, the significance of Heraclitus, Plato, the Stoics, and Plotinus in the early church and the necessity for Aquinas to introduce heterogenous existentialist elements into Aristotle). But as in the case of artistic styles, the churches cannot force a style of thought upon the philosophers. It is a matter of autonomous creativity and historical destiny whether or not the existentialist element which is present in all philosophy breaks into the open. However, the church does not need to wait for such an event. It cannot work without the essentialist descriptions of reality, and it is able to discover the existentialist presuppositions behind them and to use them in acceptance and rejection, in naturalism as well as in idealism; theology need be afraid of neither of them.

The latter considerations, like the corresponding ones in the section on religious art, are transitions to the "theology of culture," which we will discuss later.

(c) *The communal functions in the church*.—The problem of all constructing functions of the church is the relation of their autonomous cultural form to their function as material for the life of the churches. We have carried this through with respect to the aesthetic and cognitive functions of *theoria*. We must now discuss it with respect to the functions of *praxis*: the interdependent growth of community and personality. We must ask the question: Does their functioning in the service of the churches distort their autonomous forms? In relation to *theoria* this involved the question whether expressiveness and truth can preserve their honesty and their discursive strictness if they are used for consecration and meditation. In relation to *praxis* it raises the question whether community can maintain justice and whether personality can maintain humanity if they are used for the self-construction of the churches. Concretely, the problem is whether justice can be preserved if it is used for the realization of communal holiness and whether humanity can be preserved if it is used for the realization of personal saintliness. If the constructive functions of the church, in the power of the Spiritual Presence, conquer the ambiguities of religion (though only fragmentarily), they must be able to create a communal holiness which is united with justice and a personal saintliness which is united with humanity.

The communal holiness in the churches is an expression of the Holy Community, which is their dynamic essence. The churches express, and at the same time distort, communal holiness, and the Spiritual Presence fights against the ambiguities following from this situation. Communal holiness (an abbreviation for the attempt to actualize the Holy Community in a historical group) contradicts the principle of justice whenever a church commits or permits injustice in the name of holiness. Within Christian civilization this usually does not happen in the same way as it happened in many pagan religions, where, for instance, the sacramental superiority of the king or high priest gave him a position in which the principle of justice was largely suspended. The wrath of the Old Testament prophets was directed against this attitude. But even within Christianity the problem is actual, for every system of religious hierarchies is conducive to social injustice. Even if there are no formal hierarchies there are degrees of importance in the church, and the higher degress are socially and economically dependent on and interrelated to the higher degrees in the social group. This is one of the reasons why in most cases the churches have supported the "powers that be," including their injustices against the lower classes. (Another reason is the conservative trend which we have described as "tradition against reformation.") The alliance of the ecclesiastical hierarchies with the feudal hierarchies of medieval society is an example of this "injustice of holiness"; the dependence of the parish minister on representatives of the economically and socially influential classes in his parish is another example. One could say that such holiness is not holiness at all, but this is an oversimplification, because the concept of holiness cannot be reduced to that of justice. Unjust representatives of the church may still represent the religious self-transcendence to which the churches, by their very existence, point; but, certainly, this is a distorted representation which leads finally to a repudiation of the churches, not only by those who suffer under their injustice, but also by those who suffer because they see holiness (which they do not deny) and injustice united.

The description of the ambiguities of communal life, as given above, yielded four ambiguities: first, the ambiguity of inclusiveness; second, the ambiguity of equality; third, the ambiguity of leadership; fourth, the ambiguity of the legal form. The question now is: In what sense are they overcome in the community which claims participation in the Holy Community and derived holiness for itself? The ambiguity of inclusiveness is overcome in so far as the church claims to be all-inclusive beyond any social, racial, or national limitations. This claim is unconditional, but its fulfilment is conditioned and a continuous symptom of man's estrangement from his true being (note, for example, the racial and social problems within the churches). Then there is a special form of the ambiguity of inclusiveness in the churches, and that is the exclusion of those who confess another faith. The reason for it is obvious: every church considers itself a community of faith under a set of symbols, and it excludes competing symbols. Without this exclusion it could not exist. But this exclusion makes it guilty of idolatrous adherence to its own historically conditioned symbols. Therefore, whenever the Spiritual Presence makes itself felt, the self-criticism of the churches in the name of their own symbols starts. This is possible because in every authentic religious symbol there is an element that judges the symbol and those who use it. The symbol is not simply rejected but criticized, and by this criticism it is changed. In criticizing its own symbols the church expresses its dependence on the Spiritual Community, its fragmentary character, and the continuous threat of falling into the ambiguities of religion which it is supposed to fight.

The element of equality which belongs to justice is acknowledged by the churches as the equality of everyone before God. This transcendent equality does not entail the demand for social and political equality. The only attempts to actualize social and political equality do not originate in Christianity (except in some radical sects) but in ancient and modern Stoicism. Yet the equality before God should create a desire for the equality of those who approach God, i.e., for equality in the life of the church. It is important to know that as early as the New Testament, specifically in the letter of James, the problem of equality in the devotional services was discussed and the preservation of social inequality in the church services was denounced. One of the worst consequences of the neglect of the principle of equality within the churches is the treatment of "public sinners," not only in the Middle Ages but also today. The churches rarely followed the attitude of Jesus toward the "publicans and the whores." They were and are ashamed of the way in which Jesus acted in acknowledging the equality of all men under sin (which they confess) and therefore the equality of all men under forgiveness (which they confess). The establishment of the principle of inequality between socially condemned sinners and socially acknowledged righteous ones is one of the most conspicuous and most anti-Christian denials of the principle of equality. In opposition to this attitude of many groups and individuals in the churches, the fact that secular psychology of the unconscious has rediscovered the reality of the demonic in everyone must be interpreted as an impact of the Spiritual Presence. In doing so it has, at least negatively, re-established the principle of equality as an element of justice. If the churches do not feel the call to conversion in this development, they will become obsolete, and the divine Spirit will work in and through seemingly atheistic and anti-Christian movements.

The ambiguity of leadership is closely connected with the ambiguities of inclusiveness and of equality, for it is the leading groups that exclude and produce inequality, even in the relation to God. Leadership and its ambiguities belong to the life of every historical group. The history of tyranny (which embraces the largest part of the history of mankind) is not a history of bad historical accidents but rather of one of the great and inescapable ambiguities of life, from which religion is not exempt. Religious leadership has the same profane and demonic possibilities as every other leadership. The continuous attack of the prophets and apostles on the religious leaders of their time did not injure the church but saved it. And so it is today. The fact that the Roman church does not acknowledge the ambiguity of its own papal leadership saves it from the obvious ambiguities of leadership but gives it a demonic quality. The Protestant weakness of continuous self-criticism is its greatness and a symptom of the Spiritual impact upon it.

The ambiguity of the legal form is as unavoidable as the ambiguity of leadership, equality, and inclusiveness. Nothing in human history has reality without a legal form, as nothing in nature has reality without a natural form, but the legal form of the churches is not a matter of an unconditional command. The Spirit does not give constitutional rules, but it guides the churches toward a Spiritual use of sociologically adequate offices and institutions. It fights against the ambiguities of power and prestige which are effective in the daily life of the smallest village congregation as well as in the encounter of the large denominations. No church office, not even those which existed in the apostolic churches, is a result of a direct command by the divine Spirit. But the church is, and its functions are, because they belong to its nature. The institution and offices serving the church in these functions are matters of sociological adequacy, practical expediency, and human wisdom. However, it is right to ask the question whether differences in constitution are not of indirect Spiritual significance since interpretations of the relation of God and man are involved in the form of leadership (monarchic, aristocratic, democratic). This would make the problems of constitution indirectly theological, and it would explain the struggles and divisions of the churches about constitutional forms. Considering the problem of constitution both theologically and sociologically, one can first point to the ultimate theological principles implied in the differences of constitutions, for example, the Protestant principle of the "fallibility" of all religious institutions and the consequent protest against the infallible place in history, the *cathedra papalis*, or the Protestant principle of the "priesthood of all believers" and the consequent protest against a priesthood which is separated from the laymen and which represents a sacred degree in a divine-human hierarchical structure. Such principles are matters of ultimate concern. The essential functions of the church, and therefore certain organizational provisions for their execution, are not of ultimate but of necessary concern. But which methods shall be preferred is a question of expediency under the criterion of the ultimate theological principles.

The ambiguities connected with the legal organization of the churches have produced a widespread resentment against "organized religion." Of course, the term itself formulates a prejudice, for it is not religion that is organized but a community that is centered around a set of religious symbols and traditions, and some organization in such a community is sociologically inescapable. Sectarian groups in their first, revolutionary stage have tried to escape any given organization and to live in anarchy. But the sociological necessities would not let them out of their grip; almost immediately after their separation, they started to build up new legal forms, which often became stricter and more oppressive than those of the large churches. And in some important cases such groups themselves became large churches with all their constitutional problems.

The aversion to organized religion goes even farther: it wants to eliminate the communal element from religion. But this is self-deception. Since man can become person only in the person-to-person encounter and since the language of religion—even if it is silent language—is dependent on the community, "subjective religiosity" is a reflex of the communal tradition, and it evaporates if it is not continuously nourished by life in the community of faith and love. There is no such thing as "private religion"; but there is the personal response to the religious community, and this personal response may have creative, revolutionary, and even destructive impact on the community. The prophet goes into the desert in order to return; and the hermit lives from what he has taken from the tradition of the community, and often a new desert community develops, as in the early period of Christian monasticism.

The confrontation of private and organized religion would be mere foolishness if there were not a deeper, though poorly expressed, motive behind it. i.e., the *religious* criticism of every form of religion, whether it is public or private. It is right to feel that religion in the narrower sense is an expression of man's estrangement from his essential unity with God. Taken in this sense, it is only another way of speaking of the profound ambiguity of religion, and it must be understood as a complaint that the eschatological reunion has not yet arrived. This complaint is made in the hearts of religious individuals as well as in the communities' self-expressions. But this is something more embracing and more significant than the criticism of organized religion.

(*d*) *The personal functions in the church.*—We have referred to hermits and monks as people who try to escape the ambiguities which are implied in the sociological character of every religious community. This, of course, is possible only within the limits drawn by the fact that they participate in, or themselves produce, a religious community with sociological characteristics. At any rate, their retreat is possible within these limits, and it serves the powerful symbolic function of pointing to the unambiguous life of the Spiritual Community. Through their serving of this function, they participate in a significant way in the constructive function of the churches. But the desire to avoid the ambiguities of the religious communities is not the only reason for their retreat. The problem of the personal life under the impact of the Spiritual Presence was and is basic for them.

The ambiguities of the personal life are ambiguities in the actualization of humanity as the inner aim of the person. They appear both in the person's relation to himself and in his relation to others. The ambiguity of determination, which we have mentioned, is involved in both cases: the ambiguity of self-determination and the ambiguity of the determination of others.

The first question to be asked is, How is the ideal of saintliness related to the ideal of humanity? We asked before, Does the holiness of the community destroy its justice? And we must now ask: Does the saintliness of the personality within this community destroy the person's humanity? How are they related under the impact of the Spiritual Presence? The problem raised in this question is the problem of asceticism and humanity. Saintliness has often been identified with, and has always been made partly dependent on, asceticism. Beyond asceticism, it is the transparency of the divine ground of being in a person which makes him a saint. But such transparency (which, according to the Roman doctrine, expresses itself in his ability to work miracles) is dependent on the negation of many human potentialities and, therefore, is in tension with the ideal of humanity. The basic question is whether this tension necessarily becomes a conflict. The answer is dependent on the distinction of different types of asceticism. Behind the Roman Catholic ideal of monastic asceticism lies the metaphysical-mystical concept of matter's resistance against form—a resistance from which all the negativities of existence and ambiguities of life are derived. One resigns from the material in order to reach the Spiritual; this is the way the Spirit is liberated from bondage to matter. The asceticism which is derived from this religiously founded metaphysics is an "ontological" one. It implies that those who exercise it are religiously higher in the divine-human hierarchy than those who live in the materially conditioned reality of the "world." From the point of view of our basic question, we must say that there is conflict, an irreconcilable conflict, between this kind of asceticism and the *telos* of humanity; we must add that this kind of asceticism presupposes an implicit denial of the doctrine of creation. Therefore Protestantism has rejected asceticism and, in spite of its struggle with the humanists, has paved the way for the *telos* of humanity. According to the Protestant principle, there is no Spirituality which is based on the negation of matter, because God as creator is equally near the material and the Spiritual. Matter belongs to the good creation, and its humanist affirmation does not contradict Spirituality.

But there is another form of asceticism which has developed in the Jewish and Protestant spheres, and this is the asceticism of self-discipline. We find it in Paul and Calvin. It has strong moral connotations rather than ontological ones. It presupposes the fallen state of reality and the will to resist the temptation coming from many things which in themselves are not bad. In principle this is adequate to the human situation, and no humanity is possible without elements of this kind of asceticism.

But the impact of the traditional type of asceticism was so strong that the *telos* of humanity was again threatened by the ideal of Puritan repression. The radical restriction of sex and the restraint from many other potentialities of created goodness brought this kind of disciplinary asceticism close to the ontological asceticism of the Roman church, and since it often concentrated with rigor on trespasses against its petty restrictions it became both pharisaic and ludicrous. The very word "saintly" (implying no drinking, dancing, and so on) became first moralistically empty and then ridiculous. It is, at least partially, the merit of the psychotherapeutic movement since Freud that it helped the churches get rid of this distorted image of saintliness.

There is an ideal of asceticism under the impact of the Spiritual Presence which is completely united with the *telos* of humanity: the ascetic discipline without which no creative work is possible, the discipline required by the *eros* to the object. The combination of the words *eros* and "discipline" shows that the *telos* of humanity includes the idea of saintliness, for the asceticism here demanded is the conquest of a subjective self-affirmation which prevents participation in the object. "Humanity" in all its implications, as well as "saintliness" in the sense of being open to the Spiritual Presence, includes the asceticism which makes the union of subject and object possible.

In our description of the ambiguity of personal actualization, it was shown to be the separation of subject and object which produces ambiguities. The question is: How is personal self-determination possible if the determining self needs determination as much as the determined self? There is neither saintliness nor humanity without the solution of this problem. The solution is that the determining subject is determined by that which transcends subject and object, the Spiritual Presence. Its impact on the subject which is existentially separated from its object is called "grace." The word has many meanings, some of which will be discussed later, but in all its meanings, the preceding activity of the Spiritual Presence is identical. "Grace" means that the Spiritual Presence cannot be produced but is given. The ambiguity of self-determination is overcome by grace, and there is no other way of overcoming it and of escaping the despair of the conflict between the command of self-determination and the impossibility of determining oneself in the direction of what one essentially is.

In the relation of person to person, the functions of education and guidance help to reach the *telos* of humanity. We have seen the ambiguity of these functions in the separation of subject and object which they presuppose. The educational and guiding activities of the churches cannot escape the problem, but they can fight against the ambiguities in the power of the Spiritual Presence. Whereas in the person's dealing with himself it is the Spiritual Presence as grace which makes self-determination possible, in the dealing with the other one the Spirit, as the creator of participation, makes other-determination possible. Only the Spirit can transcend the split between the subject and the object in education and guidance, because only through participation in that which grasps both from the vertical dimension is the difference overcome between him who, as educator and guide, gives and him who receives. In the grasp of the Spiritual Presence the subject in education and guidance has himself become object, and the object of education and guidance has himself become subject. Both, as bearers of the Spirit, are subject and object. In the actual processes of education and guidance, this means that he who is nearer to the *telos* of humanity is continuously aware of the fact that he is still infinitely removed from it and that therefore the attitude of superiority and the will to control the other one (for his good) is replaced by the acknowledgment that the educator or the guide is in the same predicament as the one he tries to help. And it means that he who is aware of his infinite distance from the *telos* of humanity nevertheless participates in it by the Spirit's grasping him out of the vertical dimension. The Spirit does not let the subject in any human relation remain mere subject and the object mere object; the Spirit is present wherever the conquest of the subject-object split in man's existence occurs.

(5) THE RELATING FUNCTIONS OF THE CHURCHES.—The churches, in paradoxical unity with their Spiritual essence, are sociological realities, showing all the ambiguities of the social self-creation of life. Therefore they have continuous encounters with other sociological groups, acting upon them and receiving from them. Systematic theology cannot deal with the practical problems following from these relations, but it must try to formulate the ways and principles by which the churches as churches relate themselves to other social groups.

There are three ways in which this happens: the way of silent interpenetration, the way of critical judgment, and the way of political establishment. The first can be described as the continuous radiation of the Spiritual essence of the churches into all groups of the society in which they live. Their very existence changes the whole of social existence. One could call it the pouring of priestly substance into the social structure of which the churches are a part. In view of the rapid secularization of life in the last centuries, one is inclined to overlook this influence, but if in imagination one removes the churches, the empty space left in all realms of man's personal and communal life shows the significance of their silent influence. Even if the educational possibilities of the churches are officially limited, their very existence has an educational impact on the culture of a period, whether it is directly, by communicating Spiritual reality, or indirectly, by provoking a protest against what they represent.

Moreover, the influence is mutual; the churches receive the silent influx of the developing and changing cultural forms of the society, consciously or unconsciously. The most obvious of these influences is felt in the continuous transformation of the ways of understanding and expressing experiences in a living culture. The churches silently give Spiritual substance to the society in which they live, and the churches silently receive Spiritual forms from the same society. This mutual exchange, silently exercised at every moment, is the first relating function of the church.

The second is the way of critical judgment, exercised mutually by the church and the other social groups. This relation between churches and society is most manifest in the modern period of Western history, but it has existed in all periods, even under the theocratic systems of the Eastern and Western churches. The early church's criticism of the imperial Roman society was directed against its pagan ways of life and thought, and it finally transformed the pagan society into a Christian one. If the silent penetration of a society by the Spiritual Presence can be called "priestly," the open attack on this society in the name of the Spiritual Presence can be called "prophetic." Its success may be rather limited, but the fact that the society is put under judgment and must react positively or negatively to the judgment is in itself a success. A society which rejects or persecutes the bearers of the prophetic criticism against itself does not remain the same as it was before. It may be weakened or it may be hardened in its demonic and profane traits; in either case it is transformed. Therefore the churches should not only fight for the preservation and strengthening of their priestly influence (for example, in the realm of education), but they should encourage prophetic criticism of the negativities in their society up to the point of martyrdom and in spite of their awareness that the result of a prophetic criticism of society is not the Spiritual Community but, perhaps, a state of society which approaches theonomy—the relatedness of all cultural forms to the ultimate.

But again the relation is mutual. There is, on the part of society, a criticism directed toward the churches, a criticism which is as justified as the churches' prophetic criticism of society. It is the criticism of "holy injustice" and "saintly inhumanity" within the churches and in their relation to the society in which they live. The world-historical significance of this criticism in the nineteenth and twentieth centuries is obvious. Its first consequence was to produce an almost unbridgeable gap between the churches and large groups of society, in particular the labor movements; but beyond this it had the effect of inducing the Christian churches to revise their interpretations of justice and humanity. It was a kind of reverse prophetism, an unconsciously prophetic criticism directed toward the churches from outside, just as a reverse priestly impact occurred in the effect of the changing cultural forms on the churches, an unconsciously priestly influence directed toward the churches from outside. This mutual criticism exercised and received by the churches is their second relating function.

The third is the way of political establishment. While the priestly and the prohetic ways remain within the religious sphere, the third way seems to fall completely outside this sphere. But religious symbolism has always added the royal to the priestly and the prophetic religious functions. Christology attributes the royal office to the Christ. Every church has a political function, from the local up to the international level. One task of the church leaders on all levels is to influence the leaders of the other social groups in such a way that the right of the church to exercise its priestly and prophetic function is acknowledged by them. There are many ways in which this can be done, dependent on the constitutional structure of the society and the legal position of the churches within it; but in any case, if the churches act politically, they must do it in the name of the Spiritual Community, i.e., Spiritually. This excludes the use of means which contradict its character as Spiritual Community, such as the use of military force, intoxicating propaganda, and diplomatic ruses, the arousing of religious fanaticism, and so on. The more sharply a church rejects such methods, the more power it will ultimately exercise, for its real power lies in its being a creation of the Spiritual Presence. The fact that the Roman church has disregarded these principles has contributed to the scepticism in Protestantism with regard to the royal function of the church. But such scepticism is not justified. The Protestant churches cannot escape their political responsibility, and they have always exercised it, though with uneasy conscience, having forgotten that there is a royal function of the Christ. Certainly, as the royal function belongs to the Christ Crucified, so the royal function must be exercised by the church under the Cross, the humble church.

In doing so, it acknowledges that there is also a justified political impact on the churches from the side of society. One need only think of the influence of the late ancient and medieval forms of society on the structure of the churches. Political establishment is the result of a deal between different political forces inside and outside the larger groups. Even the churches are subject to the law of political compromise. They must be ready not only to direct but also to be directed. There is only one limit in the political establishment of the churches: the character of the church as expression of the Spiritual Community must remain manifest. This is first endangered if the symbol of the royal office of the Christ, and through him of the church, is understood as a theocratic-political system of totalitarian control over all realms of life. On the other hand, if the church is forced to assume the role of an obedient servant of the state, as if it were another department or agency, this means the end of its royal office altogether and a humiliation of the church which is not the humility of the Crucified but the weakness of the disciples who fled the Cross.

If we turn now to the principles under which the churches as actualizations of the Spiritual Community relate themselves to other social groups, we find a polarity between the principle of belonging to them according to the ambiguities of life and the principle of opposing them according to the fight against the ambiguities of life. Each of these principles has far-reaching consequences. The first implies that the relation of the churches to other groups has the character of mutuality, as we have seen with respect to the three ways in which the churches are related to them. The reason for this mutuality is the equality of predicament. This principle is the antidemonic criterion of the holiness of the churches, because it prevents the arrogance of finite holiness, which is the basic temptation of all churches. If they interpret their paradoxical holiness as absolute holiness, they fall into a demonic *hubris*, and their priestly, prophetic, and royal functions toward the "world" become tools of a pseudo-Spiritual will to power. It was the experience of the demonization of the Roman church in the later Middle Ages which produced the protest of both the Reformation and Renaissance. These protests liberated Christianity in large sections from bondage to the demonically distorted power of the church by making the people aware of the ambiguities of actual religion.

But in achieving this they also frequently brought about, not only in the secular world but also in the sphere of Protestantism, the loss of the other side of the relation, the opposition of the churches to the other social groups. The danger in this respect was obvious from the beginning of the two great movements. Both propagated a nationalism of which culture as well as religion became victims. The church's opposition to nationalistic ideology, with its unjust claims and untrue assertions, became weaker with every decade of modern history. The church's prophetic voice was silenced by nationalistic fanaticism. Its priestly function was distorted by the introduction of national sacraments and rites into education at all levels, especially the lowest ones. Its royal function was not taken seriously and was made impotent either by the subjection of the churches to the national states or by the liberal ideal of separation of church and state, which pushed the churches into a narrow corner of the social fabric. The power of opposition was lost in all these cases, and when the church loses its radical otherness, it loses itself and becomes a benevolent social club. Such phrases as "the church against the world" point to the one principle which essentially determines the relation of the churches to society as a whole and which should determine it actually. Yet if such phrases are used without being balanced by other phrases, such as "the church within the world," they have an arrogant ring and miss the ambiguity of the religious life.

It is part and parcel of this ambiguity that the world which is opposed by the church is not simply not-church but has in itself elements of the Spiritual Community in its latency which work toward a theonomous culture.

3. THE INDIVIDUAL IN THE CHURCH AND THE SPIRITUAL PRESENCE

a) The entering of the individual into a church and the experience of conversion.—The Spiritual Community is the Community of Spiritual personalities, i.e., of personalities who are grasped by the Spiritual Presence and who are unambiguously, though fragmentarily, determined by it. In this sense the Spiritual Community is the community of saints. The state of saintliness is the state of transparency toward the divine ground of being; it is the state of being determined by faith and love. He who participates in the Spiritual Community is united with God in faith and love. He is a creation of the divine Spirit. All this must be said paradoxically of every member of a church, because as an active (not only a legal) member of the church he is essentially and dynamically a member of the Spiritual Community. As the Spiritual Community is the dynamic essence of the churches, so is the Spiritual personality the dynamic essence of every active member of a church. It is immensely significant for the individual member of a church to realize that his dynamic essence as a member of the church is the Spiritual personality, who is a part of the Spiritual Community and whom God sees as such. He is a saint in spite of his lack of saintliness.

It is obvious that on the basis of these considerations everyone who belongs actively to a church is a "priest" by the fact of his belonging to the Spiritual Community, and he is able to exercise all the functions of a priest, although, for the sake of order and adequacy to the situation, special individuals may be called to a regular and trained performance of priestly activities. But their functioning as experts does not give them a higher status than is given by participation in the Spiritual Community.

The question as to which precedes "ontologically," the church or the individual member, has led to the separation of two types of churches, those emphasizing the predominance of the church over the individual and those emphasizing the predominance of the individual over the church. In the first case the individual enters a church which always precedes him; he enters it consciously or unconsciously (as an infant), but the presence of the New Being in a community precedes everything he is and knows. This is the theological justification of infant baptism. It rightly points to the fact that there is no moment in the life of a person when the state of Spiritual maturity can be fixed with certainty.

The faith which constitutes the Spiritual Community is a reality which precedes the ever becoming, ever changing, ever disappearing, and ever reappearing acts of personal faith. According to the multidimensional unity of life in man, the earliest beginnings of a human being in the mother's womb are, in terms of potentiality, directly connected with the latest stages of maturity. Actual personal faith cannot be determined at any age of a person's life, and it is a temptation to dishonesty if, for example, the quasi-sacramental act of "confirmation" in the fourteenth year of a child is considered a matter of free decision for the Spiritual Community. The reactions of many children shortly after their solemn and emotionally strained declaration of commitment show the psychologically unhealthy and theologically unjustifiable character of this act.

The situation is quite different if the precedence of the individual member over against the church is emphasized. In this case the decision of individuals to form a covenant is the act which creates a church. The presupposition, of course, is that such a decision is determined by the Spiritual Presence, which implies that the individuals who form a covenant do it as members of the Spiritual Community. This assumption diminishes and almost removes the contrast between the "objective" and the "subjective" type of church. In order to be able to create a church one must already be grasped by the Spiritual Presence and thus be a member of the Spiritual Community. Conversely, the bearers of the "objective" church (into which the baptized infant enters) are in their dynamic essence Spiritual personalities. The concept of the Spiritual Community overcomes the duality of the "objective" and the "subjective" interpretation of the church.

The actual situation of the individual in the churches of voluntary decision confirms the diminished significance of the distinction. From the second generation on, they are drawn by the atmosphere of family and society into the church whose actual presence precedes their voluntary decisions as much as it does in the opposite type.

The important question is: How does an individual participate in a church in such a way that, through it, he participates in the Spiritual Community as a Spiritual personality? The answer, already given, was a negative one: There is no moment in the life of a person which could be singled out as the beginning (or the end) of such a participation. This refers not only to the person who is born and reared in the atmosphere of a church-affiliated family, community, and society in general but also to the one who has experienced only secular ways of life and then joins a church in seriousness. Neither can determine the moment in which he essentially became a member of the Spiritual Community, although the moment in which he openly became a member of a church can be exactly stated. This assertion seems to contradict the concept of conversion, which plays such a role in both Testaments, in church history, and in the life of innumerable individuals in the Christian world and beyond it in all living religions. In this concept the event of conversion marks the moment in which a person enters the Spiritual Community.

But conversion is not necessarily a momentary event; it is in most cases a long process which has been going on unconsciously long before it breaks into consciousness, giving the impression of a sudden, unexpected, and overwhelming crisis. There are New Testament stories, such as that of Paul's conversion, which provided the pattern for this understanding of conversion, and there is an abundance of other such stories, many of them genuine and powerful, some of them sentimentally distorted for the sake of giving an example. It is unquestionable that such experiences are numerous and show most conspicuously the ecstatic character of the Spiritual Presence, but they do not—as pietism thinks—constitute the essence of conversion. The true nature of conversion is well expressed in the words denoting it in different languages. The word *shûbh* in Hebrew points to a turning around on one's way, especially in the social and political spheres. It points to a turning away from injustice toward justice, from inhumanity to humanity, from idols to God. The Greek word *metanoia* implies the same idea but in relation to the mind, which changes from one direction to another, from the temporal to the eternal, from oneself to God. The Latin word *conversio* (in German *Be-kehrung*) unites the spatial image with the intellectual content. These words and the images they provoke suggest two elements: the negation of a preceding direction of thought and action and the affirmation of the opposite direction. That which is negated is the bondage to existential estrangement and that which is affirmed is the New Being, created by the Spiritual Presence. The rejection of the negative with the whole of one's being is called repentance—a concept which must be freed from emotional distortion. The acceptance of the affirmative with the whole of one's being is called faith—a concept which must be freed from intellectual distortion. The impact of the Spiritual Presence which is called conversion is effective in all the dimensions of human life because of the multidimensional unity of man. It is organic as well as psychological; it occurs under the predominance of the spirit and has a historical dimension. Nevertheless, the image of turning around in one's way produces the impression of something momentary and sudden, and, in spite of all pietistic misuse of it, the element of suddenness should not be excluded from a description of conversion. It is a decision, and the very word decision points to the momentary act of cutting off other possibilities. Yet, entering into the Spiritual Community is always prepared for by and always preserves elements of the past. It is a process that becomes manifest in an ecstatic moment. Without such preparation conversion would be an emotional outburst without consequences, soon swallowed by the old being instead of constituting the New Being.

Conversion can have the character of a transition from the latent stage of the Spiritual Community to its manifest stage. This is the real structure of conversion; it implies that repentance is not completely new and that neither is faith. For the Spiritual Presence creates both, even in the stage of the latency of the Spiritual Community. There is no absolute conversion, but there is relative conversion before and after the central event of somebody's "repenting" and "believing," of somebody's being grasped by the Spiritual Presence in a fertile moment, a *kairos*.

This has much bearing on the churches' evangelistic activity, the function of which is not that of converting people in an absolute sense but rather of converting them in the relative sense of transferring them from a latent to a manifest participation in the Spiritual Community. This means that the evangelist does not address "lost souls," men without God, but people in the stage of latency, to transform them into people who have experienced manifestation. And it should be remembered that experiences analogous to conversion have been described by Greek philosophers as experiences in which their eyes were opened. The conversion to philosophical truth is a subject discussed in all periods of history. This is an expression of the fact that the Spiritual Community is related to culture and morality as much as to religion and that where Spiritual Presence is at work a moment of radical change in the attitude to the ultimate is necessary.

*b) The individual within the church and the experience
of the New Being*

(1) THE EXPERIENCE OF THE NEW BEING AS CREATION (REGENERA-
TION).—He who enters a church, seen not as one sociological group
among others but as that group whose dynamic essence is the Spiritual
Community, and who is himself grasped by the Spiritual Presence is,
in his dynamic essence, Spiritual personality. But in his actual being
he is a member of a church who is subjected to the ambiguities of the
religious life, though under the paradoxical impact of unambiguous
life. This situation has been described in different ways according to
the different points of view from which it has been considered. It
seems to be adequate—and in line with the classical tradition—to call it
the experience of the New Being and to distinguish several elements in
it which—again in accordance with the classical tradition—can be
described as the experience of the New Being as creating (regeneration), the experience of the New Being as paradox (justification), and
the experience of the New Being as process (sanctification).

It may be asked whether it is correct to describe the ways of participating in the New Being as "experiences," since this word seems to
introduce a questionable subjective element. However, it is the subject,
that is, the Spiritual personality as a member of the church, of whom
we speak here. The objective side of regeneration, justification, and
sanctification has been discussed in the section entitled "The New Being
in Jesus as the Christ as the Power of Salvation" (Part III, Sec. II E).
"Experience" here simply means the awareness of something that happens to somebody, namely, the state of being grasped by the Spiritual
Presence. It has been asked whether this can ever become an object
of experience and whether it must not remain an object of faith, in
the sense of the sentences: "I believe that I believe," or "I have faith in the
Spiritual Presence in me but I do not experience my faith, my love,
my Spirituality." But even if I only believe that I believe, there must be a
reason for such belief, and this reason must be some kind of participation in what I believe and therefore a kind of certainty which prevents
an infinite regression of the type represented by the statement "I believe
that I believe that I believe, and so on." However paradoxical one's
theological statements may be, one cannot escape the necessity of naming a Spiritual foundation for these statements. This consideration jus-

tifies the use of the term "experience" for the awareness of the Spiritual Presence.

In biblical and theological literature, the state of being grasped by the Spiritual Presence is called "new birth" or "regeneration." The term "new birth" (like the Pauline term "New Creation") is a biblical precedent to the more abstract concept of New Being. Both point to the same reality, the event in which the divine Spirit takes hold of a personal life through the creation of faith.

The use of the word "experience," however, does not imply that he who is grasped by the Spiritual Presence can verify his experience through empirical observation. Though born anew, men are not yet new beings but have entered a new reality which can make them into new beings. Participating in the New Being does not automatically guarantee that one is new.

For this reason the theologians of the Reformation and their successors prefer to begin the description of man's participation in the New Being by emphasizing its paradoxical character, thus putting justification in the first place instead of regeneration. Their main concern was and is to avoid the impression that man's state of being born anew is the cause of his being accepted by God. In this they were certainly right, as they liberated estranged man from the anxiety of the questions: Am I really reborn? And if I am not, must not God reject me? Such questioning destroys the meaning of the "good news," which is that, although unacceptable, I am accepted. But then the question arises: How can *I* accept that I am accepted? What is the source of such faith? The only possible answer is: God himself as Spiritual Presence. Every other answer would degrade faith into a belief, an intellectual act produced by will and emotion. Such belief, however, is nothing but the acceptance of the doctrine of "justification by grace through faith"; it is not the acceptance that I am accepted, and it is not the faith meant in the word "justification." That faith is the creation of the Spirit; and it was a complete distortion of the message of justification when the doctrine appeared that the gift of the divine Spirit follows faith in divine forgiveness. For Luther there would be no greater, and in a sense no other, gift of the Spirit than the certainty of being accepted by God, the faith in God's justifying the sinner. But if this is affirmed, the participation in the New Being, the creation of the Spirit, is the first element in the state of the individual in the church in so far as it is the actualization of the Spiritual Community.

If this is accepted the question is often asked: If the Spiritual Presence must grasp me and create faith in me, what can I do in order to reach such faith? I cannot force the Spirit upon myself; so what can I do but wait without acting? Sometimes this question is asked without seriousness, in an attitude of dialectical aggression, and does not really require an answer. No answer can be given to him who asks in this way, because every answer would tell him something he should do or be; it would contradict the faith for which he asks. If, however, the question—What can I do in order to experience the New Being?—is asked with existential seriousness, the answer is implied in the question, for existential seriousness is evidence of the impact of the Spiritual Presence upon an individual. He who is ultimately concerned about his state of estrangement and about the possibility of reunion with the ground and aim of his being is already in the grip of the Spiritual Presence. In this situation the question, What shall I do to receive the divine Spirit? is meaningless because the real answer is already given and any further answer would distort it.

In practical terms this means that the merely polemical question concerning the way to reunion of the estranged cannot be answered and must be exposed in its lack of seriousness. Thus he who asks with ultimate concern should be told that the fact of his ultimate concern implies the answer and therefore that he is under the impact of the Spiritual Presence and accepted in his state of estrangement. Finally, those who oscillate in their question between seriousness and the lack of it should be brought to an awareness of this situation—an awareness they can suppress and drop the question altogether or affirm and, in so doing, realize its seriousness.

(2) THE EXPERIENCE OF THE NEW BEING AS PARADOX (JUSTIFICATION).—In discussing the relation of regeneration to justification we have already begun the discussion of the central doctrine of the Reformation, the article by which Protestantism stands or falls, the principle of justification by grace through faith. I call it not only a doctrine and an article among others but also a principle, because it is the first and basic expression of the Protestant principle itself. It is only for unavoidable reasons of expediency a particular doctrine and should,

at the same time, be regarded as the principle which permeates every single assertion of the theological system. It should be regarded as the Protestant principle that, in relation to God, God alone can act and that no human claim, especially no religious claim, no intellectual or moral or devotional "work," can reunite us with him. It was my intention and it is my hope that this aim has been reached even if it has led to many quite "unorthodox" formulations in all parts of the system. The question that has always been before us is: Do other formulations impose an intellectual "good work" on the believer, for example, a repression of doubt or a sacrifice of the cognitive conscience, which caused the final formulation? In this sense the doctrine of justification is the universal principle of Protestant theology, but it is also a particular article in a particular section of the theological system.

The doctrine of justification puts before us several semantic problems. In the struggle with Rome about the *sola fide*, the doctrine became "justification by faith"—and not by "works." This, however, has led to a devastating confusion. Faith, in this phrase, has been understood as the cause of God's justifying act, which means that the moral and ritual works of Catholic teaching are replaced by the intellectual work of accepting a doctrine. Not faith but grace is the cause of justification, because God alone is the cause. Faith is the receiving act, and this act is itself a gift of grace. Therefore one should dispense completely with the phrase "justification by faith" and replace it by the formula "justification by grace through faith." It should be a serious concern in the teaching and preaching of every minister that this profound distortion of the "good news" of the Christian message be remedied.

Another piece of semantic advice for teaching and preaching can be given in connection with the Pauline term "justification" itself. Paul used it in his discussion of the legalistic perversion of his message of the New Creation in the appearance of the Christ. The propagandists of this perversion, Christians who could not separate themselves from the commands of the Jewish law, spoke in terms of just, justice, justification (*tsedaqah* in Hebrew, *dikiosyne* in Greek). Paul himself had been educated in this terminology, which he could not abandon in the discussion with former members of the synagogue. Since it is a biblical term, it cannot be rejected in the Christian churches either, but it should be replaced in the practice of teaching and preaching by the term "acceptance," in the sense that we are accepted by God although being unacceptable according to the criteria of the law (our essential being put against us) and that we are asked to accept this acceptance. Such terminology is itself acceptable by people for whom the Old and New Testament phrasing has lost all meaning, although there is a most serious existential meaning for them in the reality to which this phrasing points.

A third semantic question appears if one uses the term "forgiveness of sins" to express the paradoxical character of the experience of the New Being. It is a religious-symbolic expression taken from such human relations as that between the debtor and the one to whom he is in debt, the child and the father, the servant and the master, or the accused and the judge. As in every symbol, the analogy is limited. One limitation is that the relation between God and man does not have the character of a finite relationship between finite and estranged beings but is infinite and universal and unconditional in meaning and that divine forgiveness does not, as does every human forgiveness, require that he who forgives shall himself be forgiven. The second limitation of the analogy lies in the plural form of sin. Men forgive particular sins, for example, offenses against themselves or the trespass of concrete commands and laws. In relation to God, it is not the particular sin as such that is forgiven but the act of separation from God and the resistance to reunion with him. It is sin which is forgiven in the forgiving of a particular sin. The symbol of forgiveness of sins has proved dangerous because it has concentrated the mind on particular sins and their moral quality rather than on the estrangement from God and its religious quality. Nevertheless, the plural "sins" can stand for the singular "Sin" and point to the situation of man before God, and a particular trespass can even be experienced as a manifestation of Sin, the power of estrangement from our true being. It is one of the steps taken by Paul, as a theologian, beyond the symbolic language of Jesus, that he interpreted the acceptance of the divine forgiveness by the concept of justification by grace through faith. In doing so he answered the questions raised by the symbol of forgiveness, the questions of the relation of forgiveness to justice and of the basis for the certainty that one is forgiven. These questions are answered objectively in christological terms, an answer which underlies the doctrine of atonement, i.e., the doctrine of God's participation in man's existential estrangement and victory over it. Yet at the present point we seek the subjective answer to the questions:

How can man accept that he is accepted; how can he reconcile his feeling of guilt and his desire for punishment with the prayer of forgiveness; and what gives him the certainty that he is forgiven?

The answer lies in the unconditional character of the divine act in which God declares him who is unjust to be just. The paradox *simul justus, simul peccator* points to this unconditional divine declaration. If God accepted him who is half-sinner and half-just, his judgment would be conditioned by man's half-goodness. But there is nothing God rejects as strongly as half-goodness and every human claim based on it. The impact of this message, mediated by the Spiritual Presence, turns the eyes of man away from the bad and the good in himself to the infinite divine goodness, which is beyond good and bad and which gives itself without conditions and ambiguities. The moral demand for justice and the fearful desire for punishment are valid in the realm of the ambiguity of goodness. They express the human situation in itself. But within the New Being they are overcome by a justice which makes him who is unjust just, by acceptance. This transcendent justice does not negate but fulfils the ambiguous human justice. It fulfils also the truth in the demand for punishment by destroying what must be destroyed if reuniting love is to reach its aim. And, according to the profound psychology of Paul and Luther, this is not the evil in one's being as such but the *hubris* of trying to conquer it and to reach reunion with God by one's own good will. Such *hubris* avoids the pain of surrender to God's sole activity in our reunion with him, a pain which infinitely surpasses the pain of moral toil and ascetic self-torture. This surrender of one's own goodness occurs in him who accepts the divine acceptance of himself, the unacceptable. The courage to surrender one's own goodness to God is the central element in the courage of faith. In it the paradox of the New Being is experienced, the ambiguity of good and evil is conquered, unambiguous life has taken hold of man through the impact of the Spiritual Presence.

All this is manifest through the picture of Jesus the Crucified. God's acceptance of the unacceptable, God's participation in man's estrangement, and his victory over the ambiguity of good and evil appear in a unique, definite, and transforming way in him. It appears in him, but it is not caused by him. The cause is God and God alone.

The paradox of the New Being, the principle of justification by grace through faith, lies at the center of the experiences of Paul, Augustine, and Luther, but it is differently colored in each of them. In Paul the emphasis lies on the conquest of the law in the new eon which has been brought by the Christ. This message of justification has a cosmic frame in which individuals may or may not participate. In Augustine grace has the character of a substance, infused into men, which creates love and establishes the last period of history in which the Christ rules through the church. It is God and God alone who does this. The fate of man is dependent on predestination. The forgiveness of sins is a presupposition of the infusion of love, but it is not an expression of the continuous relation to God. Therefore the individual becomes dependent on his relation to the church. In Luther justification is the individual person's experience of both the divine wrath against his sin and the divine forgiveness which leads to a person-to-person relation with God without the cosmic and ecclesiastical framework of Paul or Augustine. This is the limitation in Luther's thought which has led both to an intellectual orthodoxy and to an emotional pietism. The subjective element was not counterbalanced in him. But his "psychology of acceptance" is the profoundest one in church history and confirmed by the best insights of contemporary "psychology of depth."

There is one question which was neither asked nor answered by Paul or Luther, although an awareness of it was shown by John and Augustine: How is the faith through which justification comes to us related to the situation of radical doubt? Radical doubt is existential doubt concerning the meaning of life itself; it may include not only the rejection of everything religious in the narrow sense of the word but also the ultimate concern which constitutes religion in the larger sense. If a person in this predicament hears the message of God's accepting the unacceptable, it cannot concern him because the term "God" and the problem of being accepted or rejected by God has no meaning for him. Paul's question, How do I become liberated from the law? and Luther's question, How do I find a merciful God? are replaced in our period by the question, How do I find meaning in a meaningless world? The question of John about the manifestation of truth and his assertion that the Christ *is* the truth, as well as the statements of Augustine concerning the truth that appears in the very nature of doubt, are nearer to our present situation than the questions and answers of Paul and Luther. But our answer must be derived from the special situation which we encounter, though on the basis of the message of the New Being.

The first part of every answer to this problem must be negative: God as the truth and the source of meaning cannot be reached by intellectual work, as he cannot be reached by moral work. The question, What can I do to overcome radical doubt and the feeling of meaninglessness? cannot be answered, because every answer would justify the question, which implies that something can be done. But the paradox of the New Being is just that nothing can be done by man who is in the situation in which he asks the question. One can only say, while rejecting the form of the question, that the seriousness of despair in which the question is asked is itself the answer. This is in the line of Augustine's argument, that in the situation of doubt the truth from which one feels separated is present in so far as in every doubt the formal affirmation of truth as truth is presupposed. But the analogous affirmation of meaning within meaninglessness is also related to the paradox of justification. It is the problem of the justification, not of the sinner, but of him who doubts, which has led to this solution. Since in the predicament of doubt and meaninglessness God as the source of the justifying act has disappeared, the only thing left (in which God reappears without being recognized) is the ultimate honesty of doubt and the unconditional seriousness of the despair about meaning. This is the way in which the experience of the New Being as paradox can be applied to the cognitive function. It is the way in which the people of our time can be told that they are accepted with respect to the ultimate meaning of their lives, although unacceptable in view of the doubt and meaninglessness which has taken hold of them. In the seriousness of their existential despair, God is present to them. To accept this paradoxical acceptance is the courage of their faith.

(3) THE EXPERIENCE OF THE NEW BEING AS PROCESS (SANCTIFICATION)

(a) Contrasting types in the description of the process.—The impact of the Spiritual Presence on the individual results in a life process based on the experience of regeneration, qualified by the experience of justification, and developing as the experience of sanctification. The character of the experience of sanctification cannot be derived from the word itself. Originally, justification and sanctification pointed to the same reality, i.e., the conquest of the ambiguities of the personal life. But slowly, especially under the influence of Paul, the term "justification" received the connotation of the paradoxical acceptance of him who is unacceptable, while "sanctification" received the connotation of actual transformation. In this sense it is synonymous with life process under the impact of the Spirit. It has always been an important theological task to describe the character of this process, and different descriptions were often expressions of different ways of life which, at the same time, received confirmation from the theological emphasis.

If we compare the attitudes of Lutheran, Calvinist, and Evangelical-Radical theology toward the character of the Christian life, differences appear which had and have consequences for religion and culture in all Protestant countries. Although all Protestants rejected the "law" as preached and administered by the Roman church, important differences arose when the Protestant churches tried to formulate their own doctrines of the law. Luther and Calvin agreed about two functions of the law, the function of directing the life of the political group by preventing or punishing transgressions and the function of showing man what he essentially is and therefore ought to be and the extent to which his actual state contradicts the image of his true being. By showing his essence, the law reveals man's estranged existence—and drives him to the quest for a reunion with what essentially belongs to him and from which he is estranged. This is the common position of Luther and Calvin. But Calvin spoke of a third function of the law, namely, the function of guiding the Christian who is grasped by the divine Spirit but who is not yet free from the power of the negative in knowledge and action. Luther rejected this solution, asserting that the Spirit itself leads to decisions in which the ambiguity of life is conquered. The Spirit, by liberating a person from the letter of the law, gives both insight into the concrete situation and the power to act in this situation according to the call of *agape*. Calvin's solution is more realistic, more able to support an ethical theory and a disciplined life of sanctification. Luther's solution is more ecstatic, unable to support a "Protestant ethics" but full of creative possibilities in the personal life. The churches born from the Evangelical Radicalism of the Reformation period accepted from Calvinism the doctrine of the third use of the law and the discipline as a tool in the process of sanctification. But in contrast to Calvin, they have lost the understanding of the paradoxical character of the churches and of the life of the individuals in them. They practically deny the lasting significance of the great "in spite of" in the process of sanctification. In this point they return to ascetic Catholic traditions: perfection can be attained in this life in those individuals and groups who are selected as bearers of the divine Spirit.

The consequences for the understanding of the Christian life based on these different attitudes toward the law are far-reaching. In Calvinism sanctification proceeds in a slowly upward-turning line; both faith and love are progressively actualized. The power of the divine Spirit in the individual increases. Perfection is approached, though never reached. The original Evangelical Radicals rejected this restriction and reaffirmed the concept of the perfect ones but in such a way that the paradoxical character of Christian perfection becomes invisible. Actual perfection is demanded and deemed to be possible. In the selected group the holiness of the whole and the saintliness of the individuals are actual, in contrast to the "world," which includes the large churches. Obviously, the situation became rather problematic when the holiness sects themselves became large churches. Then, although the ideal of the unparadoxical holiness of every member of the group could not be sustained, the perfectionist ideal remained in force and produced the identification of the Christian message of salvation with moral perfection in the individual members. Calvinism, with its perfectionist elements (though not perfectionism), has produced a type of Protestant ethics in which progressive sanctification is the aim of life. It had a tremendous effect in shaping powerful, self-controlled personalities. Desirous of observing within themselves symptoms of their election, they produced these symptoms by what has been called "inner-worldly asceticism," i.e., by work, self-control, and repression of vitality, especially in relation to sex. These perfectionistic tendencies were strengthened when the perfectionism of the Evangelicals merged with the perfectionist elements of Calvinism.

In Lutheranism the emphasis on the paradoxical element in the experience of the New Being was so predominant that sanctification could not be interpreted in terms of a line moving upward toward perfection. It was seen instead as an up-and-down of ecstasy and anxiety, of being grasped by *agape* and being thrown back into estrangement and ambiguity. This oscillation between up and down was experienced radically by Luther himself, in the change between moments of courage and joy and moments of demonic attacks, as he interpreted his states of doubt and profound despair. The consequence of the absence in Lutheranism of the Calvinistic and Evangelistic valuation of discipline was that the ideal of progressive sanctification was taken less seriously and replaced by a great emphasis on the paradoxical character of the Christian life. In the period of orthodoxy, this led Lutheranism to that disintegration of morality and practical religion against which the Pietistic movement arose. But Luther's experience of demonic attacks led also to a deep understanding of the demonic elements in life in general and in the religious life in particular. The second period of romanticism, in which the existentialist movement of the twentieth century was prepared, could hardly have sprung from Calvinist-Evangelical soil, whereas it was genuine in a culture permeated by Lutheran traditions. (An analogy can be observed in Russian literature and philosophy arising from the basis of Greek Orthodox traditions.)

(b) *Four principles determining the New Being as process.*—The exclusiveness of the different types of interpreting the process of sanctification is diminishing under the impact of secular criticism which questions the significance of all of them. Therefore we must ask whether we can find criteria for a future doctrine of life under the Spiritual Presence. One may give the following principles: first, increasing awareness; second, increasing freedom; third, increasing relatedness; fourth, increasing transcendence. How these principles will unite in a new type of life under the Spiritual Presence cannot be described before it happens, but elements of such a life can be seen in individuals and groups who anticipated what may possibly lie in the future. The principles themselves unite religious as well as secular traditions and can, in their totality, create an indefinite but distinguishable image of the "Christian life."

The principle of awareness is related to contemporary depth psychology, but it is as old as religion itself and is sharply expressed in the New Testament. It is the principle according to which man in the process of sanctification becomes increasingly aware of his actual situation and of the forces struggling around him and his humanity but also becomes aware of the answers to the questions implied in this situation. Sanctification includes awareness of the demonic as well as of the divine. Such awareness, which increases in the process of sanctification, does not lead to the Stoic "wise man," who is superior to the ambiguities of life because he has conquered his passions and desires, but rather to an awareness of these ambiguities in himself, as in everyone, and to the power of affirming life and its vital dynamics in spite of its ambiguities. Such awareness includes sensitivity toward the demands of one's own growth, toward the hidden hopes and disappointments within others, toward the voiceless voice of a concrete situation, toward the grades of authenticity in the life of the spirit in others and oneself. All this is not a matter of cultural education or sophistication but of growth under the impact of the Spiritual power and it is therefore noticeable in every human being who is open to this impact. The aristocracy of the spirit and the aristocracy of the Spirit are not identical, although they overlap in part.

The second principle of the process of sanctification is the principle of increasing freedom. The emphasis on it is especially conspicuous in Paul's and Luther's descriptions of life in the Spirit. In contemporary literature the oracles of Nietzsche and the existentialist struggle for the freedom of man's personal self from slavery to the objects he has produced are most important. Here also depth psychology contributes by its claim to liberate men from particular compulsions which are impediments to growth in Spiritual freedom. Growth in Spiritual freedom is first of all growth in freedom from the law. This follows immediately from the interpretation of the law as man's essential being confronting him in the state of estrangement. The more one is reunited with his true being under the impact of the Spirit, the more one is free from the commandments of the law. This process is most difficult, and maturity in it is very rare. The fact that reunion is fragmentary implies that freedom from the law is always fragmentary. In so far as we are estranged, prohibitions and commandments appear and produce an uneasy conscience. In so far as we are reunited, we actualize what we essentially are in freedom, without command. Freedom from the law in the process of sanctification is the increasing freedom from the commanding form of the law. But it is also freedom from its particular content. Specific laws, expressing the experience and wisdom of the past, are not only helpful, they are also oppressive, because they cannot meet the ever concrete, ever new, ever unique situation. Freedom from the law is the power to judge the given situation in the light of the Spiritual Presence and to decide upon adequate action, which is often in seeming contradiction to the law. This is what is meant when the spirit of the law is contrasted with its letter (Paul) or when the Spirit-determined self is empowered to write a new and better law than Moses (Luther) or—in a secularized form—when the bearer of freedom revaluates all values (Nietzsche) or when the existing subject resolves the impasse of existence by resoluteness (Heidegger). The mature freedom to give new laws or to apply the old ones in a new way is an aim of the process of sanctification. The danger that such freedom may turn out to be wilfulness is overcome wherever the reuniting power of the Spiritual Presence is effective. Wilfulness is a symptom of estrangement and a surrender to enslaving conditions and compulsions. Mature freedom from the law implies the power of resisting the forces which try to destroy such freedom from inside the personal self and from its social surroundings; and, of course, the enslaving powers from outside can succeed only because there are inside trends toward servitude. Resistance against both may include ascetic decisions and readiness for martyrdom, but the significance of these actions lies in the demand upon them to help preserve freedom in the concrete situation and not in their providing a higher degree of sanctity itself. They are tools under special conditions but are not themselves aims in the process of sanctification.

The third principle is that of increasing relatedness. It balances, so to speak, the principle of increasing freedom which, through the necessity of resisting enslaving influences, may isolate the maturing person. Both freedom and relatedness, as well as awareness and self-transcendence, are rooted in the Spiritual creations of faith and love. They are present whenever the Spiritual Presence is manifest. They are the conditions of participation in regeneration and acceptance of justification, and they determine the process of sanctification. But the way in which they do so is characterized by the four principles which qualify the New Being as process. For example, the principle of increasing freedom cannot be imagined without the courage to risk a wrong decision on the basis of faith, and the principle of increasing relatedness cannot be imagined without the reuniting power of *agape* to overcome *self-seclusion* fragmentarily. But in both cases the principles of sanctification make the basic manifestation of the Spiritual Presence concrete for the progress toward maturity.

Relatedness implies the awareness of the other one and the freedom to relate to him by overcoming self-seclusion within oneself and within the other one. There are innumerable barriers to this process as may be learned from the large body of literature (with analogies in the visual arts) in which the self-seclusion of the individual from others is described. The analyses of introversion and hostility given in these works are interdependent with the psychotherapeutic analyses of the same structures. And the biblical accounts of relatedness within the Spiritual Community presuppose the same unrelatedness in the pagan world out of which its members came, an unrelatedness still ambiguously present in actual congregations.

The New Being as process drives toward a mature relatedness. The divine Spirit has rightly been described as the power of breaking through the walls of self-seclusion. There is no way of overcoming self-seclusion lastingly other than the impact of the power which elevates the individual person above himself ecstatically and enables him to find the other person—if the other person is also ready to be elevated above himself. All other relations are transitory and ambiguous. They certainly exist and fill the daily life, but they are symptoms of estrangement as much as of reunion. All human relations have this character. Alone, they cannot conquer loneliness, self-seclusion, and hostility. Only a relation which is inherent in all other relations, and which can even exist without them, is able to do so. Sanctification, or the process toward Spiritual maturity, conquers loneliness by providing for solitude and communion in interdependence. A decisive symptom of Spiritual maturity is the power to sustain solitude. Sanctification conquers introversion by turning the personal center not outward, in extroversion, but toward the dimension of its depth and its height. Relatedness needs the vertical dimension in order to actualize itself in the horizontal dimension.

This is also true of self-relatedness. The state of loneliness, introversion, and hostility is just as contrary to self-relatedness as it is to relatedness to others. The species of terms having self as the first syllable is dangerously ambiguous. The term "self-centeredness" can be used to describe the greatness of man as a fully centered self or an ethically negative attitude of bondage to one's self; the terms "self-love" and "self-hate" are difficult to understand because it is impossible to separate the self as subject of love or hate from the self as object. But there is no real love or real hate without such separation. The same ambiguity damages the term "self-relatedness." Nevertheless we must use such terms, conscious of the fact that they are used analogically and not properly.

In the analogical sense, one can speak of the process of sanctification as creating a mature self-relatedness in which self-acceptance conquers both self-elevation and self-contempt in a process of reunion with one's self. Such a reunion is created by transcending both the self as subject, which tries to impose itself in terms of self-control and self-discipline on the self as object, and the self as object, which resists such imposition in terms of self-pity and flight from one's self. A mature self-relatedness is the state of reconciliation between the self as subject and the self as object and the spontaneous affirmation of one's essential being beyond subject and object. As the process of sanctification approaches a more mature self-relatedness, the individual is more spontaneous, more self-affirming, without self-elevation or self-humiliation.

The "search for identity" is the search for what has here been called "self-relatedness." Properly understood, this search is not the desire to preserve an accidental state of the existential self, the self in estrangement but rather the drive toward a self which transcends every contingent state of its development and which remains unaltered in its essence through such changes. The process of sanctification runs toward a state in which the "search for identity" reaches its goal, which is the identity of the essential self shining through the contingencies of the existing self.

The fourth principle determining the process of sanctification is the principle of self-transcendence. The aim of maturity under the impact of the Spiritual Presence comprises awareness, freedom, and relatedness, but in each case we have found that the aim cannot be reached without an act of self-transcendence. This implies that sanctification is not possible without a continuous transcendence of oneself in the direction of the ultimate—in other words, without participation in the holy.

This participation is usually described as the devotional life under the Spiritual Presence. This description is justified if the term "devotion" is understood in such a way that the holy embraces both itself and the secular. If it is used exclusively in the ordinary sense of the devotional life—a life centered in prayer as a particular act—it does not exhaust the possibilities of self-transcendence. In the mature life, determined by the Spiritual Presence, participation in the devotional life of the congregation may be restricted or refused, prayer may be subordinated to meditation, religion in the narrower sense of the word may be denied in the name of religion in the larger sense of the word; but all this does not contradict the principle of self-transcendence. It may even happen that an increased experience of transcendence leads to an increase in criticism of religion as a special function. But in spite of these qualifying statements, "self-transcendence" is identical with the attitude of devotion toward that which is ultimate.

In discussion of the devotional life the distinction is often made between organized or formalized and private devotion. This distinction has a very limited significance. He who prays in solitude prays in the words of the religious tradition which has given him the language, and he who contemplates without words also participates in a long tradition which is represented by religious men inside and outside the churches. The distinction is meaningful only in so far as it affirms that there is no law which requires participation in the religious services in the name of the Spiritual Presence. Luther reacted violently against such a law, but at the same time he created a liturgy for Protestant services and one can say in general that withdrawal from communal devotion is dangerous because it easily produces a vacuum in which the devotional life disappears altogether.

The self-transcendence which belongs to the principles of sanctification is actual in every act in which the impact of the Spiritual Presence is experienced. This can be in prayer or meditation in total privacy, in the exchange of Spiritual experiences with others, in communications on a secular basis, in the experience of creative works of man's spirit, in the midst of labor or rest, in private counseling, in church services. It is like the breathing-in of another air, an elevation above average existence. It is the most important thing in the process of Spiritual maturity. Perhaps one can say that with increasing maturity in the process of sanctification the transcendence becomes more definite and its expressions more indefinite. Participation in communal devotion may decrease and the religious symbols connected with it may become less important, while the state of being ultimately concerned may become more manifest and the devotion to the ground and aim of our being more intensive.

This element in the reality of the New Being as process has caused the so-called resurgence of religion in the decades following the Second World War. People have felt that the experience of transcendence is necessary for a life in which a New Being becomes actual. The awareness of such a demand is widespread, the freedom from prejudice against religion as the mediator of transcendence increasing. In the present situation what one wants is concrete symbols of self-transcendence.

In light of the four principles which determine the New Being as process we can say: The Christian life never reaches the state of perfection—it always remains an up-and-down course—but in spite of its mutable character it contains a movement toward maturity, however fragmentary the mature state may be. It is manifest in the religious as well as the secular life, and it transcends both of them in the power of the Spiritual Presence.

(c) *Images of perfection.*—The differences in the description of the Christian life lead to differences in the description of the ideal goal of sanctification, the *sanctus*, the saint. In the New Testament the term "saint," *hagios*, designates all members of the congregation, including those who, in terms of what saintliness means today, were certainly not saints. The term "saint" has the same paradoxical implication, when applied to the individual Christian, as the term "holiness" has when applied to the church. Both are holy because of the holiness of their function, the New Being in the Christ. This paradoxical meaning of saintliness was lost when the early church attributed a special saintliness to the ascetics and the martyrs. In comparison with them the ordinary members of the church ceased to be saints, and a double standard of judging saintliness was introduced. Nevertheless, the idea was not that the saint represented moral superiority over the others; his saintliness was his transparency to the divine. This transparency expressed itself not only in his words and his personal excellence but also—and decisively so—in his power over nature and man. A saint, according to this doctrine, is one who has performed some miracles. Miracles prove the superiority of the saint over nature, not in a moral, but in a Spiritual sense. Saintliness is transmoral in essence. Nevertheless, Protestantism has rejected the concept of the saint altogether. There are no Protestant saints or, more precisely, no saints under the criterion of the Protestant principle. One can distinguish three reasons for this rejection. First, it seems unavoidable that the distinction between those who are called saints and the other Christians establishes a state of perfection which contradicts the paradox of justification, according to which it is the sinner who is justified. Saints are justified sinners; in this they are equal to anyone. Second, the Reformation protest was directed against a situation in which the saints had become objects of a cult. One cannot deny that this was the case in the Roman church, in spite of the theological precautions the church had taken to prevent it. The church could not succeed because it gave in too readily to the superstitions connected with it and because it was successful in crushing the iconoclastic movements which tried to reduce the danger by removing the visible representations of the saints. Finally, Protestantism could not accept the Roman idea of the saint because it was connected with a dualistic valuation of asceticism. Protestantism does not recognize saints, but it does recognize sanctification, and it can accept representations of the impact of the Spiritual Presence on man. These representative persons are no more saints than any member of the Spiritual Community, however fragmentary his participation may be, but they represent the others as symbols of sanctification. They are examples of the embodiment of the Spirit in bearers of a personal self and as such are of tremendous importance for the life of the churches. But they are also, in every moment of their lives, both estranged and reunited, and it may be that in their inner selves not only the divine but also the demonic forces are extraordinarily strong—as medieval art expressively shows. Protestantism can find representatives of the power of the New Being in the religious as well as in the secular realm, not as a particular grade of sanctity, but as representatives and symbols of that in which all participate who are grasped by the Spirit.

The image of perfection is patterned after the creations of the Spirit, faith and love, and after the four principles determining the process of sanctification—increasing awareness, increasing freedom, increasing relatedness, increasing transcendence.

There are two realms of problems connected with the foundation of perfection on faith and love which need some further discussion. The first is the question of doubt in relation to the increase in faith; the second is the question of the relation of the *eros*-quality of love to the increase in its *agape*-quality. Both questions, which have been partly discussed in earlier contexts, appear at this point in connection with the New Being as process and the fourfold form of its increase toward maturity.

The first question is: What does doubt mean within the process of sanctification? Does the state of perfection include the removal of doubt? In Roman Catholicism such a question can only mean whether the Catholic believer in the state of perfection, for example, as a saint, can doubt the system of doctrines, or any part of it, laid down by the authority of the church without losing the state of perfection. The answer is obviously no, because whenever sanctification has been attained the authority of the church is, according to Roman teaching, unconditionally accepted. This answer is of course imposed by the identification of the Spiritual Community with a church and must, consequently, be rejected in the name of the Protestant principle.

In practice both orthodox Protestantism and pietism agree fundamentally with the Catholic answer—in spite of the Protestant principle. The intellectualistic distortion of faith into acceptance of the literal authority of the Bible (which in practice means the authority of the ecclesiastical creeds) leads orthodoxy to an idea of perfection in which doubt is banned while sin is considered unavoidable. Against this assertion, one could point to the fact that there is a doubt that is an unavoidable implication of sin, both being expressions of the state of estrangement. But the problem is not that of doubt as a consequence of sin; the problem is that of doubt as an element of faith. And just this must be asserted from the point of view of the Protestant principle. The infinite distance between God and man is never bridged; it is identical with man's finitude. Therefore creative courage is an element of faith even in the state of perfection, and where there is courage, there is risk and the doubt implied in risk. Faith would not be faith but mystical union were it deprived of the element of doubt within it.

Pietism, in contrast to orthodoxy, is aware of the fact that subjection to doctrinal laws cannot overcome doubt. Therefore it seeks for the conquest of doubt in experiences which are anticipations of the mystical union with God. The feeling of regeneration, of a reunion with God, of a resting in the saving power of the New Being, drives doubt away. In contrast to orthodoxy, pietism represents the principle of immediacy. Immediacy gives certainty, a certainty which obedience to a doctrinal authority cannot give. But one must ask: Does the religious experience of a man in an advanced stage of sanctification remove the possibility of doubt? Again we must answer no. Doubt is unavoidable as long as there is separation of subject and object, and even the most immediate and intimate feeling of union with the divine, as in the bride-mysticism describing the union of the Christ and the soul, cannot bridge the infinite distance between the finite self and the infinite by which it is grasped. In the oscillations of feeling, this distance is perceived and often throws him who is advanced in sanctification into a profounder doubt than people with less intensity in their religious experience. The question asked here is not a psychological one; it does not refer to the psychological possibility but to the theological necessity of doubt in the faith of the pietist. The psychological possibility is always present; the theological necessity may or may not appear in reality. But theology must state the necessity of doubt which follows from man's finitude under the conditions of existential estrangement.

The second question is that of the relation of the *eros*-quality of love to its increase in *agape*-quality. We touched on this problem when we rejected the higher religious quality of asceticism in describing the image of the saint and the Protestant image of a personality who represents conspicuously the impact of the Spiritual power in him. The problem has been confused by the gap which has been established between *eros* and *agape—eros* embracing *libido, philia,* and *eros* in the Platonic sense, and *agape* designating the New Testament concept of love. Although the establishment of this contrast has been criticized from several sides, its effect is still very strong, partly because it drew attention to a fundamental problem of life under the impact of the divine Spirit. At the same time the psychoanalytic movement in all its branches has destroyed the ideologies of Christian and humanist moralism. It has shown how deeply even the most sublime functions of the spirit are rooted in the vital trends of human nature. Further, the doctrine of the multidimensional unity of life in man requires the rejection of any attempt to suppress vitality for the sake of the spirit and its functions. An increase in awareness, freedom, relatedness, and transcendence does not imply a decrease in vital self-expression; on the contrary, spirit and life in the other dimensions are interdependent. This does not mean that all of them must always be actualized, for this would contradict man's finitude. And often a non-ascetic, yet equally strict, discipline supported by creative *eros* and wisdom is required. But directing one's life toward an integration of as many elements as possible is not identical with an acceptance of repressive practices as they are used in Roman asceticism as well as in Protestant moralism. The uncovering of the distorting consequences of such repression has been shown most convincingly by analytic psychotherapy and its application to the normal human being. This is one of its great services to theology. If the theologian tries to describe the New Being as process, he cannot afford to neglect analytic psychology's insights into the psychodynamics of repression.

Theology should not take the consequences of these insights too lightly; they are, indeed, most serious in their effect on the image of perfection. It is not sufficient, and almost a caricature, if pastoral preaching and counseling recommend the "innocent pleasures of life," thus opening the way to the wrong assumption that some pleasures are in themselves innocent and others guilty instead of encouraging a recognition of the ambiguity of creativity and destruction in every pleasure as well as in everything that is called serious. No pleasure is harmless, and seeking for harmless pleasures leads to a shallow valuation of the power of the vital dynamics in human nature. This condescension toward the vital life of man together with a kind of permissiveness toward childish pleasures is worse than genuine asceticism; it leads to continuous explosions of the repressed and only superficially admitted forces in the totality of man's being. And such explosions are personally and socially destructive. He who admits the vital dynamics in man as a necessary element in all his self-expressions (his passions or his *eros*) must know that he has accepted life in its divine-demonic ambiguity and that it is the triumph of the Spiritual Presence to draw these depths of human nature into its sphere, instead of replacing them with the help of suppression by the niceties of "harmless" pleasures. There is no nicety in the images of perfection in the saints of the Catholic church or in representatives of the new piety of the Reformation. He who tries to avoid the demonic side of the holy also misses its divine side and gains but a deceptive security between them. The image of perfection is the man who, on the battlefield between the divine and the demonic, prevails against the demonic, though fragmentarily and in anticipation. This is the experience in which the image of perfection under the impact of the Spiritual Presence transcends the humanistic ideal of perfection. It is not a negative attitude to human potentialities that produces the contrast but the awareness of the undecided struggle between the divine and the demonic in every man, which in humanism is replaced by the ideal of harmonious self-actualization. And it is the quest for the Spiritual Presence and the New Being as the conquest of the demonic that is lacking in the humanistic image of man and against which humanism rebels.

In Protestant orthodoxy the highest point reached in the process of sanctification is the *unio mystica* (mystical union). This idea, which was easily accepted by pietism, was radically rejected—as was all mysticism—by the personalistic theology of the Ritschlian school. There is, certainly, much mysticism in the image of perfection in the saints of the Roman church. But Protestantism—as the Ritschlian theologians contended—must get rid of these elements which contradict both the aim of sanctification, the personal relation to God, and the way to this aim, the faith which rejects any ascetic preparation for mystical experiences together with these experiences themselves.

The question which arises from the extended discussions about faith and mysticism in Protestant theology is that of the compatibility and, even more, the interdependence of the two. They are compatible only if the one is an element of the other; two attitudes toward the ultimate could not exist beside each other if the one were not given with the other. This is the case in spite of all antimystical tendencies in Protestantism; there is no faith (but only belief) without the Spirit's grasping the personal center of him who is in the state of faith, and this is a mystical experience, an experience of the presence of the infinite in the finite. As an ecstatic experience, faith is mystical, although it does not produce mysticism as a religious type. But it does include the mystical as a category, that is, the experience of the Spiritual Presence. Every experience of the divine is mystical because it transcends the cleavage between subject and object, and wherever this happens, the mystical as category is given. The same is true from the other side. There is faith in mystical experience. This follows from the fact that both faith and mystical experience are states of being grasped by the Spiritual Presence. But the mystical experience is not identical with faith. In faith the elements of courage and risk are actual, whereas in the mystical experience these elements, which presuppose the cleavage between subject and object, are left behind. The question is not whether faith and mysticism contradict each other; they do not. The real question is whether the transcending of the split of subject and object is a possibility in man's existential situation. The answer is that it is a reality in every encounter with the divine ground of being but within the limits of human finitude and estrangement—fragmentary, anticipatory and threatened by the ambiguities of religion. However, this is no reason to exclude the mystical experience from the Protestant interpretation of sanctification. Mysticism as a quality of every religious experience is universally valid. Mysticism as a type of religion stands under the same qualifications and ambiguities as the opposite type, which is often called—wrongly—the type of faith. The fact that Protestantism did not understand its relation to mysticism has produced tendencies which reject Christianity altogether for Eastern mysticism, for example, of the Zen Buddhist type. The alliance of psychoanalysis and Zen Buddhism in some members of the upper classes of Western society (those within the Protestant tradition) is a symptom of dissatisfaction with a Protestantism in which the mystical element is lost.

If the question is raised as to how such a Protestant mysticism can be described, I would refer to what was said about prayer transforming itself into contemplation, and I would refer to the sacred silence which has entered most Protestant liturgies and to the emphasis on the liturgical over against preaching and teaching. Only that is impossible in the spirit of Protestantism which attempts to produce a mysticism through ascetic or other means, which ignores human guilt and divine acceptance, i.e., which ignores the principles of the New Being as justification.

4. The Conquest of Religion by the Spiritual Presence and the Protestant Principle

In so far as the Spiritual Presence is effective in the churches and their individual members, it conquers religion as a particular function of the human spirit. When contemporary theology rejects the name "religion" for Christianity, it is in the line of New Testament thought. The coming of the Christ is not the foundation of a new religion but the transformation of the old state of things. Consequently, the church is not a religious community but the anticipatory representation of a new reality, the New Being as community. In the same way, the individual member of the church is not a religious personality but the anticipatory representation of a new reality, the New Being as personality. Everything said heretofore about the churches and the life of their members points in the direction of a conquest of religion. Conquest of religion does not mean secularization but rather the closing of the gap between the religious and the secular by removing both through the Spiritual Presence. This is the meaning of faith as the state of being grasped by that which concerns us ultimately and not as a set of beliefs, even if the object of belief is a divine being. This is the meaning of love as reunion of the separated in all dimensions, including that of the spirit, and not as an act of negation of all dimensions for the sake of a transcendence without dimensions.

In so far as religion is conquered by the Spiritual Presence, profanization and demonization are conquered. The inner-religious profanization of religion, its transformation into a sacred mechanism of hierarchical structure, doctrine, and ritual, is resisted by the participation of church members in the Spiritual Community, which is the dynamic essence of the churches and of which the churches are both the existential representation and the existential distortion. The freedom of the Spirit breaks through mechanizing profanization—as it did in the creative moments of the Reformation. In doing so it also resists the secular form of profanization, for the secular as secular lives from the protest against the profanization of religion within itself. If this protest becomes meaningless, the functions of morality and culture are opened again for the ultimate, the aim of the self-transcendence of life.

Demonization is also conquered in so far as religion is conquered by the Spiritual Presence. We have distinguished between the demonic that is hidden—the affirmation of a greatness which leads to the tragic conflict with the "great itself"—and the openly demonic—the affirmation of a finite as infinite in the name of the holy. Both the tragic and the demonic are conquered in principle by the Spiritual Presence. Christianity has always claimed that neither the death of the Christ nor the suffering of Christians is tragic, because neither is rooted in the affirmation of its greatness but in the participation in the predicament of estranged man to which each belongs and does not belong. If Christianity teaches that the Christ and the martyrs suffered "innocently," this means that their suffering is not based on the tragic guilt of self-affirmed greatness but on their willingness to participate in the tragic consequences of human estrangement.

Self-affirmed greatness in the realm of the holy is demonic. This is true of the claim of a church to represent in its structure the Spiritual Community unambiguously. The consequent will to unlimited power over all things holy and secular is in itself the judgment against a church which makes this claim. The same is true of individuals who, as adherents of a group making such a claim, become self-assured, fanatical, and destructive of life in others and the meaning of life within themselves. But in so far as the divine Spirit conquers religion, it prevents the claim to absoluteness by both the churches and their members. Where the divine Spirit is effective, the claim of a church to represent God to the exclusion of all other churches is rejected. The freedom of the Spirit resists it. And when the divine Spirit is effective, a church member's claim to an exclusive possession of the truth is undercut by the witness of the divine Spirit to his fragmentary as well as ambiguous participation in the truth. The Spiritual Presence excludes fanaticism, because in the presence of God no man can boast about his grasp of God. No one can grasp that by which he is grasped—the Spiritual Presence.

In other connections I have called this truth the "Protestant principle." It is here that the Protestant principle has its place in the theological system. The Protestant principle is an expression of the conquest of religion by the Spiritual Presence and consequently an expression of the victory over the ambiguities of religion, its profanization, and its demonization. It is Protestant, because it protests against the tragic-demonic self-elevation of religion and liberates religion from itself for the other functions of the human spirit, at the same time liberating these functions from their self-seclusion against the manifestations of the ultimate. The Protestant principle (which is a manifestation of the prophetic Spirit) is not restricted to the churches of the Reformation or to any other church; it transcends every particular church, being an expression of the Spiritual Community. It has been betrayed by every church, including the churches of the Reformation, but it is also effective in every church as the power which prevents profanization and demonization from destroying the Christian churches completely. It alone is not enough; it needs the "Catholic substance," the concrete embodiment of the Spiritual Presence; but it is the criterion of the demonization (and profanization) of such embodiment. It is the expression of the victory of the Spirit over religion.

B. THE SPIRITUAL PRESENCE AND THE AMBIGUITIES OF CULTURE

1. Religion and Culture in the Light of the Spiritual Presence

The relation of the Spiritual Presence to religion has two aspects, because both the profoundest ambiguity of life and the power of conquering the ambiguities of life are manifest in religion. This in itself is the basic ambiguity of religion and the root of all its other ambiguities.

The relation between religion and culture, their essential unity and their existential separation, has been discussed. At this point the question arises as to how this relation appears in the light of the Spiritual Presence and its basic creation, the Spiritual Community, the community of faith and love. The first thing to be emphasized is that the relation is not identical with the relation of the churches to the culture in which they live. Since the churches themselves are distortions as well as representations of the Spiritual Community, their relation to culture is itself culture and not the answer to the questions implied in culture. All relations of the churches to culture, as described in the section on the functions of the churches, in particular the function of relatedness, require a dual consideration, based on the dual relation of the churches to the Spiritual Community. In so far as the Spiritual Community is the dynamic essence of the churches, their existence is a medium through which the Spiritual Presence works toward the self-transcendence of culture. In so far as the churches represent the Spiritual Community in the ambiguous way of religion, their influence on the culture is itself ambiguous. This situation stands against all theocratic attempts to subject the culture to a church in the name of the Spiritual Community, and it also stands against all profanizing attempts to keep the churches in seclusion from the general cultural life. The impact of the Spiritual Presence on the functions of cultural creativity is impossible without an inner-historical representation of the Spiritual Community in a church. But the Spiritual impact can be experienced preliminarily in groups, movements, and personal experiences which have been characterized as the latent working of the Spiritual Presence. "Preliminarily" in our context means in preparation for the full manifestation of the Spiritual Community in a church, or it can mean in consequence of such a full manifestation if the church has lost its power of mediating but the effects of its previous power are latently present in a culture and keep the self-transcendence of the cultural creativity alive. This implies that the divine Spirit is not bound to the media it has created, the churches (and their media, word and sacrament), but that the free impact of the divine Spirit on a culture prepares for a religious community or is received because such a community has prepared human beings for the reception of the Spiritual impact.

On this basis one can establish some principles concerning the relation between religion and culture. The first principle is found in the freedom of the Spirit, according to which the problem of religion and culture is not identical with the problem of the relation between the churches and culture. One could call it "the principle of the consecration of the secular." This, of course, does not mean that the secular as such is Spiritual, but it does mean that it is open to the impact of the Spirit even without the mediation of a church. The practical consequences of this "emancipation of the secular," which was implied in the words and acts of Jesus and was rediscovered by the Reformation, are far-reaching. They are in definitive conflict with those public statements by writers, public speakers, and ministers that, in order to overcome the often destructive ambiguities of culture, "religion" must be strengthened. Such declarations are especially offensive when they introduce religion, not for its own sake, but for the sake of saving an empty or decaying culture and, by doing so, saving a particular nation. Even if the offensiveness of using the ultimate as a tool for something non-ultimate is avoided, the mistake remains of thinking that the divine Spirit is bound to religion in order to exercise its impact on culture. This "mistake" is actually the demonic identification of churches with the Spiritual Community and an attempt to limit the freedom of the Spirit by the absolute claim of a religious group. The principle of the "consecration of the secular" applies as well to movements, groups, and individuals who are not only on the secular pole of the ambiguities of religion but who are openly hostile to the churches and beyond this to religion itself in all its forms, including Christianity. The Spirit can and often has become manifest in such groups, for example, in the form of awakening the social conscience or in giving to man a deeper self-understanding or in breaking the bondage to ecclesiastically sustained superstitions. In this way the Spiritual Presence has used antireligious media to transform not only a secular culture but also the churches. Protestantism, in the self-critical power of the Protestant principle, is able to acknowledge the freedom of the Spirit from the churches, even the Protestant churches.

The second principle determining the relation between religion and culture is the principle of "convergence of the holy and the secular." This converging trend is the explanation of the fact, already referred to, that the latent effect of the Spiritual Presence comes from and drives toward a manifestation of it in a historical community, a church. The secular stands under the rule of all life, which we have called its self-transcending function, transcending itself in the vertical line. The secular is, as we have seen, the result of a resistance against the actualization of vertical self-transcendence. This resistance is in itself ambiguous. It prevents the finite from being swallowed by the infinite. It makes the actualization of its potentialities possible. And, above all, it creates opposition to claims on the part of the churches that they represent the transcendent directly and exclusively. In this sense the secular is the necessary corrective of the holy. Yet, it itself drives toward the holy. It cannot resist indefinitely the function of self-transcendence, which is present in every life, however secularized, for the resistance against it produces the emptiness and meaninglessness which characterizes the finite when cut off from the infinite. It produces the exhaustible, self-rejecting life which is driven to the question of an inexhaustible life above itself and so into self-transcendence. The secular is driven toward union with the holy, a union which actually is a reunion because the holy and the secular belong to each other.

For neither can the holy exist without the secular. If, in the name of the ultimate concern, it tries to isolate itself, it either falls into self-contradictions or becomes empty in a way opposite to the secular. The self-contradiction of the attempt of the holy to dispense with the secular is that every such attempt must make use of culture in all its secular forms, from language to cognition and expression and from the technical act to personal and communal self-creativity. The simplest proposition in which the holy tries to isolate itself from the secular is secular in form. But if the holy wants to avoid this problem, it must become silent and empty of all finite contents, thus ceasing to be a genuine possibility of a finite being. The holy tends to fill the "world," the realm of the secular, with holiness. It tries to take the secular into the life of ultimate concern. But this claim of the Spiritual Presence is resisted by the claim of the secular to stand by itself. So we have claim and counterclaim. But actually there is a convergent movement of the one toward the other; the principle of the convergence of the holy and the secular is always effective.

These two principles are rooted in a third, that of the "essential belongingness of religion and culture to each other." I have expressed this principle frequently in the statement that religion is the substance of culture and culture the form of religion. We have pointed to it in the discussion of the essential relation of morality, culture, and religion.

At this point we must only restate that religion cannot express itself even in a meaningful silence without culture, from which it takes all forms of meaningful expression. And we must restate that culture loses its depth and inexhaustibility without the ultimacy of the ultimate.

With these principles in mind we now turn to an analysis of the humanist idea, its ambiguities, and the question of its relation to the Spiritual Presence.

2. Humanism and the Idea of Theonomy

In the discussion of the humanist aim of the self-creation of life, we asked the question, Into what, for example, does the educational guidance toward this aim actually guide? The development of all human potentialities, the principle of humanism, does not indicate in what direction they shall be developed. This is clear in the very term "education," which means a "leading out," i.e., out of the state of crudeness, but which does not indicate into what one shall be led. We indicated that "initiation" into the mystery of being could be this aim. This, of course, presupposes a community in which the mystery of life, particularly expressed, is the determining principle of its life. There the idea of humanism is transcended without being denied. The example of education and the necessity of transcending humanism in it brings us to a more embracing consideration, namely, the question: What happens to culture as a whole under the impact of the Spiritual Presence? The answer I want to give is summed up in the term "theonomy." One could also speak of the Spirituality of culture, but this would give the impression—certainly not intended—that culture should be dissolved into religion. The term "self-transcendence of culture" would be more adequate, but since this is a general function of life, which under the dimension of spirit appears as religion, another term for the self-transcendence of culture (and another for the self-transcendence of morality) is desirable. On the basis of my Religious Socialist experience and theory, I keep the term "theonomy." It has been explained before, and it will appear again in the last part of the system. At this point the word is used for the state of culture under the impact of the Spiritual Presence. The *nomos* (law) effective in it is the directedness of the self-creation of life under the dimension of the Spirit toward the ultimate in being and meaning. It is certainly unfortunate that the term "theonomy" can indicate the subjection of a culture to divine laws, imposed from outside and mediated by a church. But this disadvantage is smaller than those connected with the other terms, and it is balanced by the possibility of using the word "heteronomy" for a situation in which a law from outside, a strange law (*heteros nomos*) is imposed and destroys the autonomy of cultural creativity, its *autos nomos*, its inner law. Out of the relation of theonomy to heteronomy, it becomes obvious that the idea of a theonomous culture does not imply any imposition from outside. Theonomous culture is Spirit-determined and Spirit-directed culture, and Spirit fulfils spirit instead of breaking it. The idea of theonomy is not antihumanistic, but it turns the humanistic indefiniteness about the "where-to" into a direction which transcends every particular human aim.

Theonomy can characterize a whole culture and give a key to the interpretation of history. Theonomous elements can come in conflict with a rising heteronomy, for example, of ecclesiastical or political provenience, and the autonomous elements in it can be defeated and temporarily suppressed (as in the late Middle Ages). They can come in conflict with a victorious autonomy, for example, of rationalistic or nationalistic provenience, and can be pushed into the underground of a culture (as in the eighteenth and nineteenth centuries). Or they may be able to effect a balance between heteronomous and autonomous trends (as in the twelfth and thirteenth centuries). But theonomy can never be completely victorious, as it can never be completely defeated. Its victory is always fragmentary because of the existential estrangement underlying human history, and its defeat is always limited by the fact that human nature is essentially theonomous.

It is difficult to give general characteristics of a theonomous culture apart from its particular functions, but one may point to the following qualities of theonomy which are derived from its very nature. First of all, the style, the over-all form, of theonomous works of cultural creation expresses the ultimacy of meaning even in the most limited vehicles of meaning—a painted flower, a family habit, a technical tool, a form of social intercourse, the vision of a historical figure, an epistemological theory, a political document, and so on. None of these things is unconsecrated in a theonomous situation; they are perhaps not consecrated by a church, but they are certainly consecrated in the way they are experienced even without external consecration.

In trying to characterize theonomy, one should be aware of the fact that the image of theonomy one develops is never independent of a concrete historical situation which is seen as a symbol of a theonomous culture. Much of the enthusiasm of the romantics for the Middle Ages was rooted in this transformation of the past into a symbol of theonomy. The romantics, of course, went wrong the moment in which they understood a theonomous situation not symbolically but empirically. Then began their historically untenable and almost ridiculous glorification of some periods of the past. But if the past is taken as the model of a future theonomy, it is taken symbolically and not empirically. The first quality of a theonomous culture is that it communicates the experience of holiness, of something ultimate in being and meaning, in all its creations.

The second quality is the affirmation of the autonomous forms of the creative process. Theonomy would be destroyed the moment in which a valid logical conclusion was rejected in the name of the ultimate to which theonomy points, and the same is true in all other activities of cultural creativity. There is no theonomy where a valid demand of justice is rejected in the name of the holy, or where a valid act of personal self-determination is prevented by a sacred tradition, or where a new style of artistic creation is suppressed in the name of assumedly eternal forms of expressiveness. Theonomy is distorted into heteronomy in all these examples; the element of autonomy in it is removed—the freedom which characterizes the human spirit as well as the divine Spirit is repressed. And then it may happen that autonomy breaks through the suppressive forces of heteronomy and discards not only heteronomy but also theonomy.

This situation leads to the third characteristic of theonomy, i.e., its permanent struggle against both an independent heteronomy and an independent autonomy. Theonomy is prior to both; they are elements within it. But theonomy, at the same time, is posterior to both; they tend to be reunited in the theonomy from which they come. Theonomy both precedes and follows the contrasting elements it contains. The process in which this happens can be described in the following way: The original theonomous union is left behind by the rise of autonomous trends which necessarily lead to a reaction of the heteronomous element. Without the liberation of autonomy from the bondage to an "archaic," mythologically founded theonomy, the culture could not develop its potentialities. Only after their liberation from the uniting myth and the theonomous state of consciousness can philosophy and the sciences, poetry and the other arts, appear. But if they achieve independence, they lose their transcendent foundation which gave them depth, unity, and ultimate meaning; and therefore, the reaction of heteronomy starts: the experience of the ultimate, as expressed in the religious tradition, reacts against the creations of an empty autonomy. This reaction easily appears as a simple negation of autonomous creativity and as an attempt to suppress the justified demands of truth, expressiveness, humanity, and justice. But this is not the whole story. A justified warning against the loss of being and meaning is expressed in the distorted form of heteronomous reactions against cultural autonomy. If a scientific theory with a high degree of probability is rejected in the name of a religiously consecrated tradition, one must find out precisely what is rejected. If it is the theory itself, a heteronomous attack on the idea of truth takes place and has to be resisted in the power of the Spirit. If, however, it is an underlying metaphysical—and ultimately religious—assumption which is attacked in the name of religion, the situation has ceased to be a conflict between heteronomy and autonomy and has become a confrontation of two ultimates which may lead to a conflict between religious attitudes but not to a conflict between autonomy and heteronomy.

The permanent struggle between autonomous independence and heteronomous reaction leads to the quest for a new theonomy, both in particular situations and in the depth of the cultural consciousness in general. This quest is answered by the impact of the Spiritual Presence on culture. Wherever this impact is effective, theonomy is created, and wherever there is theonomy, traces of the impact of the Spiritual Presence are visible.

3. THEONOMOUS MANIFESTATIONS OF THE SPIRITUAL PRESENCE

a) Theonomy: truth and expressiveness.—The Spiritual Presence drives toward the conquest of the ambiguities of culture by creating theonomous forms in the different realms of the cultural self-creation of life. In order to present these forms it is necessary to refer to the enumeration of cultural ambiguities given before and to indicate what happens to them under the impact of the Spiritual Presence. But this must be preceded by a discussion of the basic ambiguity which has appeared, more or less obviously, in all cultural functions, the cleavage of subject and object, and of the way in which it is conquered under the impact of the Spiritual Presence. Is there a general theonomous answer to the question of subject against object? Philosophers, mystics, lovers, seekers of intoxication—even of death—have tried to conquer this cleavage. In some of these attempts the Spiritual Presence is manifest; in others the desperate and often demonic desire to escape the cleavage by escaping reality is visible. Psychology has become aware of this problem; the unconscious desire to return to the mother's womb or to the devouring womb of nature or to the protective womb of contemporary society is an expression of the will to dissolve one's subjectivity into something transsubjective, which is not objective (otherwise it would reinstate the subject) but lies beyond subjectivity and objectivity. The most pertinent answers have been given by two phenomena that are related in this respect—mysticism and *eros*. Mysticism answers with the description of a state of mind in which the "universe of discourse" has disappeared but the experiencing self is still aware of this disappearance. Only in eternal fulfilment does the subject (and consequently the object) disappear completely. Historical man can only anticipate in a fragmentary way the ultimate fulfilment in which subject ceases to be subject and object ceases to be object.

A similar phenomenon is human love. The separation of the lover and the beloved is the most conspicuous and painful expression of the subject-object cleavage of finitude. The subject of love is never able to penetrate fully into the object of love, and love remains unfulfilled, and necessarily so, for if it were ever fulfilled it would eliminate the lover as well as the loved; this paradox shows the human situation and with it the question to which theonomy, as the creation of the Spiritual Presence, gives the answer.

The subject-object cleavage underlies language. Our enumeration of its ambiguities—as poverty in richness, particularity in universality, enabling and preventing communication, being open to expression and to the distortion of expression, and so on—can be summed up in the statement that no language is possible without the subject-object cleavage and that language is continuously brought to self-defeat by this very cleavage. In theonomy, language is fragmentarily liberated from the bondage to the subject-object scheme. It reaches moments in which it becomes a bearer of the Spirit expressing the union of him who speaks with that of which he speaks in an act of linguistic self-transcendence. The word which bears the Spirit does not grip an object opposite to the speaking subject, but it witnesses to the sublimity of life beyond subject and object. It witnesses, it expresses, it gives voice, to what transcends the subject-object structure. One of the ways in which this happens is the creation of the symbol. Whereas the ordinary symbol is open to an interpretation which throws it back into the subject-object scheme, the Spirit-created symbol overcomes this possibility and with it the ambiguities of language. Here we are at the point where the term "Word of God" receives its final justification and characterization. Word of God is the Spirit-determined human word. As such it is not bound to a particular revelatory event, Christian or non-Christian; it is not bound to religion in the narrower sense of the term; it is not tied up with a special content or a special form. It appears wherever the Spiritual Presence imposes itself on an individual or a group. Language, under such impact, is beyond poverty and abundance. A few words become great words! This is the ever repeated experience of mankind with the holy literature of a particular religion or of a theonomous culture. But the experience surpasses the "holy scriptures" of any particular religion. In all literature and every use of language, the Spiritual Presence can grasp him who speaks and elevate his words to the state of bearers of the Spirit, conquering the ambiguity of poverty and abundance. In the same way it conquers the ambiguities of particularity and universality. Every language is particular because it expresses a particular encounter with reality, but the language which is a bearer of the Spirit is at the same time universal because it transcends the particular encounter which it expresses in the direction of that which is universal, the Logos, the criterion of every particular logos. The Spiritual Presence also conquers the ambiguity of the indefiniteness of language. Indefiniteness is unavoidable in all ordinary speech because of the infinite distance between the language-forming subject (collective or individual) and the inexhaustible object (every object) it tries to grasp. The word, determined by the Spiritual Presence, does not try to grasp an ever escaping object but expresses a union between the inexhaustible subject and the inexhaustible object in a symbol which is by its very nature indefinite and definite at the same time. It leaves the potentialities of both sides of the symbol-creating encounter open—and in this sense it is indefinite—but it excludes other symbols (and any arbitrariness of symbolism) because of the unique character of the encounter. One more example of the power of the Spiritual Presence to conquer the ambiguities of language is the power over the ambiguity of its communicative and anticommunicative possibilities. Since language cannot penetrate to the very center of the other self, it is always a mixture of revealing and concealing; and from the latter, the possibilities of intentional concealment—of lying, deceiving, distorting, and emptying of language—follow. The Spirit-determined word reaches the center of the other one but not in terms of definitions or circumscriptions of finite objects or finite subjectivity (for example, emotions); it reaches the center of the other one by uniting the centers of the speaker and the listener in the transcendent unity. Where there is spirit, there estrangement in terms of language is overcome—as the story of Pentecost tells. And if it is overcome, the possibility of distorting the language from its natural meaning is also overcome. In all these respects one could say that the ambiguities of the human word are conquered by that human word which becomes divine Word.

To overcome the ambiguities of cognition the divine Spirit must conquer the cleavage between subject and object even more drastically than in the case of language. The cleavage appears, for example, in the circumstances that every cognitive act must use abstract concepts, thus disregarding the concreteness of the situation; that it must give a partial answer, although "the truth is the whole" (Hegel); and that it must use patterns of conceptualization and argumentation which fit only the realm of objects and their relation to each other. This necessity cannot be dismissed on the level of finite relations; and so the question arises whether there is another relation in which the wholeness of the truth can be reached and the "demonry of abstraction" overcome. This cannot be done in the dialectical manner of Hegel, who claimed to have the whole by combining all parts in a consistent system. In doing so he became, in a conspicuous way, the victim of the ambiguities of abstraction (without reaching the totality to which he aspired). The divine Spirit embraces both the totality and the concrete, not by avoiding universals—without which no cognitive act would be possible—but by using them only as vehicles for the elevation of the partial and concrete to the eternal, in which totality as well as uniqueness are rooted. Religious knowledge is knowledge of something particular in the light of the eternal and of the eternal in the light of something particular. In this kind of knowledge the ambiguities of subjectivity as well as objectivity are overcome; it is a self-transcending cognition which comes out of the center of the totality and leads back to it. The impact of the Spiritual

Presence is also manifest in the method of theonomous cognition. Within the structure of subject-object separation, observation and conclusion are the way in which the subject tries to grasp the object, remaining always strange to it and never certain of success. To the degree in which the subject-object structure is overcome, observation is replaced by participation (which includes observation) and conclusion is replaced by insight (which includes conclusions). Such insight on the basis of participation is not a method which can be used at will but a state of being elevated to what we have called the transcendent unity. Such Spirit-determined cognition is "revelation," just as Spirit-determined language is "Word of God." And as "Word of God" is not restricted to the Holy Scriptures, so "revelation" is not restricted to the revelatory experiences on which all actual religions are based. The acknowledgment of this situation lies behind the assertion of many theologians of the classical tradition, Catholics and Protestants alike, that in the wisdom of some non-Christian wise men the divine Wisdom—the Logos—was present and that the presence of the Logos meant for them—as for us—Spiritual Presence. Wisdom can be distinguished from objectifying knowledge (*sapientia* from *scientia*) by its ability to manifest itself beyond the cleavage of subject and object. The biblical imagery describing Wisdom and Logos as being "with" God and "with" men makes this point quite obvious. Theonomous knowledge is Spirit-determined Wisdom. But as the Spirit-determined language of theonomy does not dispense with the language which is determined by the cleavage between subject and object, so Spirit-determined cognition does not contradict the knowledge which is gained within the subject-object structure of encountering reality. Theonomy never contradicts autonomously created knowledge, but it does contradict a knowledge which claims to be autonomous but is actually the result of a distorted theonomy.

The aesthetic function of man's cultural self-creation presents the same problem as language and cognition: in seeking for expressiveness in its creations it is confronted by the question of whether the arts express the subject or the object. But before a theonomous answer is sought to this question, another arises, and that is the relation of man as self-integrating personality to the whole realm of aesthetic expression—the problem of aestheticism. Like the preceding question, it is rooted in the subject-object structure of finite being. The subject can transform any object into "nothing but an object" by using it for itself instead of trying to enter it in a reunion of the separated. The aesthetic function—whether pre-artistic or artistic—creates images which are objects of aesthetic enjoyment. The enjoyment is based on the expressive power of an aesthetic creation even if the subject matter expressed is ugly or terrifying. The enjoyment of aesthetically created images, pre-artistic or artistic, is in agreement with the creativity of the spirit. But aestheticism, while accepting the enjoyment, withdraws from participation. The impact of the Spiritual Presence, in uniting subject and object, makes aestheticism impossible.

Thus to the question of whether the arts express the subject or the object, we must give the obvious answer: neither the one nor the other. Subject and object must be united in a theonomous creation of the Spiritual Presence through the aesthetic function. This question has bearing on the valuation of different artistic styles. In each style the relation of subject and object is different; so the question arises whether there is a style which is more theonomous than the others or which is theonomous over against the others. It is very difficult to make such a statement, but it must be made. In analogy to the cognitive function, the question is usually asked in the form of whether a certain philosophy (for example, the Platonic, Aristotelian, Stoic, or Kantian) has more theonomous potentiality than the others. This question must be and has always been answered by the actual work of theologians, who used one or another of these philosophies in the conviction that it was most adequate to the human situation and for the construction of a theology. But it seems impossible to do the same thing with an enumeration of styles. In relation to the question of theonomy, we cannot distinguish styles; we can only distinguish stylistic elements. This is obvious, in view of the fact that no concrete style can be imitated as long as there is the will to original artistic expression. One can stand within a stylistic tradition, but one cannot change from one tradition to another at will. (This is the same situation that exists in relation to theonomous philosophy. No philosophical system can be duplicated by another philosopher, but all take over elements from their predecessors, and there are certainly elements which have more theonomous potentialities than others. But the decisive thing for the search for truth is that, under the principle of autonomy, all potentialities of man's cognitive encounter with reality are developed.)

With respect to stylistic elements (which reappear in all historical styles), the realistic, the idealistic, and the expressionistic elements can be distinguished. Each appears in every style, but normally one element is predominant. From the point of view of theonomy, one can say that the expressionistic element is most able to express the self-transcendence of life in the vertical line. It breaks away from the horizontal movement and shows the Spiritual Presence in symbols of broken finitude. This is the reason why most of the great religious art in all periods has been determined by the expressionist element in its stylistic expression. When the naturalistic and idealistic elements are predominant, the finite is either accepted in its finitude (though not copied) or is seen in its essential potentialities but not in its disruption and salvation. Naturalism, when predominant, produces acceptance, idealism, anticipation, and expressionism the breakthrough into the vertical. Thus expressionism is the genuinely theonomous element.

b) Theonomy: purpose and humanity.—The basic ambiguity of subject and object is expressed in relation to the technical activity of man in the conflicts caused by the unlimited possibilities of technical progress and the limits of his finitude in adapting himself to the results of his own productivity. The ambiguity of subject and object also expresses itself in the productions of means for ends which themselves become means without an ultimate end and in the technical transformation of parts of nature into things which are only things, i.e., technical objects. If one asks what theonomy could mean in relation to these ambiguities or, more precisely, how the split between subject and object can be overcome in this realm of complete objectivation, the answer can only be: by producing objects which can be imbued with subjective qualities; by determining all means toward an ultimate end and, by so doing, limiting man's unlimited freedom to go beyond the given. Under the impact of the Spiritual Presence, even technical processes can become theonomous and the split between the subject and the object of technical activity can be overcome. For the Spirit, no thing is merely a thing. It is a bearer of form and meaning and, therefore, a possible object of *eros*. This is true even of tools, from the most primitive hammer to the most delicate computer. As in the earliest periods when they were bearers of fetish powers, so today they can be considered and artistically valuated as new embodiments of the power of being itself. This *eros* toward the technical *Gestalt* is a way in which a theonomous relation to technology can be achieved. One can observe such *eros* in the relation of children and adults to such technical *Gestalten* as ships, cars, planes, furniture, impressive machines, factory buildings, and so on. If the *eros* toward these objects is not corrupted by competitive or mercenary interests, it has a theonomous character. The technical object—the only complete "thing" in the universe—is not in essential conflict with theonomy, but it is a strong factor in causing the ambiguities of culture and needs sublimation by *eros* and art.

The second problem which demands a theonomous solution is the indeterminate freedom of producing means for ends which in turn become means, and so on without limit. Theonomous culture includes technical self-limitation. Possibilities are not only benefits; they are also temptations, and the desire to actualize them can lead to emptiness and destruction. Both consequences are visible at present.

The first has been seen and denounced for a long time. It is fostered by the business- and advertisement-supported drives toward the production of what is called the "gadget." The gadget itself is not evil, but gearing a whole economy to it and repressing the question of an ultimate end of all production of technical goods is. This problem is necessarily raised under the impact of the Spiritual Presence and may revolutionize the attitude toward technical possibilities in such a way that actual production will be changed. This, of course, cannot be done from outside by ecclesiastical or quasi-religious political authorities; it can only be done by influencing the attitude of those for whom the things are produced— as advertisers well know. The divine Spirit, cutting out of the vertical direction to resist an unlimited running-ahead in the horizontal line, drives toward a technical production that is subjected to the ultimate end of all life processes—Eternal Life.

The problem caused by the unlimited possibilities of technical production is even more difficult when the consequences are almost inescapably destructive. Such consequences have become visible since the Second World War and have produced strong emotional and moral reactions in most people, above all in those who are mainly responsible for the technical "structures of destruction"—atomic weapons—which, according to the nature of the demonic, cannot be rejected and cannot be accepted. Therefore the reaction of these men, as well as of the people, to the demonic character inherent in the stupendous technical possibilities of the atomic discoveries is split. Under the impact of the Spiritual

Presence, the destructive side of that human possibility will be "banned" (the term used in the book of *Revelation* for the preliminary conquest of the demonic). Again, this "ban" is not a matter of authoritarian restriction on technical possibilities but a change in attitude, a change in the will to produce things which are in their very nature ambiguous and structures of destruction. No solution is imaginable without the Spiritual Presence, because the ambiguity of production and destruction cannot be conquered on the horizontal level, even fragmentarily. To realize this, one must remember that the Spiritual Presence is not bound to the religious realm (in the narrower sense of religion) but can even be effective through outspoken foes of religion and Christianity.

From the discussion of the technical function of culture and its ambiguities, we turned to the personal (and communal) function and the ambiguities of self-determination, other-determination, and personal participation. In all three cases the split between subject and object, as in all cultural functions, is the necessary condition as well as the inescapable cause of ambiguities. The ambiguity of self-determination is rooted in the fact that the self as subject and the self as object are split and that the self as subject tries to determine the self as object in a direction from which the self as subject is itself estranged. The "good will" is only ambiguously good, just because it is not united with the self as object which it is supposed to direct. No centered self under the conditions of existence is fully identical with itself. Whenever the Spiritual Presence takes hold of a centered person, it re-establishes his identity unambiguously (though fragmentarily). The "search for identity" which is a genuine problem of the present generation is actually the search for the Spiritual Presence, because the split of the self into a controlling subject and a controlled object can be overcome only from the vertical direction, out of which reunion is given and not commanded. The self which has found its identity is the self of him who is "accepted" as a unity in spite of his disunity.

The split between subject and object also produces the ambiguities of educating and guiding another person. In both activities it is necessary, though impossible, to find a way between self-restriction and self-imposition on the part of the educator or guide. Complete self-restriction, as exemplified in some types of progressive schools, leads to complete ineffectiveness. The object is not asked to unite with the subject in a common content but is left alone in bondage to himself and to his ambiguities as a person, while the subject, instead of educating or guiding, remains an irrelevant observer. The opposite attitude violates the object of education and guidance by transforming him into an object without subjectivity and therefore incapable of being educated to his own fulfilment or guided toward his ultimate aim. He can only be controlled by indoctrination, commands, tricks, "brainwashing," and so on, and in extreme cases, as in concentration camps, by methods of dehumanization which deprive him of his subjectivity by depriving him of the necessary biological and psychological conditions for existing as a person. They transform him into a perfect example of the principle of conditioned reflexes. The Spirit liberates both from mere subjectivity and from mere objectivity. Under the impact of the Spiritual Presence the educational act creates theonomy in the centered person by directing him toward the ultimate from which he receives independence without internal chaos. It belongs to the very nature of the Spirit that it unites freedom and form. If the educational or guiding communion between person and person is raised beyond itself by the Spiritual Presence, the split between subject and object in both relations is fragmentarily conquered and humanity is fragmentarily achieved.

The same is true of other person to person encounters. The other person is a stranger, but a stranger only in disguise. Actually he is an estranged part of one's self. Therefore one's own humanity can be realized only in reunion with him—a reunion which is also decisive for the realization of his humanity. In the horizontal line this leads to two possible but equally ambiguous solutions: the effort to overcome the split between the subject and object in a person-to-person encounter (whereby each person is both subject and object) either by surrendering one's self to the other one or by taking the other one into one's self. Both ways are continually tried, in many degrees of predominance of the one or the other element, and both are failures because they destroy the persons they seek to unite. It is again the vertical dimension out of which the answer comes: both sides in the encounter belong to some third thing that transcends them both. Neither surrender nor subjection are adequate means of reaching the other one. He cannot be reached directly at all. He can be reached only through that which elevates him above his self-relatedness. Sartre's assertion of the mutual objectivation of human beings in all of their encounters cannot be denied except from the point of view of the vertical dimension. Only through the impact of the Spiritual Presence is the shell of self-seclusion pierced. The stranger who is an estranged part of one's self has ceased to be a stranger when he is experienced as coming from the same ground as one's self. Theonomy saves humanity in every human encounter.

c) *Theonomy: power and justice.*—In the communal realm, too, the gap between subject and object leads to a great number of ambiguities. We have referred to some of them, and we must now show what happens to them under the impact of the Spiritual Presence. Where there is Spirit, they are conquered, though fragmentarily. The first problem following from the establishment of any kind of community is the exclusiveness which corresponds to the limitation of its inclusiveness. As every friendship excludes the innumerable others with whom there is no friendship, so every tribe, class, town, nation, and civilization excludes all those who do not belong to it. The justice of social cohesion implies the injustice of social rejection. Under the impact of the Spiritual Presence, two things happen in which the injustice within communal justice is conquered. The churches, in so far as they represent the Spiritual Community, are transformed from religious communities with demonic exclusiveness into a holy community with universal inclusiveness, without losing their identity. The indirect effect this has on the secular communities is one side of the impact of the Spiritual Presence in the communal realm. The other is the direct effect the Spirit has on the understanding and actualizing of the idea of justice. The ambiguity of cohesion and rejection is conquered by the creation of more embracing unities through which those who are rejected by the unavoidable exclusiveness of any concrete group are included in a larger group—finally in mankind. On this basis family-exclusiveness is fragmentarily overcome by friendship-inclusiveness, friendship-rejection by acceptance in local communities, class-exclusiveness by national-inclusiveness, and so on. Of course, this is a continuous struggle of the Spiritual Presence, not only against exclusiveness, but also against an inclusiveness which disintegrates a genuine community and deprives it of its identity (as in some expressions of mass society).

This example leads directly to another of the ambiguities of justice, that of inequality. Justice implies equality; but equality of what is essentially unequal is as unjust as inequality of what is essentially equal. Under the impact of the Spiritual Presence (which is the same as saying, determined by faith and love), the ultimate equality of everyone who is

called to the Spiritual Community is united with the preliminary inequality that is rooted in the self-actualization of the individual as
individual. Everyone has his own destiny, based partly on the given
conditions of his existence and partly on his freedom to react in a
centered way to the situation and the different elements in it, as provided
by his destiny. The ultimate equality, however, cannot be separated
from the existential inequality; the latter is under a continuous Spiritual
judgment, because it tends to produce social situations in which ultimate
equality becomes invisible and ineffective. Although it was the influence
of Stoic philosophy more than that of the Christian churches that reduced the injustice of slavery in its dehumanizing power, it was (and
is) the Spiritual Presence which acted through the philosophers of Stoic
provenience. But here also the struggle of the Spirit against the ambiguities of *praxis* is directed not only toward communal inequality but
also toward forms of communal equality in which essential inequality
is disregarded, for example, in the principle of equal education in a
mass society. Such education is an injustice to those whose charisma is
their ability to transcend the conformity of an equalizing culture. With
the affirmation of the ultimate equality of all men, the Spiritual Presence
affirms the polarity of relative equality and relative inequality in the
actual communal life. The theonomous solution of the ambiguities of
equality produces a genuine theonomy.

Among the most conspicuous ambiguities of community is that of
leadership and power. It also most obviously shows the subject-object
split as the source of the ambiguities. Because of the lack of a physiological centeredness such as we find in the individual person, the community
must create centeredness, as far as it is possible at all, by a ruling group
which itself is represented by an individual (king, president, and so on).
In such an individual, communal centeredness is embodied in psychosomatic centeredness. He represents the center, but he *is* not the center in
the way in which his own self is the center of his whole being. The
ambiguities of justice which follow from this character of communal
centeredness are rooted in the unavoidable fact that the ruler and the
ruling group actualize their own power of being when they actualize
the power of being of the whole community they represent. The tyranny
which pervades all systems of power, even the most liberal, is one consequence of this highly dialectical structure of social power. The other
consequence, resulting from opposition to the implications of power, is

a powerless liberalism or anarchism, which is usually soon succeeded by a conscious and unrestricted tyranny. Under the impact of the Spiritual Presence, the members of the ruling group (including the ruler) are able to sacrifice their subjectivity in part by becoming objects of their own rule along with all other objects and by transferring the sacrificed part of their subjectivity to the ruled. This partial sacrifice of the subjectivity of the rulers and this partial elevation of the ruled to subjectivity is the meaning of the "democratic" idea. It is not identical with any particular democratic constitution which attempts to actualize the democratic principle. This principle is an element in the Spiritual Community and its justice. It is present even in aristocratic and monarchic constitutions—and it may be greatly distorted in historical democracies. Wherever it is fragmentarily actual the Spiritual Presence is at work—through or in opposition to the churches or outside the overtly religious life.

Justice in communal life is, above all, justice of the law, law in the sense of a power-supported legal system. Its ambiguities are twofold: the ambiguity of the establishment of the law and the ambiguity of its execution. The first is partly identical with the ambiguity of leadership. Legal power, exercised by the ruling group (and the individual who represents the group), is first of all legislative power. The justice of a system of laws is inseparably tied to justice as conceived by the ruling group, and this justice expresses both principles of right and wrong and principles by which the ruling group affirms and sustains and defends its own power. The spirit of a law inseparably unites the spirit of justice and the spirit of the powers in control, and this means that its justice implies injustice. Under the impact of the Spiritual Presence, the law can receive a theonomous quality to the extent that the Spirit is effective. It can represent justice unambiguously though fragmentarily; in symbolic language, it can become "the justice of the Kingdom of God." This does not mean that it can become a rational system of justice above the life of any communal group, such as some Neo-Kantian philosophers of law have tried to develop. There is no such thing, because the multidimensional unity of life does not admit a function of the spirit in which the preceding dimensions are not effectively present. The spirit of the law is necessarily not only the spirit of justice but also the spirit of a communal group. There is no justice that is not someone's justice—not the justice of an individual but of a society. The Spiritual Presence does not suppress the vital basis of the law but removes its injustices by fighting against the ideologies which justify them. This fight has sometimes been waged through the voice of the churches as images of the Spiritual Community and sometimes in a direct way by the creation of prophetic movements within the secular realm itself. Theonomous legislation is the work of the Spiritual Presence through the medium of prophetic self-criticism in those who are responsible for it. Such a statement is not "idealistic" in the negative sense of the word as long as we maintain the "realistic" statement that the Spirit works indirectly through all dimensions of life, though directly only through the dimensions of man's spirit.

The other ambiguity of the legal form of communal life is the ambiguity of the execution of the law. Here two considerations are needed. One is related to the fact that the execution of the law is dependent on the power of those who render judgments and who are, in so doing, dependent, like the lawgivers, upon their own total being in all its dimensions. Each of their judgments expresses not only the meaning of the law, not only its spirit, but also the spirit of the judge, including all the dimensions which belong to him as a person. One of the most important functions of the Old Testament prophet was to exhort the judges to exercise justice against their class interest and against their changing moods. The dignity with which the office and functions of the judge are vested is a reminder of the theonomous origin of, and theonomous ideal in, the execution of the law.

However, there is another ambiguity of the legal form of communal life, one which is rooted in the very nature of the law—its abstraction and inability to fit precisely any concrete case in which it is applied. History has shown that the situation is not improved, but rather worsened, when new, more specific laws are added to the more general ones. They are equally inadequate to any concrete situation. The wisdom of the judge lies between the abstract law and the concrete situation, and this wisdom can be theonomously inspired. In so far as this is the case, the demand of the particular case is perceived and obeyed. The law in its abstract majesty does not overrule individual differences, nor does it deprive itself of its general validity in acknowledging differences.

The last remarks have prepared the transition to what underlies justice and humanity directly and all cultural functions indirectly— morality. We must now turn to the impact of the Spiritual Presence on morality.

C. THE SPIRITUAL PRESENCE AND THE AMBIGUITIES
OF MORALITY

1. RELIGION AND MORALITY IN THE LIGHT OF THE SPIRITUAL PRESENCE: THEONOMOUS MORALITY

The essential unity of morality, culture, and religion is destroyed under the conditions of existence, and in the processes of life only an ambiguous version of it remains. However, an unambiguous, though fragmentary, reunion is possible under the impact of the divine Spirit. The Spiritual Presence creates a theonomous culture and it creates a theonomous morality. The term "theonomous," as applied to culture and morality, has the meaning of the paradoxical phrases "transcultural culture" and "transmoral morality." Religion, the self-transcendence of life under the dimension of spirit, gives self-transcendence to both the self-creation and the self-integration of life under the dimension of spirit. We have discussed the relation of religion and culture in the light of the Spiritual Presence; we must now discuss the relation of religion and morality under the same aspect.

The question of the relation of religion and morality can be discussed in terms of the relation of philosophical and theological ethics. This duality is analogous to the duality of autonomous and Christian philosophy and is actually a part of the latter. We have already rejected the idea of a Christian philosophy, which would inevitably betray the honesty of search by determining before inquiry what results must be found. This refers to all parts of the philosophical enterprise, including ethics. If the phrase means what it says, "theological ethics" is consciously prejudiced ethics. However, this is not true of theonomous ethics, as it is not true of a theonomous philosophy. A philosophy is theonomous which is free from external interferences and in which, in the actual process of thought, the impact of the Spiritual Presence is effective. An ethics is theonomous in which the ethical principles and processes are described in the light of the Spiritual Presence. Theonomous ethics is part of theonomous philosophy. Theological ethics as an independent theological discipline must be rejected, although every theological statement has ethical implications (as it has ontological presuppositions). If theological ethics (or philosophy of religion) is dealt with academically in a separate course, this is merely a matter of expediency and should not become a matter of principle. Otherwise, an intolerable dualism between philosophical and theological ethics is set up, leading logically to the schizophrenic position of "double truth." One would affirm in the one course of study the autonomy of practical reason in the Kantian or Humean sense of the word, and in the other the heteronomy of revelatory divine commandments that is to be found in biblical and ecclesiastical documents. On the basis of the distinction between religion in the larger and the narrower sense of the word, we can establish *one* course of study in ethics which analyzes the nature of the moral function and judges the changing contents in the light of this analysis. Within the analysis, the unconditional character of the moral imperative and with it the theonomous quality of ethics may be affirmed or denied, but both affirmation and negation remain in the arena of philosophical controversy and are not decided by an external ecclesiastical or political authority. The theologian enters these controversies as a philosophical ethicist whose eyes are opened by the ultimate concern that has taken hold of him, but his arguments have the same experiential basis and the same rational cogency claimed for the arguments of those who deny the unconditional character of the moral imperative. The teacher of ethics is a philosopher, whether or not his ethics is theonomous. He is a philosopher even if he is a theologian and although his ultimate concern is dependent on the subject matter of his theological work, for example, the Christian message. But as an ethicist he does not bring his theological assertions into the arguments about the nature of the moral imperative.

One may ask whether such a combination of ultimate concern and partly detached argument is possible. Empirically speaking, it is impossible, because the theonomous quality of an ethics is always concrete and therefore dependent on concrete traditions, whether Jewish, Christian, Greek, or Buddhist. From this one would draw the conclusion that theonomy must be concrete and, therefore, in conflict with the autonomy of ethical research. But this argument disregards the fact that even the seemingly autonomous research in philosophy in general and in ethics in particular is dependent on a tradition which expresses an ultimate concern, at least indirectly and unconsciously. Autonomous ethics can be autonomous only with respect to scholarly method, not with respect to its religious substance. There is a theonomous element in all such ethics, however hidden, however secularized, however distorted. Theonomous ethics in the full sense of the phrase, therefore, is ethics in which, under the impact of the Spiritual Presence, the religious substance—the experience of an ultimate concern—is consciously expressed through the process of free arguing and not through an attempt to determine it. Intentional theonomy is heteronomy and must be rejected by ethical research. Actual theonomy is autonomous ethics under the Spiritual Presence.

In relation to the biblical and ecclesiastical ethical material, this means that it cannot be taken over and systematized as "theological ethics," based on revelatory "information" about ethical problems. Revelation is not information, and it is certainly not information about ethical rules or norms. All the ethical material, for example, of the Old and New Testaments, is open to ethical criticism under the principle of *agape*, for the Spirit does not produce new and more refined "letters," i.e., commandments. Rather, the Spirit judges all commandments.

2. The Spiritual Presence and the Ambiguities of Personal Self-integration

In our description of the ambiguities of the integration of the moral personality, we pointed to the polarity of self-identity and self-alteration and the loss of a centered self either in an empty self-identity or in a chaotic self-alteration. The problems implied in this polarity led us to the concept of sacrifice and its ambiguities. The continual alternative— to sacrifice either the actual for the possible or the possible for the actual—appeared as an outstanding example of the ambiguities of self-integration. The ever returning questions are: How many contents of the encountered world *can* I take into the unity of my personal center without disrupting it? And, How many contents of the encountered world *must* I take into the unity of my personal center in order to avoid an empty self-identity? Into how many directions *can* I push beyond a given state of my being without losing all directedness of the life process? And, Into how many directions *must* I try to encounter reality in order to avoid a narrowing-down of my life process to monolithic poverty? And the basic question is: How many potentialities, given to me by virtue of my being man and, further, by being this particular man, *can* I actualize without losing the power to actualize anything seriously? And, How many of my potentialities *must* I actualize in order to avoid the state of mutilated humanity? These sets of questions, of course, are not asked *in abstracto* but always in the concrete form: Shall I sacrifice this that I have for this that I could have?

The alternative is resolved, though fragmentarily, under the impact of the Spiritual Presence. The Spirit takes the personal center into the universal center, the transcendent unity which makes faith and love possible. When taken into the transcendent unity, the personal center is superior to encounters with reality on the temporal plane, because the transcendent unity embraces the content of all possible encounters. It embraces them beyond potentiality and actuality, because the transcendent unity is the unity of the divine life. In the "communion of the Holy Spirit," the essential being of the person is liberated from the contingencies of freedom and destiny under the conditions of existence. The acceptance of this liberation is the all-inclusive sacrifice which, at the same time, is the all-inclusive fulfilment. This is the only unambiguous sacrifice a human being can make. But since it is made within the processes of life, it remains fragmentary and open to distortion by the ambiguities of life.

The consequences of this consideration for the three double questions asked above can be described as follows: In so far as the personal center is established in relation to the universal center, the encountered contents of finite reality are judged for their significance in expressing the essential being of the person before they are allowed to enter, or are barred from entering, the unity of the centered self. The element of Wisdom in the Spirit makes such judgment possible (compare, for example, the judging function of the Spirit in I Corinthians, chapter 3). It is a judgment directed toward what we have distinguished as the two poles in the self-integration of the moral self, self-identity and self-alteration. The Spiritual Presence maintains the identity of the self without impoverishing the self, and it drives toward the alteration of the self without disrupting it. In this way the Spirit conquers the double anxiety which logically (but not temporally) precedes the transition from essence to existence, the anxiety of not actualizing one's essential being and the anxiety of losing oneself within one's self-actualization. Where there is Spirit, the actual manifests the potential and the potential determines the actual. In the Spiritual Presence, man's essential being appears under the conditions of existence, conquering the distortions of existence in the reality of the New Being. This statement is derived from the basic christological assertion that in the Christ the eternal unity of God and man becomes actual under the conditions of existence without being conquered by them. Those who participate in the New Being are in an analogous way beyond the conflict of essence and existential predicament. The Spiritual Presence actualizes the essential within the existential in an unambiguous way.

The question of the amount of strange content which can be taken into the unity of the centered self has led to an answer which refers to all three questions asked above and especially to the question of the sacrifice of the potential for the actual. But more concrete answers are necessary. The ambiguity of the life processes with respect to their directions and aims must be conquered by an unambiguous determination of the life processes. Where Spiritual Presence is effective, life is turned into the direction which is more than one direction among others—the direction toward the ultimate within all directions. This direction does not replace the others but appears within them as their ultimate end and therefore as the criterion of the choice between them. The "saint" (he who is determined by the Spiritual Presence) knows *where* to go and where *not* to go. He knows the way between impoverishing asceticism and disrupting libertinism. In the life of most people the question of where to go, in which directions to spread and which direction to make predominant, is a continuous concern. They do not know where to go, and therefore many cease to go at all and permit their life processes to fall into the poverty of anxious self-restriction; others start off in so many directions that they cannot follow up any of them. The Spirit conquers restriction as well as disruption by preserving the unity in divergent directions, both the unity of the centered self who takes the divergent directions and the unity of the directions which reconverge after they have diverged. They reconverge in the direction of the ultimate.

With respect to the double question of how many potentialities—in general human and in particular individual—one *can* actualize and how many one *must* actualize, the answer is the following: Finitude demands the sacrifice of potentialities which can be actualized only by the sum of all individuals, and even the power of these potentialities to be actualized is restricted by the external conditions of the human race and its finitude. Potentialities remain unactualized in every moment of history because their actualization has never become a possibility. In the same way, in every moment of every individual life potentialities remain unactualized because they have never reached the state of possibility. However, there are potentialities that are also possibilities that, nevertheless, must be sacrificed because of human finitude. Not all the creative possibilities of a person, or all the creative possibilities of the human race, have been or will be actualized. The Spiritual Presence does not change that situation—for although the finite can participate in the infinite, it cannot become infinite—but the Spirit can create an acceptance of man's and. mankind's finitude, and in so doing can give a new meaning to the sacrifice of potentialities. It can remove the ambiguous and tragic character of the sacrifice of life possibilities and restore the genuine meaning of sacrifice, namely, the acknowledgement of one's finitude. In every religious sacrifice, finite man deprives himself of a power of being which seems to be his but which is not his in an absolute sense, as he acknowledges by the sacrifice; it is his only because it is given to him and, therefore, not ultimately his, and the acknowledgment of this situation is the sacrifice. Such an understanding of the sacrifice excludes the humanistic ideal of the all-round personality in which every human potentiality is actualized. It is a God-man idea, which is quite different from the God-man image created by the divine Spirit as the essence of the man Jesus of Nazareth. This image shows the sacrifice of all human potentialities for the sake of the one which man himself cannot actualize, the uninterrupted unity with God. But the image also shows that this sacrifice is indirectly creative in all directions of truth, expressiveness, humanity, justice—in the picture of the Christ as well as in the life of the churches. In contrast to the humanist idea of man which actualizes what man can be directly and without sacrifice, the Spirit-determined fulfilment of man sacrifices all human potentialities, to the extent that they lie on the horizontal plane, to the vertical direction and receives them back into the limits of man's finitude from the vertical direction, the direction of the ultimate. This is the contrast between autonomous and theonomous personal fulfilment.

3. THE SPIRITUAL PRESENCE AND THE AMBIGUITIES OF THE MORAL LAW

The intention of the following consideration is to establish a theonomous foundation for the moral law. The ambiguities of the moral law in its heteronomous and autonomous expressions have been shown above, and the paradox of a "transmoral morality" has been considered.

It has been considered under three aspects: the validity of the moral imperative, the relativity of the moral content, the power of the moral motivation. *Agape*, the love which reunites centered person with centered person, was the answer in each case. If this answer is valid, the moral law is both accepted and transcended. It is accepted as the expression of what man essentially or by creation is. It is transcended in its form as law, that is, as that which stands against man in his existential estrangement, as commandment and threat. Love contains and transcends the law. It does voluntarily what the law commands. But now the question arises: Is not love itself a law, the all-embracing law? "Thou *shalt* love. . . ." And if love itself is a law, does it not fall under the ambiguities of the law even more than any particular law? Why is it valid; what are its contents; how does it get motivating power? The possibility of summing up all laws in the law of love does not solve the problem of the law and its ambiguities. The question cannot be answered as long as love appears as law. It has been said that the commandment "Thou shalt love . . ." is impossible because love, as an emotion, cannot be commanded. But this argument is not valid because the interpretation of love as an emotion is wrong. Love as commandment is impossible because man in existential estrangement is incapable of love. And since he cannot love, he denies the unconditional validity of the moral imperative, he has no criterion by which to choose within the flux of ethical contents, and he has no motivation for the fulfilment of the moral law. However, love is not a law; it is a reality. It is not a matter of ought-to-be—even if expressed in imperative form—but a matter of being. Theonomous morals are morals of love as a creation of the Spirit. This refers to the three problems of validity, content, and motivation.

The Spiritual Presence shows the validity of the moral imperative unambiguously, just by showing its law-transcending character. The Spirit elevates the person into the transcendent unity of the divine life and in so doing it reunites the estranged existence of the person with his essence. And this reunion is just what the moral law commands and what makes the moral imperative unconditionally valid. The historical relativity of all ethical contents does not contradict the unconditional validity of the moral imperative itself, because all contents must, in order to be valid, confirm the reunion of man's existential with his essential being; they must express love. In this way the Kantian formalism of the moral imperative is accepted and surpassed. Love unites the unconditional character of the formalized moral imperative with the conditional character of the ethical content. Love is unconditional in its essence, conditional in its existence. It is against love to elevate any moral content, except love itself, to unconditional validity, for only love is by its very nature open to everything particular while remaining universal in its claim.

This answer anticipates the second question arising from the ambiguities of the moral law, the question of its content. The contents of the moral imperative are the moral demands implied in concrete situations and abstract norms derived from ethical experiences in relation to concrete situations. The ambiguity of the law, which we have described before, leads to an oscillation of man's deciding center between the lists of general laws which never reach down to a concrete situation and the riddle of a unique case which pushes the mind back to general laws. This oscillation makes every ethical judgment ambiguous and leads to the question of an unambiguous criterion for ethical judgments. Love, in the sense of *agape*, is the unambiguous criterion of all ethical judgments. It is unambiguous but, like every creation of the Spiritual Presence in time and space, remains fragmentary. This answer implies that love overcomes the oscillation between the abstract and the concrete elements in a moral situation. Love is as near the abstract norms as it is near the particular demands of a situation, but the relation of love to each of these two elements of an ethical problem is different. In relation to the abstract element, the formulated moral laws, love is effective through wisdom. The wisdom of the ages and the ethical experiences of the past (including revelatory experiences) are expressed in the moral laws of a religion or philosophy. This origin gives an overwhelming significance to the formulated ethical norms, but it does not give them unconditional validity. Under the impact of the prophetic criticism, moral laws change their meaning or are abrogated altogether. If they have become powerless to help the ethical decision in concrete situations, they are obsolete and—if preserved—destructive. Once created by love, they are now in conflict with love. They have become "letter," and the Spirit has left them.

The concrete situation is the continuous source of ethical experience. In itself it is mute—like every fact unaccompanied by interpretative concepts. It needs ethical norms in order to give voice to its meaning.

But the norms are abstract and do not reach the situation. Only love can do that, because love unites with the particular situation out of which the concrete demand grows. Love itself uses wisdom, but love transcends the wisdom of the past in the power of another of its elements, courage. It is the courage to judge the particular without subjecting it to an abstract norm—a courage which can do justice to the particular. Courage implies risk, and man must take the risk of misconceiving the situation and of acting ambiguously and against love—perhaps because he acts against a traditional ethical norm or perhaps because he subjects himself to a traditional ethical norm. To the degree that Spirit-created love prevails in a human being, the concrete decision is unambiguous, but it never can escape the fragmentary character of finitude. With respect to moral content, theonomous morality is determined by Spirit-created love. It is supported by the Spirit-created wisdom of the ages, expressed in the moral laws of the nations. It is made concrete and adequate by the application of the courage of love to the unique situation.

Love is also the motivating power in theonomous morality. We have seen the ambiguities of the law's demanding obedience—even if it is the law of love. Love is unambiguous, not as law, but as grace. Theologically speaking, Spirit, love, and grace are one and the same reality in different aspects. Spirit is the creative power; love is its creation; grace is the effective presence of love in man. The very term "grace" indicates that it is not a product of any act of good will on the part of him who receives it but that it is given gratuitously, without merit on his side. The great "in spite of" is inseparable from the concept of grace. Grace is the impact of the Spiritual Presence that makes the fulfilment of the law possible—though fragmentarily. It is the reality of that which the law commands, the reunion with one's true being, and this means the reunion with oneself, with others, and with the ground of one's self and others. Where there is New Being, there is grace, and vice versa. Autonomous or heteronomous morality is without ultimate moral motivating power. Only love or the Spiritual Presence can motivate by giving what it demands.

This is the judgment brought against all non-theonomous ethics. They are unavoidably ethics of the law, and the law makes for the increase of estrangement. It cannot conquer it but instead produces hatred of itself as law. The many forms of ethics without Spiritual Presence are judged by the fact that they cannot show the power of motivation, the principle of choice in the concrete situation, the unconditional validity of the moral imperative. Love can do it, but love is not a matter of man's will. It is a creation of the Spiritual Presence. It is grace.

D. THE HEALING POWER OF THE SPIRITUAL PRESENCE AND THE AMBIGUITIES OF LIFE IN GENERAL

1. THE SPIRITUAL PRESENCE AND THE AMBIGUITIES OF LIFE IN GENERAL

All the preceding discussions concerning the Spirit are related to the functions of the human spirit: morality, culture, religion. But the descriptions of the ambiguities of life in the dimensions which precede the appearance of the dimensions of the spirit take a large space and are a preparation for the descriptions of the ambiguities of life under the dimension of the spirit. The question which thus arises is whether the Spirit has a relation to these dimensions of life as definite as to the human spirit. Has the Spiritual Presence a relationship to life in general?

The first answer we must give is that there is no direct impact of the Spiritual Presence on life in the dimensions of the inorganic, of the organic, and of self-awareness. Divine Spirit appears in the ecstasy of human spirit but not in anything which conditions the appearance of spirit. The Spiritual Presence is not an intoxicating substance, or a stimulus for psychological excitement, or a miraculous physical cause. This must be emphasized in view of the many instances in the history of religion, including biblical literature, in which physical or psychological effects are derived from the Spirit in its quality as divine power, for example, the removal of a person from one place to another "through the air," the killing of a healthy but morally disintegrated person by mere words, the generation of an embryo in the mother's womb without male participation, or the knowledge of foreign languages without a process of learning. All these effects are considered as caused by the Spiritual Presence. Obviously, if these stories are taken literally, they make the divine Spirit a finite, though extraordinary, cause beside other causes. In this view Spirit is a kind of physical matter. Both its Spirituality and its divinity are lost. If, in spiritualistic movements, the Spirit is described as a substance of higher power and dignity than that of the ordinary natural substances, this is an abuse of the word "Spirit." Even if there were "higher" natural substances than we know, they would not deserve the name "Spirit"; they would be "lower" than spirit in man and not under the direct impact of the Spiritual Presence. This is the first answer to the question of the relation of the Spirit to life in general.

The second answer is that the multidimensional unity of life implies an indirect and limited influence of the Spiritual Presence on the ambiguities of life in general. If the presupposition is true that all dimensions of life are potentially or actually present in each dimension, happenings under the predominance of one dimension must imply happenings in other dimensions. This means that all we have said about the impact of the Spiritual Presence on man's spirit and its three basic functions implies changes in all dimensions which constitute man's being and condition the appearance of spirit in him. The impact, for example, of the Spiritual Presence on the creation of theonomous morality implies effects on the psychological self and its self-integration, and this implies effects on biological self-integration and the physiological and chemical processes out of which it arises. However, these implications should not be misunderstood as a chain of causes and effects, starting with the impact of the Spiritual Presence on the human spirit and causing changes in all other realms through the human spirit. The multidimensional unity of life means that the impact of the Spiritual Presence on the human spirit is *at the same time*, an impact on the *psyche*, the cells, and the physical elements which constitute man. And although the term "impact" unavoidably uses causal imagery, it is not a cause in the categorical sense but a presence which participates in the object of its impact. Like the divine creativity in all respects, it transcends the category of causality, although human language must make use of causality in a symbolic way. As the "impact" of the Spiritual Presence is not a cause in the categorical sense, so it does not start a chain of causes into all dimensions of life but is "present" to all of them in one and the same Presence. However, this presence is restricted to those beings in whom the dimension of the spirit has appeared. Although qualitatively it refers to all realms, quantitatively it is limited to man as the being in whom spirit is actualized.

If we look at the processes of self-integration, self-creation, and self-transcendence with these limitations in mind, we understand why their ambiguities cannot be conquered totally and universally by the Divine Spirit. The Spirit grasps the spirit and only indirectly and in a limited way the *psyche* and the *physis*. The universe is not yet transformed; it "waits" for transformation. But the Spirit transforms actually in the dimension of the spirit. Men are the "first fruits" of the New Being; the universe will follow them. The doctrine of the Spirit leads to the doctrine of the Kingdom of God as eternal fulfilment.

But there is a function which unites the universality of the Kingdom of God with the limited impact of the Spiritual Presence—the function of healing. All dimensions of life are involved in it. It is produced by actions in all realms, including the realm which is determined by the dimension of spirit. It is an effect of the Spiritual Presence and an anticipation of eternal fulfilment. Therefore it requires a special consideration. Salvation means healing, and healing is an element in the work for salvation.

2. HEALING, SALVATION, AND THE SPIRITUAL PRESENCE

The life process under all dimensions unites self-identity with self-alteration. Disintegration occurs if one of the two poles is so predominant that the balance of life is disturbed. The name of this disturbance is disease, and its final result is death. Healing forces within organic processes, whether they lie inside or originate outside the organism, try to break the predominance of one of the poles and revive the influence of the other one. They work for the self-integration of a centered life, for health. Since disease is a disruption of centeredness under all dimensions of life, the drive for health, for healing, must also occur under all dimensions. There are many processes of disintegration leading to disease, and there are many ways of healing, of trying to reintegrate, and many kinds of healers, depending on the different processes of disintegration and the different ways of healing. The question in our context is whether there is Spiritual healing, and if it exists, how it is related to the other ways of healing, and further, how it is related to that kind of healing which in the language of religion is called "salvation."

The multidimensional unity of life is most conspicuous in the realm of health, disease, and healing. Each of these phenomena must be described in terms of multidimensional unity. All dimensions of life are included in each of them. Health and disease are states of the whole person; they are "psychosomatic," as a contemporary technical term incompletely indicates. Healing must be directed to the whole person. But such statements need drastic qualification in order to give a true picture of the reality. The different dimensions which constitute the human being are not only united; they are also distinct and capable of being affected and of reacting with relative independence. Certainly, there is no absolute independence in the dynamics of the different dimensions, but neither is there an absolute dependence. An injury of a small part of the body (for example, an injured finger) always has some impact on the biological and psychological dynamics of a person as a whole, although it does not make the whole person sick and the healing can be limited (for example, surgery). The degree in which unity or independence prevails decides the most adquate kind of healing. It decides, above all, how many kinds should be used together and whether it is not better for the health of the person as a whole that a limited disease not be subjected to an attempt at healing at all (for example, some neurotic compulsions). All this refers to healing under the different dimensions of life, without considering the healing power of the Spiritual Presence. It shows the variety of mixtures between interdependence and independence of the factors which determine health, disease, and healing. It shows that any one-sided approach to healing must be strongly rejected and that even an approach from many or all sides is inadequate in some causes. The conflicts, for example, between chemical and psychological ways of healing, are unavoidable only if the one or the other method claims exclusive validity. Sometimes both ways should be used together; sometimes one alone is preferable. But in all cases the question of the relations of the different methods to each other should be asked without a dogmatic prejudice, whether for chemical medicine, for example, or for psychotherapy.

If we now ask how these different approaches are related to healing under the impact of the Spiritual Presence, a very ambiguous concept is offered as answer: the concept of faith healing. Since faith is the first creation of the Spirit, the term "faith healing" could simply mean healing under the impact of the Spiritual Presence. But this is not the case. The term "faith healing" is currently used for psychological phenomena which suggest the term "magic healing." Faith, in the faith-healing movements or by individual faith healers, is an act of concentration and autosuggestion, produced ordinarily, but not necessarily, by acts of another person or of a group. The genuinely religious concept of faith, as the state of being grasped by an ultimate concern or, more specifically, by the Spiritual Presence, has little in common with this autosuggestive concentration called "faith" by the faith healers. In a sense it is just the opposite, because the religious concept of faith points to its receptive character, the state of being grasped by the Spirit, whereas the faith-healer's concept of faith emphasizes an act of intensive concentration and self-determination.

In calling faith healing "magic" we do not intend to use a pejorative term. Faith healing can be and has been quite successful, and there is probably no healing of any kind which is completely free from elements of magic. For magic must be defined as the impact of one being upon another which does not work through mental communication or physical causation but which nevertheless has physical or mental effects. The propagandist, the teacher, the preacher, the counselor, the doctor, the lover, the friend, can combine an impact on the perceiving and deliberating center with an impact on the whole being by magic influence, and the latter can subdue the former to such a degree that dangerous consequences result from by-passing the deliberating, deciding, and responsible self. All communication would be only intellectual and all influence of one human being upon another a matter of physical causes or arguments, without the magic element. Magic healing, of which faith healing is a conspicuous form, is one of many ways of healing. In the name of the Spiritual Presence it can be neither unambiguously accepted nor unambiguously rejected. But three things must be stated with respect to it: first, that it is not healing through faith but by magic concentration; second, that it is justified as an element in many human encounters, though it has destructive as well as creative possibilities; and third, that if it excludes other ways of healing in principle (as some faith-healing movements and individuals do) it is predominantly destructive.

There is faith healing within the Christian churches as well as in particular groups and circles. Intensive and often repeated prayers are the main tool, to which sacramental performances are added for psychological support. Since prayers and intercessions for health belong to the normal intercourse between man and God, it is difficult to draw a sharp boundary line between Spirit-determined and magical praying. Generally speaking, one can say that a Spirit-determined prayer seeks to bring one's own personal center, including one's concern for the health of one's self or of someone else, before God, and that it is willing to accept the divine acceptance of the prayer whether its overt content is fulfilled or not. Conversely, a prayer which is only a magical concentration on the desired aim, using God for its realization, does not accept an unfulfilled prayer as an accepted prayer, for the ultimate aim in the magic prayer is not God and the reunion with him but the object of the prayer, for example, health. A prayer for health in faith is not an attempt at faith healing but an expression of the state of being grasped by the Spiritual Presence.

It is now possible to relate the different ways of healing to the reality of the New Being and its significance for healing. The basic statement, derived from all the previous considerations of this part of the theological system, is that the integration of the personal center is possible only by its elevation to what can be called symbolically the divine center and that this is possible only through the impact of the divine power, the Spiritual Presence. At this point health and salvation are identical, both being the elevation of man to the transcendent unity of the divine life. The receiving function of man in this experience is faith; the actualizing function is love. Health in the ultimate sense of the word, health as identical with salvation, is life in faith and love. In so far as it is created by the Spiritual Presence, the health of unambiguous life is reached; and although unambiguous, it is not total but fragmentary, and it is open to relapses into the ambiguities of life in all its dimensions.

The question now is how this unambiguous though fragmentary health, created by the Spirit, is related to the healing activities under the different dimensions. The first answer is negative from both sides: The healing impact of the Spiritual Presence does not replace the ways of healing under the different dimensions of life. And, conversely, these ways of healing cannot replace the healing impact of the Spiritual Presence. The first statement rejects not only the wrong claims of the faith healers but also the much more serious but rather popular error that derives disease directly from a particular sin or from a sinful life. Such an error produces a despairing conscience in those who are stricken and a pharisaic self-righteousness in those who are not. To be sure there is often a simple line of cause and effect between a sinful act or behavior and a particular incidence of disease. But even then, healing is not a matter of forgiveness alone but also a matter of medical or psychological care. It is decisive for judging this situation that the sinful state itself is not a matter of the responsible self alone but also a matter of the destiny which includes ambiguities in all the dimensions which constitute the person. The different dimensions in which diseases occur have a relative independence of each other and of the Spiritual impact on the person, and demand a comparatively independent way of healing. But the other answer to our question is equally important, and that is that the other ways of healing cannot replace the healing power of the Spirit. In periods when the medical and the priestly functions were completely separate, this was not a serious problem, especially when medical healing claimed absolute validity, even against any striving of psychotherapy for independence. In this situation salvation had nothing to do with healing; it was the salvation from hell in a future life and the medical profession gladly left it to the priest. But the situation changed when mental diseases ceased to be derived from demonic possession or, in contrast, from physically observable causes. With the development of psychotherapy as an independent way of healing, problems arose in the directions both of medicine and of religion. Today psychotherapy (including all schools of psychological healing) often tries to eliminate both medical healing and the healing function of the Spiritual Presence. The first is usually a matter of practice rather than of theory, the second mostly a matter of principle. The psychoanalyst, for example, claims that he can overcome the negativities of man's existential situation—anxiety, guilt, despair, emptiness, and so on. But in order to support his claim the analyst must deny both the existential estrangement of man from himself and the possibility of his transcendent reunion with himself; that is, he must deny the vertical line in man's encounter with reality. If he is not willing to deny the vertical line, because he is aware of an unconditional concern in himself, he must accept the question of an existential estrangement. He must, for example, be willing to distinguish between existential anxiety to be conquered by a courage created by the Spiritual Presence and a neurotic anxiety to be conquered by analysis, perhaps in combination with methods of medical healing. It seems that the insight into these structures is gaining among representatives of the several ways of healing. In any case, the "struggle of the faculties" has lost its theoretical foundation as well as practical ground. The ways of healing do not need to impede each other, as the dimensions of life do not conflict with each other. The correlate of the multidimensional unity of life is the multidimensional unity of healing. No individual can exercise all the ways of healing with authority, although more than one way may be used by some individuals. But even if there is a union of different functions, for example, of the priestly and medical functions in one man, the functions must be distinguished and neither confused with the other, nor may one be eliminated by the other.

Healing is fragmentary in all its forms. Manifestations of disease struggle continuously with manifestations of health, and it often happens that disease in one realm enhances health in another realm and that health under the predominance of one dimension increases disease under another dimension (for example, the healthy athlete with all the symptoms of neurosis or the healthy activist who hides an existential despair). Not even the healing power of the Spirit can change this situation. Under the condition of existence it remains fragmentary and stands under the "in spite of" of which the Cross of the Christ is the symbol. No healing, not even healing under the impact of the Spiritual Presence, can liberate the individual from the necessity of death. Therefore the question of healing, and this means the question of salvation, goes beyond the healing of the individual to the healing through history and beyond history; it leads us to the question of the Eternal Life as symbolized by the Kingdom of God. Only universal healing is total healing—salvation beyond ambiguities and fragments.

IV

THE TRINITARIAN SYMBOLS

A. THE MOTIVES OF THE TRINITARIAN SYMBOLISM

THE Spiritual Presence is the Presence of God under a definite aspect. It is not the aspect expressed in the symbol of creation, nor is it the aspect expressed in the symbol of salvation, although it presupposes and fulfils both. It is the aspect of God ecstatically present in the human spirit and implicitly in everything which constitutes the dimension of the spirit. These aspects are reflections of something real in the nature of the divine for religious experience and for the theological tradition. They are not merely different subjective ways of looking at the same thing. They have a *fundamentum in re*, a foundation in reality, however much the subjective side of man's experience may contribute. In this sense we can say that the trinitarian symbols are a religious discovery which had to be made, formulated, and defended. What then, we ask, led to their discovery? One can distinguish at least three factors which have led to trinitarian thinking in the history of religious experience: first, the tension between the absolute and the concrete element in our ultimate concern; second, the symbolic application of the concept of life to the divine ground of being; and third, the threefold manifestation of God as creative power, as saving love, and as ecstatic transformation. It is the last of the three which suggests the symbolic names, Father, Son, and Spirit; but without the two preceding reasons for trinitarian thinking the last group would lead only into a crude mythology. We have dealt with the first two groups in describing the development of the idea of God and in discussing the application of the symbol of life to God. In the first consideration we have found that the more the ultimacy of our ultimate concern is emphasized, the more the religious need for a concrete manifestation of the divine develops, and that the tension between the absolute and the concrete elements in the idea of God drives toward the establishment of divine figures between God and man. It is the possible conflict between these figures and the ultimacy of the ultimate which motivates the trinitarian symbolism

283

in many religions and which remained effective in the trinitarian discussions of the early church. The danger of falling into tritheism and the attempts to avoid this danger were rooted in the inner tension between the ultimate and the concrete.

The second reason for the trinitarian symbolism has been discussed under the heading "God as Life." It led to the insight that if God is experienced as a living God and not as a dead identity an element of nonbeing must be seen in his being, that is, the establishment of otherness. The Divine Life then would be the reunion of otherness with identity in an eternal "process." This consideration brought us to the distinction of God as ground, God as form, and God as act, a pretrinitarian formula which makes trinitarian thinking meaningful. Certainly, the trinitarian symbols express the divine mystery as do all symbols which state something of God. This mystery, which is *the* mystery of being, remains unapproachable and impenetrable; it is identical with the divinity of the divine. It was the mistake of the classical German philosophers (whose thought is basically a philosophy of life) that, although seeing the trinitarian structure of life, they did not safeguard the divine mystery against cognitive *hubris*; but they were right (and so were most classical theologians) in using the dialectics of life in order to describe the eternal process of the divine ground of being. The doctrine of the Trinity—this is our main contention—is neither irrational nor paradoxical but, rather, dialectical. Nothing divine is irrational—if irrational means contradicting reason—for reason is the finite manifestation of the divine Logos. Only the transition from essence to existence, the act of self-estrangement, is irrational. Nor is the doctrine of the Trinity paradoxical. There is only one paradox in the relation betewen God and man, and that is the appearance of the eternal or essential unity of God and man under the conditions of their existential separation—or in Johannine language, the Logos has become flesh, i.e., has entered historical existence in time and space. All other paradoxical statements in Christianity are variations and applications of this paradox, for example, the doctrine of justification by grace alone or the participation of God in the suffering of the universe. But the trinitarian symbols are dialectical; they reflect the dialectics of life, namely the movement of separation and reunion. The statement that three is one and one is three was (and in many places still is) the worst distortion of the mystery of Trinity. If this is meant as a numerical identity, it is a trick or simply nonsense. If it is meant as the description of a real process, it is not paradoxical or irrational at all but a precise description of all life processes. And in the trinitarian doctrine it is applied to the Divine Life in symbolic terms.

But all this is preparatory for the developed trinitarian doctrine in Christian theology which is motivated by the third basic reason for trinitarian thinking, that is, the manifestation of the divine ground of being in the appearance of Jesus as the Christ. With the statement that the historical Jesus is the Christ, the trinitarian problem became a part of the christological problem, the first and basic part, as indicated by the fact that the trinitarian decision in Nicaea preceded the definitely christological decision of Chalcedon. This sequence was logical, but in terms of motivation the sequence is reversed; the christological problem gives rise to the trinitarian problem.

For this reason it is adequate in the context of the theological system to discuss the trinitarian symbolism after having discussed the christological assertions of Christianity. But christology is not complete without pneumatology (the doctrine of the Spirit), because "the Christ is the Spirit" and the actualization of the New Being in history is the work of the Spirit. It was an important step in the direction of an existential understanding of theological doctrines when Schleiermacher put the doctrine of the Trinity at the end of the theological system. Certainly, the basis of his system, the Christian consciousness, with the lines drawn from it to its divine causation, was too weak to carry the burden of the system. It is not the Christian consciousness but the revelatory situation of which the Christian consciousness is only the receiving side that is the source of religious knowledge and theological reflection, including the trinitarian symbols. But Schleiermacher is right when he derives these symbols from the different ways in which faith is related to its divine cause. It was a mistake of Barth to start his Prolegomena with what, so to speak, are the Postlegomena, the doctrine of the Trinity. It could be said that in his system this doctrine falls from heaven, the heaven of an unmediated biblical and ecclesiastical authority.

Like every theological symbol, the trinitarian symbolism must be understood as an answer to the questions implied in man's predicament. It is the most inclusive answer and rightly has the dignity attributed to it in the liturgical practice of the church. Man's predicament, out of which the existential questions arise, must be characterized by three concepts: finitude with respect to man's essential being as creature, estrangement with respect to man's existential being in time and space, ambiguity with respect to man's participation in life universal. The questions arising out of man's finitude are answered by the doctrine of God and the symbols used in it. The questions arising out of man's estrangement are answered by the doctrine of the Christ and the symbols applied to it. The questions arising out of the ambiguities of life are answered by the doctrine of the Spirit and its symbols. Each of these answers expresses that which is a matter of ultimate concern in symbols derived from particular revelatory experiences. Their truth lies in their power to express the ultimacy of the ultimate in all directions. The history of the trinitarian doctrine is a continuous fight against formulations which endanger this power.

We have referred to several motifs effective in trinitarian thought. All of them are based on revelatory experiences. The road to monotheism and the corresponding rise of mediating figures has appeared under the impact of the Spiritual Presence; the experience of God as a "living God" and not as dead identity is a work of the Spiritual Presence as is the experience of the creative ground of being in every being, the experience of Jesus as the Christ, and the ecstatic elevation of the human spirit toward the union of unambiguous life. On the other hand, the trinitarian doctrine is the work of theological thought which uses philosophical concepts and follows the general rules of theological rationality. There is no such thing as trinitarian "speculation" (where "speculation" means conceptual phantasies). The substance of all trinitarian thought is given in revelatory experiences, and the form has the same rationality that all theology, as a work of the Logos, must have.

B. THE TRINITARIAN DOGMA

It is not possible within the framework of this system to go into the intricacies of the trinitarian struggles. Only a few remarks in the light of our methodological procedures are possible. The first remark concerns the interpretation of the trinitarian dogma as given by the Ritschlian school, above all by the histories of dogma of Harnack and Loofs. It seems to me that the criticism of this theology by the different antiliberal schools of contemporary theology has in no way undercut its basic insights. Harnack and Loofs have shown both the greatness of the fundamental decision the church made at Nicaea and the impasse into which Christian theology was driven by the conceptual form used for the decision. The liberating influence these insights had is still felt even in the antiliberal groups of contemporary theology and should never be lost in Protestantism. The limits of a work like Harnack's lie, from a historical point of view, in his misrepresentation of classical Greek, and even more of Hellenistic thought, as "intellectualistic." This leads him to a rejection of the whole of early Christian theology as an invasion of Hellenistic attitudes into the preaching of the Gospel and the life of the church. But Greek thought is existentially concerned with the eternal, in which it seeks for eternal truth and eternal life. Hellenism could receive the Christian message only in these categories, as the mind of the Jews of the Diaspora could receive it only in categories similar to those used by Paul and as the first disciples could receive it only in categories used by contemporaneous eschatological movements. In the light of these facts, it would be as false to reject a theology because it uses such categories as it would be to bind all future theology to the use of these categories.

Harnack's criticism of the trinitarian dogma of the early church shows full awareness of the latter point. But it betrays a lack of positive valuation of what the synodal decisions achieved in spite of their questionable formulations. This, of course, is connected with the attempt of the Ritschlian school to replace the ontological categories of Greek thought by the moral categories of modern, particularly Kantian, thought. But, as the later development of the Neo-Kantian school itself has proved, ontological categories are always used, if not explicitly, implicitly! Therefore one should approach the trinitarian dogma of the early church with neither a positive nor a negative prejudice but with the question: What has been and what has not been achieved by it?

If God is the name for what concerns us ultimately, the principle of exclusive monotheism is established: there is no god besides God! But the trinitarian symbolism includes a plurality of divine figures. This presents the alternative either of attributing to some of these divine figures a diminished divinity or of dropping the exclusive monotheism and with it the ultimacy of the ultimate concern. The ultimacy of the ultimate concern is replaced by half-ultimate concerns and monotheism by quasi-divine powers as its expressions. This was the situation when the divinity of the Christ became a problem of theological interpretation instead of remaining an act of liturgical devotion. The problem was unavoidable, not only because of the reception of the message of the

Christ by the Greek mind, but also because man cannot repress his cognitive function in dealing with the content of his religious devotion. The great attempt of early Greek theology to solve the problem with the help of the Logos doctrine was the basis of all its later achievements and difficulties. It is understandable that the difficulties into which the doctrine was driven induced some theological schools to dismiss the doctrine altogether. But even if it were possible to develop a christology without applying the predicate Logos to the Christ, it is impossible to develop a doctrine of the living God and of the creation without distinguishing the "ground" and the "form" in God, the principle of abyss and the principle of the self-manifestation in God. Therefore one can say that even aside from the christological problem some kind of Logos doctrine is required in any Christian doctrine of God. On this basis it was and is necessary to merge the prechristological and the christological assertions about the divine life into a fully developed trinitarian doctrine. This synthesis has so great an inner necessity that even the sharpest and most justified criticism of the Logos doctrine of the classical theologians cannot annihilate it. He who sacrifices the Logos principle sacrifices the idea of a living God, and he who rejects the application of this principle to Jesus as the Christ rejects his character as Christ.

The question put before the church in Nicaea as well as in the preceding and subsequent struggles was not the establishment of the Logos principle—this was done long before the Christian era and not only in Greek philosophy—nor was it the application of this principle to Jesus as the Christ—this was done definitively in the Fourth Gospel. It was rather the question of the relation betwen God and his Logos (also called Son). This question was so existential for the early church because the valuation of Jesus as the Christ and his revelatory and saving power depends on the answer to it. If the Logos is defined as the highest of all creatures, as the left-wing theologians of the Origenistic school asserted, the Christ, in whom the Logos is manifest as historical personality, is himself, with all creatures, in need of revelation and salvation. In having him, men would have something less than "God with us." Neither error nor guilt nor death would have been conquered. This is the existential concern behind the fight of the right wing of the Origenistic school under the leadership of Athanasius. In the trinitarian decision of Nicaea their position prevailed theologically, devotionally, and politically. The half-god Jesus of Arian teaching was avoided. But the trinitarian problem was more stated than solved. In the terminology of Nicaea, the divine "nature" (*ousia*) is identical in God and his Logos, in the Father and the Son. But the *hypostasis* is different. *Ousia* in this context means that which makes a thing what it is, its particular *physis*. *Hypostasis* in this context means the power of standing upon itself, the independence of being which makes mutual love possible. The decision of Nicaea acknowledged that the Logos-Son, like the God-Father, is an expression of ultimate concern. But how can ultimate concern be expressed in two divine figures who, although identical in substance, are different in terms of mutual relations? In the post-Nicaean struggles the divinity of the Spirit was discussed, denied, and finally affirmed in the second ecumenical synod. The motive for it was again christological. The divine Spirit who created and determined Jesus as the Christ is not the spirit of the man Jesus; and the divine Spirit who creates and directs the church is not the spirit of a sociological group. And the Spirit who grasps and transforms the individual person is not an expression of his spiritual life. The divine Spirit is God himself as Spirit in the Christ and through him in the church and the Christian. The consistency of this transformation of a binitarian strain in the early church into a fully developed Trinity is obvious, but it did not help to solve the basic problem: How can ultimate concern be expressed in more than one divine *hypostasis*?

In terms of religious devotion, one can ask: Is the prayer to one of the three *personae* in whom the one divine substance exists directed toward someone different from another of the three to whom another prayer is directed? If there is no difference, why does one not simply address the prayer to God? If there is a difference, for example, in function, how is tritheism avoided? The concepts of *ousia* and *hypostasis* or of *substantia* and *persona* do not answer this basic devotional problem. They only confuse it and open the way to the unlimited number of objects of prayer which appeared in connection with the veneration of Mary and the saints—in spite of the theological distinctions between a genuine prayer, directed to God (adoration), and the evocation of the saints.

The difficulty appears as soon as the question is asked as to what the historical Jesus, the man in whom the Logos became "flesh," means for the interpretation of the Logos as the second *hypostasis* in the Trinity? We have spoken about it in connection with the symbols of the pre-existence and postexistence of the Christ. From the point of view of the trinitarian doctrine, any non-symbolic interpretation of these symbols would introduce into the Logos a finite individuality with a particular life history, conditioned by the categories of finitude. Certainly the Logos, the divine self-manifestation, has an eternal relation to his self-manifestation in the Christ as the center of man's historical existence, as the Logos has an eternal relation to all potentialities of being; but one cannot attribute to the eternal Logos in himself the face of Jesus of Nazareth or the face of "historical man" or of any particular manifestation of the creative ground of being. But certainly, the face of God manifest *for* historical man is the face of Jesus as the Christ. The trinitarian manifestation of the divine ground is Christocentric for man, but it is not Jesu-centric in itself. The God who is seen and adored in trinitarian symbolism has not lost his freedom to manifest himself for other worlds in other ways.

The trinitarian doctrine was accepted in the West as well as in the East, but its spirit was Eastern and not Western. This became visible in Augustine's attempt to interpret the difference of the hypostases by psychological analogies, his acknowledgment that the statements about the mutual relations of the *personae* are empty, and his emphasis on the unity of the acts of the Trinity *ad extra*. All this reduced the danger of tritheism, which could never be fully removed from the traditional dogma and which was always connected with a kind of subordination of the Son to the Father and the Spirit to the Son. Behind the subordinational element in the Greek Orthodox understanding of the Trinity lies one of the most fundamental and most persistent traits of the classical Greek encounter with reality, the interpretation of reality in grades, leading from the lowest to the highest (and conversely). This profoundly existential understanding of reality runs from Plato's *Symposium* to Origen and through him to the Eastern church and to Christian mysticism. In the monarchianistic tendencies of the Roman church and in Augustine's voluntaristic emphasis, it came into conflict with a strangely personalistic world view. After the sixth century the dogma could not be changed any further. Not even the reformers attempted it, in spite of Luther's biting criticism of some of the concepts used in it. It had become the politically guaranteed symbol of all forms of Christianity and the basic liturgical formula in all churches. But we must ask whether, after the historical analysis and the systematic criticism of the dogma in Protestant theology since the eighteenth century, this state of things can last—in spite of its reaffirmation in the so-called basis of the World Council of Churches, which in any case falls short of the real achievement of Nicaea and Chalcedon.

C. REOPENING THE TRINITARIAN PROBLEM

The situation of the dogma of the Trinity, as indicated in the preceding paragraph, has several dangerous consequences. The first one is a radical change in the function of the doctrine. While originally its function was to express in three central symbols the self-manifestation of God to man, opening up the depth of the divine abyss and giving answers to the question of the meaning of existence, it later became an impenetrable mystery, put on the altar, to be adored. And the mystery ceased to be the eternal mystery of the ground of being; it became instead the riddle of an unsolved theological problem and in many cases, as shown before, the glorification of an absurdity in numbers. In this form it became a powerful weapon for ecclesiastical authoritarianism and the suppression of the searching mind.

It is understandable that the autonomous revolt against this situation in the period of the Renaissance and Reformation led to a radical rejection of the doctrine of Trinity in Socinianism and Unitarianism. The smallness of the direct effect of this revolt was due to the fact that it did not do justice to the religious motives of the trinitarian symbolism, as analyzed above; however, its indirect effect on most Protestant churches since the eighteenth century has been great. One may cite the general rule that an organ which has lost its function becomes crippled and an impediment to life. Protestantism generally did not attack the dogma, but it did not use it either. Even in denominations with a "high" Christology and an emphatic confession of the divinity of the Christ (for example, the Protestant Episcopal church), no new understanding of the Trinity was produced. But in most Protestant churches something developed which one could call a "Christocentric Unitarianism," It removed the emphasis on God as God, on the mystery of the divine ground and his creativity. It prevented an understanding of the Spiritual Presence and the ecstatic character of faith, love, and prayer. It reduced Protestant Christianity to a tool for moral education, accepted by society for this reason. The source book for this education is the "teachings of Jesus." In spite of all this, the trinitarian creeds and prayers of the liturgy are still used, the hymns with their trinitarian implications are sung, and the Unitarians are excluded from the World Council of Churches.

Will it ever again be possible to say without theological embarrassment or mere conformity to tradition the great words, "In the name of the Father and the Son and the Holy Spirit"? (The term "Holy Ghost" must be purged from every liturgical or other use.) Or will it be possible again to pray for blessings through the "love of God, the Father, and the grace of Jesus Christ and the fellowship of the Holy Spirit" without awakening superstitious images in those who hear the prayer? I believe it is possible, but it requires a radical revision of the trinitarian doctrine and a new understanding of the Divine Life and the Spiritual Presence.

Besides the attempts in this direction which are made in all parts of the present system, some questions remain to be answered. The first concerns the number three implied in the word "trinity." What is the justification for keeping this number? Why was the early binitarian trend of thinking about God and Christ overcome by trinitarian symbolism? And after this, why was the Trinity not enlarged to a quaternity and beyond? These questions have a historical ground as well as a systematic one. Originally the distinction between the Logos and the Spirit was indefinite or non-existent. The christological problem developed independently of the concept of the Spirit. The concept of the Spirit was reserved for the divine power which drives individuals and groups into ecstatic experiences. There was also a trend toward quaternity in theological thought. One of the reasons for the trend is the possibility of distinguishing the common divine nature of the three *personae* from the three *personae* themselves, either by establishing a divinity above them or by considering the Father both as one of the three *personae* and as the common source of divinity. Another motive for the enlargement of the Trinity was the elevation of the Holy Virgin to a position in which she more and more approached divine dignity. For the devotional life of most Roman Catholics, she has by far surpassed the Holy Spirit and in modern Catholicism all three *personae* of the Trinity. If the doctrine which has already been discussed among Catholics, that she is to be considered as co-savior with the Christ, should become dogma, the Virgin would become a matter of ultimate concern and, consequently, a *persona* within the divine life. No scholastic distinctions would then be able to prevent the Trinity from becoming a quaternity.

These facts show that it is not the number "three" which is decisive in trinitarian thinking but the unity in a manifoldness of divine self-manifestations. If we ask why, in spite of this openness to different numbers, the number "three" has prevailed, it seems most probable that the three corresponds to the intrinsic dialectics of experienced life and is, therefore, most adequate to symbolize the Divine Life. Life has been described as the process of going out from itself and returning to itself. The number "three" is implicit in this description, as the dialectical philosophers knew. References to the magic power of the number "three" are unsatisfactory because other numbers for example, four, surpass three in magic valuation. In any case, our earlier assertion that the trinitarian symbolism is dialectical is confirmed by the persistence of the number "three" in devotional formulas and theological thought.

The symbolic power of the image of the Holy Virgin from the fifth century after Christ up to our own time raises a question for Protestantism, which has radically removed this symbol in the struggle of the Reformation against all human mediators between God and man. In this purge the female element in the symbolic expression of ultimate concern was largely eliminated. The spirit of Judaism with its exclusively male symbolism prevailed in the Reformation. Without doubt, this was one of the reasons for the great successes of the Counter Reformation over against the originally victorious Reformation. It gave rise within Protestantism itself to the often rather effeminate pictures of Jesus in Pietism; it is the cause of many conversions to the Greek or Roman churches, and it is also responsible for the attraction of Oriental mysticism for many Protestant humanists.

It is highly unlikely that Protestantism will ever reinstate the symbol of the Holy Virgin. As the whole history of religion shows, a concrete symbol of this kind cannot be reestablished in its genuine power. The religious symbol may become a poetic symbol, but poetic symbols are not objects of veneration. The question can only be whether there are elements in genuine Protestant symbolism which transcend the alternative male-female and which are capable of being developed over against a one-sided male-determined symbolism.

I want to point to the following possibilities. The first is related to the concept "ground of being" which is—as previously discussed—partly conceptual, partly symbolical. In so far as it is symbolical, it points to the mother-quality of giving birth, carrying, and embracing, and, at the same time, of calling back, resisting independence of the created, and swallowing it. The uneasy feeling of many Protestants about the first (not the last!) statement about God, that he is being-itself or the ground of being, is partly rooted in the fact that their religious consciousness and, even more, their moral conscience are shaped by the demanding father-image of the God who is conceived as a person among others. The attempt to show that nothing can be said about God theologically ᴊefore the statement is made that he is the power of being in all being is, at the same time, a way of reducing the predominance of the male element in the symbolization of the divine.

With respect to the Logos, as manifest in Jesus as the Christ, it is the symbol of the self-sacrifice of his finite particularity which transcends the alternative male-female. Self-sacrifice is not a character of male as male or of female as female, but it is, in the very act of self-sacrifice, the negation of the one or the other in exclusion. Self-sacrifice breaks the contrast of the sexes, and this is symbolically manifest in the picture of the suffering Christ, in which Christians of both sexes have participated with equal psychological and spiritual intensity.

If we finally turn to the divine Spirit, we are reminded of the image of the Spirit brooding over the chaos, but we cannot use it directly because the female element, implied in this image, was dropped in Judaism, although it never became an outspoken male symbol—not even in the story of the virginal birth of Jesus, where the Spirit replaces the male principle but does not become male itself. It is the ecstatic character of the Spiritual Presence which transcends the alternative of male and female symbolism in the experience of the Spirit. Ecstasy transcends both the rational element and the emotional element, which usually are attributed respectively to the male and female types. Again it is Protestant moralistic personalism which is distrustful of the ecstatic element in the Spiritual Presence and drives many people, in protest, toward an apersonal mysticism.

The doctrine of the Trinity is not closed. It can be neither discarded nor accepted in its traditional form. It must be kept open in order to fulfil its original function—to express in embracing symbols the self-manifestation of the Divine Life to man.

PART V
HISTORY AND THE KINGDOM OF GOD

INTRODUCTION

THE SYSTEMATIC PLACE OF THE FIFTH PART OF THE THEOLOGICAL SYSTEM AND THE HISTORICAL DIMENSION OF LIFE

I N THE analysis of the dimensions of life given in the fourth part of the system, the historical dimension was put in brackets. It requires a special treatment because it is the most embracing dimension, presupposing the others and adding a new element to them. This element is fully developed only after the dimension of the spirit has been actualized by the processes of life. But the processes of life themselves are horizontally directed, actualizing the historical dimension in an anticipatory way. This actualization is begun but unfulfilled. It would certainly be possible to call the birth, growth, aging, and dying of a particular tree its history; and it is even easier to call the development of the universe or of the species on earth history. The term "natural history" directly attributes the dimension of history to every process in nature. But the term history is ordinarily and predominantly used of human history. This points to the awareness that, although the historical dimension is present in all realms of life, it comes into its own only in human history. Analogues to history proper are found in all realms of life. There is no history proper where there is no spirit. It is therefore necessary to distinguish the "historical dimension," which belongs to all life processes, from history proper, which is something occurring in mankind alone.

The fifth part of the theological system is an extension of the fourth part, separated from it for traditional and practical reasons. Any doctrine of life must include a doctrine of the historical dimension of life in general and of human history as the most comprehensive life process in particular. Any description of the ambiguities of life must include a description of the ambiguity of life under the historical dimension. And finally, the answer of "life unambiguous" to the questions implied in life's ambiguities leads to the symbols "Spiritual Presence," "Kingdom of God," and "Eternal Life." Nevertheless, a separate treatment of the historical dimension within the whole of theological thought is advisable. As in the first part of the system the correlation between reason and revelation was taken out of the context of the second, third, and fourth parts and treated first, so in the fifth part the correlation between history and the Kingdom of God is taken out of the context of the three central parts and treated last. In both cases the theological tradition is partly responsible for this procedure: the questions of the relation of revelation to reason and of the Kingdom of God to history have always received a comparatively independent and extensive treatment. But there is also a more theoretical reason for dealing separately with the ambiguities of history and the symbols which answer the questions implied in them. It is the embracing character of the historical dimension and the equally embracing character of the symbol "Kingdom of God" that give particular significance to the discussion of history. The historical quality of life is potentially present under all its dimensions. It is actualized under them in an anticipatory way, i.e., it is not only potentially but in part actually present under them, whereas it is fully actualized in human history. Therefore it is adequate to discuss, first, history in its full and proper sense, i.e., human history, then to strive to understand the historical dimension in all realms of life, and finally, to relate human history to the "history of the universe."

A theological discussion of history must, in view of its particular question, deal with the structure of historical processes, the logic of historical knowledge, the ambiguities of historical existence, the meaning of the historical movement. It must also relate all this to the symbol of the Kingdom of God, both in its inner-historical and in its transhistorical sense. In the first sense it reaches back to the symbol "Spiritual Presence", in the second sense it goes over into the symbol "Eternal Life."

With the symbol "Eternal Life," problems appear which are normally discussed as "eschatological," that is, concerned with the doctrine of the "last things." As such their place at the end of the theological system seems natural. But it is not. Eschatology deals with the relation of the temporal to the eternal, but so do all parts of the theological system. Therefore it would be quite possible to begin a systematic theology with the eschatological question—the question of the inner aim, the *telos* of everything that is. Besides reasons of expediency, there is only one systematic reason for the traditional order, which is followed here, and that is that the doctrine of creation uses the temporal mode of "past" in order to symbolize the relation of the temporal to the eternal, whereas eschatology uses the temporal mode of "future" in order to do the same— and time, in our experience, runs from what is past to what is future.

Between the questions "where from" and "where to" lies the whole system of theological questions and answers. But it is not simply a straight line from the one to the other. The relation is more intrinsic: "where to" is inseparably implied in "where from"; the meaning of creation is revealed in its end. And conversely, the nature of the "where to" is determined by the nature of the "where from"; that is, only the valuation of the creation as good makes an eschatology of fulfilment possible; and only the idea of fulfilment makes the creation meaningful. The end of the system leads back to its beginning.

I

HISTORY AND THE QUEST
FOR THE KINGDOM OF GOD

A. LIFE AND HISTORY

1. MAN AND HISTORY

a) *History and historical consciousness.*—A semantic consideration may help us to discover a particular quality of history. The well-known fact that the Greek word *historia* means primarily inquiry, information, report, and only secondarily the events inquired about and reported is a case in point. It shows that for those who originally used the word "history" the subjective side preceded the objective side. Historical consciousness, according to this view, "precedes" historical happenings. Of course, historical consciousness does not precede in temporal succession the happenings of which it is conscious. But it transforms mere happenings into historical events, and in this sense it "precedes" them. Strictly speaking, one should say that the same situation produces both the historical occurrences and the awareness of them as historical events.

Historical consciousness expresses itself in a tradition, i.e., in a set of memories which are delivered from one generation to the other. Tradition is not a casual collection of remembered events but the recollection of those events which have gained significance for the bearers and receivers of the tradition. The significance which an occurrence has for a tradition-conscious group determines whether it will be considered as a historical event.

It is natural that the influence of the historical consciousness on the historical account should mold the tradition in accordance with the active needs for the historical group in which the tradition is alive. Consequently the ideal of pure, unbiased historical research appears at a rather late stage in the development of the writing of history. It is preceded by combinations of myth and history, by legends and sagas, by epic poetry. In all these cases, occurrences are elevated to historical significance, but the way in which it is done transforms the occurrences into symbols of the life of a historical group. Tradition unites historical reports with symbolic interpretations. It does not report "naked facts," which itself is a questionable concept; but it does bring to mind significant events through a symbolic transformation of the facts. This does not mean that the factual side is mere invention. Even the epic form in which tradition is expressed has historical roots, however hidden they may be, and saga and legend reveal their historical origins rather obviously. But in all these forms of tradition it is virtually impossible to separate the historical occurrence from its symbolic interpretation. In every living tradition the historical is seen in the light of the symbolic, and historical research can disentangle this amalgamation only in terms of higher or lower probability. For the way in which historical events are experienced is determined by their valuation in terms of significance, which implies that in their original receptions the records are partly dependent on their symbolic element. The biblical records, discussed in the third part of the system, are classical examples of this situation.

But one must ask whether the scholarly approach to historical facts is not also dependent on concealed symbols of interpretation. It seems this cannot be denied. There are several points in every historical statement of an intentionally detached character which show the influence of a symbolic vision. The choice of occurrences which are to be established as facts is the most important. Since in every moment of time at every point of space an inexhaustible number of occurrences takes place, the choice of the object of historical inquiry is dependent on the valuation of its importance for the establishment of the life of a historical group. In this respect history is dependent on historical consciousness. But this is not the only point in which this is the case. Every piece of historiography evaluates the weight of concurring influences on a person or a group and on their actions. This is one cause of the endless differences in historical presentations of the same factual material. Another cause, which is less obvious but even more decisive, is the context of the active life of the group in which the historian works, for he participates in the life of his group, sharing its memories and traditions. Out of this factor questions arise to which the presentation of the facts gives the answer. Nobody writes history on a "place above all places." Such a claim would be no less utopian than the claim that perfect social conditions are just approaching. All history-writing is dependent both on actual occurrences and on their reception by a concrete historical consciousness. There is no history without factual occurrences, and there is no history without the reception and interpretation of factual occurrences by historical consciousness.

These considerations do not conflict with the demands of the methods of historical research; the scientific criteria used by historical scholarship are as definite, obligatory and objective as those in any other realm of inquiry. But precisely in and through the act of applying them the influence of the historical consciousness becomes effective—though unintentionally in the case of honest historical work.

Another implication of the subject-object character of history must be mentioned. Through the interpretative element of all history, the answer to the question of the meaning of history has an indirect, mediated impact on a historical presentation. One cannot escape the destiny of belonging to a tradition in which the answer to the question of the meaning of life in all its dimensions, including the historical, is given in symbols which influence every encounter with reality. It is the purpose of the following chapters to discuss the symbols in which Christianity has expressed its answer to the question of the meaning of historical existence. There can be no doubt that even the most objective scholar, if he is existentially determined by the Christian tradition, interprets historical events in the light of this tradition, however unconscious and indirect its influence may be.

b) *The historical dimension in the light of human history.*—Human history, as the semantic study of the implications of the term *historia* has shown, is always a union of objective and subjective elements. An "event" is a syndrome (i.e., a running-together) of facts and interpretation. If we now turn from the semantic to the material discussion, we find the same double structure in all occurrences which deserve the name "historical event."

The horizontal direction under the dimension of the spirit has the character of intention and purpose. In a historical event, human purposes are the decisive, though not the exclusive, factor. Given institutions and natural conditions are other factors, but only the presence of actions with a purpose makes an event historical. Particular purposes may or may not be actualized, or they may lead to something not intended (according to the principle of the "heterogony of purposes");

but the decisive thing is that they are a determining factor in historical events. Processes in which no purpose is intended are not historical.

Man, in so far as he sets and pursues purposes, is free. He transcends the given situation, leaving the real for the sake of the possible. He is not bound to the situation in which he finds himself, and it is just this self-transcendence that is the first and basic quality of freedom. Therefore, no historical situation determines any other historical situation completely. The transition from one situation to another is in part determined by man's centered reaction, by his freedom. According to the polarity of freedom and destiny, such self-transcendence is not absolute; it comes out of the totality of elements past and present, but within these limits it is able to produce something qualitatively new.

Therefore, the third characteristic of human history is the production of the new. In spite of all abstract similarities of past and future events, every concrete event is unique and in its totality incomparable. This assertion, however, needs qualification. It is not only human history in which the new is produced. The dynamics of nature create the new by producing individuality in the smallest parts as well as in the largest composites of nature and also by producing new species in the evolutionary process and new constellations of matter in the extensions and contractions of the universe. But there is a qualitative difference between these forms of the new and the new in history proper. The latter is essentially related to meanings or values. Both terms can be adequate if correctly defined. Most philosophies of history in the last one hundred years have spoken of history as the realm in which values are actualized. The difficulty of this terminology is the necessity of introducing a criterion which distinguishes arbitrary values from objective values. Arbitrary values, unlike objective values, are not subject to such norms as truth, expressiveness, justice, humanity, holiness. The bearers of objective valuations are personalities and communities. If we call such valuations "absolute" (where by "absolute" we mean that their validity is independent of the valuating subject), it is possible to describe the creation of the new in human history as the creation of new actualizations of value *in* centered personalities. However, if one is hesitant about the term "value," an alternative is "meaning." Life in meanings, according to previous considerations, is life determined by the functions of the spirit and the norms and principles controlling them. The word "meaning," of course, is not unambiguous. But the merely logical use of the term ("a word has a meaning") is transcended if one speaks of "life in meanings." If the term "meaning" is used in this sense, one should describe the production of the new in history as the production of new and unique embodiments of meaning. My preference for this latter terminology is based partly on the rejection of the anti-ontological value theory and partly on the importance of terms like "the meaning of life" for the philosophy of religion. A phrase like "the value of life" has neither the depth nor the breadth of "the meaning of life."

The fourth characteristic of history proper is the significant uniqueness of a historical event. The unique, novel quality of all processes of life is shared by the historical processes. But the unique event has significance only in history. To signify something means to point beyond one's self to that which is signified—to represent something. A historical personality is historical because it represents larger events, which themselves represent the human situation, which itself represents the meaning of being as such. Personalities, communities, events, and situations are significant when more is embodied in them than a transitory occurrence within the universal process of becoming. These occurrences, of which innumerable ones come and go in every second of time, are not historical in the proper sense, but a combination of them may assume historical significance if it represents a human potentiality in a unique, incomparable way. History describes the sequence of such potentialities but with a decisive qualification: it describes them as they appear under the conditions of existence and within the ambiguities of life. Without the revelation of human potentialities (generally speaking, potentialities of life), historical accounts would not report significant events. Without the unique embodiment of these potentialities, they would not appear in history; they would remain pure essences. Yet they are both significant, because they are above history, and unique, because they are within history. There is, however, another reason for the significance of unique historical events: the significance of the historical process as a whole. Whether there is such a thing as "world history" or not, the historical processes within historical mankind have an inner aim. They go ahead in a definite direction, they run toward a fulfilment, whether they reach it or not. A historical event is significant in so far as it represents a moment within the historical movement toward the end. Thus, historical events are significant for three reasons:

they represent essential human potentialities, they show these potentialities actualized in a unique way, and they represent moments in the
development toward the aim of history—in which way the aim itself
is symbolized.

The four characteristics of human history (to be connected with
purpose, to be influenced by freedom, to create the new in terms of
meaning, to be significant in a universal, particular, and teleological
sense) lead to the distinction between human history and the historical
dimension in general. The distinctions are implicit in the four characteristics of human history and can also be shown from the other side, i.e.,
from the dimension of the historical in the realms of life other than
human history. If we take as examples the life of higher animals, the
evolution of species, and the development of the astronomical universe,
we observe first of all that in none of these examples are purpose and
freedom effective. Purposes, e.g., in the higher animals, do not transcend the satisfaction of their immediate needs; the animals do not
transcend their natural bondage. Nor is there any particular intention
operating in the evolution of the species or in the movements of the
universe. The question becomes more complicated when we ask whether
there is absolute meaning and significant uniqueness in these realms of
life, e.g., whether the genesis of a new species in the animal realm has
meaning comparable to the rise of a new empire or a new artistic style
in human history. Obviously, the new species is unique, but the question
is whether it is significantly unique in the sense of an embodiment of
absolute meaning. Again we must answer negatively: there is no absolute meaning and there is no significant uniqueness where the dimension of the spirit is not actual. The uniqueness of a species or of a
particular exemplar within a species is real but not ultimately significant, whereas the act in which a person establishes himself as a person,
a cultural creation with its inexhaustible meaning, and a religious experience in which ultimate meaning breaks through preliminary meanings are infinitely significant. These assertions are based on the fact
that life under the dimension of the spirit is able to experience ultimacy
and to produce embodiments and symbols of the ultimate. If there
were absolute meaning in a tree or a new animal species or a new
galaxy of stars, this meaning could be understood by men, for meaning
is experienced by man. This factor in human existence has led to
the doctrine of the infinite value of every human soul. Although such

a doctrine is not directly biblical, it is implied in the promises and threats pronounced by all biblical writers: "heaven" and "hell" are symbols of ultimate meaning and unconditional significance. But no such threat or promise is made about other than human life.

Nevertheless, there is no realm of life in which the historical dimension is not present and actualized in an anticipatory way. Even in the inorganic, and certainly in the organic, realm, there is *telos* (inner aim) which is quasi-historical, even though it is not a part of history proper. This is also true of the genesis of species and the development of the universe; they are analogues to history, but they are not history proper. The analogy appears in the spontaneity in nature, in the new produced by the progress in biological evolution, in the uniqueness of cosmic constellations. But it remains analogy. Freedom and absolute meaning are lacking. The historical dimension in life universal is analogous to life in history proper, but it is not history itself. In life universal the dimension of spirit is actualized only in anticipation. There are analogies between life under the biological dimension and life under the dimension of the spirit, but the biological is not spirit. Therefore, history remains an anticipated, but unactualized, dimension in all realms except that of human history.

c) Prehistory and posthistory.—The development from anticipated to actual history can be described as the stage of prehistorical man. He is already man in some respects, but he is not yet historical man. For if that being which eventually will produce history is called "man," he must have the freedom to set purposes, he must have language and universals, however limited these may be, and he must also have artistic and cognitive possibilities and a sense of the holy. If he had all this he would already be historical in a way in which no other being in nature is historical, but the historical potentiality in him would only be in transition from possibility to reality. It would be, metaphorically speaking, the state of "awakening" humanity. There is no way of verifying such a state; yet it can be postulated as the basis for the later development of man, and it can be used as a critical weapon against unrealistic ideas about the early state of mankind which attribute to prehistorical man either too much or too little. Too much is attributed to him if he is endowed with all kinds of perfections which anticipate either later developments or even a state of fulfilment. Examples of this are theological interpretations of the paradise myth which attribute to Adam the perfections of the Christ and the secular interpretations of the original state of mankind which attribute to the "noble savage" the perfections of the humanist ideal of man.

On the other hand, too little is attributed to prehistorical man if he is considered as a beast without at least the possibility of universals and, consequently, of language. If this were true, there would be no prehistorical man, and historical man would be a "creation out of nothing." But all empirical evidence stands against such an assumption. Prehistorical man is that organic being which is predisposed to actualize the dimensions of spirit and history and which in his development drives toward their actualization. There is no identifiable moment when animal self-awareness becomes human spirit and when human spirit enters the historical dimension. The transition from one dimension to the other is hidden, although the result of this transition is obvious when it appears. We do not know when the first spark of historical consciousness dawned in the human race, but we do recognize expressions of this consciousness. We can distinguish historical from prehistorical man though we do not know the moment of transition from one to the other because of the mixture of slow transformation and sudden leap in all evolutionary processes. If evolution proceeded only by leaps, one could identify the result of each leap. If evolution proceeded only by a slow transformation, no radical change could be noticed at all. But evolutionary processes combine both the leap and the slow change, and therefore, although one can distinguish the results, one cannot fix the moments in which they appear. The darkness which veils prehistorical mankind is not a matter of preliminary scholarly failure but rather of the indefiniteness of all evolutionary processes with respect to the appearance of the new. Historical man is new, but he is prepared for and anticipated by prehistorical man, and the point of transition from the one to the other is essentially indefinite.

A similar consideration must be brought to bear upon the idea of posthistory. The question is whether one must anticipate a stage of the evolutionary process in which historical mankind, though not as human race, comes to an end. The significance of this question lies in its relation to utopian ideas with respect to the future of mankind. The last stage of historical man has been identified with the final stage of fulfillment—with the Kingdom of God actualized on earth. But the "last" in the temporal sense is not the "final" in the eschatological sense. It is not by chance that the New Testament and Jesus resisted the attempt to put the symbols of the end into a chronological frame. Not even Jesus knows when the end will come; it is independent of the historical-post-historical development of mankind, although the mode of "future" is used in its symbolic description. This leaves the future of historical mankind open for possibilities derived from present experience. For example, it is not impossible that the self-destructive power of mankind will prevail and bring historical mankind to an end. It is also possible that mankind will lose not its potential freedom of transcending the given—this would make of him something no longer man—but the dissatisfaction with the given and consequently the drive toward the new. The character of the human race in this state would be similar to what Nietzsche has described as the "last man" who "knows everything" and is not interested in anything; it would be the state of "blessed animals." The negative utopias of our century, such as *Brave New World*, anticipate—rightly or wrongly—such a stage of evolution. A third possibility is a continuation of the dynamic drive of the human race toward unforeseeable actualizations of man's potentialities, up to the gradual or sudden disappearance of the biological and physical conditions for the continuation of historical mankind. These and perhaps other chances of posthistorical mankind must be envisaged and liberated from any entanglement with the symbols of the "end of history" in their eschatological sense.

d) The bearers of history: communities, personalities, mankind.— Man actualizes himself as a person in the encounter with other persons within a community. The process of self-integration under the dimension of the spirit actualizes both the personality and the community. Although we have described the actualization of the personality in connection with moral principles, we have postponed the discussion of the actualization of the community to this point because life processes in a community are immediately determined by the historical dimension in accordance with the fact that the direct bearers of history are groups rather than individuals, who are only indirect bearers.

History-bearing groups are characterized by their ability to act in a centered way. They must have a centered power which is able to keep the individuals who belong to it united and which is able to preserve its power in the encounter with similar power groups. In order to fulfil the first condition a history-bearing group must have a central, lawgiving, administering, and enforcing authority. In order to fulfil the second condition a history-bearing group must have tools to keep itself in power in the encounter with other powers. Both conditions are fulfilled in what is called, in modern terminology, a "state," and in this sense history is the history of states. But this statement needs several qualifications. First, one must point to the fact that the term "state" is much younger than the statelike organizations of large families, clans, tribes, cities, and nations, in which the two conditions of being bearers of history were previously fulfilled. Second, one must emphasize that historical influence can be exercised in many ways by economical, cultural, or religious groups and movements that work within a state or that cut across many states. Still, their historical effect is conditioned by the existence of the organized internal and external power of history-bearing groups. The fact that in many countries even the periods of artistic style are named for emperors or sequences of emperors indicates the basic character of political organization for all historical existence.

The history-bearing group was described as a centered group with internal and external power. This, however, does not mean that the political power in both directions is a mechanism independent of the life of the group. In every power structure *eros* relations underlie the organizational form. Power through administering and enforcing the law, or power through imposing law by conquest, presupposes a central power group whose authority is acknowledged at least silently; otherwise it would not have the support necessary for enforcement and conquest. A withdrawal of such silent acknowledgment by the supporters of a power structure undercuts it. The support is based on an experience of belonging, a form of communal *eros* which does not exclude struggles for power within the supporting group but which unites it against other groups. This is obvious in all statelike organizations from the family up to the nation. Blood relations, language, traditions, and memories create many forms of *eros* which make the power structure possible. Preservation by enforcement and increase by conquest follow, but do not produce, the historical power of a group. The element of compulsion in every historical power structure is not its foundation but an unavoidable condition of its existence. It is at the same time the cause of its destruction if the *eros* relations disappear or are completely replaced by force.

One way among others in which the *eros* relations that underlie a power

structure express themselves is in the legal principles that determine
the laws and their administration by the ruling center. The legal system
of a history-bearing group is derived neither from an abstract concept
of justice nor from the will to power of the ruling center. Both factors
contribute to the concrete structure of justice. They also can destroy it
if one of them prevails, for neither of them is the basis of a statelike
structure. The basis of every legal system is the *eros* relations of the
group in which they appear.

It is, however, not only the power of the group in terms of enforce-
able internal unity and external security but also the aim toward which
it strives which makes it a history-bearing group. History runs in a
horizontal direction, and the groups which give it this direction are
determined by an aim toward which they strive and a destiny they try
to fulfill. One could call this the "vocational consciousness" of a history-
bearing group. It differs from group to group not only in character but
also in the degree of consciousness and of motivating power. But vocational feeling has been present since the earliest times of historical mankind. Its most conspicuous expression is perhaps the call to Abraham
in which the vocational consciousness of Israel finds its symbolic expression; and we find analogous forms in China, in Egypt, and in
Babylon. The vocational consciousness of Greece was expressed in the
distinction between Greeks and barbarians, that of Rome was based
on the superiority of the Roman law, that of medieval Germany on the
symbol of the Holy Roman Empire of German nationality, that of Italy
on the "rebirth" of civilization in the Renaissance, that of Spain on the
idea of the Catholic unity of the world, that of France on its leadership
in intellectual culture, that of England on the task of subjecting all
peoples to a Christian humanism, that of Russia on the salvation of the
West through the traditions of the Greek church or through the Marxist
prophecy, that of the United States on the belief in a new beginning in
which the curses of the Old World are overcome and the democratic
missionary task fulfilled. Where the vocational consciousness has van-
ished or was never fully developed, as in nineteenth-century Germany
and Italy and smaller states with artificial boundaries, the element of
power becomes predominant either in an aggressive or in a merely de-
fensive sense. But even in these cases, as the recent examples of Germany
and Italy show, the need for a vocational self-understanding is so strong

that the absurdities of Nazi-racism were accepted because they filled a vacuum.

The fact of a vocational consciousness shows that the content of history is the life of the history-bearing group in all dimensions. No dimension of life is excluded from the living memory of the group, but there are differences in choice. The political realm is always predominant because it is constitutive of historical existence. Within this frame, social, economic, cultural, and religious developments have an equal right to consideration. In some periods, more—and in other periods, less—emphasis can be given any one of them. Certainly, the history of man's cultural functions is not confined to any concrete history-bearing group, not even the largest. But if the cultural or religious historian crosses the political boundaries he is aware that this is an abstraction from actual life, and he does not forget that the *political* unities, whether large or small, remain the conditions of all cultural life. The primacy of political history cannot be disregarded, either for the sake of an independent intellectual history demanded by idealistic historians or for the sake of a determining economic history demanded by materialistic historians. History itself has refuted the demands of the latter whenever they seemed to be near fulfilment, as in Zionist Israel or Communist Russia. It is significant that the symbol in which the Bible expresses the meaning of history is political: "Kingdom of God," and not "Life of the Spirit" or "economic abundance." The element of centeredness which characterizes the political realm makes it an adequate symbol for the ultimate aim of history.

This leads to the question of whether one could call mankind, rather than particular human groups, the bearer of history. For the limited character of groups necessarily seems to disrupt the unity which is intended in the symbol "Kingdom of God." But the form of this question prejudices the answer; the aim of history does not lie in history. There is no united mankind within history. It certainly did not exist in the past; nor can it exist in the future because a politically united mankind, though imaginable, would be a diagonal between convergent and divergent vectors. Its political unity would be the framework for a disunity that is the consequence of human freedom with its dynamic that surpasses everything given. The situation would be different only if the unity of mankind were the end of history and the frame for the posthistorical stage in which man's aroused freedom would have come to rest. This would be the state of "animal blessedness." As long as there is history, a "united mankind" is the frame for a "disunited mankind." Only in posthistory could the disunity disappear, but such a stage would not be the Kingdom of God, for the Kingdom of God is not "animal blessedness."

Historical groups are communities of individuals. They are not entities alongside or above the individuals of whom they are constituted; they are products of the social function of these individuals. The social function produces a structure which gains a partial independence from the individuals (as is the case in all other functions), but this independence does not produce a new reality, with a center of willing and acting. It is not "the community" that wills and acts; it is individuals in their social quality and through their representatives who make communal actions possible by making centeredness possible. The "deception of personifying the group" should be revealed and denounced, especially to point out tyrannical abuses of this deception. So we must ask again: In what sense is the individual a bearer of history? In spite of the criticism of any attempt to personalize the group, the answer must be that the individual is a bearer of history only in relation to a history-bearing group. His individual life process is not history, and therefore biography is not history. But it can become significant either as the story of somebody who actively and symbolically represents a history-bearing group (Caesar, Lincoln) or as an individual who represents the average situation within a group (*the* peasant, *the* bourgeois). The relation to the group of historically significant individuals is especially obvious in persons who have left the community to go into seclusion in the "desert" or into "exile." In so far as they are historically significant, they remain related to the group from which they come and to which they might return, or they establish a relation with the new group which they enter and in which they may become historically significant. But as mere individuals they have no historical significance. History is the history of groups.

This, however, does not answer the question: Who determines the historical processes, "great" individuals or mass movements? The question in this form is unanswerable because no empirical evidence can be found to support the one or the other point of view. The question is also misleading. The adjective "great," in history, is attributed to persons who are great as leaders in the movements of history-bearing groups.

The term "great" in this sense implies the relation to masses. Individuals who have had potential historical greatness but have never reached actualization are not called great, because the potentiality to greatness can be tested only by its actualization. Concretely speaking, one would have to say that no one can achieve historical greatness who is not received by history-bearing groups. On the other hand, the movements of the masses would never occur without the productive power of individuals in whom the potentialities and actual trends of the many become conscious and formulated. The question of whether individuals or "masses" determine history must be replaced by an exact description of their interplay.

2. History and the Categories of Being

a) *Life processes and categories.*—In the second part of the theological system, "Being and God," we discussed the principal categories—time, space, causality, and substance—and showed their relation to the finitude of being. When in the fourth part we characterized the different dimensions of life, we did not deal with the relations of the categories to the dimensions. This was omitted in order to consider these relations in their totality, including the historical dimension.

Each category is differentiated within itself according to the dimension under which it is effective. There is, for example, not *one* time for all dimensions, for the inorganic, the organic, the psychological, the historical; but in each of them, there is time. Time is both an independent and a relational concept: time remains time in the whole realm of finitude; but the time of the amoeba and the time of historical man are different. And the same is true of the other categories. However, one can describe that which gives each of the four categories identity, justifying the identity of the term in the following way: one can define that which makes time time, under all dimensions, as the element of "after-each-other-ness." Temporality is after-each-other-ness in each of its forms. Of course, such a definition is not possible without using the category of time, which is implied in the phrase "after-each-other-ness." Nevertheless, it is not useless to extrapolate this element, because it is qualified in different ways under different dimensions, though remaining the basis in every form of temporality. In the same way one can define that which makes space space under all dimensions as the element of "beside-each-other-ness." Again, this is not a true definition, because it uses that which is to be defined in the definition: the category of space is implied in the phrase "beside-each-other-ness." Here again it appears useful to extrapolate this element, because it identifies space as space, however qualified by other elements it may be. That which makes a cause a cause is the relation in which a consequent situation is conditioned by a preceding one, though the character of this conditioning is different under the different dimensions of life. The conditioning exercised by a solid body in motion upon another solid body is different from the conditioning of a historical event by preceding ones. The category of substance expresses the remaining unity within the change of what are called "accidents." It is literally that which underlies a process of becoming and gives it its unity, making it into a definite, relatively lasting thing. Substance in this sense characterizes objects under all dimensions, but not in the same way. The relation of a chemical substance to its accidents is different from the relation of the substance of the feudal culture to its manifestations. But "remaining unity in change" characterizes both substances equally.

The question now arises whether, in spite of the differences in the relations of the categories to the dimensions of life, there is a unity in each category, not only of the element which determines the definition, but also of the actualized forms in which it is applied and qualified. Concretely speaking, one would ask: Is there time which comprises all forms of temporality, space which comprises all forms of spatiality, causality which implies all forms of causality, substantiality which implies all forms of substantiality? The fact that all parts of the universe are contemporal, conspatial, causally conditioned by each other, and substantially distinct from each other demands an affirmative answer to the question of the categorical unity of the universe. But this unity cannot be known, as the universe qua universe cannot be known. The character of a time which is not related to any of the dimensions of life but to all of them, thus transcending all of them, belongs to the mystery of being-itself. Temporality, not related to any identifiable temporal process, is an element in the transtemporal, time-creating ground of time. Spatiality, not related to any identifiable space, is an element in the trans-spatial, space-creating ground of space. Causality, not related to any identifiable causal nexus, is an element in the transcausal, cause-creating ground of causality. Substantiality, not related to any identifiable substantial form, is an element in the transubstantial, substance-creating ground of substantiality. These considerations, besides their immediate significance for the question raised before, give the basis for symbolic use of the categories in the language of religion. This use is justified, because the categories have in their very nature a point of self-transcendence.

The following examples are chosen according to their importance for the understanding of historical processes, as the four categories themselves are chosen—in the whole system—on the basis of their importance for the understanding of the religious language. Other categories as well as other examples of their functions under the different dimensions of life could have been chosen. The analysis is not complete and probably, as the history of the doctrine of categories has shown, cannot be complete by its very nature; the boundary line between categories and realms is open to an indefinite process of reformulation.

b) *Time, space, and the dimensions of life in general.*—It is expedient and in some ways unavoidable (as Kant has shown), to treat time and space interdependently. There is a kind of proportional relation in the degree to which time or space is predominant in a realm of beings. Generally speaking, one can say that the more a realm is under the predominance of the inorganic dimension, the more it is also under the predominance of space; and conversely, the more a realm is under the predominance of the historical dimension, the more it is also under the predominance of time. In the interpretations of life and history, this fact has led to the "struggle between time and space," which appears most conspicuously in the history of religion.

In the realms which are determined by the dimension of the inorganic, space is, almost without restriction, the dominant category. Certainly, inorganic things are moving in time, and their movements are calculated in temporal measures; but this calculation has been taken into the calculation of physical processes as a "fourth dimension" of space. The spatial solidity of physical objects, i.e., their power of providing an impenetrable, particular place for themselves, is continuously encountered in everybody's average existence. Existing means above all to have a place among the places of all other beings and to resist the threat of losing one's place and with it existence altogether.

The quality of beside-each-other-ness which characterizes every space has the quality of exclusiveness in the inorganic realm. The same exclusiveness characterizes time under the predominance of the dimension of the inorganic. In spite of the continuity of the time-flux, every discernible moment of time in a physical process excludes the preceding and the following moments. A drop of water running down the riverbed is here in this moment and there in the next, and nothing unites the two moments. It is this character of time which makes the after-each-other-ness of temporality exclusive. And it is a bad theology that uses the endless continuation of this kind of time as the symbolic material for eternity.

In the realms which are determined by the dimension of the biological, a new quality, both of time and space, appears: the exclusive character of beside-each-other-ness and after-each-other-ness is broken by an element of participation. The space of a tree is not the space of an aggregate of unconnected inorganic parts but the space of a unity of interdependent elements. The roots and the leaves have an exclusive space only in so far as they are also determined by the dimension of the inorganic; but under the predominance of the organic, they participate in each other, and what happens in the roots also happens in the leaves, and conversely. The distance between roots and leaves does not have the quality of exclusiveness. In the same way the exclusive after-each-other-ness of temporality is broken by the participation of the stages of growth within each other; in the present now, the past and the future are effective. And only here do the modes of time become actual and qualify reality. In the young tree, the old tree is included as "not yet," and conversely, the young tree is included in the old as "no longer." The immanence of all the stages of growth in every stage of the growth of a living being overcomes temporal exclusiveness. As the space of all parts of a tree is the whole tree, so the time of all moments of a process of growth is the whole process.

When, in animal life, the dimension of self-awareness appears, the immanence of past and future in the present now is experienced as memory and anticipation; here the immanence of the modes of time is not only real but also known as real. In the psychological realm (under the predominance of self-awareness), the time of a living being is experienced time, the experienced present which includes the remembered past and the anticipated future in terms of participation. Participation is not identity, and the element of after-each-other-ness is not removed; but its exclusiveness is broken, both in reality and in awareness. Under the dimension of self-awareness, spatiality is correlative with temporality. It is the space of self-directed movement in which the beside-each-other-ness of all forms of space is partly overcome. The space of an animal is not only the space taken by the physical existence of its body but also the space of its self-directed movement, which can be very small, as in some lower animals, or very large, as, for example, in migrating birds. The space covered by their movement is *their* space. In the time and space of growth and self-awareness, space is still predominant over time, but its absolute predominance is broken. In the directedness of growth and the futuristic character of self-awareness, time, so to speak, prepares for the full breakthrough of its bondage to space which occurs in time under the dimension of history ("historical time").

With the emergence of the dimension of the spirit as predominant, another form of beside-each-other-ness and after-each-other-ness appears; the time and space of the spirit. Their first characteristic, given with the power of abstraction, is essential unlimitedness. The mind experiences limits by transcending them. In the act of creativity, basically in language and technique, the limited is posited as limited in contrast to the possibility of going beyond it without limit. This is the answer to the question of the finite or infinite character of time and space (as Kant has seen, following in this respect the Augustinian-Cusanian tradition). The question cannot be answered in the context of inorganic or biological or psychological time and space; it can be answered only in the context of the time and space of the creative spirit. The time of the creative spirit unites an element of abstract unlimitedness with an element of concrete limitedness. The very nature of creation as an act of the spirit implies this duality: creating means transcending the given in the horizontal direction without a priori limits, and it means bringing something into a definite, concrete existence. The saying "Self-limitation shows the master" implies both the possibility of the unlimited and the necessity of limitation in the creative act. The concreteness of time under the dimension of the spirit gives time a qualitative character. The time of a creation is not determined by the physical time in which it is produced but by the creative context which is used and transformed by it. The time of a painting is neither the stretch of time in which it is painted nor the date when it is finished, but the time which is qualified by the situation in the development of painting to which it belongs and which it changes to a lesser or greater degree. The spirit has a time which cannot be measured by physical time although it lies within the whole of physical time. This, of course, leads to the question of how physical time and the time of the spirit are related, i.e., to the question of historical time.

Analogous statements must be made about the space of the spirit. The combination of the words space and spirit seems strange, but it is so only if spirit is understood as a bodiless level of being instead of as a dimension of life, in unity with all other dimensions. In reality spirit has its space as well as its time. The space of the creative spirit unites an element of abstract unlimitedness with an element of concrete limitation. The creative transformation of a given environment has no limits imposed by this environment; the creative act runs ahead without limit into space, not only in imagination, but also in reality (as shown in the so-called conquest of space in our period). But creation implies concreteness, and the imagination must return to the given environment, which through the act of transcending and returning becomes a section of space universal with a particular character. It becomes a space of settlement—a house, a village, a city. It becomes a space of social standing within a social order. It becomes a space of community such as family, neighborhood, tribe, nation. It becomes a space of work, such as land, factory, school, studio. These spaces are qualitative, lying within the frame of physical space but incapable of being measured by it. And thus the question arises as to how physical space and the space of the spirit are related to each other, i.e., the question of historical space.

c) *Time and space under the dimension of history.*—The question of the relation of physical time and space to time and space under the dimension of spirit has led us to the problem of history and the categories. In the processes which we call historical in the proper sense, those which are restricted to man, all forms of after-each-other-ness and beside-each-other-ness are directly effective; history moves in the time and the space of the inorganic realm. In history there are centered groups which grow and age and develop organs, in a way analogous to that in the dimension of self-awareness. Therefore history includes time and space, qualified by growth and self-awareness. And history determines and is determined by interdependence, by life under the dimension of spirit. In history the creative act of the spirit and with it the time and space of the spirit are always present.

But historical time and space show qualities beyond the temporal and spatial qualities of the preceding dimensions. First of all, in history time becomes predominant over space as in the inorganic realm space is predominant over time. But the relation of these two extremes is not that of a simple polarity: in history potentialities of the inorganic become actual; therefore the actualized historical realm includes the actualized inorganic realm, but not vice versa. This relation also applies to time and space. Historical time includes inorganic time actually; inorganic time includes historical time only potentially. In every historical event the atoms move according to the order of inorganic time, but not every movement of atoms provides a basis for a historical event. This difference of the contrasted dimensions with respect to time is analogously true of space. Historical space includes the space of the physical realm as well as the space of growth, of self-awareness, of creativity. But as in the organic and inorganic realms time was subordinated to space, so under the historical dimension space is subordinated to time. This particular relation of space to time in the realm of history requires first an analysis of historical time.

Historical time is based on a decisive characteristic of form of after-each-other-ness, and that characteristic is irreversibility. Under no dimension does time go backward. Some qualities of a particular moment of time can repeat themselves, but only those qualities which are abstracted from a whole situation. The situation in which they reappear, for example, a sunset or the rejection of the creatively new by most people, is different each time, and consequently, even the abstracted elements have only similarity and not identity. Time, so to speak, runs ahead toward the new, the unique, the novel, even in repetitions. In this respect time has an identifying mark under all dimensions; the after-each-other-ness cannot be reversed. But, given this common basis, historical time possesses a quality of its own. It is united with the time of the spirit, the creative time, and it appears as time running toward fulfilment. Every creative act aims at something. Its time is the time between the vision of the creative intention and the creation brought into existence. But history transcends every creative act horizontally. History is the place of all creative acts and characterizes each of them as unfulfilled in spite of their relative fulfilment. It drives beyond all of them toward a fulfilment which is not relative and which does not need another temporality for its fulfilment. In historical man, as the bearer of the spirit, time running toward fulfilment becomes conscious of its nature. In man, that toward which time is running becomes a conscious aim. Historical acts by a historical group drive toward a fulfilment which transcends every particular creation and is considered to be the aim of historical existence itself. But historical existence is embedded in universal existence and cannot be separated from it. "Nature participates in history" and in the fulfilment of the universe. With respect to historical time, this means that the fulfilment toward which historical time runs is the fulfilment toward which time under all dimensions runs. In the historical act the fulfilment of time universal becomes a conscious aim. The question of the symbols in which this aim has been expressed and in which it should be expressed is identical with the question of the "end of history," and it must be answered with the answer to this question. The answer given in our context is "Eternal Life."

Time under the non-historical dimensions is neither endless nor ending. The question of its beginning cannot be asked (which should deter theology from identifying an assumed beginning of physical time with the symbol of creation). Nor can the question of its end be asked (which should deter theology from identifying an assumed physical end with the symbol of consummation). The end of history is the aim of history, as the word "end" indicates. The end is the fulfilled aim, however this aim may be envisioned. Yet, where there is an end there must be a beginning, the moment in which existence is experienced as unfulfilled and in which the drive toward fulfilment starts. The beginning and the end of time are qualities which belong to historical time essentially and in every moment. According to the multidimensional unity of all dimensions of life, there can be no time without space and, consequently, no historical time without historical space. Space in the historical dimension stands under the predominance of time. The beside-each-other-ness of all spatial relations appears in the historical dimension as the encounter of the history-bearing groups, their separations, struggles, and reunions. The space on which they stand is characterized by the different kinds of beside-each-other-ness under the different dimensions. But beyond it, they have the quality of driving toward a unity which transcends all of them without annihilating them and their creative potentialities. In the symbol "Kingdom of God," pointing to the aim toward which historical time is running, the spatial element is obvious: a "kingdom" is a realm, a place beside other places.

Of course, the place of which God is ruler is not a place beside others but a place above all places; nevertheless it is a place and not spaceless "spirituality" in the dualistic sense. Historical time, driving toward fulfilment, is actual in the relations of historical spaces. And as historical time includes all other forms of time, so historical space includes all other forms of space. As in historical time the meaning of after-each-other-ness is raised to consciousness and has become a human problem, so in historical space the meaning of beside-each-other-ness is raised to consciousness and has also become a problem. The answer in both cases is identical with the answer to the question of the aim of the historical process.

d) Causality, substance, and the dimensions of life in general.—Causality in the dimension of the historical must be considered in contrast to and in unity with substance; but in order to understand the special character of both of them under the historical dimension, their nature in the other realms must be analyzed. As in the case of time and space, there is an element which is common to causality in all its varieties, namely, the relation in which one complex precedes another in such a way that the other would not be what it is without the preceding one. A cause is a conditioning precedent, and causality is the order of things according to which there is a conditioning precedent for everything. The implications of this order for the understanding of finitude have been discussed in another part of the system.[1] Here the question is: How does the conditioning occur under the different dimensions?

In the same way, the category of substance under the dimension of the historical must first be considered by an analysis of the meaning of substance in general, then under the non-historical dimensions, and finally under the dimension of the historical itself. The general character of substance is "underlying identity," that is, identity with respect to the changing accidents. This identity which makes a thing a thing has different characteristics and different relations to causality under the different dimensions. It is of the utmost importance for theology to be aware of these distinctions if it uses both causality and substance in its description of the relation of God and the world, of the divine Spirit and the human spirit, of providence and *agape*.

Under the predominance of the dimension of the inorganic, the conditioning precedent and conditioned consequent (cause and effect) are

[1] *Systematic Theology,* I, 164–66, 195–96.

separated, as in the corresponding character of time the observed moments are separated from each other. Causation in this sense keeps the effect at a distance from the cause by which the effect is, at the same time, determined. In the ordinary encounter with reality (except at the microcosmic and macrocosmic boundary lines of the inorganic realm), the determination can be expressed in quantitative terms and mathematical equations. Causality under the dimension of the inorganic is a quantitative, calculable conditioning of the consequent by the precedent.

Substance in the same realm is the transitory identity of the causing precedent with itself and the transitory identity of the caused consequent with itself. It goes without saying that substance in this sense is not seen as an "underlying immovable thing" (as the immortal soul-substance of earlier metaphysics). Substance is that amount of identity within the changing accidents which makes it possible to speak of their complex as a "thing." Obviously, substance in this realm is dependent on arbitrary divisions which are indefinitely possible. There is no substantial unity between two pieces of a metal after they have been split from each other; but each of them then has now a transitory substantial identity with itself. They are subject to the radical beside-each-other-ness of space in the inorganic realm.

The dependence of theological literalism on the ordinary understanding of the categories is shown when causality and substance are endowed with characteristics that appear only in the inorganic realm and are surpassed in the other realms. We see examples of this dependence when God is conceived as cause and the world as effect or when we make God a substance and the world another substance.

Under the dimensions of the organic and the psychological, causality and substance change both in their character and in their relations to each other. The element of separation between cause and effect and between one individual substance and another is balanced by an element of participation. Within an organism the conditioning precedent is a state of the organism and the conditioned consequent is another state of the same organism. There may be causal influences on an organic system from outside, but they are not the cause of the consequent state of the organism; they are an occasion for the organic processes which lead from the one to to the other state. Organic causality is effective through a centered whole—which definitively includes the chemical-physical processes internal to the organism and their quantitatively measurable causation. Under the dimension of self-awareness, we find the same situation. There is no quantitatively measurable relation between stimulus and response in centered self-awareness. Here also the external cause is effective through the psychological whole which moves under the occasioning impact from one state to another. This does not exclude the validity of the calculable element in the processes of association, reaction, and so on, but its calculability is limited by the individual center of self-awareness within whose circle those processes occur.

The centered self within which organic and psychological causality are effective is an individual substance with a definite identity. It is not transitory because (in so far as it is centered) it cannot be divided. Its contents can change but only in a continuity which, in the realm of self-awareness, is experienced as memory. If the continuity (biological or psychological) is completely interrupted, the individual substance has ceased to exist (normally by death, sometimes by a complete loss of memory). Under the dimensions of the organic and the psychological, causality is, so to speak, the prisoner of substance. Causation takes place in the unity of a centered whole, and causes from outside the circle are effective through the whole—if they do not destroy it. This is the reason why an individual substance comes to an end if it is not able to take external influences into its substantial identity but is disrupted by them. Then quantitatively calculable processes (chemical, associative, and so on,) take over, as in bodily sickness and mental disease, and lead to an annihilation of the substance.

Although under the dimension of self-awareness causality is contained within substance, under the dimension of the spirit causality breaks through this containment. Causality must participate in the quality of spirit to be creative. The conditioning precedent determines the margin within which the creative act is possible, and it also determines the impulse to an act which might be creative. But it does not determine the content of the creation, for the content is the new, which makes the creative act creative. The concept of the new needs further consideration. Since actual being has the character of becoming, one can say that everything that happens in the smallest moment of time is new in comparison with what has happened in the previous moment. If "new" means each situation in the process of becoming, everything is always new, and this certainly is true—in spite of the assertion of Ecclesiastes that there is nothing new under the sun. But the concept of the new demands as many distinctions as the meaning of the categories—according to the dimensions in which the new appears. The new which results from causation qua quantitative transformation is different from the new which results from causation qua qualitative transformation within an individual substance, and both kinds of newness are different from that newness which is the result of causation through a creative act of man's spirit. In the first two cases, determination is predominant over the freedom of positing the new. In the case of the spirit, freedom prevails over determination, and the underivably new is created. In the creation of *Hamlet* by Shakespeare the material, particular form, personal presuppositions, occasioning factors, and so on, are derivable. All these elements are effective in the artistic process which created *Hamlet*; but the result is new in the sense of the underivable. It is in this sense that we speak when we say that under the dimension of the spirit, general causality becomes causality as creating the new.

The new is not bound to the individual substance, but it rises out of the substance and has effects on the character of the substance. The individual substance becomes spirit-determined; the center of self-awareness becomes a person. In the person the substantial identity has the character of oughtness in an unconditional sense. This has led former metaphysics into the error of establishing an immortal substance as a separated being which maintains its identity in the process of inorganic time. Such a conclusion contradicts the nature of all categories to be manifestations of finitude. But the basis of the argument is sound, for it involves the insight into the unconditional element which makes a person a person and gives him his infinite significance. The spirit-determined, centered being, the person, is the source of creative causality; but the creation surpasses the substance out of which it comes—the person.

e) *Causality and substance under the dimension of history.*—Historical causality is the embracing form of causality because of the fact that in historical events all dimensions of life are actively participant. It is dependent on the freedom of creative causality, but it is equally dependent on the inorganic and organic developments which have made historical man possible and which remain as the frame or substructure of his whole history. And this is not all; since the bearers of history are historical groups, the nature of these groups represents the decisive interpenetration of determining and free causality in the historical process. In a historical group a double causation can be observed; the causation from a given sociological structure to the creation of cultural content and the causation from this content toward a transformed sociological structure. The "givenness" of the sociological is an ideal point in an infinite past in which the historical process started. From this point on (the transition from prehistory to history), creativity has broken through the given culture and in this way contributed to it, so that a transformed culture was caused, out of which new creativity arose, and so on. Therefore it is as impossible to derive the contents of the creative act from the given culture, as some anthropologists do, as it is to derive a given culture exclusively from creative acts, as classical idealism did.

Substance under the historical dimension can be called the "historical situation." A given culture, as discussed before, is such a situation. It can appear on a family, tribal, national, or international basis. It can be restricted to a particular history-bearing group; it can be enlarged to a combination of such groups; it can embrace continents. In any case, where there is a situation out of which historical causality drives toward the new, there is substance under the historical dimension. If a history-creating situation is called a substance, this means that there is a point of identity in all its manifestations. A situation in this sense reaches into all dimensions: it has a geographical basis, a space in the inorganic realm; it is borne by biological groups, by the self-awareness of groups and individuals, and by sociological structures. It is a system of sociological, psychological, and cultural tensions and balances. But it ceases to be substance in the historical sense. Names of historical periods (such as Renaissance, Enlightenment) express this point of identity if the balances fail and tensions destroy the element of identity which constitutes the substance. Without applying the category of substance to history, either implicitly or explicitly, no historiography would be possible. Historical names, such as Hellenism, Renaissance, Absolutism, "West and East" in the cultural sense, "eighteenth century" in a qualitative sense, or India in a geographical and cultural sense, would be meaningless if they did not point to a historical substance, a situation out of which historical causation can or did grow and which, at the same time, is the result of historical causation.

Like historical time, historical causality is future-directed; it creates the new. And as historical time draws historical space into its "futuristic" movement, so historical causality draws historical substance into the direction toward the future. Historical causality drives toward the new beyond every particular new, toward a situation or historical substance beyond every particular situation or substance. In this it transcends the particular creations under the dimension of the spirit. The very concept of the new which belongs to creative causality implies the transcending character of the historical movement. The ever repeated creation of particular newness has in itself an element of oldness. Not only do the creations become old (they become static in a given substance), but the process of creating the particular new in endless variations has in itself the quality of oldness. Therefore man's historical consciousness has always looked ahead beyond any particular new to the absolutely new, symbolically expressed as "New Creation." The analysis of the category of historical causality can lead up to this point, but it cannot give an answer to the question of the "New-Itself."

Historical situation or substance, if drawn into the dynamics of historical causality, contains the quest for a universal historical substance (including all forms of dimensionally qualified substance) or a situation which transcends every situation. It would be a situation in which all possible historical tensions are universally balanced. Here again man's historical consciousness has been aware of this implication of the category of historical substance and has looked ahead beyond any situation to symbols of an ultimate situation, for example, the universal unity of the Kingdom of God.

3. The Dynamics of History

a) The movement of history: trends, structures, periods.—Having discussed the categorical structure of history, we now turn to a description of the movement of history within this structural frame. The categories under the dimension of history provide the basic elements for such a description: time provides the element of irreversibility of the historical movement; causality provides the element of freedom, creating the underivably new; space and substance provide the relatively static element out of which the dynamics of time and causality break and to which they return. With these elements in mind we can approach several questions arising out of the historical movement.

The question of the relation of necessity and contingency in the dynamics of history is first in importance. It is important not only for the method of historiography but also for historical decisions and actions.

The element of necessity arises out of the historical situation; the element of contingency arises out of historical creativity. But neither of these elements is ever alone. Considered under the predominance of the element of necessity, I call their unity "trend," and under the predominance of the element of contingency, "chance."

The nature of trends (as well as the irreversibility of historical time) should prevent any attempt to establish historical laws. Such do not exist, because every moment in history is new in relation to all preceding moments, and a trend, however powerful it may be, can be changed. History is never without changes of seemingly unchangeable trends. There are, however, certain regularities in the sequences of events, rooted in sociological and psychological laws, which, in spite of their lack of strictness, participate in determining a historical situation. But these regularities cannot be predicted with that certainty which makes natural laws the scientific ideal. Trends can be produced by sociological laws—of which point the rule that successful revolutions have the tendency to annihilate their original leaders is an example. Trends can also be produced by creative acts, such as new inventions and their impact on society, or by increasing reactions against such impacts. There are situations in which trends are almost irresistible. There are situations in which trends are less manifest even if no less effective. There are situations in which trends are balanced by chances, and there are trends hidden under an abundance of chances.

As every historical situation contains trends, so it contains chances. Chances are occasions to change the determining power of a trend. Such occasions are produced by elements in the situation which are contingent with respect to the trend and have for the observer the character of the unforeseeable. The chance-giving occasion, in order to become a real chance, must be used by an act of creative causality; and the only proof that there is a real occasion is the historical act in which a trend is successfully transformed. Many chances never come into the open because there is nobody who takes them, but in no historical situation can one say with certainty that no chance is present. Of course, neither chances nor trends are absolute. The determining power of the given situation limits the margin of chances and often makes it very small. Nevertheless, the existence of chances, balancing the determining power of trends, is the decisive argument against all forms of historical determinism—naturalistic, dialectical, or predestinarian. All three envisage a world without chances—a vision, however, which is continually contradicted by the thoughts and actions through which even their own adherents see chances and take them, for example, the chance to work for socialism or for one's own salvation or for a deterministic metaphysics. In every creative act chances are presupposed, consciously or unconsciously.

The second question about the dynamics of history refers to structures of the historical movement. It is the merit of Arnold Toynbee's *A Study of History* that he has tried to show such structures which appear again and again, without rendering them universal and without making them laws. Geographical, biological, psychological, and sociological factors are effective in the structures, producing situations out of which creative acts can arise.

Other structures, such as those of progress and regression, action and reaction, tension and solution, and growth and decay, and most important of all, the dialectical structure of history, have been described in earlier efforts. The general judgment with respect to all of them must be that they have a limited truth and, even more, that they are used in practice in every historical work, even by those who reject them when formulated *in abstracto*. For without them no meaningful description of the texture of events would be possible. But they share a danger which has produced the strong resistance against them on the part of empirical historians: they are often used not as particular structures but as universal laws. As soon as this happens they distort facts, even if, in consequence of their particular truth, they reveal facts. Just because it is the character of historical causality to be creative and to use chances, it cannot be said that a universal structure of historical movement exists. In some cases the attempt to formulate such a law is based on a confusion of the historical dimension with the self-transcendent function of history. It is a confusion between a scientific description and a religious interpretation of history. For instance, progress in some realms (like regression in other realms) is observable in all periods of history, but the law of universal progress is a secularized and distorted form of the religious symbol of divine providence. Stories of growth and decay are contained in all historical works; yet even this most obvious of all structures of the historical movement is not an empirical law. Empirically, there are many instances which contradict it. However, if it is made into a universal law, it assumes a religious character and is an application of the circular interpretation of existence to historical movements—which is a confusion of dimensions.

The dialectical structure of historical events demands special consideration. It has influenced world history more profoundly than any of the other structural analyses. First of all, one must emphasize that it is true not only of many historical phenomena but of life-processes in general. It is an important scientific tool for the analysis and description of the dynamics of life as life. If life is dissolved into elements and these elements are recomposed according to purposes, dialectics have no place; but if life is left unviolated, dialectical processes go on and can be described. Such descriptions are much older than Plato's use of dialectics in his dialogues and Hegel's application of the dialectical method to all dimensions of life and especially to history. Wherever life comes into conflict with itself and drives toward a new stage beyond the conflict, objective or real dialectics take place. Whenever such processes are described in terms of "yes" and "no," subjective or methodological dialectics are used. The movement of life from self-identity to self-alteration and back to self-identity is the basic scheme of dialectics, and we have seen that it is adequate even for the symbolic description of the divine life.

Nevertheless, one cannot make a universal law of dialectics and subsume the universe in all its movements under it. When elevated to such a function, it is no longer empirically verifiable but presses reality into a mechanized scheme which ceases to mediate knowledge, as is shown, for example, in Hegel's *Encyclopedia*. Obviously—and it was so intended by Hegel—his dialectics are the religious symbols of estrangement and reconciliation conceptualized and reduced to empirical descriptions. But again, this is a confusion of dimensions.

The term "materialistic dialectics" is ambiguous and dangerous because of its ambiguity. The term "materialistic" can be understood as metaphysical materialism (which was strongly rejected by Marx) or as moral materialism (which he attacked as the characteristic of bourgeois society). Both interpretations are wrong. Rather, materialism, in connection with dialectics, expresses the belief that the economic-social conditions of a society determine all other cultural forms and that the movement of the economic-social basis has a dialectical character which produces tensions and conflicts in a social situation and drives beyond them toward a new economic-social stage. It is obvious that the dialectical character of this materialism excludes metaphysical materialism and includes the element of the new which Hegel called "synthesis" and which cannot be reached without historical action—as Marx himself realized and applied in practice. The relative truth of social dialectics, rooted in economic conflicts, cannot be denied, but truth becomes error if this kind of dialectics is raised to the status of a law for all history. Then it becomes a quasi-religious principle and loses any empirical verifiability.

A third problem raised by the dynamics of history is the problem of the rhythm of the historical movement. It is the question of historical periods. In the discussion of substance under the dimension of history, we pointed to the identity of a historical situation and emphasized that without naming historical periods historiography would be impossible. In early chronicles the sequence of imperial dynasties provided names for historical periods because the character of each dynasty was supposed to represent the historically significant character of the period in which it ruled. Such characterization has not disappeared, as is shown by the use of the term "Victorian period" for the second half of the nineteenth century in England and large parts of Europe. Other names are taken from predominant styles in the arts, in politics, and in social structures, as, for example, "baroque", "absolutism", "feudalism", or from a total cultural situation, as, for example, "Renaissance." Sometimes the numbers of centuries have received a qualitative character and designate a historical period in abbreviated form ("eighteenth century"). The most universal periodization is based on religion: the time before and after Christ in the Christian era. It implies a universal change in the quality of historical time through the appearance of Jesus as the Christ, making him the "center of history" in the Christian view.

The question to be asked at this point is only: What is the validity of these periodizations? Does history move in such a way that the distinction of periods has a foundation in reality and not only in the mind of the historian? The answer is implied in two earlier observations: the first concerns the subjective-objective character of history, and the second concerns the concept of historical importance. Periods are subjective-objective according to the valuation of importance in a history-bearing group. No periodization is meaningful if it is not based on events in time and space, but no periodization would take place without a valuation of these events as historically decisive by history-conscious representatives of a historical group. The period-creating events can be sudden, dramatic, and widespread, as in the Reformation, or they can be slow, undramatic, and restricted to small groups, as in the Renaissance. In each case the consciousness of western Europe has seen in these events the beginning of a new period, and it is impossible to confirm or to deny this view by research into the events themselves. In the same way it is impossible to discuss the historical centrality of the event of Jesus as the Christ by positive or negative arguments based on new discoveries about the historical circumstances of this event. Something happened which for two thousand years has induced people to see in it, in terms of existential significance, the boundary between the two main periods of human history.

History moves in a periodic rhythm, but periods are periods only for those who can see them as such. In the sequence of events there are continuous transitions, overlappings, advances, and delays, and no signpost marks a new period. But for those who valuate these events according to the principle of importance, signposts become visible, marking the boundary line between qualitatively different stretches of historical time.

b) History and the processes of life.—The processes of life, together with their ambiguities, which we have described in all dimensions, are not absent under the dimension of history. Life strives toward self-integration and may disintegrate in every history-creating act. Life creates and may destroy itself when the dynamics of history drive toward the new. Life transcends itself and may fall into profanity when it runs toward the ultimately new and transcendent.

All this happens in the bearers of history. It occurs directly in the historical groups and indirectly in the individuals who both constitute the historical groups and are constituted by them. We have discussed the nature and the ambiguities of social groups in the sections of the fourth part of the system dealing with the cultural function of man's spirit, especially the function of *praxis*: the personal and the communal act. And we have discussed the ambiguities of *praxis* under the headings of the ambiguities of technical and personal and, above all, of communal transformation. In these discussions the historical dimension was "put into brackets"; we described the historical groups only from the point of view of their character as cultural creations, subject to the criteria of humanity and justice. It was especially the relation of power and justice in the communal realm that was the center of our attention. This, however, was a preparation for the description of the movement of the history-bearing groups in history.

At the present point the focus is on the relation of the historical dimension to the processes of life in the personal-communal realm. In all three processes it is the character of historical time that makes the difference: history runs ahead toward the ever new and toward the ultimately new. From this point of view both the nature and the ambiguities of the drive toward self-integration, self-creativity, and self-transcendence must be seen. This, however, as indicated in the former discussions ("the ambiguities of communal transformation"), has the consequence that the three processes of life are united in *one* process: the movement toward an aim. There is still self-integration, but not as an end in itself; self-integration under the historical dimension serves the drive toward universal and total integration. There is still self-creativity, but not for the sake of particular creations; self-creativity under the historical dimension serves the drive toward that which is universally and totally new. And there is still self-transcendence, but not toward a particular sublimity; self-transcendence under the historical dimension serves the drive toward the universally and totally transcendent. History runs toward fulfilment through all processes of life, notwithstanding the fact that while it runs toward the ultimate it remains bound to the preliminary, and in running toward fulfilment it defeats fulfilment. It does not escape the ambiguities of life by striving in all processes toward unambiguous life.

The aim of history can now be expressed in terms of the three processes of life and their unity in the following way: History, in terms of the self-integration of life, drives toward a centeredness of all history-bearing groups and their individual members in an unambiguous harmony of power and justice. History, in terms of the self-creativity of life drives toward the creation of a new, unambiguous state of things. And history, in terms of the self-transcendence of life, drives toward the universal, unambiguous fulfilment of the potentiality of being.

But history, like life in general, stands under the negativities of existence and therefore under the ambiguities of life. The drive toward universal and total centeredness, newness, and fulfilment is a question and remains a question as long as there is history. This question is implied in the great ambiguities of history which have always been felt and powerfully expressed in myth, religious and secular literature, and art.

They are the questions to which (in the sense of the method of correlation) the religious (and quasi-religious) interpretations of history as well as the eschatological symbolism relate. They are the questions to which, within the circle of Christian theology, the Kingdom of God is the answer.

c) *Historical progress: its reality and its limits.*—In every creative act progress is implied, namely, a step (*gressus*) beyond the given. In this sense the whole movement of history is progressive. It progresses to the particularly new and tries to reach the ultimately new. This applies to all sides of the cultural function of the human spirit, to the functions of *theoria* as well as to the functions of *praxis*, and it applies to morality and religion in so far as cultural content and cultural forms are implied in them. There is intended and sometimes actual progress from the beginning to the end of a political action or a lecture or a scientific inquiry, and so on. In every centered group, even the most conservative, creative acts aiming at progress are continuous.

Beyond these indisputable facts, progress has become a symbol, defining the meaning of history itself. It has become a symbol beyond reality. As such it expresses the idea that history progressively approaches its ultimate aim or that infinite progress itself is the aim of history. We shall discuss these answers to the question of the meaning of history later; at this point we have to ask in which realm of being progress is possible and in which realm it is impossible, according to the nature of the reality at stake.

There is no progress where individual freedom is decisive. This implies that there is no progress in the moral act. Each individual, in order to become a person, must make moral decisions of his own. They are the absolute precondition for the appearance of the dimension of spirit in any individual with self-awareness. But there are two kinds of progress in connection with the moral function, the two kinds being those of ethical content and of educational level. Both are cultural creations and open to the new. The ethical content of moral action has progressed from primitive to mature cultures in terms of refinement and breadth, although the moral act in which the person is created is the same whatever content is actualized. This distinction is fundamental if one speaks of moral progress. It is in the cultural element within the moral act that progress takes place, not in the moral act itself.

In the same way moral education belongs to culture and not to the moral act itself. Such education appears both as education by others and as education by oneself. In both cases it consists of repetitions, exercises, and the resulting habit which is a matter of progress. In this way mature moral personalities can be created and the level of moral habits in a group can be raised. But the actual moral situation demands free decision on every level of maturity and in every degree of ethical sensitivity; and it is by these decisions that the person is confirmed as person (even if the moral habit and the ethical sensitivity are creations of the Spirit, that is, grace). This is the reason for the stories of the temptations of the saints in the Catholic tradition, for the need to receive forgiveness at every stage of sanctification in Protestant experience, for the struggle with despair about one's self in the greatest and maturest representatives of humanism, and for the self-limitation of psychotherapeutic healing to the point where the patient is set free for moral decisions of his own.

Within the realm of cultural creation there is no progress beyond the classical expressions of man's encounter with reality, whether it is in the arts, in philosophy, or in the personal or communal realms. There is often, although not always, progress from inadequate attempts to reach the classical expression of a style, but there is no progress from one mature style to the other. It was the great mistake of the classicistic art criticism to see in the Greek and Renaissance styles the norm for visual arts, by which everything else was to be measured as either progress toward it or regression from it or relegated to a state of primitive impotence. The justified reaction against this doctrine in our century has sometimes gone to unjustified extremes in the opposite direction, but it has established the principle of the essentially non-progressive character of the history of the arts.

The same must be said for philosophy—in so far as it is defined as the attempt to answer in the most universal concepts the question of the nature and structure of being. Here again one can distinguish between undeveloped and mature types of the philosophical encounter with reality and see a progress from one to the other. And certainly the logical tools and scientific materials used in philosophical systems are being progressively refined, corrected, and enlarged. But there is an element in the central vision of the representative philosophers which is not derived from their scientific material or their logical analysis but which has its source in an encounter with ultimate reality, i.e., in a quasi-revelatory experience. It has been called *sapientia* in contrast to *scientia* and appears, for example, in the book of Job, personified as the companion of God at which he looked in creating the world, or in Heraclitus, as the Logos which is present equally in the laws of the universe and in the wisdom of a few among men. In so far as philosophy is Logos-inspired, it can have many faces, according to its inner potentialities and the receiving organs of individuals and periods, but there is no progress from one face to another. Each, of course, presupposes a new creative endeavor, in addition to a critical use of logical form and scientific material, and it requires the discipline gained by a knowledge of earlier solutions. The Logos-inspired character of philosophy does not mean that it is arbitrary. But it does mean that philosophy is enabled to give an answer to the question of being—which answer, therefore, lies above progress and obsolescence. The history of philosophy clearly shows that none of the great philosophical solutions has ever become obsolete, although their scientific observations and theories soon become antiquated. And it is only consistent that some analytic philosophers reject the entire history of philosophy before the rise of analytic philosophy because they see no, or little, progress in it toward what they believe to be the only task of philosophy: logical and semantic analysis.

Although the moral act as an act of freedom is beyond progress, the question remains whether there is progress in approaching the principle of humanity and creating the formed personality and in approaching the principle of justice and creating the organized community. As in aesthetic and cognitive creativity, one must distinguish between two elements, the qualitative and the quantitative elements. Only in the latter is progress possible—that is, in breadth and refinement—and not in the former. Persons embodying the principle of humanity in a mature way are not dependent on the changing developments of culture, whether progressive or obsolescent or regressive. Certainly, humanity is a new creation in every individual in which it is actualized and in every period in which the cultural situation affords new potentialities. But there is no progress from one representative of personal humanity to another in a later period. He who knows sculptural representations from the earliest cultures to the present knows examples of expressive humanity (in terms of dignity, seriousness, serenity, wisdom, courage, compassion) in the images of every period.

The situation with respect to justice is no different. This, of course, is a bold statement in a culture which considers its own social-political system as not only the adequate expression of its own idea of justice but the ideal of justice to which all previous forms are but insufficient approaches. Nevertheless, the assertion must be made that the justice of democracy represents progress above other forms of justice only in its quantitative elements, not in its qualitative character. Systems of justice in the history of mankind develop out of geographical, economic, and human conditions through the encounter of man with man and the quest for justice that results from this encounter. Justice becomes injustice to the degree that the change of conditions is not matched by a correlative change in the systems of justice. But in itself every system includes an element which is essential for the encounter of man with man and a valid principle for a concrete situation. Each of such systems points to the "Justice of the Kingdom of God," and there is no progress from the one to the other in this respect. However, as in the previous considerations, we must distinguish those stages in which the principle is still undeveloped and those stages in which it disintegrates from the stage of mature fulfilment. There is progress or obsolescence or regression on the way from one stage to the other. Only mature systems, embodying qualitatively different visions of justice, are beyond progress.

The most important question in this context is that of a possible progress in religion. Obviously there is no progress in the religious function as such. The state of ultimate concern admits no more of progress than of obsolescence or regression. But the question of progress arises with the existence of historical religions and their foundations, revelatory experiences. It might seem that the question of progress has already been answered affirmatively when we called the revelation in Jesus as the Christ the final revelation, and the history of religion the process in which the "center of history" is prepared for or received. But the situation is more complex.

In discussions about the "absoluteness" of Christianity, the evolutionary-progressivistic scheme has been applied to the relation of the Christian religion to the others. The classical formulation of this idea is Hegel's philosophical interpretation of the history of religion, but analogous constructions are also openly present or hidden in the anti-Hegelian systems of liberal theology. Even secular philosophers of religion distinguish between primitive and great religions. But against this evolutionary scheme stands the claim of each of the great religions that it itself is absolute in contrast to the other religions which are considered as relatively true or completely false. Analogously to the previous discussions, we must first emphasize the distinction between the essentially religious and the cultural elements in the historical religions. There is certainly progress, obsolescence, and regression in the cultural side of every religion, in its cognitive self-interpretation and in its aesthetic self-expression, as in its way of forming personality and community. But of course this progress is limited by the extent to which these functions are themselves open to progress. The decisive question, however, is whether the foundations of religions, the revelatory experiences on which they are based, have progressive possibilities. Can one speak of a progressive history of revelation? This is the same question as whether one can speak of a progressive "history of salvation" (*Heilsgeschichte*). The first answer must be that the revelatory and saving manifestation of the Spiritual Presence is always what it is, and that in this respect there is no more or less, no progress or obsolescence or regression. But the content of such manifestations and their symbolic expressions, like styles in the arts and visions in philosophy, are dependent on the potentialities implied in the human encounter with the holy, on the one hand, and on the receptivity of a human group for one or another of these potentialities, on the other. The human receptivity is conditioned by the totality of external and internal factors which constitute historical destiny—religiously speaking, historical providence. Progress in this respect is possible between different cultural stages in which the revelatory experience takes place or between different degrees of clarity and power with which the manifestation of the Spiritual is received. (This corresponds to the progress from immaturity to maturity in the cultural realms.)

In the light of these considerations, a particular religion could not maintain a claim to be based on the final revelation. The only possible answer to the question of progress in religion would be the coexistence of different types without a universal claim. But there is one point of view which can change the picture—the conflict between the divine and the demonic in every religion. Out of this conflict the question arises: Upon which religious basis and in which revelatory event is the power of the demonic, outside and inside the religious reality, broken? Christianity answers that this has happened on the basis of the prophetic type of religion in the event of Jesus as the Christ. According to Christianity this event is not the result of a progressive approximation, nor is it the actualization of another religious potentiality, but it is the uniting and judging fulfilment of all potentialities implied in the encounter with the holy. Therefore the whole history of religion, past and future, is the universal basis, and the prophetic type of revelatory experience is the particular basis of the central event. This view excludes the idea of a horizontal progress from the universal to the particular basis and from the particular basis to the unique event, out of which Christianity has grown. The idea which claims that Christianity as a religion is "absolute" and that the other religions are a progressive approximation to it is also excluded. It is not Christianity as a religion that is absolute but the event by which Christianity is created and judged to the same extent as any other religion, both affirmatively and negatively. This view of the history of religions—derived from the Christian claim that it is based on the final, victoriously antidemonic revelatory event—is not horizontal but vertical. The unique event, which is both the criterion of all religions and the power which has, in principle, broken the demonic for all time, stands at one point on the larger basis of past and future religious developments and on the particular basis of prophetism in past and future. There is no progressivistic scheme in this view.

It is now necessary to sum up the realms in which progress has its place, as indicated in the preceding discussions. The first and almost unlimited realm in which progress is decisive is technology. The phrase "better and better" has its proper field here and only here. The better tool, and generally the technically better means for whatever end, is a cultural reality of never ending consequences. A non-progressive element appears only if the questions are raised: For which ends? Or, are there tools which by their consequences may defeat the ends for which they are produced (e.g., atomic weapons)? The second realm in which progress is essential is that of the sciences in all realms of methodological research, not in the natural sciences alone. Every scientific statement is a hypothesis open for testing, rejecting, and changing; and in so far as there is a scientific element in philosophy, the philosopher must use the same method. A non-progressive element appears only where philosophical elements are presupposed consciously or unconsciously or where decisions must be made as to what subject matter shall be investigated or where existential participation in the subject matter is required in order to penetrate it. The third realm in which progress is real is that of education, whether it is by training for skills, by the mediation of cultral contents, or by introduction into given systems of life. This is obvious in individual education which directs the progress of a person toward maturity, but it is also true of social education, by which every generation is heir to the gains of the preceding ones. A non-progressive element is present only in the assertion of an ultimate educational aim in the interpretation of human nature and destiny and in the kind of an educational community between educators and educated. The fourth realm in which progress is real is the increasing conquest of spatial divisions and separations within and beyond mankind. Partly parallel with this conquest of space is the increasing participation of human beings in all cultural creations. In these respects, which can be measured quantitatively, progress was and is real and may remain real in an indefinite future. A non-progressive element in these movements is the fact that quantitative changes can have qualitative consequences and create a new age which, in relation to others, is unique but in itself is neither a progess nor a regression.

This analysis of the reality and the limits of progress in history gives a basis for the valuation of progress as a symbol in the religious interpretation of history.

B. THE AMBIGUITIES OF LIFE
UNDER THE HISTORICAL DIMENSION

1. The Ambiguities of Historical Self-integration: Empire and Centralization

History, while running ahead toward its ultimate aim, continuously actualizes limited aims, and in so doing it both achieves and defeats its ultimate aim. All ambiguities of historical existence are forms of this basic ambiguity. If we relate them to the processes of life, we can distinguish the ambiguity of historical self-integration, the ambiguity of historical self-creativity, and the ambiguity of historical self-transcendence.

The greatness of man's political existence—his striving toward universality and totality in the process of the self-integration of life under the historical dimension—is expressed in the term "empire." In biblical literature the ambiguity of the empires plays an important role. The same is true of all phases of church history, and it is equally true of secular movements up to the present day. Empires are built and grow and fall before they have reached their aim, which is to become all-inclusive. It would be rather superficial to derive this striving for universality simply from the will to power, whether political or economic. The will to power, in all its forms, is a necessary element in the self-integration of the history-bearing groups, for it is only through their centered power that they are able to act historically. But there is another element in the drive toward all-inclusiveness: the vocational self-interpretation of a historical group. The stronger and more justified this element is, the greater the group's empire-building passion becomes; and the more it has the support of all its members, the better its chance is to last a long time. The history of mankind is full of examples. In Western history the greatest, though not the only, examples of vocational consciousness are the following: the Roman empire's bidding to represent the law, the Germanic empire's representation of the Body Christian, the British empire's representation of Christian civilization, the Russian empire's representation of the depth of humanity against a mechanized culture, and the American empire's call to represent the principle of liberty. And there are corresponding examples in the Eastern section of mankind. The great conquerors are, as Luther visualized them, the demonic "masks" of God through whose drive toward universal centeredness he performs his providential work. In this vision the "ambiguity of the empire" is symbolically expressed. For the disintegrating, destructive, and profanizing side of empire-building is as obvious as the integrating, creative, and sublimating side. No imagination can grasp the amount of suffering and destruction of structure, life, and meaning that is inevitably connected with the growth of empires. In our period the trend toward all-inclusiveness in the two great imperial powers, the United States and Russia, has led to the deepest and most universal split of mankind, and this has happened just because neither of the two empires has come into existence by a simple will to economic or political power; they have risen and become powerful by their vocational consciousness in unity with their natural self-affirmation. But the tragic consequences of their conflict are noticeable in every historical group and every individual human being, and they may become destructive for mankind itself.

This situation gives us a clue to what has been called world history. "World," in this phrase, means mankind; it means the history of all mankind. But there is no such thing; all we have had up to the present century are histories of human groups, and the compilation of their histories as far as they are known may be called world history but certainly not a history of mankind. However, in our century, the technical conquest of space has produced a unity which makes a history of mankind as a whole possible and has started to make it real. This, of course, does not change the isolated character of former histories, but it is a new stage for man's historical integration. In this sense our century belongs with the great centuries in regard to the creation of the new. But the first direct result of mankind's technical (and more than technical) union has been the tragic split, the "schizophrenia," of mankind. The moment of greatest integration in all history implies the danger of the greatest disintegration, even of radical destruction.

In view of this situation, one must ask: Is it justifiable to speak of *one* aim? This question becomes even more urgent if one realizes that not all tribes and nations have striven or are striving toward all-inclusiveness, that not every conquest has the ambiguity of empire-building, and that even those in whom the drive toward universal integration has been effective have often made it ineffective by withdrawing to a limited tribal or national centeredness. These facts show that there is in history-bearing groups a tendency against the universalistic element in the dynamics of history. The daring, ultimately prophetic character of the idea of empire produces reactions toward tribal or regional or national isolation and the defense of a limited spatial unity; such reactions have indirectly contributed much to the movement of history as a whole. But one can show that in all important cases of this kind the isolationist movement was and is not a genuine action but a reaction, a withdrawal from involvement in universalist movements. Historical existence stands under the "star" of historical time and runs ahead against every particularist resistance. Therefore the isolationist attempts are never ultimately successful; they are frustrated by the dynamics of history which are universalist by their very nature. No individual and no group can avoid the dynamics of history in order to avoid the tragic implications of the greatness of history as it is expressed in the symbol of empire. But even so the concept of world history remains doubtful in view of past unknown or unconnected historical movements. It cannot be defined empirically but must be understood in terms of an interpretation of history as self-transcending.

The ambiguities of centeredness refer not only to the extensive but also to the intensive aspect of historical integration. Every history-bearing group has a power structure without which it would not be able to act historically. This structure is the source of the ambiguities of centeredness within a historical group. We have discussed the structural side in the discussion of the ambiguities of leadership. Under the historical dimension the dynamic side must be considered; we must look at the relation of intensive to extensive centeredness, which, in political terms, is the relation of politics to international relations. There are two contradictory tendencies, the one toward a totalitarian control of the life of everyone who belongs to a history-bearing and especially to an imperial group, the other toward the personal freedom that fosters creativity. The first tendency is strengthened if external conflicts demand an increase in centered power or if disintegrating forces within the group endanger the centeredness itself. In both cases the necessity of a powerful center reduces and tends to annihilate the element of freedom which is the precondition for all historical creativity. The group is able to act historically because of its severe centralization, but it cannot use its power creatively because it has suppressed those creative potencies which drive into the future. Only the dictatorial elite—or the dictator alone— is free to act historically, and then actions, because they are deprived of the meaning which can appear only in the encounter of free, moral, cultural, and religious agents, become empty power drives, though often on a grand scale. They may serve as tools of historical destiny, but they pay for their loss of meaning by the destruction of the historical group they use. For power which has lost meaning also loses itself as power.

The opposite attitude toward political centeredness and historical creativity is the sacrifice of the former to the latter. This can result from a diversity of power centers within a history-bearing group, if the center of the group as a whole is changing from one subcenter to another or if no embracing center can be established at all. These are the most tragic and often the most creative periods in history. It is also possible that the center, in spurring individual creativity, may deprive itself of the power which is necessary for centered historical action—a situation which is usually followed by a dictatorial period. In this case the effect, even of great individual creation, on history as a whole remains indirect because a centered historical action is lacking.

These considerations drive to the question: How can the ambiguities of the external imperial trend and of internal centralization be conquered within an unambiguous historical integration?

2. The Ambiguities of Historical Self-creativity:
Revolution and Reaction

Historical creativity takes place in the non-progressive as well as in the progressive element of the dynamics of history. It is the process in which the new is created in all realms under the historical dimension. Everything new in history keeps within itself elements of the old out of which it grows. Hegel has expressed this fact in the well-known phrase that the old is in the new, both negated and preserved (*aufgehoben*). But Hegel did not take seriously the ambiguity of this structure of growth and its destructive possibilities. These factors appear in the relation between the generations, in the struggles of artistic and philosophical styles, in the ideologies of the political parties, in the oscillation between revolution and reaction, and in the tragic situations to which these conflicts lead. The greatness of history is that it runs toward the new, but greatness, because of its ambiguity, is also the tragic character of history.

The problem of the relation between the generations is not that of authority (which has been discussed earlier) but that of the old and the new in the dynamics of history. In order to make a place for the new the young generation has to disregard the creative processes out of which the old has arisen. Representatives of the new attack the final results of those processes, unaware of the answers to former problems which are implied in these results. Therefore the attacks are necessarily unfair; their unfairness is an unavoidable element of their strength to break through the given. Naturally, their unfairness produces negative reactions on the side of the old—negative not so much in terms of unfairness as in terms of inability to understand. Representatives of the old see in the given results the toil and greatness of their own creative past; they do not see that they constitute stumbling blocks in the way of the new generation to creativity. In this conflict partisans of the old become hardened and bitter, and partisans of the new frustrated and empty.

It is natural that political life is largely structured by the ambiguity of historical creativity. Every political act is directed toward something new; but the difference is whether this new step is taken for the sake of the new itself or for the sake of the old. Even in non-revolutionary situations the struggle between the conservative and progressive forces leads to the disruption of human ties, to a partly unconscious, partly conscious, distortion of factual truth, to promises the fulfilment of which was not even intended, and to the suppression of the creative forces belonging to the other side. Finally, a revolutionary situation may develop with its devastating struggles between revolution and re-action. There are situations in which only a revolution (not always a bloody one) can achieve the breakthrough to a new creation. Such violent breakthroughs are examples of destruction for the sake of crea-tion, a destruction sometimes so radical that a new creation becomes impossible and a slow reduction of the group and its culture to the stage of an almost vegetative existence takes place. It is this danger of utter chaos that gives the established powers the ideological justification to suppress revolutionary forces or to try to overcome them in a counter-revolution. Often the revolution itself runs in a direction which contra-dicts its original meaning and annihilates those who have created it. If the reaction is victorious, history has not returned to the "ideal" stage in the name of which the counterrevolution was undertaken but to something new which disclaims newness and is slowly eroded by the forces of the new, which cannot be excluded in the long run, however distorted their emergence may be. The immensity of personal sacrifice and destruction of things in these processes drives to the question of unambiguous historical creativity.

3. The Ambiguities of Historical Self-transcendence:
    The "Third Stage" as Given and as Expected

The historical conflicts between the old and the new reach their most destructive stage if either side claims ultimacy for itself. This self-elevating claim to ultimacy is the definition of the demonic, and no-where is the demonic as manifest as under the historical dimension. The claim to ultimacy takes the form of the claim to have or to bring the ultimate toward which history runs. This has happened not only in the political but even more directly in the religious sphere. The struggle between the sacred old and the prophetic new is a central theme of the history of religions, and, according to the fact that the demonic's favored place is the holy, these conflicts reach an all-surpassing destructiveness in religious wars and persecutions. From the point of view of historical dynamics, this is the conflict between different groups which claim to represent the aim of history either in terms of its actual or in terms of its anticipated fulfilment. In this connection we can use the traditional symbol of the "third stage." Its mythological background is the cosmic drama of paradise, fall, and restitution. Its application to history has led to apocalyptic visions of several world ages and the expected coming of the new and last age. In Augustine's interpretation of history, the last age begins with the foundation of the Christian church. In opposition to him, Joachim de Fiore, following Montanist ideas, speaks of three ages, of which the third has not yet appeared but which will appear in a few decades. The feeling of being at the beginning of the last stage of history was expressed by sectarian movements in religious terminology, for example, by the symbol of the thousand years in which the Christ will rule history before the final end. In the periods of Enlightenment and idealism, the symbol of the third stage was secularized and assumed a revolutionary function. Both bourgeoisie and proletariat construed their world historical role respectively as that of the bearers of the "age of reason" or of the "classless society," terms which are variations of the symbol of the third stage. In each form of the symbol, religious or secular, the conviction is expressed that the third stage has started, that history has reached a point which cannot be surpassed in principle, that the "beginning of the end" is at hand, and that we can see the ultimate fulfilment toward which history moves, in the course of which it transcends itself and each of its moments. In these ideas the self-transcendence of life under the dimension of history is expressed and leads to two utterly ambiguous attitudes: the first being the self-absolutizing one, in which the present situation is identified with the third stage, and the second being the utopian one, in which the third stage is seen as immediately at hand or already beginning. The self-absolutizing attitude is ambiguous because, on the one hand, it makes the self-transcendence of life manifest in religious or quasi-religious symbols and, on the other, it conceals the self-transcendence of life by identifying these symbols with the ultimate itself. The classical expression of this ambiguity is the Roman church's claim that it is the fulfilment of the apocalyptic vision of the thousand-year reign of Christ on earth, receiving from this self-interpretation both its divine and its demonic traits. In sectarian as well as secular utopianism, the ambiguity is most manifest when we contrast the way in which these movements create new historical realities through the enthusiasm of their expectation and the sacrifices they make to fulfill it, with the result of profound existential disappointment, followed by cynicism and indifference, when and if the state of things fails to corroborate their expectations. History expresses the ambiguity of its self-transcendence most conspicuously in these oscillations. In them, above all, the riddle of history becomes an existential concern as well as a philosophical and theological problem.

The last three considerations have shown that it is possible and revealing to apply the distinction of the three functions of life also to history and that, as in the other dimensions of life, they lead to conflicts which are inescapable and which cause both the greatness and the tragedy of historical existence. Such analyses can liberate us from both utopianism and despair with regard to the meaning of history.

4. THE AMBIGUITIES OF THE INDIVIDUAL IN HISTORY

Most religions and philosophies agree with Hegel's judgment that "history is not the place in which the individual can find happiness." Even a superficial look into world history shows the truth of this statement, and a deeper and more embracing view overwhelmingly confirms it. Nevertheless, this is not the whole truth. The individual receives his life as a person from the history-bearing group to which he belongs. History has given to everyone the physical, social, and spiritual conditions of his existence. Nobody who uses language is outside history, and nobody can withdraw from it. The monk and the hermit, those who try to cut all social and political ties, are dependent on the history they want to avoid, and further, they influence the historical movement from which they try to separate themselves. It is an often repeated fact that those who have refused to act historically have had a greater impact on history than those who were near the centers of historical action.

History is not only political; all sides of man's cultural and religious activity have a historical dimension. Therefore everyone, in every realm of human activity, acts historically. The smallest and lowest services help to uphold the technical and economic basis of society and consequently support its historical movement. However, the universal participation of every human being in history does not exclude the predominance of the political function in historical activity. The reason for this predominance is the internal and external political character of the history-bearing groups. The precondition of all life, including life in history, is the centeredness of the agents of life—in the case of history, the centeredness of historical groups in their static and dynamic qualities. And the function in which this centeredness is actualized is the political. Therefore the image of history, whether in the popular view or in scholarly books, is dominated by political personalities and their actions. Even historical accounts of economics, science, art, or the church cannot avoid continual reference to the political frame within which cultural and religious activities take place.

The predominance of the political function and, at the same time, the ambiguity of the individual in history are most conspicuous in the democratic organization of the political realm. As stated before, democracy is not an absolute political system, but it is the best way discovered so far to guarantee the creative freedom of determining the historical process to everyone within a centered historical group. The predominance of politics includes the dependence of all other functions in which creative freedom is presupposed upon the political organization. For verification of this, it is sufficient to look at the dictatorial systems and their attempts to subject all forms of cultural creativity, including ethics and religion, to the central political power. The result is the deprivation not only of freedom of political creativity but also of the freedom of creativity of any kind except where the central authorities desire it (as in scientific work in Soviet Russia). Democracy makes it possible to fight for freedom in all realms which contribute to the historical movement by fighting for freedom in the political realm. Nevertheless, the participation of the individual in democratic systems of politics is not without limits and ambiguities. In political activity in particular, the techniques of representation drastically reduce the participation of the individual, sometimes even to the vanishing point in mass societies with an all-powerful party bureaucracy. A majority can be produced and maintained by methods which deprive a large number of individuals of political influence altogether and for an indefinite time. The channels of public communication in the hands of ruling groups can become instruments of a conformity which kills creativity in all realms as successfully as under dictatorships, the realm of politics being the chief example. On the other hand, democracy can become unworkable because of disruptive splits within the group—for example, the rise of so many parties that a majority capable of action becomes impossible. Or parties can arise which are absolutistic in ideology and which wage a life and death struggle against opposing parties. In such cases, dictatorship is not far away.

There are ambiguities of the individual in history which are valid under every political system. They can be summed up in the ambiguity of historical sacrifice. It is this basic character of the individual's participation in history which induces in many people the desire to escape history altogether. In Hamlet's monologue "To be or not to be," many of the historical causes for such a desire are enumerated. Today the breakdown of the progressivistic ideology has produced a widespread indifference, and the East-West split with its thread of universal self-destruction has driven innumerable individuals to cynicism and despair; they feel with the Jewish apocalyptics that the earth has become "old"—a realm in which demonic forces rule—and they look above history in resignation or mystical elevation. The symbols of hope expressing the goal toward which history runs, whether secular or religious, have lost their moving power. The individual feels himself a victim of forces which he cannot influence. For him history is negativity without hope.

The ambiguities of life under the dimension of history and the implication of these ambiguities for the life of the individual within his historical group lead to the question: What is the significance of history for the meaning of existence universally? All interpretations of history try to give an answer to this question.

C. INTERPRETATIONS OF HISTORY AND THE QUEST FOR THE KINGDOM OF GOD

1. The Nature and the Problem of an Interpretation of History

Every legend, every chronicle, every report of past events, every scholarly historical work, contains interpreted history. This is the consequence of the subject-object character of history that we discussed before. Such interpretation, however, has many levels. It includes the selection of facts according to the criterion of importance, the valuation of causal dependences, the image of personal and communal structures, a theory of motivation in individuals, groups, and masses, a social and political philosophy, and underlying all this, whether admitted or not, an understanding of the meaning of the history in unity with the meaning of existence in general. Such understanding influences consciously or unconsciously all other levels of interpretation, and it, conversely, is dependent on a knowledge of historical processes, both specifically and universally. This mutual dependence of historical knowledge in all its levels and an interpretation of history should be realized by everyone who deals with history on *any* level.

Our problem is the interpretation of history in the sense of the question: What is the significance of history for the meaning of existence in general? In what way does history influence our ultimate concern? The answer to this question must be related to the ambiguities implied in the processes of life under the dimension of history, all of which are expressions of the basic antinomy of historical time.

How is an answer to the question of the meaning of history possible? Obviously, the subject-object character of history precludes an objective answer in any detached, scientific sense. Only full involvement in historical action can give the basis for an interpretation of history. Historical activity is the key to understanding history. This, however, would lead to as many interpretations as there are types of historical activity, and the question arises: Which type provides the right key? Or, in other words, in which historical group must one participate to be given the universal view that opens up the meaning of history? Every historical group is particular, and participation in its historical acitivities implies a particular view of the aim of historical creativity. It is the vocational consciousness, referred to above, that decides upon the key and what it opens in the understanding of history. For example, the Greek vocational self-interpretation, as given in Aristotle's *Politics*, sees in the contrast between Greeks and barbarians the key to an interpretation of history, while the Jewish vocational self-interpretation, as given in the prophetic literature, sees such a key in the establishment of the rule of Jahweh over the nations of the world. More examples will be given later. At this point the question is: Which group and which vocational consciousness are able to give a key to history as a whole? Obviously, if we try to answer, we have already presupposed an interpretation of history with a claim to universality; we have already used the key in justifying its use. This is an unavoidable consequence of the "theological circle" within which systematic theology moves; but it is an unavoidable circle wherever the question of the ultimate meaning of history is asked. The key and what the key opens are experienced in one and the same act; the affirmation of the vocational consciousness in a definite historical group and the vision of history implied in this consciousness go together. Within the circle of this theological system, it is Christianity in which key and answer are found. In the Christian vocational consciousness, history is affirmed in such a way that the problems implied in the ambiguities of life under the dimension of history are answered through the symbol "Kingdom of God." This, however, is an assertion which must be tested by contrasting this symbol with the other main types of understanding history and by reinterpreting the symbol in light of these contrasts.

The interpretation of history includes more than an answer to the question of history. Since history is the all-embracing dimension of life, and since historical time is the time in which all other dimensions of time are presupposed, the answer to the meaning of history implies an answer to the universal meaning of being. The historical dimension is present in all realms of life, though only as a subordinated dimension. In human history, it comes into its own. But after it has come into its own, it draws into itself the ambiguities and problems under the other dimensions. In terms of the symbol of the Kingdom of God, this means that "Kingdom" includes life in all realms, or that everything that is participates in the striving toward the inner aim of history: fulfilment or ultimate sublimation.

Such an assertion, of course, is more than an answer to the question of the interpretation of history. It implies an interpretation; therefore, the question now is: How can this particular understanding of the inner aim of history, as it appears in the theological system, be described and justified?

2. Negative Answers to the Question of the Meaning of History

The ambiguities of history, as the final expression of the ambiguities of life under all its dimensions, have led to a basic split in the valuation of history and life itself. We have referred to it in the discussion of the New Being and its expectation by the two contrasting types of interpreting history—the non-historical and the historical. The non-historical type, our first subject of consideration, presupposes that the "running ahead" of historical time has no aim either within or above history but that history is the "place" in which individual beings live their lives unaware of an eternal *telos* of their personal lives. This is the attitude toward history for the largest number of human beings. One can distinguish three forms of such non-historical interpretations of history: the tragic, the mystical, the mechanistic.

The tragic interpretation of history receives its classical expression in Greek thought but is by no means restricted to it. History, in this view, does not run toward a historical or transhistorical aim but in a circle back to its beginning. In its course it provides genesis, acme, and decay for every being, each one at its time and with definite limits; there is nothing beyond or above this stretch of time which itself is determined by fate. Within the cosmic circle, periods can be distinguished which as a whole constitute a process of deterioration, starting with an original perfection and falling by degrees into a stage of utter distortion of what the world and man essentially are. Existence in time and space and in the separation of individual from individual is tragic guilt, which leads necessarily to self-destruction. But tragedy presupposes greatness, and in this view there is heavy emphasis on greatness in terms of centeredness, creativity, and sublimation. The glory of life in nature, nations, and persons is praised, and it is just for this reason that the shortness and misery and tragic quality of life are deplored. But there is no hope, no expectation of an immanent or transcendent fulfilment of history. It is non-historical, and the tragic circle of genesis and decay is its last word. None of the ambiguities of life is conquered; there is no consolation for the disintegrating, destructive, profanizing side of life, and its only resource is the courage which raises both hero and wise man above the vicissitudes of historical existence.

This way of transcending history points to the second type of the non-historical interpretation of history, the mystical. Although it appears also in Western culture (as, for example, in Neoplatonism and Spinozism), it is most fully and effectively developed in the East, as in Vedanta Hinduism, in Taoism, and in Buddhism. Historical existence has no meaning in itself. One must live in it and act reasonably, but history itself can neither create the new nor be truly real. This attitude, which demands elevation above history while living in it, is the most widespread of all within historical mankind. In some Hindu philosophies there is a speculation similar to that of Stoicism about cosmic cycles of genesis and decay and the deteriorization of historical mankind from one period to another up to the last in which we are living. But in general there is no awareness of historical time and of an end toward which it is running in this type of non-historical interpretation of history. The emphasis is on the individual and particularly on the comparatively few illuminated individuals who are aware of the human predicament. The others are objects of a pharisaic judgment about their *karma* for which they are responsible in a former incarnation, or they are objects of compassion and adaptation of the religious demands to their unenlightened stage, as in some forms of Buddhism.

In any case, these religions contain no impulse to transform history in the direction of universal humanity and justice. History has no aim, either in time or in eternity. And again, the consequence is that the ambiguities of life under all dimensions are unconquerable. There is only one way to cope with them and that is to transcend them and live within them as someone who has already returned to the Ultimate One. He has not changed reality but he has conquered his own involvement in reality. There is no symbol analogous to that of the Kingdom of God. But there is often a profound compassion for the universality of suffering under all dimensions of life—an element often lacking under the influence of historical interpretations of history in the Western world.

Under the impact of the modern scientific interpretation of reality in all its dimensions, the understanding of history has undergone a change, not only in relation to the mystical interpretation of history, but also in relation to the tragic interpretation. Physical time controls the analysis of time so completely that there is little place for the special characteristics of biological, and even less of historical, time. History has become a series of happenings in the physical universe, interesting to man, worthy to be recorded and studied, but without a special contribution to the interpretation of existence as such. One could call this the mechanistic type of non-historical interpretation of history (where the term "mechanistic" is used in the sense of a "reductionistic naturalism"). Mechanism does not emphasize the tragic element in history as the classical naturalism of the Greeks did. Since it is intimately related to the technical control of nature by science and technology, it has in some cases a progressivistic character. But it is also open to the opposite attitude of cynical devaluation of existence in general and of history in particular. The mechanistic view usually does not share the Greek emphasis on the greatness and tragedy of man's historical existence, and it shares to an even lesser extent the interpretation of history from the point of view of an inner-historical or transhistorical aim toward which history is supposed to run.

3. Positive but Inadequate Answers to the Question of the Meaning of History

In some cases the mechanistic interpretation of history is allied with "progressivism," the first type of a historical interpretation of history that will be discussed. In it "progress" is more than an empirical fact (which it also is); it has become a quasi-religious symbol. In the chapter on progress we discussed the empirical validity and empirical limitations of the concept of progress. Here we must look at its use as a universal law determining the dynamics of history. The significant side of progressivistic ideology is its emphasis on the progressive intention of every creative action and its awareness of those areas of the self-creativity of life in which progress is of the essence of the reality concerned, for example, technology. In this way the symbol of progress includes the decisive element of historical time, its running ahead toward an aim. Progressivism is a genuinely historical interpretation of history. Its symbolic power was in some periods of history as strong as any of the great religious symbols of historical interpretation, including the symbol of the Kingdom of God. It gave impetus to historical actions, passion to revolutions, and a meaning to life for many who had lost all other faith and for whom the eventual breakdown of the progressivistic faith was a spiritual catastrophe. In short, it was a quasi-religious symbol in spite of its inner-historical aim.

One can distinguish two forms of it: the belief in progress itself as an infinite process without an end, and the belief in a final state of fulfilment, for example, in the sense of the concept of the third stage. The first form is progressivism in the proper sense; the second form is utopianism (which requires separate discussion). Progressivism, as the belief in progress as progress without a definite end, has been produced by the idealistic wing of the philosophical self-interpretation of modern industrial society; Neo-Kantianism was most important for the development of the idea of infinite progress. Reality is the never finished creation of man's cultural activity. There is no "reality in itself" behind this creation. Hegel's dialectical processes have the element of infinite progress in their structure and that element is the driving power of negation, which, as Bergson has strongly emphasized, requires an infinite openness for the future—even in God. The fact that Hegel stopped the dialectical movement with his own philosophy was incidental to his principle and has not prevented his becoming one of the most powerful influences for progressivism in the nineteenth century. The positivistic wing of nineteenth-century philosophy—as Comte and Spencer show— could accept progressivism on its own terms; and this school has given a large amount of material for a scientific justification of progress as a universal law of history, appearing under all dimensions of life but becoming conscious of itself only in human history. The progressivistic belief was undercut by the experiences of our century: the world-historical relapses to stages of inhumanity supposed to have been conquered long ago, the manifestation of the ambiguities of progress in the realms in which progress takes place, the feeling of the meaninglessness of an infinite progress without an end, and the insight into the freedom of every newborn human being to start again for good and evil. It is astonishing to notice how sudden and radical the breakdown of progressivism was, so radical that today many (including this writer) who twenty years ago fought against the progressivistic ideology now feel driven to defend the justified elements of this concept.

Perhaps the sharpest attack on the belief in infinite progress came from an idea which originally has grown out of the same root—the utopian interpretation of history. Utopianism is progressivism with a definite aim: arrival at that stage of history in which the ambiguities of life are conquered. In discussing utopianism it is important to distinguish, as in the case of progressivism, the utopian impetus from the literally interpreted symbol of utopia, the latter being the "third stage" of the historical development. The utopian impetus results from an intensification of the progressive impetus, and is distinguishable from it by the belief that present revolutionary action will bring about the final transformation of reality, that stage of history in which the *ou-tópos* (no-place) will become the universal place. This place will be the earth, the planet which in the geocentric world view was farthest removed from the heavenly spheres and which, in the heliocentric world view, has become a star among the others, of equal dignity, equal finitude, and equal internal infinity. And it will be man, the microcosm, the representative of all dimensions of the universe, through whom the earth will be transferred into the fulfilment of what in paradise was mere potentiality. These ideas of the Renaissance lie behind the many forms of secular utopianism in the modern period and have given incentive to revolutionary movements up to the present day.

The problematic character of the utopian interpretation of history has been clearly betrayed in the developments of the twentieth century. Certainly, the power and truth of the utopian impetus has become manifest in the immensity of success in all those realms in which the law of progress is valid, as foreseen in the Renaissance utopias; but at the same time, there has appeared a complete ambiguity between progress and relapse in those realms in which human freedom is involved. Realms involving human freedom were also envisaged in a state of unambiguous fulfilment by the utopianists of the Renaissance and all their successors in the revolutionary movements of the last three hundred years. But these expectations were disappointed with that profound disappointment which follows every idolatrous reliance on something finite. A history of such "existential disappointments" in modern times would be a history of cynicism, mass indifference, a split consciousness in leading groups, fanaticism, and tyranny. Existential disappointments produce individual and social diseases and catastrophes: the price for idolatrous ecstasy must be paid. For utopianism, taken literally, is idolatrous. It gives the quality of ultimacy to something preliminary. It makes unconditional what is conditioned (a future historical situation) and at the same time disregards the always present existential estrangement and the ambiguities of life and history. This makes the utopian interpretation of history inadequate and dangerous.

A third form of inadequate historical interpretation of history could be called the "transcendental" type. It is implicit in the eschatological mood of the New Testament and the early church up to Augustine. It was brought to its radical form in orthodox Lutheranism. History is the place in which, after the Old Testament preparation, the Christ has appeared to save individuals within the church from bondage to sin and guilt and to enable them to participate in the heavenly realm after death. Historical action, especially in the decisive political realm, cannot be purged from the ambiguities of power, internally or externally. There is no relation between the justice of the Kingdom of God and the justice of power structures. The two worlds are separated by an unbridgeable gap. Sectarian utopian and Calvinistic theocratic interpretations of history are rejected. Revolutionary attempts to change a corrupt political system contradict God's will as expressed in his providential action. After history has become the scene of saving revelation, nothing essentially new can be expected from it. The attitude expressed in these ideas was quite adequate to the predicament of most people in the late feudal period of central and eastern Europe, and it contains an element which is relevant to the situation of innumerable individuals in all periods of history. In theology it is a necessary counterbalance to the danger of secular as well as religious utopianism. But it falls short of an adequate historical interpretation of history. Its most obvious shortcoming is the fact that it contrasts the salvation of the individual with the transformation of the historical group and the universe, thus separating the one from the other. This error was sharply criticized by Thomas Muenzer, who in his criticism of Luther's attitude pointed to the fact that the masses have no time and strength left for a spiritual life, a judgment which was repeated by Religious Socialists in their analysis of the sociological and psychological situation of the proletariat in the industrial cities of the late nineteenth and early twentieth centuries. Another shortcoming of the transcendental interpretation of history is the way in which it contrasts the realm of salvation with the realm of creation. Power in itself is created goodness and an element in the essential structure of life. If it is beyond salvation—however fragmentary the salvation may be—life itself is beyond salvation. In such consequences the Manichaean danger of the transcendental view of history becomes visible.

Finally, this view interprets the symbol of the Kingdom of God as a static supranatural order into which individuals enter after their death—instead of understanding the symbol, with the biblical writers, as a dynamic power on earth for the coming of which we pray in the Lord's Prayer and which, according to biblical thought, is struggling with the demonic forces which are powerful in churches as well as empires. The transcendental type of historical interpretation, consequently, is inadequate because it excludes culture as well as nature from the saving processes in history. It is ironical that this happened in that type of Protestantism which—following Luther himself—has had the most positive relation to nature and has made the greatest contribution to the artistic and cognitive functions of culture. But all this remained without decisive consequence for modern Christianity because of the transcendental attitude toward politics, social ethics, and history in Lutheranism.

It was the dissatisfaction with the progressivistic, utopian, and transcendental interpretations of history (and the rejection of the non-historical types) that induced the Religious Socialists of the early 1920's to try a solution which avoids their inadequacies and is based on biblical prophetism. This attempt was made in terms of a reinterpretation of the symbol of the Kingdom of God.

4. THE SYMBOL "KINGDOM OF GOD" AS THE ANSWER TO THE
   QUESTION OF THE MEANING OF HISTORY

a) The characteristics of the symbol "Kingdom of God."—In the chapter on the three symbols of unambiguous life we have described the relationship of the symbol "Kingdom of God" to the symbols "Spiritual Presence" and "Eternal Life." We found that each of them includes the other two but that, because of the differences in the symbol materials, we are justified in using Spiritual Presence as the answer to the ambiguities of the human spirit and its functions, Kingdom of God as the answer to the ambiguities of history, and Eternal Life as the answer to the ambiguities of life universal. Nevertheless, the connotations of the symbol of the Kingdom of God are more embracing than those of the two others. This is a consequence of the double character of the Kingdom of God. It has an inner-historical and a transhistorical side. As inner-historical, it participates in the dynamics of history; as transhistorical, it answers the questions implied in the ambiguities of the dynamics of history. In the former quality it is manifest through the Spiritual Presence; in the latter it is identical with Eternal Life. This double quality of the Kingdom of God makes it a most important and most difficult symbol of Christian thought and—even more—one of the most critical for both political and ecclesiastical absolutism. Because it is so critical, the ecclesiastical development of Christianity and the sacramental emphasis of the two Catholic churches has pushed the symbol aside, and today, after its use (and partial secularization) by the social gospel movement and some forms of religious socialism, the symbol has again lost in power. This is remarkable in view of the fact that the preaching of Jesus started with the message of the "Kingdom of Heaven at hand" and that Christianity prays for its coming in every Lord's Prayer.

Its reinstatement as a living symbol may come from the encounter of Christianity with the Asiatic religions, especially Buddhism. Although the great India-born religions claim to be able to receive every religion as a partial truth within their self-transcending universality, it seems impossible that they can accept the symbol of the Kingdom of God in anything like its original meaning. The symbolic material is taken from spheres—the personal, social and political—which in the basic experience of Buddhism are radically transcended, whereas they are essential and never missing elements of the Christian experience. The consequences of this difference for religion and culture in East and West are world-historical, and it would seem that there is no other symbol in Christianity which points to the ultimate source of the differences as clearly as the symbol "Kingdom of God," especially when it is contrasted with the symbol "Nirvana."

The first connotation of the Kingdom of God is political. This agrees with the political sphere's predominance in the dynamics of history. In the Old Testament development of the symbol, the Kingdom of God is not so much a realm in which God rules as it is the controlling power itself which belongs to God and which he will assume after the victory over his enemies. But, although the kingdom as realm is not in the foreground, it is not altogether absent, and it is identical with Mount Zion, Israel, the nations, or the universe. Later in Judaism and in the New Testament the realm of the divine rule becomes more important: it is a transformed heaven and earth, a new reality in a new period of history. It results from a rebirth of the old in a new creation in which God is everything in everything. The political symbol is transformed into a cosmic symbol, without losing its political connotation. The word "king" in this and many other symbolizations of the divine majesty does not introduce a special constitutional form into the symbol material, against which other constitutional forms, such as that of a democracy, must react; for "king" (in contrast to other forms of rule) has since earliest times been a symbol in its own right for the highest and most consecrated center of political control. Its application to God, therefore, is a generally understandable double symbolization.

The second characteristic of the Kingdom of God is social. This characteristic includes the ideas of peace and justice—not in contrast to the political quality and, therefore, not in contrast to power. In this way the Kingdom of God fulfils the utopian expectation of a realm of peace and justice while liberating them from their utopian character by the addition "of God," for with this addition the impossibility of an earthly fulfilment is implicitly acknowledged. But even so the social element in the symbol is a permanent reminder that there is no holiness without the holy of what ought to be, the unconditional moral imperative of justice.

The third element implied in the Kingdom of God is the personalistic one. In contrast to symbols in which the return to the ultimate identity is the aim of existence, the Kingdom of God gives eternal meaning to the individual person. The transhistorical aim toward which history runs is not the extinction but the fulfilment of humanity in every human individual.

The fourth characteristic of the Kingdom of God is its universality.

It is a kingdom not only of men; it involves the fulfilment of life under all dimensions. This agrees with the multidimensional unity of life: fulfilment under one dimension implies fulfilment in all dimensions. This is the quality of the symbol "Kingdom of God" in which the individual-social element is transcended, though not denied. Paul expresses this in the symbols "God being all in all" and "the Christ surrendering the rule over history to God" when the dynamics of history have reached their end.

b) The immanent and the transcendent elements in the symbol "Kingdom of God."—The symbol "Kingdom of God," in order to be both a positive and an adequate answer to the question of the meaning of history, must be immanent and transcendent at the same time. Any one-sided interpretation deprives the symbol of its power. In the section on inadequate answers to the question of the meaning of history we discussed the utopian and transcendental interpretation, adducing examples for both of them from the Christian-Protestant tradition. This indicates that the mere use of the symbol "Kingdom of God" does not guarantee an adequate answer. Although its history gives all the elements of an answer, the same history shows that each of these elements can be suppressed and the meaning of the symbol distorted. Therefore it is important to point to the emergence of these elements in the basic development of the idea of the Kingdom of God.

The emphasis in the prophetic literature is inner-historical-political. The destiny of Israel is the revelatory medium for the prophetic understanding of Jahweh's character and actions, and Israel's future is seen as the victory of the God of Israel in the struggle with her enemies. Mount Zion will become the religious center of all nations, and although the "day of Jahweh" is first of all judgment, it is also fulfilment in a historical-political sense. But this is not the whole story. The visions about judgment and fulfilment include an element which could hardly be called inner-historical or immanent. It is Jahweh who wins the battle against enemies infinitely superior in numbers and power to Israel. It is God's holy mountain that, in spite of its geographical insignificance, will be the place to which all nations come to worship. The true God, the God of justice, conquers a concentration of partly political, partly demonic, forces. The Messiah, who will bring about the new eon, is a human being with superhuman traits. The peace between the nations includes nature, so that the most hostile species of animals will live peacefully beside each other. These transcendent elements within the predominantly immanent-political interpretation of the idea of the Kingdom of God point to its double character. God's Kingdom cannot be produced by the inner-historical development alone. In the political upheavals of Judaism during the Roman period, this double character of the prophetic anticipation was almost forgotten—which led to the complete destruction of the national existence of Israel.

Experiences such as this, long before the Roman period, brought about a change in emphasis from the immanent-political to the transcendent-universal side in the idea of the Kingdom of God. This was most impressive in the so-called apocalyptic literature of the intertestamental period, with some predecessors in the latest parts of the Old Testament. The historical vision is enlarged upon and superceded by a cosmic vision. The earth has become old, and demonic powers have taken possession of it. Wars, disease, and natural catastrophes of a cosmic character will precede the rebirth of all things and the new eon in which God will finally become the ruler of the nations and in which the prophetic hopes will be fulfilled. This will not happen through historical developments but through divine interference and a new creation, leading to a new heaven and a new earth. Such visions are independent of any historical situation and are not conditioned by human activities. The divine mediator is no longer the historical Messiah, but the Son of Man, the Heavenly Man. This interpretation of history was decisive for the New Testament. Inner-historical-political aims within the Roman empire were beyond reach. The empire has to be accepted according to its elements of goodness (Paul), and it will be destroyed by God because of its demonic structure (Revelation). Obviously, this is far removed from any inner-historical progressivism or utopianism; nevertheless, it is not without immanent-political elements. The reference to the Roman empire—sometimes seen as the last and greatest in a series of empires—shows that the vision of the demonic powers is not merely imaginary. It is related to the historical powers of the period in which it is conceived. And the cosmic catastrophes include historical events within the world of nations. The final stages of human history are described with inner-historical colors. Again and again in later times people have found their own historical existence described in the mythical imagery of the apocalyptics. The New Testament adds a new element to these visions: the inner-historical appearance of Jesus as the Christ and the foundation of the church in the midst of the ambiguities of history. All this shows that the emphasis on transcendence in the symbol "Kingdom of God" does not exclude inner-historical features of decisive importance—just as the predominance of the immanent element does not exclude transcendent symbolism.

These developments show that the symbol "Kingdom of God" has the power to express both the immanent and the transcendent sides, though one side is normally predominant. With this in mind the reality of the Kingdom of God in and above history will be discussed in the remaining sections of the system.

II

THE KINGDOM OF GOD WITHIN HISTORY

A. THE DYNAMICS OF HISTORY AND THE NEW BEING

1. THE IDEA OF "HISTORY OF SALVATION"

IN THE chapter, "The manifestation of the Spiritual Presence in historical mankind" (Part IV, Sec. II B), we related the doctrine of the Spirit to man's historical existence, but we did not consider the historical dimension as such. In discussing the Spiritual Presence and its relation to the human spirit we put history into brackets, not because it is not effective in every moment of the spiritual life, but because the different points of view can only be dealt with consecutively. We must now look at the Spiritual Presence and its manifestations from the point of view of their participation in the dynamics of history.

Theology has spoken of this problem under the originally German term *Heilsgeschichte* ("history of salvation"). Since this term connotes many unsolved problems, I am using it tentatively, subject to serious qualification. The first question refers to the relation of the history of salvation to the history of revelation. The basic answer has been given (Part I, Sec. II B): Where there is revelation there is salvation! Turning this statement around we can also say: Where there is salvation there is revelation. Salvation embraces revelation, emphasizing the element of truth in the saving manifestation of the ground of being. Therefore, by speaking of universal (not "general") revelation, we have spoken implicitly of universal salvation. The second question refers to the relation of history as the result of human creativity to the history of salvation. They are not identical. Their identification was the error of classical idealism and some forms of theological liberalism, often in connection with a progressivistic interpretation of history. It is impossible to identify world history and the history of salvation because of the ambiguities of life in all its dimensions, including the historical. Salvation is the conquest of these ambiguities; it stands against them and cannot be identified with a realm in which they are effective. Later, we shall also see that the history of salvation is not identical with the history of religion either, or even with the history of the churches, although the churches represent the Kingdom of God. Saving power breaks into history, works through history, but is not created by history.

The third question, therefore, is: How is the history of salvation manifest in world history? In the description of revelatory experiences (given in Part I, Sec. II, "The Reality of Revelation," which was an anticipation of some ideas belonging to this part), the manifestation of Spiritual Power was pictured with respect to its cognitive elements. And in the chapters dealing with the effects of the Spiritual Presence on individuals and communities (Part IV, Sec. III) the manifestation of the saving power was described in its totality. But we did not discuss the historical dimension of these manifestations, their dynamics in relation to the dynamics of world history.

If the term "history of salvation" is justified at all, it must point to a sequence of events in which saving power breaks into historical processes, prepared for by these processes so that it can be received, changing them to enable the saving power to be effective in history. Seen in this way, the history of salvation is a part of universal history. It can be identified in terms of measured time, historical causality, a definite space and a concrete situation. As an object of secular historiography, it must be subjected to the tests prescribed by a strict application of the methods of historical research. Simultaneously, however, although it is within history, it manifests something which is not from history. For this reason the history of salvation has also been called sacred history. It is sacred and secular in the same series of events. In it history shows its self-transcending character, its striving toward ultimate fulfilment. There is no reason to call the history of salvation "suprahistorical." The prefix "supra" indicates a higher level of reality in which divine actions take place without connection with world history. In this way the paradox of the ultimate appearing in history is replaced by a supranaturalism which disconnects world history from the history of salvation. But if they are disconnected, it is impossible to understand how the supranatural events can have saving power within the processes of world history.

Because of these misinterpretations to which the term "history of salvation" is exposed, it might be preferable to avoid the term altogether and to speak about the manifestations of the Kingdom of God in history. And of course, where there is manifestation of the Kingdom of God, there is revelation and salvation. However, the question remains as to whether there is a rhythm in these manifestations—a kind of progress, or an up and down, or a repetition of some structures—or no rhythm at all. This question cannot be answered in general terms. Its answer is an expression of the concrete revelatory experience of a religious group and is therefore determined by the character of the theological system within which the question is raised. The following answer is based on Christian symbolism and the central Christian assertion that Jesus of Nazareth is the Christ, the final manifestation of the New Being in history.

2. The Central Manifestation of the Kingdom of God in History

Whatever the rhythm of manifestations of the Kingdom of God in history may be, Christianity claims to be based on its central manifestation. Therefore it considers the appearance of Jesus as the Christ as the center of history—if history is seen in its self-transcending character. The term "center of history" has nothing to do with quantitative measurements, which would understand it as the middle between an indefinite past and an indefinite future, nor does the term describe a historical moment in which the cultural process came to a point where the lines of the past were united and determined the future. There is no such point in history. And what is true of the relation of the center of history to culture is also true of its relation to religion. The metaphor "center" expresses a moment in history for which everything before and after is both preparation and reception. As such it is both criterion and source of the saving power in history. The third and fourth parts of the present system contain the full development of these assertions, but they do not consider the historical dimension.

If we call the appearance of the Christ the center of history, we imply that the manifestation of the Kingdom of God in history is not an incoherent series of manifestations, each with a relative validity and power. In the very term "center" a critique of relativism is expressed. Faith dares to assert its dependence on that event which is the criterion of all revelatory events. Faith has the courage to dare such an extraordinary assertion, and it takes the risk of error. But without this courage and without the risk, it would not be faith. The term "center of history"

also includes a critique of all forms of a progressivistic view of the manifestations of the Kingdom of God in history. Obviously, there can be
no progress beyond that which is the center of history (except in the
realms in which progress is essential). Everything succeeding it stands
under its criterion and partakes of its power. Nor is the appearance of
the center the result of a progressive development as discussed before
under the heading "Historical Progress: Its Reality and Its Limits" (Part
V, Sec. IA, 3c).

The only progressive element in the preparatory history of revelation
and salvation is its movement from immaturity to maturity. Mankind
had to mature to a point in which the center of history could appear
and be received as the center. This maturing process is working in all
history, but a particular development was necessary in order to prepare
for Him in whom the final revelation would occur. This is the function
of the development of which the Old Testament is the document. The
Old Testament manifestations of the Kingdom of God produced the
direct preconditions for its final manifestation in the Christ. The maturity was reached; the time was fulfilled. This happened once in the
original revelatory and saving stretch of history, but it happens again
wherever the center is received as center. Without the larger basis of
history of religion and the smaller basis of prophetic criticism and transformation of the larger basis, there is no possibility of accepting the
center. Therefore all missionary activity inside and outside the Christian
culture must use the religious consciousness that is present or can be
evoked in all religions and cultures. And every missionary activity,
inside and outside Christian culture, must follow the Old Testament's
prophetic purification of the religious consciousness. Without the Old
Testament, Christianity relapses into the immaturities of the universal
history of religion—including the history of the Jewish religion (which
was the main object of criticism and purification by the Old Testament
prophets). The maturing or preparatory process toward the central
manifestation of the Kingdom of God in history is, therefore, not restricted to the pre-Christian epoch; it continues after the center's appearance and is going on here and now. The theme of Israel's leaving
Egypt is that of maturation toward the center, which is the theme of
the East-West encounter in present-day Japan, and which was and still
is the theme of the development of modern Western culture in the last
five hundred years. In biblical and theological language, this has been

expressed as the symbol of the transtemporal presence of the Christ in every period.

Conversely, there is always a process of receiving from the central manifestation of the Kingdom of God in history. Of course, as there is an original history of preparation for the center, leading to its appearance in time and space, so is there an original history of reception from the center, derived from its appearance in time and space; and this is the history of the church. But the church does not exist in a simply manifest way, by receiving from what has happened in the past; it also exists latently, by anticipating what will happen in the future. In its latency the church is dependent, by anticipation, on what is to come as the center of history. This is the meaning of "prophecy" in the sense of announcing the future, and it is the meaning of such passages as those in which the Fourth Gospel points to the pre-existence of the Christ, passages that symbolize the potential presence of the center in all periods of history.

In view of these connotations of the term "center of history," we can say that human history, seen from the point of view of the self-transcendence of history, is not only a dynamic movement, running ahead, but also a structured whole in which one point is the center.

Where there is a central point, the question of the beginning and end of the movement of which it is the center arises. We are not here speaking of the beginning and end of the historical process as such. That was discussed in the chapter on prehistory and posthistory. The problem here is: When did that movement start of which the Christ's appearance is the center, and when will it come to an end? The answer, of course, cannot be given in terms of numbers. Whenever this has been done, it has been refuted by history itself with respect to the end and by historical knowledge with respect to the beginning. All calculations about the imminent end came to naught when the calculated day appeared, and all records about the beginning of historical time, including the biblical ones, have been infinitely surpassed by our knowledge of the origins of mankind on earth. Beginning and end in relation to the center of history can mean only the beginning and end of the manifestations of the Kingdom of God in history, and the answer to the question is determined by the character of the center itself. That history which is a history of revelation and salvation begins the moment man becomes aware of the ultimate question of his estranged predicament and of his destiny to overcome this predicament. This awareness has been expressed in myths and rites of earliest human record, but there is no possibility of marking a definite moment or a definite person or group. The end of history, in the same sense in which we spoke of its beginning, comes at the moment in which mankind ceases to ask the question of its predicament. This can happen by an external extinction of historical mankind through destruction caused cosmically or humanly, or it can happen by biological or psychological transformations which annihilate the dimension of the spirit or by an inner deterioration under the dimension of the spirit which deprives man of his freedom and consequently of the possibility of having a history.

When Christianity claims that the event on which it is based is the center of the history of revelation and salvation, it cannot overlook the fact that there are other interpretations of history which make the same claim for another central event. For the choice of a center of history is universal wherever history is taken seriously. The center of national interpretations of history—often in an imperial sense—is the moment in which the nation's vocational consciousness arose, whether in an actual event or in a legendary tradition. The exodus of the Israelites from Egypt, the foundation of the city of Rome, and the revolutionary war in America are such centers of particular histories. They can be raised to universal significance, as in Judaism, or can become a motivation of imperial aspirations, as in Rome. For the followers of a world religion, the event of their foundation is the center of history. This is true not only of Christianity and Judaism but also of Mohammedanism, Buddhism, Zoroastrianism, and Manichaeism. In view of these analogies in political and religious history, the question is unavoidable as to how Christianity can justify its claim to be both rooted in time and based in the universal center of the manifestations of the Kingdom of God in history. The first answer, to which we already have referred, is a positivistic one: this claim is an expression of the daring courage of the Christian faith. But this is not sufficient for a theology which calls Jesus as the Christ the central manifestation of the divine Logos. The Christian claim must have a "logos," not an argument in addition to faith, but a logos-determined explanation of faith. Theology undertakes such an explanation by saying that questions implied in historical time and in the ambiguities of historical dynamics have been answered in none of the other assumed centers of history. The principle by which politically determined centers of history are chosen is particular and cannot lose its particularity however much it tries imperialistically to become universal. This is even true of Judaism, in spite of the universalistic element in its prophetic self-criticism.

The prophetic and apocalyptic expectations of Judaism remain expectations and do not lead to an inner-historical fulfilment as in Christianity. Therefore no new center of history after the Exodus is seen, and the future center is not center but end. At this point the fundamental and unbridgeable gap between Jewish and Christian interpretations of history appears. In spite of all the possible demonizations and sacramental distortions of the central manifestation of the Kingdom of God in actual Christianity, the message of the center which *has* appeared must be maintained if Christianity is not to become another preparatory religion of the Law. Islam (with the exception of Sufism) is a religion of the law and has, as such, a great function of educational progress toward maturity. But educational maturity in relation to the ultimate is ambiguous. The breakthrough of the law is most difficult in the religious life of individuals as well as of groups. Therefore Judaism from the beginning of Christianity on and Islam in a later period were the greatest barriers against the acceptance of Jesus as the Christ and as the center of history. These religions themselves, however, were not and are not able to give another center. The appearance of Mohammed as the prophet does not constitute an event in which history receives a meaning which is universally valid. Nor is a universal center of history provided by the foundation of a nation which, in the sense in which the prophets interpreted it, *is* the "elected" nation. And this is so because its universality has not yet been liberated from its particularity. It is not necessary to say much of Buddhism in this context, after our discussion of the non-historical interpretations of history. Buddha is not for the Buddhist a dividing line between before and after. He is the decisive example of an embodiment of the Spirit of Illumination which has happened and can happen at any time, but he is not seen in a historical movement which leads to him and is derived from him. This survey shows that the only historical event in which the universal center of the history of revelation and salvation can be seen—not only for daring faith but also for a rational interpretation of this faith—is the event on which Christianity is based. This event is not only the center of the history of the manifestation of the Kingdom of God; it is also the only event in which the historical dimension is fully and universally affirmed. The appearance of Jesus as the Christ is the historical event in which history becomes aware of itself and its meaning. There is—even for an empirical and relativistic approach—no other event of which this *could* be asserted. But the *actual* assertion is and remains a matter of daring faith.

3. "Kairos" and "Kairoi"

We spoke of the moment at which history, in terms of a concrete situation, had matured to the point of being able to receive the breakthrough of the central manifestation of the Kingdom of God. The New Testament has called this moment the "fulfilment of time," in Greek, *kairos*. This term has been frequently used since we introduced it into theological and philosophical discussion in connection with the religious socialist movement in Germany after the First World War. It was chosen to remind Christian theology of the fact that the biblical writers, not only of the Old but also of the New Testament, were aware of the self-transcending dynamics of history. And it was chosen to remind philosophy of the necessity of dealing with history, not in terms of its logical and categorical structure only, but also in terms of its dynamics. And, above all, *kairos* should express the feeling of many people in central Europe after the First World War that a moment of history had appeared which was pregnant with a new understanding of the meaning of history and life. Whether or not this feeling was empirically confirmed—in part it was, in part it was not—the concept itself retains its significance and belongs in the whole of systematic theology.

Its original meaning—the right time, the time in which something can be done—must be contrasted with *chronos*, measured time or clock time. The former is qualitative, the latter quantitative. In the English word "timing," something of the qualitative character of time is expressed, and if one would speak of God's "timing" in his providential activity, this term would come near to the meaning of *kairos*. In ordinary Greek language, the word is used for any practical purpose in which a good occasion for some action is given. In the New Testament it is the translation of a word used by Jesus when he speaks of his time which has not yet come—the time of his suffering and death. It is used by both John the Baptist and Jesus when they announce the fulfilment of time with respect to the Kingdom of God, which is "at hand." Paul uses *kairos* when he speaks in a world-historical view of the moment of time in which God could send his Son, the moment which was selected to become the center of history. In order to recognize this "great *kairos*," one must be able to see the "signs of the times," as Jesus says when he accuses his enemies of not seeing them. Paul, in his description of the *kairos*, looks at the situation both of paganism and of Judaism, and in the Deutero-Pauline literature the world-historical and cosmic view of the appearance of the Christ plays an increasingly important role. We have interpreted the fulfilment of time as the moment of maturity in a particular religious and cultural development—adding, however, the warning that maturity means not only the ability to receive the central manifestation of the Kingdom of God but also the greatest power to resist it. For maturity is the result of education by the law, and in some who take the law with radical seriousness, maturity becomes despair of the law, with the ensuing quest for that which breaks through the law as "good news."

The experience of a *kairos* has occurred again and again in the history of the churches, although the term was not used. Whenever the prophetic Spirit arose in the churches, the "third stage" was spoken of, the stage of the "rule of Christ" in the "one thousand-year" period. This stage was seen as immediately imminent and so became the basis for prophetic criticism of the churches in their distorted stage. When the churches rejected this criticism or accepted it in a partial, compromising way, the prophetic Spirit was forced into sectarian movements of an originally revolutionary character—until the sects became churches and the prophetic Spirit became latent. The fact that *kairos*-experiences belong to the history of the churches and that the "great *kairos*," the appearance of the center of history, is again and again re-experienced through relative "*kairoi*," in which the Kingdom of God manifests itself in a particular breakthrough, is decisive for our consideration. The relation of the one *kairos* to the *kairoi* is the relation of the criterion to that which stands under the criterion and the relation of the source of power to that which is nourished by the source of power. *Kairoi* have occurred and are occurring in all preparatory and receiving movements in the church latent and manifest. For although the prophetic Spirit is latent or even repressed over long stretches of history, it is never absent and breaks through the barriers of the law in a *kairos*.

Awareness of a *kairos* is a matter of vision. It is not an object of analysis and calculation such as could be given in psychological or sociological terms. It is not a matter of detached observation but of involved experience. This, however, does not mean that observation and analysis are excluded; they serve to objectify the experience and to clarify and enrich the vision. But observation and analysis do not produce the experience of the *kairos*. The prophetic Spirit works creatively without any dependence on argumentation and good will. But every moment which claims to be Spiritual must be tested, and the criterion is the "great *kairos*." When the term *kairos* was used for the critical and creative situation after the First World War in central Europe, it was used not only by the religious socialist movement in obedience to the great *kairos*—at least in intention—but also by the nationalist movement, which, through the voice of naziism, attacked the great *kairos* and everything for which it stands. The latter use was a demonically distorted experience of a *kairos* and led inescapably to self-destruction. The Spirit naziism claimed was the spirit of the false prophets, prophets who spoke for an idolatrous nationalism and racialism. Against them the Cross of the Christ was and is the absolute criterion.

Two things must be said about *kairoi*: first, they can be demonically distorted, and second, they can be erroneous. And this latter characteristic is always the case to a certain extent, even in the "great *kairos*." The error lies not in the *kairos*-quality of the situation but rather in the judgment about its character in terms of physical time, space, and causality, and also in terms of human reaction and unknown elements in the historical constellation. In other words, the *kairos*-experience stands under the order of historical destiny, which makes foresight in any scientific-technical sense impossible. No date foretold in the experience of a *kairos* was ever correct; no situation envisaged as the result of a *kairos* ever came into being. But something happened to some people through the power of the Kingdom of God as it became manifest in history, and history has been changed ever since.

A last question arises as to whether there are periods in history in which no *kairos* is experienced. Obviously the Kingdom of God and the Spiritual Presence are never absent in any moment of time, and by the very nature of the historical processes, history is always self-transcendent. But the experience of the presence of the Kingdom of God as determining history is not always given. History does not move in an equal rhythm but is a dynamic force moving through cataracts and quiet stretches. History has its ups and downs, its periods of speed and of slowness, of extreme creativity and of conservative bondage to tradition.

The men of the late Old Testament period complained that there was a dearth of Spirit, and in the history of the churches this complaint has been reiterated. The Kingdom of God is always present, but the experience of its history-shaking power is not. *Kairoi* are rare and the great *kairos* is unique, but together they determine the dynamics of history in its self-transcendence.

4. HISTORICAL PROVIDENCE

We discussed the doctrine of providence under the title "God's directing creativity" (Part II, Sec. II B, 5c). We have seen that providence must not be understood in a deterministic way, in the sense of a divine design decreed "before the creation of the world," which is now running its course and in which God sometimes interferes miraculously. Instead of such supranatural mechanism we applied the basic ontological polarity of freedom and destiny in the relation of God and the world and asserted that God's directing creativity works through the spontaneity of creatures and human freedom. Now that we are including the historical dimension we can say that the "new" toward which history runs, both the particularly new and the absolutely new, is the aim of historical providence. It is misleading to speak of a divine "design," even if it is not understood in a deterministic way. For the term "design" has the connotation of a preconceived pattern, including all the particulars which constitute a design. This restricts the element of contingency in the processes of history to the extent that destiny annihilates freedom. But the texture of history includes the contingent, the surprising, the underivably new. We must enlarge the symbol of divine providence to include the omnipresent element of contingency. There is an element of contingency in the spontaneity of the bird which contributes to its providential death here and now, and there is contingency in the rise of a tyrant who destroys individuals and nations under the divine providence.

The last example points to the question of historical providence and the powers of evil in history. The immensity of moral and physical evil and the overwhelming manifestation of the demonic and its tragic consequence in history have always been an existential as well as a theoretical argument against the acceptance of any belief in historical providence. And, indeed, only a theology which takes these aspects of reality into its concept of providence has a right to use this concept at all. A concept of providence which takes evil into account radically excludes that teleological optimism which characterized the philosophy of the Enlightenment—with some important exceptions—and the progressivism of the nineteenth and early twentieth centuries. First of all, no future justice and happiness can annihilate the injustice and suffering of the past. The assumed well-being of a "last generation" does not justify the evil and the tragedy of all previous generations. And second, the progressivist-utopian assumption contradicts the elements of "freedom for good and evil" with which every individual is born. Where the power for good increases, the power for evil increases also. Historical providence includes all this and is creative through it toward the new, both in history and above history. This concept of historical providence also includes the rejection of reactionary and cynical pessimism. It provides the certainty that the negative in history (disintegration, destruction, profanization) can never prevail against the temporal and eternal aims of the historical process. This is the meaning of Paul's words about the conquest of the demonic powers by the love of God as manifest in the Christ (Romans, chapter 8). The demonic forces are not destroyed, but they cannot prevent the aim of history, which is reunion with the divine ground of being and meaning.

The way in which this happens is identical with the divine mystery and beyond calculation and description. Hegel made the mistake of claiming that he knew this way and that he was able to describe it by applying the dialectics of logic to the concrete events of recorded history. One cannot deny that his method opened his eyes for many important observations concerning the mythical and metaphysical background of different cultures. But he did not take into consideration unrecorded historical developments, the inner struggles in every great culture which limit any general interpretation, the openness of history toward the future which prevents a consistent design, the survival and rebirth of great cultures and religions which, according to the evolutionary scheme, should have lost their historical significance long ago, or the breakthrough of the Kingdom of God into the historical processes, creating the permanence of Judaism and the uniqueness of the Christian event. There have been other attempts to give a concrete design of historical providence, even if they do not speak of providence. None of them is as rich and concrete as that of Hegel, not even that of his positivistic counterpart, Comte. Most of them are more cautious, restricting themselves to certain regularities in the dynamics of history, as is illustrated, for example, by Spengler's law of growth and decay or Toynbee's general categories, such as "withdrawal" and "return," "challenge" and "response." Such attempts give precious insights into concrete movements, but they do not provide a picture of historical providence. The Old Testament prophets were even less concrete than these men. The prophets dealt with many of the surrounding nations, not in order to show their world-historical significance, but to show the divine acting through them, in creation, judgment, destruction, and promise. The prophetic messages imply no concrete design; they imply only the universal rule of divine action in terms of historical creativity, judgment, and grace. The whole of the particular providential acts remains hidden in the mystery of the divine life.

This necessary foregoing of a concrete interpretation of world history does not exclude the understanding, from a special point of view, of particular developments in their creative sequences. We attempted this when discussing the idea of *kairos* and describing the situation of the "great *kairos*." From the Christian point of view, the providential character of Judaism is a lasting example of a particular interpretation of historical developments. The Danielic description of the sequence of world powers can be understood in this sense, and this also justifies the critical analysis of a contemporary situation in light of past developments. Awareness of a *kairos* actually includes an image of past developments and their meaning for the present. But any step beyond this must be countered by the arguments given against Hegel's grandiose attempt to "set himself on the chair of the divine providence."

B. THE KINGDOM OF GOD AND THE CHURCHES

1. THE CHURCHES AS THE REPRESENTATIVES OF THE KINGDOM OF GOD IN HISTORY

In our discussion of the Spiritual Community we called the churches the ambiguous embodiment of the Spiritual Community, and we spoke of the paradox that the churches reveal as well as hide the Spiritual Community. Now that we are considering the historical dimension and the symbols of its religious interpretation, we must say that the churches are the representatives of the Kingdom of God. This characterization does not contradict the other one. "Kingdom of God" embraces more than "Spiritual Community"; it includes all elements of reality, not only those, i.e., persons, who are able to enter into a Spiritual Community.

The Kingdom of God includes the Spiritual Community, but, just as the historical dimension embraces all other dimensions, the Kingdom of God embraces all realms of being under the perspective of their ultimate aim. The churches represent the Kingdom of God in this universal sense.

The representation of the Kingdom of God by the churches is as ambiguous as is the embodiment of the Spiritual Community in the churches. In both functions the churches are paradoxical: they reveal and hide. We have already indicated that the churches may even represent the demonic kingdom. But the demonic kingdom is a distortion of the divine Kingdom and it would have no being without that of which it is the distortion. The power of the representative, however much he misrepresents what he is supposed to represent, is rooted in his function of representing. The churches remain churches even if they are forces hiding the ultimate instead of revealing it. Just as man, the bearer of spirit, cannot cease to be such, so the churches, which represent the Kingdom of God in history, cannot forfeit this function even if they exercise it in contradiction to the Kingdom of God. Distorted spirit is still spirit; distorted holiness is still holiness.

Since we developed the doctrine of the church fully in the fourth part of the system, we have only to add, at this point, certain observations related to its historical dimension. As representatives of the Kingdom of God, the churches share actively both in the running of historical time toward the aim of history and in the inner-historical struggle of the Kingdom of God against the forces of demonization and profanization that fight against this aim. The Christian church in its original self-interpretation was well aware of this double task and expressed it quite conspicuously in its liturgical life. It asked the newly baptized to separate themselves publicly from the demonic forces to which they had been subjected in their pagan past. Many contemporary churches in the act of "confirmation" take the younger generation into the ranks of the fighting church. At the same time all churches in liturgy, hymns, and prayers speak of the coming of the Kingdom of God and the duty of everyone to be prepared for it. In spite of the reduction of these ideas to an individualistic idea of salvation, it is hard for hierarchical and orthodox conservativism to remove eschatological dynamics completely from the awareness of the churches. Wherever prophetic Spirit appears, it revives expectation of the coming Kingdom and awakens the churches to their task of witnessing to it and preparing for it. This causes the ever repeated, eschatological movements in the history of the churches, which are often very powerful and often very absurd. The churches have been and always should be communities of expectation and preparation. They should point to the nature of historical time and the aim toward which history runs.

The struggle against demonization and profanization draws passion and power from this consciousness of the "end". In carrying on this struggle through all history the churches are tools of the Kingdom of God. They are able to serve as tools because they are based on the New Being in which the forces of estrangement are conquered. The demonic, according to popular symbolism, cannot stand the immediate presence of the holy if it appears in holy words, signs, names, or materials. But beyond this the churches believe that the power of the New Being, active in them, will conquer the demonic powers as well as the forces of pro-fanization in history universally. They feel—or should feel—that they are fighting agents of the Kingdom of God, leading forces in the drive toward the fulfilment of history.

There were no manifest churches before the central manifestation of the New Being in the event on which the Christian church is based, but there was and is a latent church in all history, before and after this event: the Spiritual Community in the state of its latency. Without it and its preparatory work the churches would not be able to represent the Kingdom of God. The central manifestation of the holy itself would not have been possible without the preceding experience of the holy, both of being and of ought-to-be. Consequently, churches would not have been possible. Therefore, if we say that the churches are the lead-ing forces in the drive toward the fulfilment of history, we must include the latent church (not churches) in this judgment. And we may say that the Kingdom of God in history is represented by those groups and individuals in which the latent church is effective and through whose preparatory work in past and future the manifest church, and with it the Christian churches, could and can become vehicles of history's movement toward its aim. This is the first of several considerations which call the churches to humility in their function as representatives of the Kingdom of God in history.

At this point we must ask: What does it mean that the churches are not only embodiments of the Spiritual Community but also representa-tives of the Kingdom of God in its all-embracing character? The answer lies in the multidimensional unity of life and the consequences it has for the sacramental manifestation of the holy. To the degree in which a church emphasizes the sacramental presence of the divine, it draws the realms preceding spirit and history, the inorganic and organic universe, into itself. Strongly sacramental churches, such as the Greek Orthodox, have a profound understanding for the participation of life under all dimensions in the ultimate aim of history. The sacramental consecration of elements of all of life shows the presence of the ultimately sublime in everything and points to the unity of everything in its creative ground and its final fulfilment. It is one of the shortcomings of the churches of the "word," especially in their legalistic and exclusively personalistic form, that they exclude, along with the sacramental element, the universe outside man from consecration and fulfilment. But the Kingdom of God is not only a social symbol; it is a symbol which comprises the whole of reality. And if the churches claim to represent it, they must not reduce its meaning to one element alone.

This claim, however, raises another problem. The churches which represent the Kingdom of God in its fight against the forces of profanization and demonization are themselves subject to the ambiguities of religion and are open to profanization and demonization. How, then, can that which is itself demonized represent the fight against the demonic and that which is profanized represent the fight against the profane? The answer was given in the chapter on the paradox of the churches: they are profane and sublime, demonic and divine, in a paradoxical unity. The expression of this paradox is the prophetic criticism of the churches by the churches. Something in a church reacts against this distortion of the church as a whole. Its fight against the demonic and the profane is first directed against the demonic and the profane in the church itself. Such fights can lead to reformation movements, and it is the fact of such movements that gives the churches the right to consider themselves vehicles of the Kingdom of God, struggling in history, including the history of the churches.

2. The Kingdom of God and the History of the Churches

The history of the churches is the history in which the church is actual in time and space. The church is always actual in churches and that which is actual in churches is the one church. Therefore one can speak of the history of the church as well as of the history of the churches.

However, one should not claim that up to a certain time (A.D. 500 or 1500) there was the one church, actual in time and space, and that after this period splits occurred which produced the churches. A consequence of such an assertion is that one of the churches in one period or in all periods calls itself *the* church. The Anglican churches are inclined to elevate the first five hundred years of church history to superiority over the other periods and to elevate themselves because of their similarity to the early church to superiority over the other churches. The Roman church attributes unrestricted absoluteness to itself in all periods. The Greek Orthodox churches derive their claim to superiority from the first seven ecumenical councils with which they live in an essentially unbroken tradition. The Protestant churches could make similar claims if they considered the history between the apostolic age and the Reformation as a period in which the church was only latent (as it is in Judaism and paganism). And there are some theological and ecclesiastical radicals who, at least by implication, assert this. Each of these is erroneous, and as a consequence, demonic attitudes often result from disregard of the truth that the church, the Spiritual Community, *always* lives in the churches and that where there are churches confessing their foundation in the Christ as the central manifestation of the Kingdom of God in history there the church is.

If we look at church history in light of this two-way relationship between the church and the churches, we can say that church history is at no point identical with the Kingdom of God and at no point without manifestation of the Kingdom of God. With this in mind one should look at the many riddles of church history which express the paradoxical character of churches. It is impossible to avoid the question: How can the claim of the churches to be based on the central manifestation of the Kingdom of God in history be united with the reality of church history? In particular this means: Why are the churches overwhelmingly limited to one section of mankind, where they belong to a particular civilization, and why are they tied-up with the cultural creation of this civilization? And further: Why, for almost five hundred years, have secular movements arisen within Christian civilization which have radically changed human self-interpretation and have in many cases turned against Christianity, notably in scientific humanism and naturalistic communism? This is a question to which another must be added today:

Why do these two forms of secularism have such tremendous power in nations with a non-Christian civilization, such as those of the Far East? In spite of all Christian missionary efforts and successes in some parts of the world, the spread of these outgrowths of the Christian civilization is far more impressive. Such considerations are, of course, not arguments, but they are reactions to one of the riddles of church history. Other riddles appear in the inner development of the churches. The great splits among the churches are the most obvious, for each claims truth—even if not absolute and exclusive truth as the Roman church does. Certainly a Christian church which does not assert that Jesus is the Christ has ceased to be a manifest Christian church (though the latent church may remain in it). But if churches which acknowledge Jesus as the Christ differ in their interpretations of this event because of their exclusiveness, one must ask: How was it possible that the history of the church, embodied in the history of the churches, produced such contradictory interpretations of the one event to which they refer? One may even ask what divine providence intends by leading the churches (which are based on the central creation of historical providence) to a split which in the human view is without healing? A further question is: How could it happen that there is so much profanization of the holy in church history, in both of the senses of profanization, i.e., by ritualization and by secularization? The first distortion happens more often in Catholic, the second more often in Protestant, types of Christianity. One must ask, sometimes with prophetic wrath, how the name of Christ as the center of history can be identified with the enormous amount of superstitious devotion in some sections of the Catholic world, both Greek and Roman, in both national and social groups. One does not doubt the genuine piety of many of these people, however primitive it may be, but one does doubt that the rituals performed by them in devotional acts for the sake of the fulfilment of earthly or heavenly wishes has anything to do with the New Testament picture of the Christ. And one must add the serious question as to how it could happen that this ritualization of the Spiritual Presence was justified or at least condoned by a theology which knew better and was defended by a hierarchy which rejected the reformation of these conditions. If one turns to Protestantism, the other form of the profanization of the ultimately sublime appears—secularization. It appears under the heading of the Protestant principle, which makes of the priest a layman, of the sacrament words, of the holy the secular. Of course, Protestantism does not intend to secularize priesthood, sacraments, and the holy, but rather it tries to show that the holy is not restricted to particular places, orders, and functions. In so doing, however, it does not escape the tendency to dissolve the holy into the secular and to pave the way for a total secularization of Christian culture, whether it is by moralism, intellectualism, or nationalism. Protestantism is less armed against secular trends on its soil than Catholicism. But Catholicism is more threatened by a direct onslaught of secularism against everything Christian, as the histories of France and Russia have shown.

The secular form of profanization of the ultimately sublime, which is now spreading all over the world, is a further great riddle of church history especially in the last centuries. It is probably the most puzzling and urgent problem of present-day church history. In any case, the question is: How can this development in the midst of Christian civilization be reconciled with the claim that Christianity has the message of that event which is the center of history? Early theology was able to absorb the secular creation of Hellenistic-Roman culture. Through the Stoic Logos-doctrine, it used the ancient civilization as material for building up the universal church, which in principle includes all positive elements in man's cultural creativity. The question then arises as to why a secular world broke away from this union in modern Western civilization. Was not and is not the power of the New Being in the Christ strong enough to subject the creations of modern autonomous culture to the Logos, who became personal presence in the center of history? This question, of course, should be a decisive motive in all contemporary theology, as it is in the present system.

The last question, and perhaps the most offensive riddle of church history, is the manifest power of the demonic in it. This is an offensive riddle in view of the fact that the highest claim of Christianity, as expressed in Paul's triumphant hymn in Romans, chapter 8, is the victory of the Christ over the demonic powers. In spite of the victory over the demonic, the presence of demonic elements in primitive and priest-condoned ritualizations of the holy can no more be denied than can that more basic demonization which occurs whenever Christian churches have confused their foundation with the buildings they erected on it and have attributed the ultimacy of the former to the latter. There is one line of demonization in Christianity, from the first persecution of heretics immediately after the elevation of Christianity to the position of state religion of the Roman empire, through formulas of condemnation in the declarations of the great councils, through wars of extirpation against medieval sects and the principles of the inquisition, through the tyranny of Protestant orthodoxy, the fanaticism of its sects, and the stubbornness of fundamentalism, to the declaration of the infallibility of the pope. The event in which the Christ sacrificed all claims to a particular absoluteness into which the disciples wanted to force him occurred in vain for all these examples of demonization of the Christian message.

In view of this one must ask: What is the meaning of church history? One thing is obvious: one cannot call church history "sacred history" or a "history of salvation." Sacred history is in church history but is not limited to it, and sacred history is not only manifest in but also hidden by church history. Nevertheless, church history has one quality which no other history has: since it relates itself in all its periods and appearances to the central manifestation of the Kingdom of God in history, it has in itself the ultimate criterion against itself—the New Being in Jesus as the Christ. The presence of this criterion elevates the churches above any other religious group, not because they are "better" than others, but because they have a better criterion against themselves and, implicitly, also against other groups. The struggle of the Kingdom of God in history is, above all, this struggle within the life of its own representatives, the churches. We have related this struggle to the reformations which occur again and again in the churches. But the struggle of the Kingdom of God within them is not only manifest in the dramatic form of reformations; it also goes on in the daily life of individuals and communities. The consequences of the struggle are fragmentary and preliminary but are not devoid of actual victories of the Kingdom of God. However, neither dramatic reformations nor unnoticed transformations of individuals and communities are the ultimate test for the vocation of the churches and the uniqueness of church history. The ultimate test is the relation of the churches and their history to this foundation in the center of history, even in the most distorted stages of their development.

We said before that the history of the manifest church would not be possible without the preparatory work of the church in its latency. This work is hidden in world history, and the second consideration of the struggle of the Kingdom of God in history deals with its effect in world history.

C. THE KINGDOM OF GOD AND WORLD HISTORY

1. CHURCH HISTORY AND WORLD HISTORY

The meaning of the term "world" in the context of this and the preceding chapters is determined by its contrast to the terms "church" and "the churches." It does not imply the belief that there is a world history which is a coherent and continuous history of the all-embracing historical group "mankind." As discussed before, there is no history of mankind in this sense. Mankind is the place on which historical developments occur. These developments are partly unconnected and partly interdependent, but they never have a united center of action. Even today, when a technical unity of mankind has been achieved, no centered action by mankind as such is being performed. And if, in an unforeseeable future, mankind as such were to perform centered actions particular histories would still be the main content of world history. Therefore we must look at these particular histories in our consideration of the relation of the Kingdom of God to world history. Whether they are connected or disconnected, the phenomena under discussion take place in each of them.

The first problem, in light of the preceding section, concerns the relation between church history and world history. The difficulty of this question stems from the fact that church history, as the representation of the Kingdom of God, is a part both of world history and of that which transcends world history and from the other fact that world history is both opposed to and dependent on church history (including the activities of the latent church which prepare for church history proper). This obviously is a highly dialectical relationship, including several mutual affirmations and negations. The following points must be considered.

The history of the churches shows all the characteristics of the history of the world, that is, all the ambiguities of social self-integration, self-creativity, and self-transcendence. The churches in these respects are the world. They would not exist without structures of power, of growth, of sublimation, and the ambiguities implied in these structures. Seen from this point of view the churches are nothing but a special section of world history. But in spite of its truth, this point of view cannot claim exclusive validity. In the churches there is also unconquered resistance against the ambiguities of world history and fragmentary victories over them. World history is judged by the churches in their capacity as the embodiment of the Spiritual Community. The churches as representatives of the Kingdom of God judge that without which they themselves could not exist. But they do not merely judge it theoretically while accepting it practically. Their judgment consists not only in prophetic words but also in prophetic withdrawals from the ambiguous situations in which world history moves. Churches which resign from political power are more entitled to judge the ambiguities of political power than those which never saw the questionable character of their own power politics. The Catholic judgment against communism, however justified it may be in itself, necessarily evokes the suspicion that it is done as a struggle between two competing power groups, each making ultimate claims for its particular validity. Protestant criticism is not free of this deception but instead is open to the question whether the criticism is done in the name of man's ultimate concern or in the name of a particular political group which uses the religious judgment for its political-economical purposes (as in the alliance of fundamentalism and ultra-conservativism in America). The judgment of a Protestant group against communism may be equally as justified and equally as questionable as that of the Catholic group. But it can have undergone the test of its honesty, this test being that it has first brought judgment against the churches themselves, even in their basic structure; and this is a test which the Roman church would never be able to undergo. For her church history is sacred history without any restriction in principle, although, of course, restrictions may be invoked with respect to individual members and particular events.

Church history judges world history while judging itself because it is a part of world history. Church history has an impact on world history. The last two thousand years of world history in the Western part of mankind move under the transforming influence of the churches. For example, the climate of social relations is changed by the existence of the churches. This is a fact as well as a problem. It is a fact that Christianity has changed person-to-person relations in a fundamental way, wherever it has been accepted. This does not mean that the consequences of this change have been practiced by a majority of people or even by many people. But it does mean that whoever does not practice the new way of human relations, although aware of them, is stricken by an uneasy conscience. Perhaps one can say that the main impact of church history on world history is that it produces an uneasy conscience in those who have received the impact of the New Being but follow the ways of the old being. Christian civilization is not the Kingdom of God, but it is a continuous reminder of it. Therefore one should never use changes in the state of the world as a basis for proving the validity of the Christian message. Such arguments do not convince because they miss the paradox of the churches and the ambiguities of every stage of world history. Often historical providence works through demonizations and profanizations of the churches toward the actualization of the Kingdom of God in history. Such providential developments do not excuse the churches in their distortion, but they show the independence of the Kingdom of God from its representatives in history.

Writing church history under these conditions requires a double viewpoint in the description of every particular development. First, church history must show facts and their relations with the best methods of historical research and must do so without bringing in divine providence as a particular cause in the general chain of causes and effects. The church historian is not supposed to write a history of divine interferences in world history when he writes the history of the Christian churches. Secondly, the church historian, as a theologian, must remain aware of the fact that he speaks about a historical reality in which the Spiritual Community is effective and by which the Kingdom of God is represented. The section of world history with which he deals has a providential vocation for all world history. Therefore he must not only look at world history as the large matrix within which church history moves but also from a threefold point of view: first, as that reality in which church history as the representation of the Kingdom of God has been and is being prepared; second, as that reality which is the object of the transforming activities of the Spiritual Community; and third, as that reality by which church history is judged while judging it. Church history, written in this manner, is a part of the history of the Kingdom of God, actualized in historical time. But there is another part to this history, and that is world history itself.

2. THE KINGDOM OF GOD AND THE AMBIGUITIES OF HISTORICAL SELF-INTEGRATION

We have described the ambiguities of history as consequences of the ambiguities of life processes in general. The self-integration of life under the dimension of history shows the ambiguities implied in the drive toward centeredness: the ambiguities of "empire" and of "control," the first appearing in the drive of expansion toward a universal historical unity, and the second, in the drive toward a centered unity in the particular history-bearing group. In each case the ambiguity of power lies behind the ambiguities of historical integration. So the question arises: What is the relation of the Kingdom of God to the ambiguities of power? The answer to this question is also the answer to the question of the relation of the churches to power.

The basic theological answer must be that, since God as *the* power of being is the source of all particular powers of being, power is divine in its essential nature. The symbols of power for God or the Christ or the church in biblical literature are abundant. And Spirit is the dynamic unity of power and meaning. The depreciation of power in most pacifist pronouncements is unbiblical as well as unrealistic. Power is the eternal possibility of resisting non-being. God and the Kingdom of God "exercise" this power eternally. But in the divine life—of which the divine kingdom is the creative self-manifestation—the ambiguities of power, empire, and control are conquered by unambiguous life.

Within historical existence this means that every victory of the Kingdom of God in history is a victory over the disintegrating consequences of the ambiguity of power. Since this ambiguity is based on the existential split between subject and object, its conquest involves a fragmentary reunion of subject and object. For the internal power structure of a history-bearing group, this means that the struggle of the Kingdom of God in history is actually victorious in institutions and attitudes and conquers, even if only fragmentarily, that compulsion which usually goes with power and transforms the objects of centered control into mere objects. In so far as democratization of political attitudes and institutions serves to resist the destructive implications of power, it is a manifestation of the Kingdom of God in history. But it would be completely wrong to identify democratic institutions with the Kingdom of God in history. This confusion, in the minds of many people, has elevated the idea of democracy to the place of a direct religious symbol and has simply substituted it for the symbol "Kingdom of God." Those who argue against this confusion are right when they point to the fact that aristocratic hierarchical systems of power have for long periods prevented the total transformation of men into objects by the tyranny of the strongest. And beyond this they also correctly point out that by their community and personality-creating effects aristocratic systems have developed the democratic potential of leaders and masses. However, this consideration does not justify the glorification of authoritarian systems of power as expressions of the will of God. In so far as the centering and liberating elements in a structure of political power are balanced, the Kingdom of God in history has conquered fragmentarily the ambiguities of control. This is, at the same time, the criterion according to which churches must judge political actions and theories. Their judgment against power politics should not be a rejection of power but an affirmation of power and even of its compulsory element in cases where justice is violated ("justice" is used here in the sense of protection of the individual as a potential personality in a community). Therefore, although the fight against "objectivation" of the personal subject is a permanent task of the churches, to be carried out by prophetic witness and priestly initiation, it is not their function to control the political powers and force upon them particular solutions in the name of the Kingdom of God. The way in which the Kingdom of God works in history is not identical with the way the churches want to direct the course of history.

The ambiguity of self-integration of life under the historical dimensions is also effective in the trend toward the reunion of all human groups in an empire. Again it must be stated that the Kingdom of God in history does not imply the denial of power in the encounter of centered political groups, for example, nations. As in every encounter of living beings, including individual men, power of being meets power of being and decisions are made about the higher or lower degree of such power—so it is in the encounter of political power groups. And as it is in the particular group and its structure of control, so it is in the relations of particular groups to each other that decisions are made in every moment in which the significance of the particular group for the unity of the Kingdom of God in history is actualized. In these struggles it might happen that a complete political defeat becomes the condition for the greatest significance a group gets in the manifestation of the Kingdom of God in history—as in Jewish history and, somehow analogously, in Indian and Greek history. But it also may be that a military defeat is the way in which the Kingdom of God, fighting in history, deprives national groups of a falsely claimed ultimate significance—as in the case of Hitler's Germany. Although this was done through the conquerors of naziism, their victory did not give them an unambiguous claim that they themselves were the bearers of the reunion of mankind. If they raised such a claim they would, by this very fact, show their inability to fulfil it. (See, for example, some hate propaganda in the United States and the absolutism of Communist Russia.)

For the Christian churches this means that they must try to find a way between a pacifism which overlooks or denies the necessity of power (including compulsion) in the relation of history-bearing groups and a militarism which believes in the possibility of achieving the unity of mankind through the conquest of the world by a particular historical group. The ambiguity of empire-building is fragmentarily conquered when higher political unities are created which, although they are not without the compulsory element of power, are nonetheless brought about in such a way that community between the united groups can develop and none of them is transformed into a mere object of centered control.

This basic solution of the problem of power in expansion toward larger unities should determine the attitude of the churches to empire-building and war. War is the name for the compulsory element in the creation of higher imperial unities. A "just" war is either a war in which arbitrary resistance against a higher unity has to be broken (for example, the American Civil War) or a war in which the attempt to create or maintain a higher unity by mere suppression is resisted (for example, the American Revolutionary War). There is no way of saying with more than daring faith whether a war was or is a just war in this sense. This incertitude, however, does not justify the cynical type of realism which surrenders all criteria and judgments, nor does it justify utopian idealism which believes in the possibility of removing the compulsory element of power from history. But the churches as representatives of the Kingdom of God can and must condemn a war which has only the appearance of a war but is in reality universal suicide. One never can start an atomic war with the claim that it is a just war, because it cannot serve the unity which belongs to the Kingdom of God. But one must be ready to answer in kind, even with atomic weapons, if the other side uses them first. The threat itself could be a deterrent.

All this implies that the pacifist way is not the way of the Kingdom of God in history. But certainly it is the way of the churches as representatives of the Spiritual Community. They would lose their representative character if they used military or economic weapons as tools for spreading the message of the Christ. The church's valuation of pacifist movements, groups, and individuals follows from this situation. The churches must reject political pacifism but support groups and individuals who try symbolically to represent the "Peace of the Kingdom of God" by refusing to participate in the compulsory element of power struggles and who are willing to bear the unavoidable reactions by the political powers to which they belong and by which they are protected. This refers to such groups as the Quakers and to such individuals as conscientious objectors. They represent within the political group the resignation of power which is essential for the churches but cannot be made by them into a law to be imposed on the body politic.

3. The Kingdom of God and the Ambiguities of Historical Self-creativity

While the ambiguities of historical self-integration lead to problems of political power, the ambiguities of historical self-creativity lead to problems of social growth. It is the relation of the new to the old in history which gives rise to conflicts between revolution and tradition. The relations of the generations to each other is the typical example for the unavoidable element of unfairness on both sides in the process of growth. A victory of the Kingdom of God creates a unity of tradition and revolution in which the unfairness of social growth and its destructive consequences, "lies and murder," are overcome.

They are not overcome by rejection of revolution or tradition in the name of the transcendent side of the Kingdom of God. The principal antirevolutionary attitude of many Christian groups is fundamentally wrong, whether unbloody cultural or unbloody and bloody political revolutions are concerned. The chaos which follows any kind of revolution can be a creative chaos. If history-bearing groups are unwilling to take this risk and are successful in avoiding any revolution, even an unbloody one, the dynamics of history will leave them behind. And certainly they cannot claim that their historical obsolescence is a victory of the Kingdom of God. But neither can this be said of the attempt of revolutionary groups to destroy the given structures of the cultural and political life by revolutions which are intended to force the fulfilment of the Kingdom of God and its justice "on earth." It was against such ideas of a Christian revolution to end all revolutions that Paul wrote his words in Romans, chapter 13, about the duty of obedience to the authorities in power. One of the many politico-theological abuses of biblical statements is the understanding of Paul's words as justifying the anti-revolutionary bias of some churches, particularly the Lutheran. But neither these words nor any other New Testament statement deals with the methods of gaining political power. In Romans, Paul is addressing eschatological enthusiasts, not a revolutionary political movement.

The Kingdom of God is victorious over the ambiguities of historical growth only where it can be discerned that revolution is being built into tradition in such a way that, in spite of the tensions in every concrete situation and in relation to every particular problem, a creative solution in the direction of the ultimate aim of history is found.

It is the nature of democratic institutions, in relation to questions of political centeredness and of political growth, that they try to unite the truth of the two conflicting sides. The two sides here are the new and the old, represented by revolution and tradition. The possibility of removing a government by legal means is such an attempted union; and in so far as it succeeds it represents a victory of the Kingdom of God in history, because it overcomes the split. But this fact does not remove the ambiguities inherent in democratic institutions themselves. There have been other ways of uniting tradition and revolution within a political system, as is seen in federal, pre-absolutistic organizations of society. And we must not forget that democracy can produce a mass conformity which is more dangerous for the dynamic element in history and its revolutionary expression than is an openly working absolutism. The Kingdom of God is as hostile to established conformism as it is to negativistic non-conformism.

If we look at the history of the churches we find that religion, including Christianity, has stood overwhelmingly on the conservative-traditionalistic side. The great moments in the history of religion when the prophetic spirit challenged priestly doctrinal and ritual traditions are exceptions. These moments are comparatively rare (the Jewish prophets,

Jesus and the apostles, the reformers)—according to the general law that the normal growth of life is organic, slow, and without catastrophic interruptions. This law of growth is most effective in realms in which the given is vested with the taboo of sacredness and in which, consequently, every attack on the given is felt as a violation of a taboo. The history of Christianity up to the present is full of examples of this feeling and consequently of the traditionalist solution. But whenever the spiritual power produced a spiritual revolution, one stage of Christianity (and religion in general) was transformed into another. Much tradition-bound accumulation is needed before a prophetic attack on it is meaningful. This accounts for the quantitative predominance of religious tradition over religious revolution. But every revolution in the power of the Spirit creates a new basis for priestly conservation and the growth of lasting traditions. This rhythm of the dynamics of history (which has analogies in the biological and psychological realms) is the way in which the Kingdom of God works in history.

4. THE KINGDOM OF GOD AND THE AMBIGUITIES OF HISTORICAL SELF-TRANSCENDENCE

The ambiguities of self-transcendence are caused by the tension between the Kingdom of God realized in history and the Kingdom as expected. Demonic consequences result from absolutizing the fragmentary fulfilment of the aim of history within history. On the other hand if the consciousness of realization is completely absent, utopianism alternates with the inescapable disappointments that are the seedbed of cynicism.

Therefore no victory of the Kingdom of God is given if either the consciousness of realized fulfilment or the expectation of fulfilment is denied. As we have seen, the symbol of the "third stage" can be used in both ways. But it also can be used in such a way as to unite the consciousness of the presence and the not-yet-presence of the Kingdom of God in history. This was the problem of the early church, and it remained a problem for all church history, as well as for the secularized forms of the self-transcending character of history. While it is comparatively easy to see the theoretical necessity of the union of the presence and not-yet-presence of the Kingdom of God, it is very difficult to keep the union in a state of living tension without letting it deteriorate into a shallow "middle way" of ecclesiastical or secular satisfaction. In the case of either ecclesiastical or secular satisfaction, it is the influence of those social groups which are interested in the preservation of the status quo that is largely, though not exclusively, responsible for such a situation. And the reaction of the critics of the status quo leads in each case to a restatement of the "principle of hope" (Ernst Bloch) in utopian terms. In such movements of expectation, however unrealistic they may be, the fighting Kingdom of God scores a victory against the power of complacency in its different sociological and psychological forms. But of course, it is a precarious and fragmentary victory because the bearers of it tend to ignore the given, but fragmentary, presence of the Kingdom.

The implication of this for the churches as representatives of the Kingdom of God in history is that it is their task to keep alive the tension between the consciousness of presence and the expectation of the coming. The danger for the receptive (sacramental) churches is that they will emphasize the presence and neglect the expectation; and the danger for the activistic (prophetic) churches is that they will emphasize the expectation and neglect the consciousness of the presence. The most important expression of this difference is the contrast between the emphasis on individual salvation in the one group and on social transformation in the other. Therefore it is a victory of the Kingdom of God in history if a sacramental church takes the principle of social transformation into its aim or if an activistic church pronounces the Spiritual Presence under all social conditions, emphasizing the vertical line of salvation over against the horizontal line of historical activity. And since the vertical line is primarily the line from the individual to the ultimate, the question arises as to how the Kingdom of God, in its fight within history, conquers the ambiguities of the individual in his historical existence.

5. THE KINGDOM OF GOD AND THE AMBIGUITIES OF THE INDIVIDUAL IN HISTORY

The phrase "individual in history" in this context means the individual in so far as he actively participates in the dynamics of history. Not only he who acts politically participates in history but so does everybody who in some realm of creativity contributes to the universal movement of history. And this is so in spite of the predominance of the politi-

cal in historical existence. Therefore everybody is subject to the ambiguities of this participation, the basic character of which is the ambiguity
of historical sacrifice.

It is not a victory of the Kingdom of God in history if the individual
tries to take himself out of participation in history in the name of the
transcendent Kingdom of God. Not only is it impossible, but the attempt
itself deprives the individual of full humanity by separating him from
the historical group and its creative self-realization. One cannot reach
the transcendent Kingdom of God without participating in the struggle
of the inner-historical Kingdom of God. For the transcendent is actual
within the inner-historical. Every individual is thrown into the tragic
destiny of historical existence. He cannot escape it, whether he dies as
an infant or as a great historical leader. Nobody's destiny is uninfluenced
by historical conditions. But the more one's destiny is directly determined by one's active participation, the more historical sacrifice is demanded. Where such sacrifice is maturely accepted a victory of the
Kingdom of God has occurred.

However, if there were no other answer to the question of the individual in history, man's historical existence would be meaningless and
the symbol "Kingdom of God" would have no justification. This is
obvious as soon as we ask the question: Sacrifice for what? A sacrifice
the purpose of which bears no relation to him of whom it is demanded
is not sacrifice but enforced self-annihilation. Genuine sacrifice fulfils
rather than annihilates him who makes the sacrifice. Therefore historical sacrifice must be surrender to an aim in which more is achieved than
just the power of a political structure or the life of a group or a progress
in historical movement or the highest state of human history. Rather, it
must be an aim the sacrifice for which produces also the personal fulfilment of him who surrenders himself. The personal aim, the *telos*, may
be "glory," as in classical Greece; or it may be "honor," as in feudal
cultures; or it may be a mystical identification with the nation, as in
the era of nationalism, or with the party, as in the era of neo-collectivism;
or it may be the establishment of truth, as in scientism; or the attainment
of a new stage of human self-actualization, as in progressivism. It may
be the glory of God, as in ethical types of religion; or union with the
Ultimate One, as in mystical types of religious experience; or Eternal
Life in the divine ground and aim of being, as in classical Christianity.
Wherever historical sacrifice and the certainty of personal fulfilment are

united in this way, a victory of the Kingdom of God has taken place. The participation of the individual in historical existence has received an ultimate meaning.

If we now compare the manifold expressions of the ultimate meaning of the individual's participation in the dynamics of history, we may transcend them all—by the symbol of the Kingdom of God. For this symbol unites the cosmic, social, and personal elements. It unites the glory of God with the love of God and sees in the divine transcendence inexhaustible manifoldness of creative potentialities.

This consideration leads to the last section of this part and of the whole theological system: "The Kingdom of God as the End of History (or as Eternal Life)."

III

THE KINGDOM OF GOD AS THE
END OF HISTORY

A. THE END OF HISTORY OR ETERNAL LIFE

1. THE DOUBLE MEANING OF "END OF HISTORY" AND THE PERMANENT PRESENCE OF THE END

THE FRAGMENTARY victories of the Kingdom of God in history point by their very character to the non-fragmentary side of the Kingdom of God "above" history. But even "above" history, the Kingdom of God is related to history; it is the "end" of history.

The English word "end" means both finish and aim; as such it is an excellent tool for the expression of the two sides of the Kingdom of God, the transcendent and the inner-historical. At some time in the development of the cosmos, human history, life on earth, the earth itself, and the stage of the universe to which it belongs will come to an end; they will cease to have existence in time and space. This event is a small one within the universal temporal process. But "end" also means aim, which the Latin *finis* and the Greek *telos* designate as that toward which the temporal process points as its goal. The first meaning of "end" has theological significance only because it demythologizes the dramatic-transcendent symbolism concerning the end of historical time, as given, for example, in apocalyptic literature and in some biblical ideas. But the end of the biological or physical possibility of history is not the end of history in the second sense of the word. The end of history in this sense is not a moment within the larger development of the universe (analogously called history) but transcends all moments of the temporal process; it is the end of time itself—it is eternity. The end of history in the sense of the inner aim or the *telos* of history is "eternal life."

The classical term for the doctrine of the "end of history" is "eschatology." The Greek word *eschatos* combines, as does the English "end," a spatio-temporal and a qualitative-valuating sense. It points both to the last, the most removed in space and time, and to the highest, the most

394

perfect, the most sublime—but sometimes also to the lowest in value, the extreme negative. These connotations are present, if the term "eschatology," the "doctrine of the last," or "last things," is used. Its most immediate as well as most primitive mythological connotation is "the last in the chain of all days." This day belongs to the whole of all days which constitute the temporal process; it is one of them, but after it there will be no other day. All the events that happen at that day are called "the last things" (*ta eschata*). Eschatology in this sense is the description of what will happen in the last of all days. Poetic, dramatic, and pictorial imagination has given such description in a rich way, from the apocalyptic literature to the paintings of the ultimate judgment and of heaven and hell.

But our question is: What is the theological meaning of all this imagery (which is by no means exclusively Jewish and Christian)? In order to emphasize the qualitative connotation of *eschatos* I use the singular: the *eschaton*. The theological problem of eschatology is not constituted by the many things which will happen but by the one "thing" which is not a thing but which is the symbolic expression of the relation of the temporal to the eternal. More specifically, it symbolizes the "transition" from the temporal to the eternal, and this is a metaphor similar to that of the transition from the eternal to the temporal in the doctrine of creation, from essence to existence in the doctrine of the fall, and from existence to essence in the doctrine of salvation.

The eschatological problem is given an immediate existential significance by this reduction of the *eschata* to the *eschaton*. It ceases to be an imaginative matter about an indefinitely far (or near) catastrophe in time and space and becomes an expression of our standing in every moment in face of the eternal, though in a particular mode of time. The mode of future appears in all eschatological symbolism, just as the mode of past appears in all creational symbolism. God *has* created the world, and he *will* bring the world to its end. But although in both cases the relation of the temporal to the eternal is symbolized, the existential and therefore theological meaning of the symbols is different. If the mode of past is used for the relation of the temporal to the eternal, the dependence of creaturely existence is indicated; if the mode of future is used, the fulfilment of creaturely existence in the eternal is indicated.

Past and future meet in the present, and both are included in the eternal "now." But they are not swallowed by the present; they have their independent and different functions. Theology's task is to analyze and describe these functions in unity with the total symbolism to which they belong. In this way the *eschaton* becomes a matter of present experience without losing its futuristic dimension: we stand *now* in face of the eternal, but we do so looking ahead toward the end of history and the end of all which is temporal in the eternal. This gives to the eschatological symbol its urgency and seriousness and makes it impossible for Christian preaching and theological thought to treat eschatology as an appendix to an otherwise finished system. This has never been done with respect to the end of the individual: the preaching of the *memento mori* was always important in the church, and the transcendent destiny of the individual was always a matter of high theological concern. But the question of the end of history and of the universe in the eternal was rarely asked, and if asked, not seriously answered. It is only the historical catastrophes of the first half of the twentieth century and the threat of man's self-annihilation since the middle of the century that have aroused an often passionate concern for the eschatological problem in its fullness. And it must be said here that without the consideration of the end of history and of the universe, even the problem of the eternal destiny of the individual cannot be answered.

2. The End of History as the Elevation of the Temporal into Eternity

History, we have seen, is creative of the qualitatively new and runs toward the ultimately new, which, however, it can never attain within itself because the ultimate transcends every temporal moment. The fulfilment of history lies in the permanently present end of history, which is the transcendent side of the Kingdom of God: the Eternal Life.

There are three possible answers to the question: What is the content of the life which is called eternal or what is the content of the kingdom which is ruled by God in transcendent fulfilment? The first is the refusal to answer, because it is considered an unapproachable mystery, the mystery of the divine glory. But religion has always trespassed, and theology should trespass, this restriction. For "life" and "kingdom" are concrete and particular symbols, distinguished from others that have appeared in the history of religion and in secular expressions of the ultimate. If concrete symbols are used at all, mere silence about their meaning is not permitted.

Another answer, that of popular imagination and theological supra-naturalism (its conceptual ally), is quite opposite. Popular imagination and theological supranaturalism know very much about the transcend-ent kingdom, because they see in it an idealized reduplication of life as experienced within history and under the universal conditions of exist-ence. It is characteristic of this reduplication that the negative character-istics of life as known to us, for example, finitude, evil, estrangement, and so on, are removed. All hopes, derived from the essential nature of man and his world, are fulfilled. In actuality the popular expressions of hope by far exceed the limits of essentially justified hope. They are projections of all the ambiguous materials of temporal life, and the de-sires they evoke, into the transcendent realms. Such a supranatural realm has no direct relation to history and the development of the universe. It is established in eternity, and the problem of human existence is whether and in what way individual men may enter the transcendent realm. His-tory is valuated merely as an important element in man's earthly life; it is a finite texture within which the individual must make decisions, rele-vant to his own salvation but irrelevant for the Kingdom of God above history. This obviously deprives history of an ultimate meaning. His-tory is, so to speak, the earthly realm out of which individuals are moved into the heavenly realm. Historical activity, however seriously and spiritually performed, does not contribute to the heavenly kingdom. Even the churches are institutions of salvation, that is, the salvation of individuals, but not actualizations of the New Being.

There is a third answer to the question of the relation of history to Eternal Life. It corresponds with the dynamic-creative interpretation of the symbol "Kingdom of God" as well as with the anti-supranaturalistic or paradoxical understanding of the relation of the temporal to the eternal. Its basic assertion is that the ever present end of history elevates the positive content of history into eternity at the same time that it ex-cludes the negative from participation in it. Therefore nothing which has been created in history is lost, but it is liberated from the negative element with which it is entangled within existence. The positive be-comes manifest as unambiguously positive and the negative becomes manifest as unambiguously negative in the elevation of history to eter-nity. Eternal Life, then, includes the positive content of history, liberated from its negative distortions and fulfilled in its potentialities. History in this statement is primarily human history. But since there is a historical dimension in all realms of life, they are all included in the statement, though to different degrees. Life universal moves toward an end and is elevated into eternal life, its ultimate and ever present end.

In fully symbolic language one could say that life in the whole of creation and in a special way in human history contributes in every moment of time to the Kingdom of God and its eternal life. What happens in time and space, in the smallest particle of matter as well as in the greatest personality, is significant for the eternal life. And since eternal life is participation in the divine life, every finite happening is significant for God.

Creation is creation for the end: in the "ground," the "aim" is present. But between beginning and end, the new is created. For the divine ground of being we must say both that the created is *not* new, for it is potentially rooted in the ground, and that it *is* new, for its actuality is based on freedom in unity with destiny, and freedom is the precondition of all newness in existence. The necessarily consequent is not new; it is merely a transformation of the old. (But even the term "transformation" points to an element of newness; total determination would make even transformation impossible.)

3. THE END OF HISTORY AS THE EXPOSURE OF THE NEGATIVE AS NEGATIVE OR THE "ULTIMATE JUDGMENT"

The elevation of the positive in existence into eternal life implies liberation of the positive from its ambiguous mixture with the negative, which characterizes life under the conditions of existence. The history of religion is full of symbols for this idea, such as the Jewish, Christian, and Islamic symbol of a final judgment or the Hindu and Buddhist symbol of reincarnation under the law of karma. In all these cases the judgment is not restricted to individuals but refers to the universe. The Greek and Persian symbol of the total burning of one cosmos and the birth of another expresses the universal character of the negation of the negative in the end. The Greek word for judging (*krinein*, 'to separate') points most adequately to the nature of the universal judgment: it is an act of separating the good from the bad, the true from the false, the accepted ones from the rejected ones.

In the light of our understanding of the end of history as ever present and as the permanent elevation of history into eternity the symbol of ultimate judgment receives the following meaning: here and now, in the permanent transition of the temporal to the eternal, the negative is defeated in its claim to be positive, a claim it supports by using the positive and mixing ambiguously with it. In this way it produces the appearance of being positive itself (for example, illness, death, a lie, destructiveness, murder, and evil in general). The appearance of evil as positive vanishes in the face of the eternal. In this sense God in his eternal life is called a "burning fire," burning that which pretends to be positive but is not. Nothing positive is being burned. No fire of judgment could do it, not even the fire of the divine wrath. For God cannot deny himself, and everything positive is an expression of being-itself. And since there is nothing merely negative (the negative lives from the positive it distorts), nothing that has being can be ultimately annihilated. Nothing that is, in so far as it is, can be excluded from eternity; but it can be excluded in so far as it is mixed with non-being and not yet liberated from it.

The question as to what this means for the individual person will be discussed later. At this point one naturally asks how the transition from the temporal to the eternal takes place? What happens to things and beings which are non-human in the transition from time to eternity? How, in this transition, is the negative exposed in its negativity and left to annihilation? What exactly is negated if nothing positive can be negated? Such questions can only be answered in the context of a whole system as implications of main concepts (being, non-being, essence, existence, finitude, estrangement, ambiguity, and so on) as well as of the central religious symbols (creation, the Fall, the demonic, salvation, *agape*, Kingdom of God, and so on). Otherwise, the answers would be mere opinions, flashes of insight, or mere poetry (with its revealing but non-conceptual power). In the context of the present system the following answers are possible: The transition from the temporal to the eternal, the "end" of the temporal, is not a temporal event—just as the creation is not a temporal event. Time is the form of the created finite (thus being created with it), and eternity is the inner aim, the *telos* of the created finite, permanently elevating the finite into itself. With a bold metaphor one could say that the temporal, in a continuous process, becomes "eternal memory." But *eternal* memory is living retention of the remembered thing. It is together past, present, and future in a transcendent unity of the three modes of time. More cannot be said—except in poetic imagery. But the little which can be said—mostly in negative terms—has an important consequence for our understanding of time and eternity: The eternal is not a future state of things. It is always present, not only in man (who is aware of it), but also in everything that has being within the whole of being. And with respect to time we can say that its dynamics move not only forward but also upward and that the two movements are united in a curve which moves both forward and upward.

The second question asks for an explanation of the main assertion of this chapter—that in the transition from the temporal to the eternal the negative is negated. If we apply again the metaphor of "eternal memory," we can say that the negative is not an object of eternal memory in the sense of living retention. Neither is it forgotten, for forgetting presupposes at least a moment of remembering. The negative is not remembered at all. It is acknowledged for what it is, non-being. Nevertheless it is not without effect on that which is eternally remembered. It is present in the eternal memory as that which is conquered and thrown out into its naked nothingness (for example, a lie). This is the condemning side of what is symbolically called ultimate judgment. Again one must confess that beyond these predominantly negative statements nothing can be said about the judgment of the universe, except in poetic language. But something must be said about the saving side of the ultimate judgment. The statement that the positive in the universe is the object of eternal memory requires an explanation of the term "positive" in this context. Its immediate meaning is that it has true reality—as the created essence of a thing. This leads to the further question as to how the "positive" is related to essential being and, by contrast, to existential being. A first and somewhat Platonizing answer is that being, elevated into eternity, involves a return to what a thing essentially is; this is what Schelling has called "essentialization." This formulation can mean return to the state of mere essentiality or potentiality, including the removal of everything that is real under the conditions of existence. Such an understanding of essentialization would make it into a concept which is more adequate to the India-born religions than to any of the Israel-born ones. The whole world process would not produce anything new. It would have the character of falling away from and returning to essential being. But the term "essentialization" can also mean that the new which has been actualized in time and space adds something to essential being, uniting it with the positive which is created within existence, thus producing the ultimately new, the "New Being," not fragmentarily as in temporal life, but wholly as a contribution to the Kingdom of God in its fulfilment. Such thought, however metaphorically and inadequately expressed, gives an infinite weight to every decision and creation in time and space and confirms the seriousness of what is meant in the symbol "ultimate judgment." Participation in the eternal life depends on a creative synthesis of a being's essential nature with what it has made of it in its temporal existence. In so far as the negative has maintained possession of it, it is exposed in its negativity and excluded from eternal memory. Whereas, in so far as the essential has conquered existential distortion its standing is higher in eternal life.

4. The End of History and the Final Conquest of the Ambiguities of Life

With the exposure and the exclusion of the negative in the ultimate judgment the ambiguities of life are conquered, not only fragmentarily as in the inner-historical victories of the Kingdom of God, but totally. Because the state of final perfection is the norm of fragmentary perfection and the criterion of the ambiguities of life, it is necessary to point to it, though in the negative metaphorical language which must be used in all attempts to conceptualize eschatological symbols.

With regard to the three polarities of being and the corresponding three functions of life we must ask for the meaning of self-integration, self-creativity and self-transcendence in the Eternal Life. Since Eternal Life is identical with the Kingdom of God in its fulfilment, it is the non-fragmentary, total, and complete conquest of the ambiguities of life—and this under all dimensions of life, or, to use another metaphor, in all degrees of being.

The first question then is: What do we mean by unambiguous self-integration as a characteristic of Eternal Life? The answer points to the first pair of polar elements in the structure of being: individualization and participation. In Eternal Life the two poles are in perfect balance. They are united in that which transcends their polar contrast: the divine centeredness, which includes the universe of powers of being without annihilating them into a dead identity. One can still speak of their self-integration, indicating that even within the centered unity of the divine life they have not lost self-relatedness. Eternal Life is still life, and the universal centeredness does not dissolve the individual centers. This is the first answer to the question of the meaning of Eternal Life, an answer which also gives the first condition for characterizing the fulfilled Kingdom of God as the unambiguous and non-fragmentary life of love.

The second question is: What is the meaning of unambiguous self-creativity as a characteristic of Eternal Life? The answer points to the second pair of polar elements in the structure of being: dynamics and form. In Eternal Life these two poles are also in perfect balance. They are united in that which transcends their polar contrast: the divine creativity, which includes the finite creativity without making it into a technical tool of itself. The self in self-creativity is preserved in the fulfilled Kingdom of God.

The third question is: What is the meaning of unambiguous self-transcendence as a characteristic of Eternal Life? The answer points to the third pair of polar elements in the structure of being: freedom and destiny. In Eternal Life there is also perfect balance between these two poles. They are united in that which transcends their polar contrast—in divine freedom, which is identical with divine destiny. In the power of its freedom every finite being drives beyond itself toward fulfilment of its destiny in the ultimate unity of freedom and destiny.

The preceding metaphoric "descriptions" of Eternal Life referred to the three functions of life in all its dimensions, including that of the human spirit. However, it is also important to deal separately with the three functions of the spirit in their relation to Eternal Life.

The basic statement to be made is that in the end of history the three functions—morality, culture, and religion—come to their end as special functions. Eternal Life is the end of morality. For there is no ought-to-be in it which, at the same time, is not. There is no law where there is essentialization, because what the law demands is nothing but the essence, creatively enriched in existence. We assert the same when we call Eternal Life the life of universal and perfect love. For love does what law demands before it is demanded. To use another terminology, we can say that in Eternal Life the center of the individual person rests in the all-uniting divine center and through it is in communion with all other personal centers. Therefore the demand to acknowledge them as persons and to unite with them as estranged parts of the universal unity is not needed. Eternal Life is the end of morality because what morality demanded is fulfilled in it.

And Eternal Life is the end of culture. Culture was defined as the self-creativity of life under the dimension of the spirit, and it was divided into *theoria*, in which reality is received, and *praxis*, in which reality is shaped. We have already shown the limited validity of this division in connection with the doctrine of the Spiritual Presence. In Eternal Life there is no truth which is not also "done," in the sense of the Fourth Gospel, and there is no aesthetic expression which is not also a reality. Beyond this, culture as spiritual creativity becomes, at the same time, Spiritual creativity. The human spirit's creativity in Eternal Life is revelation by the divine Spirit—as it is fragmentarily already in the Spiritual Community. Man's creativity and divine self-manifestation are one in the fulfilled Kingdom of God. In so far as culture is an independent human enterprise, it comes to an end in the end of history. It becomes eternal divine self-manifestation through the finite bearers of the Spirit.

Finally, the end of history is the end of religion. In biblical terminology this is expressed in the description of the "Heavenly Jerusalem" as a city in which there is no temple because God lives there. Religion is the consequence of the estrangement of man from the ground of his being and of his attempts to return to it. This return has taken place in Eternal Life, and God is everything in and to everything. The gap between the secular and the religious is overcome. In Eternal Life there is no religion.

But now the question arises: How can the fulfilment of the eternal be united with the element of negation without which no life is thinkable? The question can best be answered by considering a concept which belongs to the emotional sphere but which contains the problem of Eternal Life in its relation to being and non-being—the concept of blessedness as applied to the Divine Life.

5. Eternal Blessedness as the Eternal Conquest of the Negative

The concept "blessed" (*makarios, beatus*) can be applied in a fragmentary way to those who are grasped by the divine Spirit. The word designates a state of mind in which Spiritual Presence produces a feeling of fulfilment which cannot be disturbed by negativities in other dimensions. Neither bodily nor psychological suffering can destroy the "transcendent happiness" of being blessed. In finite beings this positive experience is always united with the awareness of its contrary, the state of unhappiness, despair, condemnation. This "negation of the negative" gives blessedness its paradoxical character. But there is a question as to whether this is also true of eternal blessedness. Without an element of negativity neither life nor blessedness can be imagined.

The term "eternal blessedness" is applied both to the Divine Life and to the life of those who participate in it. In the case of both God and man we must ask what the negativity is which makes possible a life of eternal blessedness. The problem has been seriously raised by the philosophers of becoming. If one speaks of the "becoming" of God, one has introduced the negative element; one raises the issue of the negation of what has been left behind in every moment of becoming. Life is most emphatically attributed to God in such a doctrine of God. But it is difficult on this basis to interpret the idea of eternal blessedness in God, for total fulfilment is implied in the concept of eternal blessedness. Fragmentary fulfilment can create temporal but not eternal blessedness; and every limitation of divine blessedness would be a restriction of the divinity of the divine. The philosophers of becoming can refer to biblical statements in which repentance, toil, patience, suffering, and sacrifice are attributed to God. Such expressions of the vision of a living God have led to ideas which were rejected by the church, the so-called patripassionist doctrine that God as father suffered in the suffering of the Christ. But such an assertion contradicts too obviously the fundamental theological doctrine of God's impassibility. In the judgment of the church it would have brought God down to the level of the passionate and suffering gods of Greek mythology. But the rejection of patripassionism does not solve the question of the negative in the blessedness of the Divine Life. Present-day theology tries—with very few exceptions— to avoid the problem altogether, either by ignoring it or by calling it an inscrutable divine mystery. But such escape is impossible in view of the question's significance for the most existential problem of theodicy. People in "boundary-situations" will not accept the escape into the divine mystery on this point if it is not used on other points, for example, in the teaching of the church about God's almighty power and his ever present love, teaching which demands interpretation in view of the daily experience of the negativity of existence. If theology refuses to answer such existential questions, it has neglected its task.

Theology must take the problems of the philosophers of becoming seriously. It must try to combine the doctrine of eternal blessedness with the negative element without which life is not possible and blessedness ceases to be blessed. It is the nature of blessedness itself that requires a negative element in the eternity of the Divine Life.

This leads to the fundamental assertion: The Divine Life is the eternal conquest of the negative; this is its blessedness. Eternal blessedness is not a state of immovable perfection—the philosophers of becoming are right in rejecting such a concept. But the Divine Life is blessedness through fight and victory. If we ask how blessedness can be united with the risk and uncertainty which belong to the nature of serious fight, we may remember what was said about the seriousness of the temptations of the Christ. In this discussion the seriousness of the temptation and the certainty of the communion with God were described as compatible. This can be an analogy—and more than an analogy—of the eternal identity of God with himself, which does not contradict his going out from himself into the negativities of existence and the ambiguities of life. He does not lose his identity in his self-alteration; this is the basis for the dynamic idea of eternal blessedness.

Eternal blessedness is also attributed to those who participate in the Divine Life, not to man only, but to everything that is. The symbol of "a new heaven and a new earth" indicates the universality of the blessedness of the fulfilled Kingdom of God. The next chapter will discuss the relation of eternity to individual persons. At this point we must ask: What does the symbol of eternal blessedness mean for the universe besides man? There are indications in biblical literature of the idea that nature participates in showing and praising the divine glory; but there are other passages in which the animals are excluded from the divine care (Paul) and man's misery is seen in the fact that he is not better off than flowers and animals (Job). In the first group of expressions, nature somehow participates (symbolically expressed in the visions of the Apocalypse) in the divine blessedness, whereas in the second group, nature *and* man are excluded from eternity (most parts of the Old Testament). In line with what we have said before about "essentialization," a possible solution would be that all things—since they are good by creation—participate in the Divine Life according to their essence (compare this with the doctrine that the essences are eternal ideas in the divine mind, as in the later Platonic school). The conflicts and sufferings of nature under the conditions of existence and its longing for salvation, of which Paul speaks (Romans, chapter 8), serve the enrichment of essential being after the negation of the negative in everything that has being. Such considerations, of course, are almost poetic-symbolic and should not be treated as if they were descriptions of objects or events in time and space.

B. THE INDIVIDUAL PERSON AND HIS ETERNAL DESTINY

1. UNIVERSAL AND INDIVIDUAL FULFILMENT

Several statements of the preceding five sections have referred to the Kingdom of God "above" history or to Eternal Life in general. All dimensions of life were included in the consideration of the ultimate *telos* of becoming. Now we must single out the dimension of the spirit and the individual persons who are its bearers. Individual persons always were in the center of eschatological imagination and thought, not only because we ourselves as human beings are persons, but also because the destiny of the person is determined by himself in a way in which it is not under the dimensions of life other than that of spirit. Man as finite freedom has a relation to Eternal Life which is different from that of beings under the predominance of necessity. Awareness of the element of "ought to be," and with it awareness of responsibility, guilt, despair, and hope, characterizes man's relation to the eternal. Everything temporal has a "teleological" relation to the eternal, but man alone is aware of it; and this awareness gives him the freedom to turn against it. The Christian assertion of the tragic universality of estrangement implies that every human being turns against his *telos*, against Eternal Life, at the same time that he aspires to it. This makes the concept of "essentialization" profoundly dialectical. The *telos* of man as an individual is determined by the decisions he makes in existence on the basis of the potentialities given to him by destiny. He can waste his potentialities, though not completely, and he can fulfil them, though not totally. Thus, the symbol of ultimate judgment receives a particular seriousness. The exposure of the negative as negative in a person may not leave much positive for Eternal Life. It can be a reduction to smallness; but it also can be an elevation to greatness. It can mean an extreme poverty with respect to fulfilled potentialities, but it can also mean an extreme richness of them. Small and great, poor and rich, are relative valuations. Because they are relative they contradict the absolute judgments that appear in religious symbolism, such as "losing or winning," "being lost or being saved," "hell or heaven," "eternal death" or "eternal life." The idea of degrees of essentialization undercuts the absoluteness of these symbols and concepts.

Absolute judgments over finite beings or happenings are impossible, because they make the finite infinite. This is the truth in theological universalism and the doctrine of the "restitution of everything" in eternity. But the word "restitution" is inadequate: essentialization can be both more and less than restitution. The church rejected Origen's doctrine of the *apokatastasis panton* (the restitution of everything) because this expectation seemed to remove the seriousness implied in such absolute threats and hopes as "being lost" or "being saved." A solution of this conflict must combine the absolute seriousness of the threat to "lose one's life" with the relativity of finite existence. The conceptual symbol of "essentialization" is capable of fulfilling this postulate, for it emphasizes the despair of having wasted one's potentialities yet also assures the elevation of the positive within existence (even in the most unfulfilled life) into eternity.

This solution rejects the mechanistic idea of a necessary salvation without falling into the contradictions of the traditional solution which described the eternal destiny of the individual either as being everlastingly condemned or as being everlastingly saved. The most questionable form of this idea, the doctrine of double predestination, has demonic implications: it introduces an eternal split into God himself. But even without predestination the doctrine of an absolutely opposite eternal destiny of individuals cannot be defended in view of both the self-manifestation of God and the nature of man.

The background of the imagery of a twofold eternal destiny lies in the radical separation of person from person and of the personal from the subpersonal as a consequence of biblical personalism. When individualization under the dimension of the spirit conquers participation, strongly centered selves are created who, through ascetic self-control and acceptance of sole responsibility for their eternal destiny, separate themselves from the creaturely unity of creation. But Christianity, in spite of its personalistic emphasis, also has ideas of universal participation in the fulfilment of the Kingdom of God. These ideas received more emphasis the less Christianity was indirectly influenced by the strong dualistic tendencies in the later period of Hellenism.

From the point of view of the divine self-manifestation the doctrine of twofold eternal destiny contradicts the idea of God's permanent creation of the finite as something "very good" (Genesis, chapter 1). If being as being is good—the great anti-dualistic statement of Augustine—nothing that is can become completely evil. If something is, if it has being, it is included in the creative divine love. The doctrine of the unity of everything in divine love and in the Kingdom of God deprives the symbol of hell of its character as "eternal damnation." This doctrine does not take away the seriousness of the condemning side of the divine judgment, the despair in which the exposure of the negative is experienced. But it does take away the absurdities of a literal understanding of hell and heaven and also refuses to permit the confusion of eternal destiny with an everlasting state of pain or pleasure.

From the point of view of human nature, the doctrine of a twofold eternal destiny contradicts the fact that no human being is unambiguously on one or the other side of divine judgment. Even the saint remains a sinner and needs forgiveness and even the sinner is a saint in so far as he stands under divine forgiveness. If the saint receives forgiveness, his reception of it remains ambiguous. If the sinner rejects forgiveness, his rejection of it remains ambiguous. The Spiritual Presence is also effective in pushing us into the experience of despair. The qualitative contrast between the good and evil ones, as it appears in the symbolic language of both Testaments, means the contrasting quality of good and evil as such (for example, truth and lie, compassion and cruelty, union with God and separation from God). But this qualitative contrast does not describe the thoroughly good or thoroughly evil character of individual persons. The doctrine of the ambiguity of all human goodness and of the dependence of salvation on the divine grace alone either leads us back to the doctrine of double predestination or leads us forward to the doctrine of universal essentialization.

There is another side to human nature which contradicts the idea of the isolation of person from person and of the personal from the sub-personal that is presupposed in the doctrine of twofold eternal destiny. The total being, including the conscious and unconscious sides of every individual, is largely determined by the social conditions which he is influenced by upon entering existence. The individual grows only in interdependence with social situations. And the functions of man's spirit, according to the mutual immanence of all dimensions of being, are in structural unity with the physical and biological factors of life. Freedom and destiny in every individual are united in such a way that it is as

impossible to separate one from the other as it is, consequently, to separate the eternal destiny of any individual from the destiny of the whole
race and of being in all its manifestations.

This finally answers the question of the meaning of distorted forms
of life—forms which, because of physical, biological, psychological, or
sociological conditions, are unable to reach a fulfilment of their essential
telos even to a small degree, as in the case of premature destruction, the
death of infants, biological and psychological disease, morally and
Spiritually destructive environments. From the point of view which
assumes separate individual destinies, there is no answer at all. The
question and the answer are possible only if one understands essentialization or elevation of the positive into Eternal Life as a matter of universal participation: in the essence of the least actualized individual, the
essences of other individuals and, indirectly, of all beings are present.
Whoever condemns anyone to eternal death condemns himself, because
his essence and that of the other cannot be absolutely separated. And he
who is estranged from his own essential being and experiences the
despair of total self-rejection must be told that his essence participates
in the essences of all those who have reached a high degree of fulfilment
and that through this participation his being is eternally affirmed. This
idea of the essentialization of the individual in unity with all beings
makes the concept of vicarious fulfilment understandable. It also gives
a new content to the concept of Spiritual Community; and finally, it
gives a basis for the view that such groups as nations and churches
participate in their essential being in the unity of the fulfilled Kingdom
of God.

2. IMMORTALITY AS SYMBOL AND AS CONCEPT

For the individual participation in Eternal Life, Christianity uses the
two terms "immortality" and "resurrection" (besides "Eternal Life" itself). Of the two, only "resurrection" is biblical. But "immortality," in
the sense of the Platonic doctrine of the immortality of the soul, was used
very early in Christian theology, and in large sections of Protestant
thought, it has replaced the symbol of resurrection. In some Protestant countries it has become the last remnant of the whole Christian message, but it has done so in the non-Christian pseudo-Platonic form of a
continuation of the temporal life of an individual after death without
a body. Where the symbol of immortality is used to express this popular

superstition, it must be radically rejected by Christianity; for participation in eternity is not "life hereafter". Neither is it a natural quality of the human soul. It is rather the creative act of God, who lets the temporal separate itself from and return to the eternal. It is understandable that Christian theologians who are aware of these difficulties reject the term "immortality" altogether, not only in its form in popular superstitions but also in its genuine Platonic form. But this is not justified. If the term is used in the way in which I Timothy 6:16 applies it to God, it expresses negatively what the term eternity expresses positively: it does not mean a continuation of temporal life after death, but it means a quality which transcends temporality.

Immortality in this sense does not contradict the symbol of Eternal Life. But the term is traditionally used in the phrase "immortality of the soul." This produces a further problem for its use in Christian thought: it introduces a dualism between soul and body, contradicting the Christian concept of Spirit, which includes all dimensions of being; and it is incompatible with the symbol "resurrection of the body." But here again we should ask whether the meaning of the term cannot be understood in a non-dualistic way. Aristotle has shown this possibility in his ontology of form and matter. If the soul is the form of the life process, its immortality includes all elements which constitute this process, though it includes them as essences. The meaning of the "immortality of the soul" then would involve the power of essentialization. And in Plato's late doctrine of the world-soul, the idea of immortality in the sense of universal essentialization seems to be implied.

In most of the discussions of immortality the question of evidence preceded in interest the question of content. The question was asked whether there is any evidence for belief in the immortality of the soul, and it was answered with the Platonist arguments that were never satisfactory but were never given up. This situation (which is analogous to that concerning the arguments for the existence of God) is rooted in the transformation of "immortality" from a symbol to a concept. As a symbol "immortality" has been used of the gods and of God, expressing the experience of ultimacy in being and meaning. As such it has the certainty of man's immediate awareness that he is finite and that he transcends finitude exactly in this awareness. The "immortal gods" are symbolic-mythical representations of that infinity from which men as mortals are excluded but which they are able to receive from the gods.

This structure remains valid even after the prophetic demythologization of the sphere of the gods into the reality of the One who is ground and aim of everything that is. He can "clothe our mortality with immortality" (I Corinthians 15:33). Our finitude does not cease to be finitude, but it is "taken into" the infinite, the eternal.

The cognitive situation is totally changed when the conceptual use of the term immortality replaces its symbolic use. In this moment immortality becomes characteristic of the part of man called soul, and the question of the experiential ground for certainty of eternal life is changed into an inquiry into the nature of the soul as a particular object. No doubt Plato's dialogues are largely responsible for this development. But it must be emphasized that in Plato himself there are breaks against the objectifying ("reifying") understanding of immortality: his arguments are arguments "ad hominem" (in present terminology, existential arguments); they can be grasped only by those who participate in the good and the beautiful and the true and who are aware of their transtemporal validity. As arguments in the objective sense, "you cannot be altogether confident of them" (Plato's *Phaidon*). Aristotle's criticism of the Platonic idea of immortality could be understood as an attempt to resist its inescapable primitivization and to take Plato's thought into his own symbol of highest fulfilment, which is man's participation in the eternal self-intuition of the divine *nous*. From here the way is not long to Plotinus' mystical union of the one with the One in the experience of ecstasy. Christian theology could not go this way because of its emphasis on the individual person and his eternal destiny. Instead, Christian theology returned to Plato, using his concept of the immortal soul as the basis for the whole eschatological imagery, unafraid of the unavoidable primitivistic and superstitious consequences. The natural theology of both Catholics and Protestants used old and new arguments for the immortality of the soul, and both demanded acceptance of this concept in the name of faith. They gave official standing to the confusion of symbol and concept, thus provoking the theoretical reaction of the philosophical critics of metaphysical psychology, of whom Locke, Hume, and Kant are examples. Christian theology should not consider their criticism as an attack on the *symbol* "immortality" but on the *concept* of a naturally immortal substance, the soul. If understood in this way, the certainty of Eternal Life has been liberated from its dangerous connection with the concept of an immortal soul.

In view of this situation it would be wise in teaching and preaching to use the term "Eternal Life" and to speak of "immortality" only if superstitious connotations can be prevented.

3. THE MEANING OF RESURRECTION

Man's participation in eternal life beyond death is more adequately expressed by the highly symbolic phrase "resurrection of the body." The churches recognized the latter as a particularly Christian expression. The phrase in the Apostles' Creed is "resurrection of the flesh," that is, of that which characterizes the body in contrast to the spirit, the body in its perishable character. But the phrase is so misleading that in any liturgical form it should be replaced by "resurrection of the body" and interpreted by the Pauline symbol "Spiritual body." Of course, this phrase also requires interpretation; it should be understood as a double negation, expressed by a paradoxical combination of words. First, it negates the "nakedness" of a merely spiritual existence, thus contradicting the assertion in the dualistic traditions of the East as well as in the Platonic and Neo-Platonic schools. The term "body" stands against these traditions as a token of the prophetic faith in the goodness of creation. The antidualistic bias of the Old Testament is powerfully expressed in the idea that the body belongs to Eternal Life. But Paul realizes—better than the Apostles' Creed—the difficulty of this symbol, the danger that it may be understood in the sense of a participation of "flesh and blood" in the Kingdom of God: He insists that they cannot "inherit" it. And against this "materialistic" danger he calls the resurrection body "Spiritual." Spirit—this central concept of Paul's theology—is God present to man's spirit, invading it, transforming and elevating it beyond itself. A Spiritual body then is a body which expresses the Spiritually transformed total personality of man. One can speak about the symbol "Spiritual body" up to this point; concepts cannot go beyond this, but poetic and artistic imagination can. And even the limited statement which is made here points more to the positive implication of the double negation than it does to something directly positive. If we forget this highly symbolic character of the symbol of resurrection, a host of absurdities appears and conceals the true and immensely significant meaning of resurrection.

Resurrection says mainly that the Kingdom of God includes all dimensions of being. The whole personality participates in Eternal Life. If we use the term "essentialization," we can say that man's psychological, spiritual, and social being is implied in his bodily being—and this in unity with the essences of everything else that has being.

The Christian emphasis on the "body of resurrection" also includes a strong affirmation of the eternal significance of the individual person's uniqueness. The individuality of a person is expressed in every cell of his body, especially in his face. The art of portrait-painting continually calls to mind the astonishing fact that molecules and cells can express the functions and movements of man's spirit which are determined by his personal center and determine it in mutual dependence. Beyond this, portraits, if they are authentic works of art, mirror what we have called "essentialization" in artistic anticipation. It is not one particular moment in the life process of an individual that they reproduce but a condensation of all these moments in an image of what this individual essentially has become on the basis of his potentialities and through the experiences and decisions of his life process. This idea can explain the Greek-Orthodox doctrine of icons, the essentialized portraits of the Christ, the apostles, and saints, and in particular the idea that the icons participate mystically in the heavenly reality of those whom they represent. The history-minded Western churches have lost this doctrine, and icons have been replaced by religious pictures which are supposed to remind one of particular traits in the temporal existence of holy persons. This was still done in the line of the older tradition, but the classical forms of expression were slowly replaced by idealistic ones, which were later replaced by naturalistic forms lacking religious transparency. This development in visual arts can be helpful for an understanding of individual essentialization in all dimensions of human nature.

The question most often raised with respect to the eternal destiny of the individual has to do with the presence of the self-conscious self in Eternal Life. The only meaningful answer here, as in the assertion of a Spiritual body, is in the form of two negative statements. The first is that the self-conscious self cannot be excluded from Eternal Life. Since Eternal Life is life and not undifferentiated identity and since the Kingdom of God is the universal actualization of love, the element of individualization cannot be eliminated or the element of participation would also disappear. There is no participation if there are no individual centers to participate; the two poles condition each other. And where there are individual centers of participation, the subject-object structure of existence is the condition of consciousness and—if there is a personal subject—of self-consciousness. This leads to the statement that the centered, self-conscious self cannot be excluded from Eternal Life. The dimension of the spirit which in all its functions presupposes self-consciousness cannot be denied eternal fulfilment, just as eternal fulfilment cannot be denied to the biological dimension and therefore to the body. More than this cannot be said.

But now the opposite negation must be expressed with equal strength: As the participation of bodily being in Eternal Life is not the endless continuation of a constellation of old or new physical particles, so the participation of the centered self is not the endless continuation of a particular stream of consciousness in memory and anticipation. Self-consciousness, in our experience, depends on temporal changes both of the perceiving subject and of the perceived object in the process of self-awareness. But eternity transcends temporality and with it the experienced character of self-consciousness. Without time and change in time, subject and object would merge into each other; the same would perceive the same indefinitely. It would be similar to a state of stupor in which the perceiving subject was unable to reflect on its perceiving and therefore lacked self-consciousness. These psychological analogies are not intended to describe self-consciousness in Eternal Life, but they are supposed to support the second negative statement, which is that the self-conscious self in Eternal Life is not what it is in temporal life (which would include the ambiguities of objectivation). Everything said which exceeds these two negative statements is not theological conceptualization but poetic imagination.

The symbol of resurrection is often used in a more general sense to express the certainty of Eternal Life rising out of the death of temporal life. In this sense it is a symbolic way of expressing the central theological concept of the New Being. As the New Being is not another being, but the transformation of the old being, so resurrection is not the creation of another reality over against the old reality but is the transformation of the old reality, arising out of its death. In this sense the term "resurrection" (without particular reference to the resurrection of the body) has become a universal symbol for the eschatological hope.

4. ETERNAL LIFE AND ETERNAL DEATH

In biblical symbolism the two main concepts which express the negative judgment against a being in relation to its eternal destiny are everlasting punishment and eternal death. The second can be considered as
a demythologization of the first, as Eternal Life is a demythologization
of everlasting happiness. The theological significance of the second is
due to the fact that it takes into consideration the transtemporal character of man's eternal destiny. It also needs interpretation, for it combines two concepts which, if taken at their face value, are completely
contradictory—eternity and death. This combination of words means
death "away" from eternity, a failure to reach eternity, being left to
the transitoriness of temporality. As such eternal death is a personal
threat against everyone who is bound to temporality and unable to
transcend it. For him Eternal Life is a meaningless symbol because he
is lacking in anticipatory experience of the eternal. In the symbolism of
resurrection, one could say that he dies but does not participate in
resurrection.

However, this contradicts the truth that everything as created is rooted
in the eternal ground of being. In this respect non-being cannot prevail against it. Therefore, the question arises as to how the two considerations can be united: How can we reconcile the seriousness of the
threat of death "away" from eternal life with the truth that everything
comes from eternity and must return to it? If we look at the history
of Christian thought we find that both sides of the contradiction are
powerfully represented: the threat of "death away from eternity" is predominant in the practical teaching and preaching of most churches and
in many of them is asserted and defended as official doctrine. The certainty of being rooted in eternity and therefore of belonging to it, even if
turning against it, is the predominant attitude in mystical and humanistic movements within churches and sects. The first type of thought is
represented by Augustine, Thomas, and Calvin, while the second type
is represented by Origen, Socinus, and Schleiermacher. The theological
concept around which the discussion has centered is the "restitution of
all things," the *apokatastasis panton* of Origen. This notion means
that everything temporal returns to the eternal from which it comes.
In the struggles between the beliefs in the particularity and in the
universality of salvation, the contradicting ideas showed their lasting
tension and their practical importance. However primitive the symbolic

framework of these controversies was and to some extent still is, the point of discussion is of great theological and perhaps even greater psychological significance. Presuppositions about the nature of God, man, and their relation are implied. Ultimate despair and ultimate hope or superficial indifference and profound seriousness can be produced by this controversy. Despite its speculative dress, it is one of the most existential problems of Christian thought.

In order to give even a very preliminary answer, it is necessary to look at the motives underlying one or the other attitude. The threat of "death away from eternity" belongs to the ethical-educational type of thinking which, quite naturally, is the basic attitude of the churches. They are (in the case of Origen and of Unitarian Universalism) afraid that the teaching of *apokatastasis* would destroy the seriousness of religious and ethical decisions. This fear is not unfounded, for it has sometimes been recommended that one preach the threat of eternal death (or even of everlasting punishment) but hold, at the same time, to the truth of the doctrine of *apokatastasis*. Probably most Christians have a similar solution for others who die and for themselves when they anticipate their own death. No one can stand the threat of eternal death either for himself or for others; yet the threat cannot be dismissed on the basis of this impossibility. Mythologically speaking, no one can affirm hell as his own or anyone else's eternal destiny. The incertitude about our ultimate destiny cannot be removed, but above this incertitude, there are moments in which we are paradoxically certain of the return to the eternal from which we come. Doctrinally, this leads to a double statement, which is analogous to the other double statements in all cases in which the relation of the temporal to the eternal is expressed: both have to be denied—the threat of eternal death and the security of the return.

Attempts have been made to overcome the sharpness of this polarity both outside and inside Christianity. Three of them are important: the ideas of "reincarnation," of an "intermediary state," and of "purgatory." All three express the feeling that one cannot make the moment of death decisive for man's ultimate destiny. In the case of infants, children, and undeveloped adults, for example, this would be a complete absurdity. In the case of mature people it disregards innumerable elements which enter every mature personal life and cause its profound ambiguity. The whole life process, rather than a particular moment, is decisive for the degree of essentialization. The idea of the reincarnation of individual life had, and, to some extent still has, great power over billions of Asiatic peoples. There, however, the assertion of "life after death" is not a consoling idea. On the contrary, the negative character of all life leads to reincarnation, the painful way of returning to the eternal. Some people, notably the great German poet and philosopher Lessing, in the eighteenth century, accepted this doctrine instead of the orthodox belief that the final decision about one's ultimate destiny is made in the moment of death. But the difficulty of every doctrine of reincarnation is that there is no way to experience the subject's identity in the different incarnations. Therefore reincarnation must be understood—similarly to immortality—as a symbol and not as a concept. It points to higher or lower forces which are present in every being and which fight with each other to determine the individual's essentialization on a higher or lower level of fulfilment. One does not *become* an animal in the next incarnation, but unhumanized qualities may prevail in a human being's personal character and determine the quality of his essentialization. This interpretation, however, does not answer the question of the possible development of the self after death. It is probably impossible to answer the question at all on the basis of the negative attitude that Hinduism and Buddhism take toward the individual self. But if the question is answered at all, the answer presupposes a doctrine which is not far removed from the Roman Catholic doctrine of purgatory. Purgatory is a state in which the soul is "purged" from the distorting elements of temporal existence. In Catholic doctrine, mere suffering does the purging. Besides the psychological impossibility of imagining uninterrupted periods of mere suffering, it is a theological mistake to derive transformation from pain alone instead of from grace which gives blessedness within pain. In any case, a development after death is guaranteed for many beings (though not for all).

Protestantism abolished the doctrine of purgatory because of the severe abuses to which clerical greed and popular superstition subjected it. But Protestantism was not able to answer satisfactorily the problems which originally led to the symbol of purgatory. Only one attempt, and that a rather weak one, was made to solve the problem of individual development after death (except for rare ideas of reincarnation); that attempt was the doctrine of the intermediary state between death and resurrection (in the day of consummation). The main weakness of this doctrine is the idea of a bodiless intermediary state which contradicts the truth of the multidimensional unity of life and involves an unsymbolic application of measurable time to life beyond death.

None of the three symbols for the individual's development after death is able to fulfil the function for which it was created: that is, to combine the vision of an eternal positive destiny of every man with the lack of physical, social, and psychological conditions for attaining this destiny in most or, in some way, in all men. Only a strictly predestinarian doctrine could give a simple answer, and it did this by asserting that God does not care for the large majority of beings who were born as men but never reached the age or state of maturity. But if this is asserted, God becomes a demon, contradicting the God who creates the world for the sake of fulfilment of all created potentialities.

A more adequate answer must deal with the relation of eternity and time or of transtemporal fulfilment in relation to temporal development. If transtemporal fulfilment has the quality of life, temporality is included in it. As in some previous cases, we need two polar assertions above which lies the truth, which, however, we are unable to express positively and directly: eternity is neither timeless identity nor permanent change, as the latter occurs in the temporal process. Time and change are present in the depth of Eternal Life, but they are contained within the eternal unity of the Divine Life.

If we combine this solution with the idea that no individual destiny is separated from the destiny of the universe, we have a framework within which the great question of the development of the individual in Eternal Life can at least find a limited theological answer.

The Catholic doctrine which recommends prayer and sacrifice for the deceased is a powerful expression of belief in the unity of individual and universal destiny in Eternal Life. This element of truth should not be forgotten because of the many superstitions and abuses in the practical carrying-out of the idea. It is hardly necessary, after all that has been said, to refer to the symbols "heaven" and "hell." First of all, they are symbols and not descriptions of localities; second, they express states of blessedness and despair. Third, they point to the objective basis of blessedness and despair, that is, the amount of fulfilment or nonfulfilment which goes into the individual's essentialization. The symbols "heaven" and "hell" must be taken seriously in this threefold sense and can be used as metaphors for the polar ultimates in the experience of the divine. The frequently evil psychological effects of a literal use of "heaven" and "hell" are not sufficient reason for removing them completely. They provide vivid expression for the threat of "death away from eternity," and for its contrast, the "promise of eternal life." One cannot "psychologize away" basic experiences of threat and despair about the ultimate meaning of existence, as one cannot psychologize away moments of blessedness in anticipated fulfilment. Psychology can only dissolve the neurotic consequences of the literalistic distortion of the two symbols, and there is ample reason for it to do so. There would be less reason if not only theology but also preaching and teaching would remove the superstitious implications of a literal use of these symbols.

C. THE KINGDOM OF GOD: TIME AND ETERNITY

1. ETERNITY AND THE MOVEMENT OF TIME

We have rejected the understanding of eternity as timelessness and as endless time. Neither the denial nor the continuation of temporality constitutes the eternal. On this basis we have been able to discuss the question of the individual's possible development in Eternal Life. Now we must face the question of time and eternity in a formalized way.

In order to do so it is useful to call upon the help of a spatial image and see the movement of time in relation to eternity with the aid of a diagram. This has been done since the Pythagoreans used circular movement as the spatial analogy to time's coming back to itself in eternal return. Because of its circular character Plato called time the "moving image of eternity." It is an open question as to whether Plato attributed some kind of temporality to the eternal. This seems to be logically unavoidable if the word "image" is taken seriously. For there must be in the original something of that which is in the image—otherwise the image would lack the character of similarity which makes it an image. It also seems that in his later dialogues Plato points to a dialectical movement within the realm of essences. But all this remained ineffectual in classical Greek thought. Because there was no aim toward which time is now supposed to run, there was, consequently, a lack of symbols for the beginning and end of time. Augustine took a tremendous step when he rejected the analogy of the circle for the movement of time and replaced it by a straight line, beginning with the creation of the temporal and ending with the transformation of everything temporal. This idea not only was possible in the Christian view of the Kingdom of God as the aim of history but was demanded by it. Time not only mirrors eternity; it contributes to Eternal Life in each of its moments. However, the diagram of the straight line does not indicate the character of time as coming from and going to the eternal. And its failure to do so made it possible for modern progressivism, naturalistic or idealistic, to prolong the temporal line indefinitely in both directions, denying a beginning and an end, thus radically cutting off the temporal process from eternity. This drives us to the question as to whether we can imagine a diagram which in some way unites the qualities of "coming from," "going ahead," and "rising to." I would suggest a curve which comes from above, moves down as well as ahead, reaches the deepest point which is the *nunc existentiale*, the "existential now," and returns in an analogous way to that from which it came, going ahead as well as going up. This curve can be drawn in every moment of experienced time, and it can also be seen as the diagram for temporality as a whole. It implies the creation of the temporal, the beginning of time, and the return of the temporal to the eternal, the end of time. But the end of time is not conceived in terms of a definite moment either in the past or in the future. Beginning from and ending in the eternal are not matters of a determinable moment in physical time but rather a process going on in every moment, as does the divine creation. There is always creation and consummation, beginning and end.

2. Eternal Life and Divine Life

God is eternal; this is the decisive characteristic of those qualities which make him God. He is subjected neither to the temporal process nor with it to the structure of finitude. God, as eternal, has neither the timelessness of absolute identity nor the endlessness of mere process. He is "living," which means that he has in himself the unity of identity and alteration which characterizes life and which is fulfilled in Eternal Life.

This leads immediately to the question: How is the eternal God, who is also the living God, related to Eternal Life, which is the inner aim of all creatures? There cannot be two eternal life processes parallel to each other, and the New Testament excludes this idea directly by calling God alone the "eternal One." The only possible answer is that Eternal Life is life in the eternal, life in God. This corresponds to the assertion that everything temporal comes from the eternal and returns to the eternal, and it agrees with the Pauline vision that in ultimate fulfilment God shall be everything in (or for) everything. One could call this symbol "eschatological pan-en-theism."

There are some problems, however, which arise from the place of this solution within the whole system of theological thought; and it is appropriate to deal with them in the last section of the theological system. The first problem is the meaning of "in," when we say that Eternal Life is life "in" God.

The first meaning of "in" in the phrase "in God" is that it is the "in" of creative origin. It points to the presence of everything that has being in the divine ground of being, a presence that is in the form of potentiality (in a classical formulation, this is understood as the presence of the essences or eternal images or ideas of everything created in the divine mind). The second meaning of "in" is that it is the "in" of ontological dependence. Here, the "in" points to the inability of anything finite to be without the supporting power of the permanent divine creativity—even in the state of estrangement and despair. The third meaning of "in" is that it is the "in" of ultimate fulfilment, the state of essentialization of all creatures.

This threefold "in-ness" of the temporal in the eternal indicates the rhythm both of the Divine Life and of life universal. One could refer to this rhythm as the way from essence through existential estrangement to essentialization. It is the way from the merely potential through actual separation and reunion to fulfilment beyond the separation of potentiality and actuality. Inasmuch as we have been pushed by the consistency of thought as well as by the religious expression in which fulfilment is anticipated to the identification of Life Eternal with the Divine Life it is appropriate to ask about the relation of the Divine Life to the life of the creature in the state of essentialization or in Eternal Life. Such a question is both unavoidable, as the history of Christian thought shows, and impossible to answer except in terms of the highest religious-poetic symbolism. We have touched upon the question at several points, particularly in the discussions of trinitarian symbolism and of the divine blessedness. There is no blessedness where there is no conquest of the opposite possibility, and there is no life where there is no "otherness." The trinitarian symbol of the Logos as the principle of divine self-manifestation in creation and salvation introduces the element of otherness into the Divine Life without which it would not be life. With the

Logos, the universe of essence is given, the "immanence of creative potentiality" in the divine ground of being. Creation into time produces the possibility of self-realization, estrangement, and reconciliation of the creature, which, in eschatological terminology, is the way from essence through existence to essentialization.

In this view the world process means something for God. He is not a separated self-sufficient entity who, driven by a whim, creates what he wants and saves whom he wants. Rather, the eternal act of creation is driven by a love which finds fulfilment only through the other one who has the freedom to reject and to accept love. God, so to speak, drives toward the actualization and essentialization of everything that has being. For the eternal dimension of what happens in the universe is the Divine Life itself. It is the content of the divine blessedness.

Such formulations concerning the Divine Life and its relation to the life of the universe seem to transcend the possibility of human assertions even within the "theological circle." They seem to violate the mystery of the divine "abyss." Theology must answer such a criticism by pointing out, first, that the language used is symbolic; it avoids the danger of subjecting the ultimate mystery to the subject-object scheme, which would distort God into an object to be analyzed and described. Second, theology must answer that, in the all-embracing symbolism, a genuine religious interest is preserved, that is, the affirmation of the ultimate seriousness of life in the light of the eternal; for a world which is only external to God and not also internal to Him, in the last consideration, is a divine play of no essential concern for God. This is certainly not the biblical view which emphasizes in many ways God's infinite concern for his creation. If we elaborate the conceptual implication of this religious certainty (which is the function of theology) then we are driven to formulations similar to those given here. And there may be a third answer to the criticism of the universal theology that embraces both God and the world, the answer that it sharply transcends a merely anthropocentric as well as a merely cosmocentric theology and expresses a theocentric vision of the meaning of existence. Although most considerations given within the theological circle deal with man and his world in their relation to God, our final consideration points in the opposite direction and speaks of God in his relation to man and his world.

Although this can only be done in terms of the symbols which have been interpreted as answers to the questions implied in human existence, it both can and must be done in a theology which starts with an analysis of the human condition. For in such a theology religious symbols can easily be misunderstood as products of man's wishful imagination. This is especially true of such eschatological symbols as "life hereafter." Therefore it is adequate to use the eschatological symbols that turn us from man to God, thereby considering man in his significance for the Divine Life and its eternal glory and blessedness.

INDEX

INDEX